Rape

Rape
Challenging contemporary thinking

Edited by

**Miranda A. H. Horvath and
Jennifer M. Brown**

WILLAN
PUBLISHING

Published by

Willan Publishing
Culmcott House
Mill Street, Uffculme
Cullompton, Devon
EX15 3AT, UK
Tel: +44(0)1884 840337
Fax: +44(0)1884 840251
e-mail: info@willanpublishing.co.uk
website: www.willanpublishing.co.uk

Published simultaneously in the USA and Canada by

Willan Publishing
c/o ISBS, 920 NE 58th Ave, Suite 300
Portland, Oregon 97213-3786, USA
Tel: +001(0)503 287 3093
Fax: +001(0)503 280 8832
e-mail: info@isbs.com
website: www.isbs.com

First published 2009

ISBN   978-1-84392-520-0 paperback
       978-1-84392-519-4 hardback

British Library Cataloguing-in-Publication Data

A catalogue record for this book is available from the British Library.

FSC
Mixed Sources
Product group from well-managed
forests and other controlled sources

Cert no. SGS-COC-2482
www.fsc.org
© 1996 Forest Stewardship Council

Project managed by Deer Park Productions, Tavistock, Devon
Typeset by GCS, Leighton Buzzard, Bedfordshire
Printed and bound by T.J. International Ltd, Padstow, Cornwall

Contents

Part 2   Victim Vulnerabilities

Part 3   The Criminal Justice System

Part 4   Concluding Remarks

List of tables and figures

Tables

Figures

List of abbreviations

ABE	Achieving Best Evidence
ACPO	Association of Chief Police Officers
AIC	Australian Institute of Criminology
AMMSA	Acceptance of Modern Myths about Sexual Aggression Scale
ATR	Attitudes Towards Rape Scale
BME	Black and Minority Ethnic
BMER	Black, Minority Ethnic and Refugee
CA	Conversation Analysis
CADS	Community, Autonomy and Divinity Scale
CJS	Criminal Justice System
CPS	Crown Prosecution Service
CResPP	Centre for Research in Political Psychology
CRIS	Crime Report Information System
CRP	Crime Reduction Programme
CRP VAWI	Crime Reduction Programme Violence Against Women Initiative
CWASU	Child and Woman Abuse Studies Unit
DPP	Director of Public Prosecutions
EKS	Evaluative Knowledge Structure
ELM	Elaboration Likelihood Model
ESRC	Economic and Social Research Council
FGM	Female Genital Mutilation
HMCPSI	Her Majesty's Crown Prosecution Service Inspectorate
HMIC	Her Majesty's Inspectorate of Constabulary
IRMA	Illinois Rape Myth Acceptance Scale

ISRA	International Society for Research on Aggression
MPS	Metropolitan Police Service
NDM	Naturalistic Decision-Making
OIC	Officer in Charge
PJAQ	Pretrial Juror Attitude Questionnaire
PTSD	Post-Traumatic Stress Disorder
Q&A	Question and Answer
RCNE	Rape Crisis Network Europe
RMA	Rape Myth Acceptance
RMAS	Rape Myth Acceptance Scale
SARC	Sexual Assault Referral Centre
SOLO	Sexual Offence Liaison Officer
SORI	Sexual Offences Research Initiative
SOTP	Sexual Offences Treatment Programme
VAW	Violence Against Women
WLM	Women's Liberation Movement
WRC	War on Rape Collective

Acknowledgments

Miranda and Jennifer would like to thank numerous people without whom this edited collection would not have been possible. This collection emerged out of a series of seminars funded by the British Psychological Society and from which the Sexual Offences Research Initiative was developed. The seminars were lively affairs and we struggled with some contentious issues and were enlivened and challenged by the different disciplinary backgrounds that the seminar participants possessed between them. It really was a privilege to be part of such a committed and inquiring group of people. We would like to thank everyone who took part and especially those who helped to organise the events. We jointly decided that we wished to share our enthusiasm for this project not least because we collectively wanted to contribute to thinking that might just address the justice gap experienced by women who have been sexually assaulted and raped. Several additional authors were approached after the seminars to contribute chapters to this collection and we would like to thank them for being so willing to engage with us in this project. Producing this collection has been a real team effort and we would like to thank all of the contributors for their insights, promptness in producing copy, openness to editorial suggestions and their tireless support for the project. We would also like to thank Brian Willan and his colleagues at Willan Publishing for their assistance and advice with the editing process. We are also grateful to Jo Edward Lewis for his invaluable work preparing the collection for publication. We would like to dedicate this collection to the women who have the courage to come forward and make complaints to the police and the many thousands of women who go unheard and unsupported and have to do the best they can to endure sexual violence.

Notes on contributors

Gerd Bohner is Professor of Social Psychology at the Department of Psychology, University of Bielefeld, Germany. He graduated in psychology (Dipl.-Psych.) in 1986 and received his doctorate in psychology (Dr.phil) in 1990, both at the University of Heidelberg. In 1997 he completed his Habilitation in psychology at the University of Mannheim. He held teaching and research positions at the University of Heidelberg, the University of Mannheim and the University of Kent at Canterbury, as well as visiting positions at New York University and the University of Würzburg. Since 2001, he has been Professor of Social Psychology at the University of Bielefeld, where he served as Dean of the Faculty of Psychology and Sports Science from 2007 to 2009. His areas of research interest include basic and applied aspects of attitudes and social cognition, gender issues and sexual violence. Currently, he is editor-in-chief of the journal *Social Psychology* and serves as consulting editor for various international journals, including *Group Processes and Intergroup Relations* and *Personality and Social Psychology Bulletin*. He is co-author of the textbook *Attitudes and Attitude Change* with Professor Michaela Wänke.

Jennifer M. Brown is Professor of Forensic Psychology at the University of Surrey, having been formerly Head of the Department of Psychology. She is currently Director of the Crime and Justice Initiative, a cross-faculty initiative of the university. She has co-written two books about policing and edited two further books, one related to environmental risk and the other about using the interview as a research method. She recently collaborated with Dr Elizabeth

Campbell on an edited collection, *The Handbook of Forensic Psychology*, to be published by Cambridge University Press. She has published a large number of papers on various aspects of women and the criminal justice system. She is particularly interested in police occupational culture and the role of women within the police service. In 2006 she was given the President's Award from the International Association of Women in Policing for her research contributions to understanding the position of women in contemporary policing.

Maddy Coy is currently a Research Fellow at the Child and Woman Abuse Studies Unit, London Metropolitan University. She obtained a BA (Hons) in Women's Studies in 1998 from Liverpool John Moores University, an MA in Research and Social Policy in 2001 from the University of Birmingham and a PhD in Sociology in 2007 from Loughborough University. She has several years' experience of residential and outreach work with sexually exploited girls and adult women in prostitution, as well as support work with vulnerable women in other settings. Her PhD research explored young women's routes into prostitution from local authority care. Ongoing research interests centre on women's ontology of prostitution, particularly the psycho-social dimension of identity and embodiment, and the socio-cultural sexualisation of girls and women.

Friederike Eyssel is a Post-Doctoral Researcher at the Department of Psychology, University of Bielefeld, Germany. She earned her Masters Degree in psychology from the University of Heidelberg in 2004 and received her PhD in psychology from the University of Bielefeld in 2007. In her work she investigates how rape myths and their acceptance influence behavioural intentions or, more generally, how rape myth acceptance affects information processing. Dr Eyssel is also interested in the assessment of implicit and explicit gender prejudice, the social psychology of disability and research on dehumanisation and anthropomorphism.

Hannah Frith is a Senior Lecturer in the Department of Applied Social Sciences, University of Brighton. She graduated in social psychology in 1993 and received her doctorate in psychology in 1998, both from Loughborough University. Her research on issues of sexuality focuses on sexual communication and negotiation and exploring the cultural discourses through which individuals make sense of themselves and their behaviours. She is currently researching discourses of orgasm and orgasmic 'failure'. Her research interests also include body image and embodiment, the construction of visual identities and the management of 'spoiled' identities, and the construction of identities and affect in reality television.

Aisha Gill BA, MA(Di), PhD (University of Essex), PGCHE is a Senior Lecturer in Criminology at Roehampton University. Her main areas of interest and research are health and criminal justice responses to violence against Black, Minority Ethnic and Refugee (BMER) women in the United Kingdom. She has been involved in addressing the problem of Violence Against Women (VAW) at the grassroots and activist levels for the past ten years. She is Chair of Newham Asian Women's Project, management committee member of Imkaan (a second-tier national VAW charity) and a member of Liberty's Project Advisory Group, 'End Violence Against Women' group (EVAW) and invited advisor (from July 2009) on the IPCC strategic support group on investigations and complaints involving gendered forms of violence against women in the UK. Dr Gill has extensive experience of providing expert advice to government and the voluntary sector on legal policy issues related to so-called 'honour' killings and forced marriage, and has challenged politicians to be more inclusive of BMER women's voices in policy-making on issues of gender-based violence and human rights. Her current research interests include the following: rights, law and forced marriage; crimes related to patriarchy; 'honour'-based violence and femicide in Iraqi Kurdistan and the Kurdish/South Asian Diaspora; post-separation violence and child contact; trafficking; missing women; and sexual violence. She has also published widely in national and international referred journals and has recently completed a manuscript on violence against women in the South Asian community in the UK with Dr Ravi Thiara.

Roger Giner-Sorolla is a Senior Lecturer in Psychology at the Centre for the Study of Group Processes, Department of Psychology, University of Kent. He has authored numerous empirical articles and chapters on defensive information processing, emotionally based attitudes and the role of specific emotions in moral judgment and self-control. He has secured a number of grants from the Economic and Social Research Council (ESRC), British Academy and European Social Foundation to investigate the role of emotions such as guilt and shame in inter-group relations and to promote research in inter-group emotions more generally. In 2007 he was principal co-editor of a special issue on inter-group emotion in the journal *Group Processes and Individual Differences*.

Miranda A. H. Horvath is a Lecturer in Forensic Psychology at the University of Surrey. Dr Horvath obtained a BSc (Hons) in Social Psychology in 2002, an MSc in Forensic Psychology in 2003 from the University of Kent and a PhD in Forensic Psychology in 2006 from the University of Surrey. She is currently an Assistant Director of the Crime & Justice @ Surrey Research Initiative. Her PhD (funded by the Economic and Social Research Council) investigated the role of alcohol and drugs in rape. The majority of her research is focused on sexual violence working from an applied social psychological perspective. She has both published and presented in a range of arenas including international peer-reviewed journals and national and international conferences. She has recently co-written a book *Understanding Criminal Investigation* (Wiley, forthcoming) with Dr Steve Tong and Dr Robin Bryant. Her current research interests include multiple perpetrator rape, offending and non-offending men's accounts and understandings of non-consensual and consensual sexual behaviour, and the links between men's use of 'lad's mags', their attitudes towards women and paying for sex.

Liz Kelly is Roddick Chair in Sexual Violence of the Child and Woman Abuse Studies Unit at London Metropolitan University. Professor Kelly has worked in the fields of woman and child abuse for over thirty years – in support services and as a researcher. She has been Director of the Child and Woman Abuse Studies Unit (CWASU) at London Metropolitan University for over a decade, and the Unit has a national and international reputation for its research and policy work on a range of forms of abuse. She is responsible for developing the concept of a continuum of violence, the recognition that child pornography is a record of abuse and the principle that woman protection is often child protection. Professor Kelly is a Commissioner for the Women's National Commission, chairing the Violence Against Women Working Group. She is also chair of the End Violence Against Women Coalition. Most recently Anita Roddick endowed a chair on Violence Against Women, which Liz Kelly holds. It is the first such chair in Europe. The MA in Woman and Child Abuse at London Metropolitan University is also the first such MA.

Jenny Kitzinger is Professor of Media and Communication Research at Cardiff University School of Journalism, Media and Cultural Studies. She specialises in researching the media coverage and audience reception of social, health and scientific issues and has written extensively about sexual violence. Her articles in this field cover issues such as the ideologies implicit in 'recovery' self-help books, survivors' experiences of medical and obstetric treatment and the media coverage of sexual violence. Her books include: *Framing Abuse: Media Influence and Public Understanding of Sexual Violence Against Children* (Pluto Press, 2004); *Developing Focus Group Research: Politics, Theory and Practice* (Sage, 1999); *The Mass Media and Power in Modern Britain* (Oxford University Press, 1997); *Great Expectations* (Hochland & Hochland, 1998); *The Circuit of Mass Communication in the AIDS Crisis* (Sage, 1999); and *Human Cloning in the Media: From Science Fiction to Science Practice* (Routledge, 2007).

Barbara Krahé is Professor of Social Psychology at the University of Potsdam, Germany. Her research interests lie in the area of applied social psychology, in particular aggression research (sexual aggression, media violence and aggression) and social cognition research applied to legal decision-making (rape myths and biases in judgments about sexual assault). Her research has been funded by the German Research Foundation and conducted in collaboration with colleagues at the University of Sussex, the University of Michigan and the Warsaw School of Social Psychology. She is an active member of the International Society for Research on Aggression (ISRA) and associate editor of its journal *Aggressive Behavior*. She is also a member of the Sexual Offences Research Initiative (SORI) and a Fellow of the British Psychological Society.

Jo Lovett is a Research Fellow at the Child and Woman Abuse Studies Unit, London Metropolitan University. Since 2001 she has conducted a number of research and evaluation projects in the field of sexual and domestic violence, as well as policy briefings on violence against women and sexual violence specifically. Her current research interests include rape attrition, alcohol/drugs in relation to sexual violence, and national and international government policy on gender equality and violence against women.

Evanthia Lyons is Professor of Psychology and a Director of the Centre for Research in Political Psychology (CResPP) at the School of Psychology, Queen's University, Belfast. She obtained her first, Masters and doctoral degrees from London University. Her research interests include the role of identities in perceptions of justice and inter-group relations and qualitative methods. Her research has been funded by the European Commission, European Science Foundation,

Economic and Social Research Council (ESRC), International Association for the Promotion of Co-operation with Scientists from new independent States of the former Soviet Union (INTAS) and industry. She has co-edited two books and published numerous articles in these areas in refereed journals. Professor Lyons has also (co-)supervised 25 doctoral students to completion.

Lesley McMillan is a Senior Lecturer in the Department of Sociology, Glasgow Caledonian University and an Associate Director of the Centre for Research in Families and Relationships at the University of Edinburgh. She is author of *Feminists Organising Against Gendered Violence* (Palgrave, 2007), a comparative study of alternative welfare provision for women survivors of violence. Her research interests include gendered and sexual violence, sexual health and the sociology of trauma. She is currently the principal investigator on a large ESRC-funded research project looking at attrition in rape cases.

Vanessa E. Munro is Professor of Socio-Legal Studies at the School of Law, University of Nottingham. She is author of *Law and Politics at the Perimeter: Re-Evaluating Key Debates in Feminist Theory* (Hart, 2007) and co-editor of both *Sexuality and the Law: Feminist Engagements* (Cavendish, 2007) and *Demanding Sex: Critical Reflections on the Regulation of Prostitution* (Ashgate, 2008). She has published widely on feminist legal and political theory and combines this with empirical research examining popular and penal responses to gender violence. With funding from the ESRC, she has conducted two large-scale studies exploring (mock) juror attitudes in rape trials, and with funding from the Nuffield Foundation, ESRC and British Academy, she has conducted interdisciplinary research on prostitution and trafficking. She is currently working on a study on rape and asylum, funded by the Nuffield Foundation. She has acted as an advisor to the government on the issues of both human trafficking and sexual offences reform, and has been invited to present her research to, among others, Metropolitan Police Sexual Assault Investigators and Crown Court Judges. She is currently co-editing a collection entitled *Rethinking Rape Law: International and Comparative Perspectives* (Routledge, forthcoming).

Stephanie O'Keeffe leads the Research and Policy function in the Crisis Pregnancy Agency, Dublin (an Irish state agency tasked with addressing reproductive and sexual health needs). She is a social psychologist with interests in research methodology, applied social science research and research dissemination and implementation in health and organisational contexts.

Afroditi Pina is a Lecturer in Forensic Psychology at the Department of Psychology, University of Kent, having obtained a BSc (Hons) in Psychology from the University of Wales, Bangor in 2002, an MSc in Forensic Psychology in 2003 and a PhD in Forensic Psychology in 2007, both from the University of Kent. Her PhD thesis examined the role of appraisals and emotions in women's strategies for coping with sexual harassment. Her research interests include gender equality issues, emotions and coping strategies, domestic violence and sexual violence, with particular focus on sexual harassment and rape.

Pascale S. Russell is a Postgraduate Researcher at the University of Kent at Canterbury. She gained her Masters in Social Psychology at the University of Kent in 2006, during which time she completed a dissertation examining the underlying factors of people's sexual prejudice such as people's emotions and perception of harm. She then continued at the University of Kent, registering for a PhD in Social Psychology, in which she is carrying out extensive research on people's emotional reactions toward various social groups, specifically comparing moral disgust and anger and the cognitive processes that are associated with these emotions.

Frank Siebler is an Associate Professor at the Department of Psychology, University of Tromsø, Norway. He graduated in Sociology at the University of Mannheim in 1995 and was awarded a PhD in Psychology from the University of Kent at Canterbury in 2002. He has held research and teaching positions at the universities of Dresden, Mannheim, Canterbury, Kassel and Bielefeld. His research interests include dual-process models of social cognition, mainly in the domains of persuasive communication and of person perception. Currently, he is involved in research on predictors of men's proclivity to sexually harass. He also has a strong interest in connectionist (artificial neural network) models of social judgment processes.

Betsy Stanko is Head of the Strategic Research and Analysis Unit in the Metropolitan Police Service. Professor Stanko began her career as a Professor of Criminology, teaching and researching at Clark University (USA), Brunel University, Cambridge University and Royal Holloway, University of London. She has published over 60 books and articles over her academic career. The most cited of these works is *Intimate Intrusions: Women's Experiences of Male Violence*, published in 1985. She has been awarded a number of lifetime achievement awards from the American Society of Criminology, most notably the Vollmer Award (1996), in recognition of the outstanding influence of her academic work on criminal justice practice. From 1997 to 2002 she was Director of the ESRC Violence Research Programme. In 2002, she joined the Cabinet Office, in the Prime Minister's Office of Public Services Reform, leading the project on citizen-focused policing for the Cabinet Office. In 2003, she joined the Metropolitan Police Service and has played a variety of development and strategic roles in one of the largest police forces in the world. She is a fellow of the Royal Society of the Arts.

Jennifer Temkin is Professor of Law at the University of Sussex. She is the author of *Rape and the Legal Process* (2nd edn, 2002), *Sexual Assault and the Justice Gap: A Question of Attitude* (2008, with Barbara Krahé) and many articles on criminal law and criminal justice. She was a member of the Home Office Advisory Group on the use of Video Recordings in Criminal Proceedings (the Pigot Committee, 1989–90), the National Children's Home Committee of Enquiry into Children Who Abuse Other Children (1990–2), the External Reference Group of the Home Office Sex Offences Review (2000) and the Council of Europe's Committee of Experts on the Treatment of Sex Offenders (2003–6). She is a barrister and Bencher of the Middle Temple.

Michelle Thomas is a Research Fellow on a study of attrition in rape cases (with Dr Lesley McMillan) in the Department of Sociology, Glasgow Caledonian University. She has a background in medical sociology and in health research, and her research interests include sexual health, gender and health, and the sociology of relationships and emotions. She is interested in methodological issues and has published on gender and danger in fieldwork and issues in recruitment for research, and has co-authored a Sage text on focus groups.

G. Tendayi Viki is a Senior Lecturer in Psychology at the Department of Psychology, University of Kent, having obtained an Honours degree in Psychology from the University of Zimbabwe in 1997. He then obtained his MSc degree in Forensic Psychology in 2000 and his PhD in Forensic Psychology in 2003, both from the University of Kent. He is interested in and has been researching various topics within social psychology and forensic psychology. These include: intra- and inter-group dynamics, social-cognitive processes, contemporary sexism, rape myth acceptance, attitudes to punishment, prison rehabilitation and behavioural variables in cancer prevention.

Emma Williams is a Lead Researcher in the Metropolitan Police Service. Prior to this she was a part-time visiting lecturer at Brunel University and North London University. She has completed various internal qualitative research projects within the MPS including work on rape victim withdrawals. Her research interests are victims of crime, sexual violence, policing and community engagement.

Foreword

Mary P. Koss, University of Arizona

In August of 1990 I received an invitation by the then Chairman of the United States Senate Committee on the Judiciary, Joseph R. Biden, Jr to testify at hearings on the Violence Against Women Act that was eventually incorporated into the Violence Crime Control and Law Enforcement Act and signed into law in 1994. It might have been at that hearing, or it might have been elsewhere, but I recall he said something to the effect that if there were a disease that affected one in five women, a bell would ring to mobilise a massive public response, but in the case of violence against women, the bell tolls very softly. Tempering the pleasure of being asked to introduce Miranda Horvath and Jennifer Brown's book, *Rape: Challenging contemporary thinking* is the recognition that its subtext is the same as Biden's: the bell is still tolling very softly.

This edited book brings together the major thinkers on rape from across Europe. I initially viewed the chapters as an odd lot – a set of chapters on factors that support and promote rape and a second set that examined law enforcement and judicial response. About halfway through the text I recognised that a greater whole emerges from the parts. The material on justice response presents data about what happens in the real world of police stations, prosecutors' offices and courtrooms, cataloguing what is most typically labelled as 'attrition' of rape cases from the system. Eureka! The opening chapters on rape-supporting myths including acceptance and alcohol use were much the same as the typical stereotypes and misperceptions that explain the scant justice accorded to rape victims. The book is a real addition to the knowledge base on rape. It is interdisciplinary, but it does not duplicate existing sources on forensic procedures, medical and psychological care and public health prevention. The voice in this book is also clearly different from other recent works because it is distinctly sociological and social psychological. The initial chapters address language in the field that we rarely question. There are thoughtful conceptual discussions and precise definitions of commonly used words like attitudes, beliefs, anger, moral disgust and ethics, and critical analysis of alcohol use in rape and media trends in coverage of rape.

Although it is not the intent of the authors, as a public health worker, I was impressed with the practical implications of the material. For example, the critical analysis of rape myth scales noted that they are dated and pose questions in a format that almost no one agrees with any more. When participants begin a programme with very little evidence of rape myths, no data-based programme impact can be measured. There is a very useful table of examples that update the various myths so that they are more likely to detect the subtle forms in which they continue to exist and exert influence. Those who provide rape prevention education should welcome this contribution because it both gives new life to how this common programme element could be taught and raises hope that with contemporary measurement we might achieve evidence of programme impacts that is thus far eluding us. Likewise, prevention in other fields such as tobacco cessation has recognised the significant negative force of media on unhealthy behaviour and has incorporated media literacy education to counter the effects. Children and young people today are surrounded by media during all their waking hours yet they often do not understand that what they see is not real; it has been shaped and messaged. The material on media preoccupation with rape and how it is distorted is an excellent core for a media education component in sexual violence prevention. We need to teach that media focuses on sensational cases, ignores common abuse, overplays contested and false allegations and makes acquaintance rape invisible.

A fascinating conceptualisation and study of the sexual scripts and the refusal process also should be provocative to prevention specialists. Recent UK legislative reform shifts the consent standard in rape from passive to active consent – it is up to everyone to ensure that their partner agrees to sexual activity. We have focused hard on teaching consent; casting an eye to how refusal is conveyed and understood expands potential modifiable targets for prevention. Important points include sexual script analysis, beliefs about the best time in the sexual intimacy progression to refuse, communicating refusal and what is hearable as a refusal. Surprisingly, the way people express refusal rarely contains the word 'no'. However, prevention efforts grounded in miscommunication theory to prevent rape by improving communication is not only naive but demonstrably ineffective. As it turns out, both men and women are already capable of understanding and communicating refusal in ways that are hearable if they are encouraged to access and verbalise their acquired knowledge of sexual matters.

The chapters that focus on justice response to rape are dismaying. Among those who reported rape to the Metropolitan Police, all but 13 per cent of the cases involved women with vulnerabilities, including being under 18 years old, having a mental health issue, having been intimate with the offender or having consumed alcohol. These vulnerabilities affected criminal justice decision-making at every stage and were significantly related to the probability that a case would be closed, a victim sent away with no sense of validation or justice, an offender would get away with rape and communities would continue to believe that many rape complaints have no merit. Apparently, quite dramatic wrongdoing by the defendant is required for the focus to be diverted away from the complainant. Often social scientists try to understand these decision-making processes experimentally. However, a fascinating discussion of naturalistic decision making points out that people take their actions with an eye to the ethical and cultural views of the influential others above them in the institutional hierarchy. Subsequent discussion focuses on the reasons/excuses of police officers for viewing rape complaints as false and what they look for as veracity cues. The stage where victims' withdraw or officers close cases occurs very early in the process; victims feel disbelieved and/or disrespected, sometimes even before reporting. The solution seems clear: train justice personnel, equip them with accurate information and the biases will disappear. However, we have been doing that since the beginning of the anti-rape movement and one wonders when our efforts will start to be reflected in justice performance statistics. Furthermore, rape education focused on attitude change has demonstrated minute or no long-lasting change in every setting where it has been evaluated. Perhaps some of the insight presented on approaches that appear to change attitudes under laboratory conditions will stimulate creative thinking about applications in the field.

The book ends with a shocking observation about rape trials in the UK (and is true of other jurisdictions as well). In 2007, rape of a female was the only sexual or violent crime where acquittals exceeded convictions. Even more appalling is that the rate is artificially inflated by inclusion of a large number of rapes of children less than 13 years of age where absence of consent does not need to be proved. Suggested questions for prosecutors to ask potential jurors in the quest to raise conviction rates are referenced and the option to draft special judicial instruction for jurors on psychological reactions to rape is considered. Subsequently, the radical suggestion that countries should abandon jury trials for rape is evaluated. Despite judges' warnings, it is becoming hard to control jury members' access to the Internet where they can learn prejudicial material about victims that is fodder for the press but would be inadmissible at trial. Having a trained jurist decide rape cases is potentially appealing and it is additionally responsive to the spate of wrongful convictions that have occurred in rape. But would it affect conviction rates? Judges are a predominately male pool not known for gender awareness. Yet again, stereotypical attitudes about rape pose a major obstacle to unbiased and fair decisions.

I recently attended a meeting in Brazil focused on involving men and boys in violence prevention. I recommend this book to that emerging sector of the anti-violence movement because, as the authors substantiate, it is predominately men who hold decision-making authority within the media that determine how rape is presented to the public, men who fail to assure they have consent and have heard any refusals who commit most rapes, and men in the criminal justice system who make fateful decisions impacting on the lives of victims. It is indeed time for the bell to ring louder.

Chapter 1

Setting the scene: introduction to understanding rape

Miranda A. H. Horvath and Jennifer M. Brown

Origins

This collection emerged out of a series of seminars funded by the British Psychological Society (held between 2005 and 2007) which brought together a network of researchers with the common focus of rape. This network evolved into the Sexual Offences Research Initiative (SORI: http://www.sori.co.uk). The contributed chapters represent the range of topics discussed in the seminars and bring together some of the leading European researchers currently thinking and developing ideas, conceptualising and researching aspects of sexual violence. Additional contributors were invited to cover topics felt to be of particular importance when considering rape and sexual violence. As originally conceived our seminar discussions addressed emerging areas of concern, specifically: attrition; drug-assisted rape, including the role of alcohol; consent and the Sexual Offences Act; and false allegations. The seminars had three major foci: Methodology; Concepts and Models; and Practice Application.

Methodology

Previous research has investigated rape using a number of techniques depending on which aspects of rape are the focus, for example: vignettes, mock juries, questionnaires, interviews, secondary analysis, trial observations, service evaluation and case tracking. There are pros and cons attached to these relating to reliability and generalisability of data. Moreover, rarely is any form of data triangulation employed.

There are particular difficulties when seeking to engage rape survivors in research, for example gaining access, particularly where this is mediated by gatekeepers, and ensuring ethical concerns and matters of confidentiality and anonymity are adequately addressed. There are also issues surrounding the researcher's role in relation to a range of potential participants (e.g. victims, police officers, prosecutors). The seminars reviewed approaches to research investigations.

Concepts and models

Previously, research has incorporated a wide variety of conceptual approaches, for example counterfactual thinking, decision-making, heuristics, social identity theory and feminist perspectives. The members of the seminar group have considerable expertise across these theoretical domains and the seminars provided an opportunity for the sharing of ideas and approaches and for examining their explanatory power and indicating the overlap and differences between them.

Practice application

A criticism that is often made of academic research is that it has very little application in the 'real world for practitioners'. We offer in the final chapter some suggestions for further research and practitioner/ academic collaboration. This is by way of an agenda for action rather than a fleshed out set of solutions. We seek to challenge both the academic community and practitioners to work on and further develop the ideas discussed in the book's chapters.

The chapters in this collection draw together the three foci outlined above. Furthermore, while this book extended authorship to cover more topics than were debated during our seminars, the core membership have developed their thinking through these interdisciplinary exchanges. In those exchanges it became apparent that other topics such as the role of the media and sociocultural issues were important and we were delighted that additional collaborators joined the project of writing contributions to this edited collection.

Rape

Many authors have identified rape as a unique crime, for numerous reasons as outlined by Liz Kelly (2008: 256):

... for centuries [rape] has been the subject of unique evidential requirements (Temkin 2002), but also because of its specific characteristics (New South Wales Standing Committee on Social Issues 1996). Unlike other forms of assault, rape violates personal, intimate and psychological boundaries – what in human rights language is designated human dignity and bodily integrity, and in feminist and critical theory is termed sexual autonomy or sexual sovereignty (Richardson 2000). The meaning of rape for women, within gender and generational relations and cultural contexts, underlies its emotional, psychological and social impacts and consequences.

Legislative reform, investigative practices and prosecutorial decision-making have been undertaken internationally since the early 1980s, however, there are huge variations in the speed and effectiveness of these changes. In fact little is still known about the efficacy of some of the more recent strategies and laws. This has been particularly evident in England and Wales where, in recent years we have seen a raft of key action plans and legislation, including the Rape Action Plan 2002, the Sexual Offences Act 2003, the Victims of Crime and Domestic Violence Act 2004, the Crown Prosecution Service (CPS) Policy for Prosecuting Cases of Rape 2004 and the Cross Government Action Plan on Sexual Violence and Abuse 2007. Also, a Home Office advertising campaign (reportedly costing £500,000) focused on urging men to ensure they get a woman's consent before they have sex with her (Home Office 2006a, 2006b). Some of these efforts have been the subject of evaluation (e.g. Temkin and Krahé 2008 show what little impact the Home Office campaign had on the perceived severity of rape or on views about length of sentences for those convicted). The conviction rates for rape remain stubbornly static at around 6 per cent of all cases reported to the police. The justice gap, i.e. the disparity between cases and conviction rates, is still very wide for this offence. So what is it about rape that makes it so difficult to successfully prosecute? The contributions reflect different stages of the route through the criminal justice system and the authors offer a range of explanations for why women might not report the rape, why police investigators or prosecutors decide to drop cases and what influences jurors when deliberating the guilt or innocence of defendants.

Aims

The key strength of this book is the integration of a diverse range of scholars with very different approaches and backgrounds. The ambition of such integration is to establish the groundwork for developing a model for in-depth, interdisciplinary engagements that may provide a stronger conceptual basis for designing successful interventions to reduce the justice gap. The book clearly is not attempting to be exhaustive. We have concentrated on adult women as victims, survivors or complainants with adult men being the perpetrators, offenders or defendants. We accept that there are other specific categories of victims – children, the elderly, men – and also other perpetrators – young offenders or women abusers. We hope these chapters provide a fresh examination of topics that will stimulate new research collaborations across disciplines and set challenges for practitioners. Our SORI meetings were lively and productive. We hope this book will encourage engagement and debate between researchers, practitioners and policymakers to address the impediments that at present see relatively few women seeking justice, and those that do not getting it.

The book presents a comprehensive and up-to-date review of research on rape stereotypes; it confronts existing stereotypes and challenges current thinking about rape. As a result it is more wide-ranging than previous texts and addresses some of the prevailing issues besetting the criminal justice system with regard to the crime of rape. The collection is multi-perspective and includes new and unpublished data. As noted above this collection does not seek to provide an account of every issue in relation to rape. The fact that our focus is on adult women as victims and adult men as perpetrators is because this is the most frequently occurring dyad (Greenfield 1997). To do full justice to other victims and perpetrators another volume would be needed. Further, like Ward's (1995) book, we are concerned with attitudes about rape but our approach reflects contemporary issues and concerns. We also echo many of the issues covered by Jennifer Temkin and Barbara Krahé in their 2008 book *Sexual Assault and the Justice Gap: A Question of Attitude* about the attrition process and methods for tackling the justice gap. However, this collection provides a wider perspective on individual psychological as well as group social processes and varieties of sexual violence.

Terminology

We have not imposed any rules on the contributors to this book about terminology; as such the reader may notice some variation in the chapters. The focus of this book is rape, broadly understood as penetration of the vagina and/or anus with a penis without consent. In England and Wales, the Sexual Offences Act 2003 expanded the definition to include oral penetration and some authors reflect this change. The term sexual assault is also used; it can include a range of behaviours from unwanted touching or kissing to penetration with an object, essentially any unwanted sexual contact.

Perhaps most controversial is the term used to describe people who have been raped. Terms in use include victim, survivor and complainant. In Chapter 7 Aisha Gill provides some discussion of the issues surrounding these terms because the women she interviewed expressed a wish to her to be identified as survivors. The majority of authors have chosen to use victims: for some this is because they are working with police data which identifies them as such, for others it might be a wish to identify the harm that has been done to them by the perpetrator. The term survivor may also imply the woman has recovered from the trauma, whereas the term victim implies she is still suffering. Complainant is the term used by O'Keeffe *et al.* in their chapter because the focus of their empirical study was women who had made a complaint of rape or sexual assault to the police and by Munro and Kelly since they are looking at the legal process.

As with the issues already discussed about what to call those who have been raped, debate exists about what we should call those who have committed the act. In some respects the distinctions here are clearer cut; if someone has been accused of rape they may simply be referred to as 'the accused'; similarly, if someone is standing trial for an alleged rape they are 'the defendant'. The term perpetrator and offender are used interchangeably and imply those accounts have yet to be tested in court. Finally, if someone has been convicted of a rape they can be labelled a rapist. However, the accused and the defendant are also alleged rapists. Rapist and rape victim are very emotive and pejorative terms which can label an individual with a social stigma they are likely to carry all their life and face the consequential opprobrium. We do not offer any 'preferred' terms but have left to the authors the usage which they felt most appropriate in the context of their chapter.

Themes

We have identified six threads that emerge across the chapters:

- attitudes;
- 'real rape';
- social knowledge/discourse;
- attrition;
- methods;
- practice application.

In order to give the reader some context we briefly outline these themes below. However, it should also be noted that not all appear in each chapter – indeed chapters can be read as free-standing entities although a cumulative reading adds much which we try and summarise in the final chapter.

Attitudes

Attitudes are summary evaluations of an object of thought. Attitudes have been defined as consisting of three component parts: affective (how a person feels about some object or class of person), cognitive (the beliefs, opinions or ideas about the attitude object) and behavioural (what a person does in relation to the attitude object) (Stahlberg and Frey 1996). Central to attitudes about rape, its victims and perpetrators are rape myths which operate to deny or minimise harm, blame victims and exonerate perpetrators (see particularly Gerd Bohner and colleagues' chapter). Rape myth acceptance influences the victim's responses to and determines whether they will even label what has happened to them as rape (see Hannah Frith's chapter on sexual scripts, Maddy Coy's accounts from prostitutes and Aisha Gill's contribution on Asian women's narratives). These attitudes also influence police decision-making (see Stephanie O'Keefe, Jennifer Brown and Evanthia Lyons' study and also the chapter by Lesley McMillan and Michelle Thomas). Jurors too are influenced by the attitudes they bring with them into the jury room and Vanessa Munro and Liz Kelly explore these in their chapter. The affective component of attitudes, feelings of anger and disgust are also important and Roger Giner-Sorolla and Pascale Russell explore this in Chapter 3. Jo Lovett and Miranda Horvath's chapter and the research reported by Betsy Stanko and Emma Williams present some convincing evidence to show that rape myths have little basis in actuality.

'Real rape'

A number of chapters use the term 'real rape' (or 'stereotypical rape') to refer to the widely held belief that genuine rapes contain the following elements: the victim and rapist are strangers; the assault occurs in an outdoors location; the victim shows active visible resistance; and the rapist uses or threatens to force the victim. The roots of this term can be found in Susan Estrich's 1987 book *Real Rape: How the Legal System Victimises Women Who Say No*, in which she argues that 'simple rapes' (a term coined by Kalven and Zeisel 1966 to mean ambiguous or contested sex between people who know each other) are also 'real' rapes and should be acknowledged as such. Estrich identifies the significant differences in treatment of victims depending on the 'type' of rape they have experienced. Specifically those who have suffered an 'aggravated rape', involving no prior relationship between the victim and perpetrator, multiple assailants or extrinsic violence (e.g. beatings, knives), are more likely to be believed and have their case prosecuted and indeed identify that they have been raped than those, who in fact make up the majority of cases (see Walby and Allen 2004), who have experienced a 'simple rape', where 'none of the aggravating circumstances were present'. Throughout this collection the implications of 'real rape' have been drawn out, for example Bohner *et al.* in Chapter 2 demonstrate how notions about what a 'typical rape' should be, in the form of rape myths, directly contribute to low levels of prosecutions and convictions. Jenny Kitzinger shows how the media continue to reinforce and perpetuate the notion of real rape through their selective reporting of serial rape or especially violent rapes. The two chapters on police decision-making (by O'Keefe *et al.* and by McMillan and Thomas) show the pragmatic reality for police officers of adhering to this notional standard of the 'real' rape when they chose to discontinue their investigations. Munro and Kelly highlight notions of 'stereotypical rape' throughout the legal process and Jo Lovett and Miranda Horvath's chapter demonstrates that rape myths are not substantiated by the research evidence.

Social knowledge and discourse

Another theme that emerges relates to the notion of social knowledge, the power of social discourse and shared understandings about what constitutes rape, a rape victim and a rapist, and conversely what does not. Social knowledge is the resource used by all members of society to formulate their attitudes and the chapters of this book testify that all the actors in a rape (victim, perpetrator, police officer, prosecutor, judge and juror) are not immune from their influence in terms of the decisions they make at key points in the criminal justice process. Hannah Frith demonstrates how this social knowledge is communicated through discourse between young women which sets up their understanding and expectations about sexual encounters. She is particularly interested in how young women communicate no to sex and the problematics of this. These problematics are heightened for women in 'honour' cultures which Aisha Gill elaborates, stigmatised women, i.e. those involved in prostitution, a group investigated by Maddy Coy, and for those with a range of vulnerabilities, investigated by Betsy Stanko and Emma Williams.

Attrition

Attrition is the process by which rape cases fall out of the criminal justice system and in doing so contribute to the justice gap whereby there is a dramatic loss of cases through key stages of the criminal justice process. Rape remains under-reported and it is thought that the largest number of cases are lost at the initial reporting stage, with the majority of victims choosing not to tell the police. The chapters by Vanessa Munro and Liz Kelly, Hannah Frith, Aisha Gill and Gerd Bohner and colleagues lay out explanations as to why women may neither identify their rape or assault as a rape nor report to the police. From the point at which a case is reported to the police there are three main stages at which attrition occurs. Firstly with the police, which can be the result of a case being 'no crimed' (where a notifiable offence has been classified by the police and a decision is subsequently made that it should not have been recorded as a crime), the victim withdrawing their complaint or the police believing there is insufficient evidence to mount a prosecution. The studies of police decision-making by O'Keeffe and colleagues and McMillan and Thomas together with the empirical data reported by Stanko and Williams and Munro and Kelly address attrition issues at this stage in the process. Once cases move to the prosecutors they can again be lost because of the victim withdrawing their complaint or refusing to cooperate with the prosecution but more often they are lost because the prosecutors do not believe there is enough evidence to proceed. Finally, at the trial stage, cases can also be lost because the victim withdraws or declines to cooperate or because the jury acquit the accused. Vanessa Munro and Liz Kelly and Lesley

McMillan and Michelle Thomas discuss factors influencing attrition at the prosecutorial and jury stages in the process.

Methods

There are a wide variety of methods for data collection and analysis described in this collection. These include data extracted from police records, laboratory-based experimental research, mock jury trials and life-story interviews. Both qualitative and quantitative analysis techniques are also included. For example, Coy, Gill and Frith report information from detailed interviews with a variety of women whereas Bohner *et al*. and Giner-Sorolla and Russell report findings from laboratory-based experimental research. Stanko and Williams and Lovett and Horvath use data extracted from police case files and conduct secondary analyses. Finally, a number of chapters employ a range of methodologies in their research to collect primary data (e.g. Munro and Kelly use jury simulations; McMillan and Thomas and O'Keeffe and colleagues collect interview data). The result is that the knowledge contributed by this collection includes a diversity of experiences of criminal justice professionals, mock jurors and victims of sexual violence.

Methods are chosen to address the research question(s) and to be epistemologically congruent with the paradigm orientation of the researcher. Secondary data analyses of police records are a useful resource especially for mapping out the phenomenology of rape and sexual assault and generating hypotheses. The strength of this approach is that exploratory work can be undertaken without having to re-engage the rape victim with the trauma she experienced. Similarly, analogue research conducted under laboratory conditions with student respondents also permits hypotheses testing, refinement of psychometric tests and development of explanatory models. Some conceptual development is difficult to achieve without the use of experimental deception and a balance must be struck between the insights gained and the troubling aspects of deceiving research participants. Once formulated hypotheses do need to be taken into the field to test their explanatory power when a wider range of victims (i.e. other than those reporting to the police) may be co-opted. Given the range of methods represented in this volume, we would argue for a mixed methods approach. As Teddlie and Tashakkori (2003: 14) suggest they are superior to single-approach designs because mixed methods:

- can answer research questions other methodologies cannot (i.e. can address explanatory and confirmatory questions at the same time thereby generating and verifying theory);
- provide stronger inferences (thereby complementing and overcoming weaknesses in single-method approaches);
- generate greater diversity of divergent views (and where findings converge, greater confidence can be expressed in the findings).

Furthermore, a mixed method approach places central importance on the experiences of the individual and alerts the researcher to the power differentials between themselves and those they research (Merton *et al.* 1990).

Practice application

In both Bohner and colleagues' and Hannah Frith's chapters rape prevention education programmes which are a common feature on college campuses in the United States are discussed. These programmes are perhaps the most visible application of the concepts and theories presented in this collection. Frith demonstrates how discursive psychology provides a valuable tool for explaining why some intervention approaches may be more successful than others. Both Bohner *et al.* and Frith discuss the limitations of existing programmes, including a lack of evaluation, and challenge the basis for such programmes, i.e. the assumption that changing attitudes leads to changes in behaviour. They also challenge the use of college graduates (often males) to derive findings which limits the generalisability of effects. These authors provide suggestions for alternative new approaches that may be more successful in changing both attitudes and behaviour. Maddy Coy's chapter highlights aspects of the lived experience of prostitution that may be instructive for the development of exit strategies and support work, as well as policy debates on the gendered harm of the sex industry.

Law and social reform are touched upon in many chapters and discussed in detail by Munro and Kelly and by Krahé and Temkin who provide comprehensive accounts of some of the options for change currently being explored in England and Wales and elsewhere. Considering these in relation to Stanko and Williams' identification of the key factors that inhibit the likelihood of cases proceeding to prosecution puts in context quite how much reform is needed at every level from encouraging more victims to report to the police to increasing the likelihood that when they do their case will progress to court.

Layout of book

The book is organised into four parts. In Part 1 the protagonist is every(wo)man, in other words people as social actors who are subject to social and societal influences that contribute to values, attitudes, social knowledge underpinning beliefs, perceptions and behaviours related to rape. The chapters in this part examine the social and societal processes and identify some of the resources that people use and call upon when making causal attributions about rape, its causes and blameworthiness. In Chapter 2 Bohner *et al.* focus on rape myth acceptance and give an overview of the findings from a series of studies they and other colleagues have conducted. Roger Giner-Sorolla and Pascale Russell use Chapter 3 to provide a comprehensive introduction to the role of emotions, focusing on anger and disgust, in evaluations and judgments of sexual crimes. Chapter 4 focuses on the representation of rape in the news media in the United States and United Kingdom. Jenny Kitzinger's analysis takes in the period from the 1970s to the beginning of the twenty-first century. In the final chapter of the first part Hannah Frith explores explanations for rape and sexual aggression focusing on sexual negotiation and communication between heterosexual couples using conversation analysis and discursive psychology and drawing on sexual miscommunication and sexual script theories. The ideas outlined in Part 1 are drawn upon in the remaining chapters of the book.

In the four chapters that comprise Part 2 the protagonist is the victim. These chapters are about her experiences/stories as examples of particular circumstances under which rape occurs. The focus is on circumstances where the victim is especially vulnerable, being viewed as: (a) an undeserving or stigmatised victim, (b) contributing to her own victimisation or (c) being incapacitated through mental health issues or intoxication. In Chapter 6 Jo Lovett and Miranda Horvath present data from two large studies of alcohol-related sexual assaults and in doing so they seek to advance a more nuanced understanding of the role of alcohol in rape. Aisha Gill uses Chapter 7 to focus on South Asian women's experience of sexual violence, drawing on interview data and exploring the sociocultural context in which these experiences occur. Chapter 8 focuses on another group of women who are frequently overlooked in the research literature, those involved in prostitution. Maddy Coy explores the ontology of violation drawing on data from life-story interviews and arts workshops. Finally, in Chapter 9 Betsy Stanko and Emma Williams use data from allegations of rape reported to the Metropolitan Police Service. While a descriptive account of the data is provided the focus of the chapter is on exploring the multiple vulnerabilities that victims have, such as mental health problems or simply being young, that were found to be a major contributor to the outcome of allegations in the criminal justice system.

The chapters in Part 3 move the focus from the victims to the criminal justice system (CJS) and the perspectives of those engaged in some formal way in investigating or prosecuting rapes. These chapters present critiques of the problems in part embedded in the process identified in the first part and compounded by the CJS that contribute to attrition and failure of the justice system. O'Keeffe *et al.* use the theoretical framework of naturalistic decision-making to explore the way police officers consider whether an allegation of rape is true or not. In Chapter 10 they draw upon interviews conducted with officers from the Republic of Ireland's National Police Service, An Garda Siochana. The focus of Chapter 11 is on the role and function of the police interview from the perspective of the different parties in the process: rape victims, police officers and judges. Lesley McMillan and Michelle Thomas use data from two different studies including interviews with police officers, a review of reported rapes to a police force, interviews with victims and observations in courtrooms. Chapter 12 is focused on developing a more holistic analysis of contemporary patterns of attrition and conviction in England and Wales. Vanessa Munro and Liz Kelly pay particular attention to those cases which do not conform to the stereotype of rape that was outlined in Part 1. Barbara Krahé and Jennifer Temkin in Chapter 13 focus their attention on rape trials and discuss some of the proposed potential strategies for decreasing attrition at this stage in the process.

Finally, in Chapter 14 which makes up Part 4, we draw together the accumulated threads and present our version of Munro and Kelly's vicious cycle whereby the poor conviction rates appear to support the prejudices inherent in rape myths which inhibit women from reporting their rapes. We also draw out the potential for practice in terms of education, training and changes in the law. The implications of both researching rape and our responsibilities to everyone (including but not exclusively victims, perpetrators, criminal justice practitioners) caught up in this vicious crime are touched upon. Rape is a crime which can impact all of those involved. Researchers and practitioners are not immune from the collateral damage of the harm caused to victims as they read their testimonies or take their accounts of their experiences.

Final introductory thoughts

On a more personal note readers should be aware that conducting research on rape with victims, perpetrators, criminal justice practitioners, the public and many others is not easy. This is not a line of research that one embarks upon lightly. Although the reader may not agree with all of the arguments presented in this book we hope that they will at least acknowledge that they were constructed with great care and consideration because ultimately the underlying hope of all the authors is to spark discussion and debate and contribute to the closing of the justice gap.

References

Crown Prosecution Service (2004) *Policy for Prosecuting Cases of Rape*. London: CPS. Available at: http://www.cps.gov.uk/publications/docs/prosecuting_rape.pdf (accessed 4 April 2009.

Estrich, S. (1987) *Real Rape: How the Legal System Victimises Women Who Say No*. Boston: Harvard University Press.

Greenfield, L. A. (1997) 'Sex offences and offenders: an analysis of data on rape and sexual assault', cited in E. F. Avakame (1999) 'Females' labour force participation and rape: an empirical test of the Backlash Hypothesis', *Violence Against Women*, 5: 926–49.

HM Government (2007) *Cross Government Action Plan on Sexual Violence and Abuse*. Available at: http://www.crimereduction.homeoffice.gov.uk/sexualoffences/finalsvaap.pdf (accessed 4 April 2009.

Home Office (2006a) *Consent Campaign*. Available at: http://www.homeoffice.gov.uk/documents/consent-campaign/ (accessed 4 April 2009.

Home Office (2006b) 'Consent Awareness Campaign – Summary of Evaluation'. Unpublished report.

Kalven, H. and Zeisel, H. (1966) *The American Jury*. Boston: Little, Brown.

Kelly, L. (2008) 'Contradictions and paradoxes: international patterns of, and responses to, reported rape cases', in G. Letherby, K. Williams, P. Birch and M. Cain (eds), *Sex as Crime?* Cullompton: Willan, pp. 253–79.

Merton, R. K., Fiske, M. and Kendall, P. L. (1990) *The Focused Interview*. New York: Free Press.

New South Wales Standing Committee on Social Issues (1996) *Sexual Violence*, Vol. 1. Sydney: Department of Justice.

Rape Action Plan (2002) Available at: http://www.crimereduction.homeoffice.gov.uk/sexual/sexual20.htm (accessed 4 April 2009.

Richardson, D. (2000) *Rethinking Sexuality*. London: Sage.

Stahlberg, D. and Frey, D. (1996) 'Attitudes: structure, measurement and functions', in M. Hewstone, W. Stroebe and G. Stephenson (eds), *Introduction to Social Psychology*, 2nd edn. Oxford: Blackwell, pp. 205–39.

Teddlie, C. and Tashakkori, A. (2003) 'Major issues and controversies in the use of mixed methods in the social and behavioural sciences', in A. Tashakkori and C. Teddlie (ed.), *Handbook of Mixed Methods in Social and Behavioural Research*. Thousand Oaks, CA: Sage, pp. 3–50.

Temkin, J. (2002) *Rape and the Legal Process*. Oxford: Oxford University Press.

Temkin, J. and Krahé, B. (2008) *Sexual Assault and the Justice Gap: A Question of Attitude*. Oxford: Hart.

Walby, S. and Allen, J. (2004) *Domestic Violence, Sexual Assault and Stalking: Findings from the British Crime Survey*, Home Office Research Study No. 276. London: Home Office.

Ward, C. (1995) *Attitudes Toward Rape: Feminist and Social Psychological Perspectives*. London: Sage.

Part I

Processes and Representations

Chapter 2

Rape myth acceptance: cognitive, affective and behavioural effects of beliefs that blame the victim and exonerate the perpetrator

Gerd Bohner, Friederike Eyssel, Afroditi Pina,
Frank Siebler and G. Tendayi Viki

Introduction

The reality of sexual violence and its harmful effects on the individual and on society are indisputable. Recent statistics indicate a serious worldwide problem, with one in three women having experienced some form of sexual violence, such as being battered, coerced into sex or otherwise abused (United Nations Development Fund for Women 2008; World Bank 1993). The health consequences of rape and sexual violence are both detrimental and long lasting (Holmes *et al.* 1998); for women aged between 15 and 44, rape and domestic violence are higher risk factors for death and disability than are cancer, war and motor vehicle accidents (United Nations Development Fund for Women 2008; World Bank 1993). In sum, 'sexual violence is the most pervasive human rights violation that we know today, it devastates lives, fractures communities and stalls development' (United Nations Development Fund for Women 2008: 1). Feminist writers have argued that the prevalence of sexual violence contributes to gender inequality and supports the status quo of male dominance by keeping all women, including those women who are not directly victimised, in a state of constant fear (Brownmiller 1975). Empirical research confirms that the fear of rape is a daily reality for many women, limiting their freedom of movement and reducing their quality of life (Dobash and Dobash 1992; Gordon *et al.* 1980; Mirrlees-Black and Allen 1998).

At the same time, the attrition rates for successful prosecution of rapes through the criminal justice system are high. The proportion of rapes reported to the police is notoriously low, and within those relatively few cases that are reported, conviction rates have been declining (Kelly *et al.* 2005; Temkin and Krahé 2008; United Nations 2000). Researchers have recognised that a major cause of this widening 'justice gap' are pervasive beliefs about rape, or *rape myths* (Brownmiller 1975; Burt 1980). These myths affect subjective definitions of what constitutes a 'typical rape', contain problematic assumptions about the likely behaviour of perpetrators and victims, and paint a distorted picture of the antecedents and consequences of rape. They are widely held by the general public (e.g. Gerger *et al.* 2007) and by those in the criminal justice system (e.g. Brown and King 1998; Feild 1978). Rape myths are propagated by the media (e.g. Franiuk *et al.* 2008), affecting the offending behaviour of perpetrators, the reporting behaviour of victims, the decision-making behaviour of investigators and prosecutors and the assessement of guilt or innocence by jurors (Temkin and Krahé 2008; Wilson and Scholes 2008).

In this chapter, we introduce and discuss the concept of rape myths and examine some of the research instruments that have been used to measure these beliefs. We then review a series of interlinked studies from our laboratory, as well as related research by others, on both general and gender-specific functions of rape myth acceptance (RMA). In doing so, we present a theoretical framework according to which RMA influences information processing, affect and behaviour by serving as a cognitive schema. We conclude with discussing applied implications of RMA research for interventions aimed at reducing RMA and improving legal procedures.

Introduction to the concept of rape myths

In the 1970s the concept of rape myths became a topic of interest and closer inspection for various researchers (e.g. Brownmiller 1975; Feild 1978; Schwendinger and Schwendinger 1974). Within social psychology, Martha Burt (1980) was the first to propose a definition of rape myths as 'prejudicial, stereotyped and false beliefs about rape, rape victims and rapists' (p. 217). Although this definition has been widely used, Lonsway and Fitzgerald (1994), in their excellent review and critique of prominent definitions of rape myths, point out that Burt's definition is not 'sufficiently articulated', nor are all the terms used explained sufficiently clearly for it to serve as a formal definition (p. 134).

Despite definitional concerns that will be outlined in more detail below, there seems to be a consensus as to what rape myths usually entail (for a full review on structural issues see Payne *et al.* 1999). We may identify four general types of rape myth: beliefs that

- *blame the victim for their rape* (e.g. 'women have an unconscious desire to be raped', 'women often provoke rape through their appearance or behaviour');

- express a *disbelief in claims of rape* (e.g. 'most charges of rape are unfounded', 'women tend to exaggerate how much rape affects them');

- *exonerate the perpetrator* (e.g. 'most rapists are over-sexed', 'rape happens when a man's sex drive gets out of control'); and

- allude that *only certain types of women are raped* (e.g. 'a woman who dresses in skimpy clothes should not be surprised if a man tries to force her to have sex', 'usually it is women who do things like hang out in bars and sleep around that are raped')

(Bohner, Reinhard *et al.* 1998; Briere *et al.* 1985; Burt 1980, 1991; Costin 1985; Gerger *et al.* 2007; Lonsway and Fitzgerald 1994, 1995; Payne *et al.* 1999).

Lonsway and Fitzgerald (1994) emphasise the characteristics of the term 'myth', highlighting the specific cultural functions that myths usually serve. Their more recent definition of rape myths as 'attitudes and beliefs that are generally false but are widely and persistently held, and that serve to deny and justify male sexual aggression against women' (Lonsway and Fitzgerald 1994: 134) integrates such functional aspects. Taking this functional view a step further, Bohner (1998: 12–14) as well as Gerger *et al.* (2007) pointed out that aspects such as whether rape myths are 'false' or 'widely held' should not be included in a formal definition. On the one hand, it is often impossible to decide whether a myth is false, for example if the myth expresses a normative belief or is stated in a way that is difficult to falsify (e.g. 'many women *secretly* desire to be raped'). Questions of prevalence, on the other hand, should be addressed empirically, otherwise a belief that was once widely held but is not widely held any more would by definition cease to be a rape myth. The most recent definition we rely on for the purposes of this chapter thus describes rape myths as 'descriptive or prescriptive beliefs about rape (i.e. about its causes, context, consequences, perpetrators, victims and their interaction) that serve to deny, downplay or justify sexual violence that men commit against women' (Bohner 1998: 14).

19

Current measures of rape myth acceptance and methodological issues

The scientific progress reflected in the evolution of conceptualisations about rape-related beliefs also becomes evident at the level of instruments to measure rape myths. We critically discuss some of the most commonly used classic measures of rape myths as well as a recently developed scale designed to measure modern myths about sexual aggression. The distinction between classic and contemporary versions of rape myths predominantly rests on the degree of subtlety of the item wordings, with classic measures being marked by rather blatant item formulations, whereas our modern measure is characterised by its more subtle item content.

Among the most widely used classic scales are the *Rape Myth Acceptance Scale* (RMAS: Burt 1980) and the *Attitudes Toward Rape Scale* (ATR: Feild 1978). To illustrate, Buhi (2005) reviews 57 studies using the 19-item RMAS scale, thus attesting to its wide usage. Most of these studies attest to the good psychometric properties of this instrument (e.g. Kopper 1996; Krahé 1988; Margolin *et al.* 1989). Other researchers developed RMA scales that were modified versions of Burt's original scale (e.g. Donnerstein *et al.* 1986; Ellis *et al.* 1992; Fonow *et al.* 1992).

Another widely used measure of RMA is Feild's (1978) ATR. The ATR is a 32-item scale that predates the RMAS (for a report on the reliability of the ATR, see Lonsway and Fitzgerald 1994). In a factor analysis, Feild identified eight interpretable subscales (e.g. *woman's responsibility in rape prevention, sex as motivation for rape, victim precipitation of rape*). Subsequent research on the differential validity of these subscales, however, is lacking. As with the RMAS, the ATR too has been subjected to modifications, including Costin's popular 20-item *R scale* (Costin 1985), which was translated into several languages (Costin and Schwarz 1987) and widely used with German samples by Bohner (1998).

Despite their wide use, these two scales have been criticised for various reasons (e.g. Payne *et al.* 1999). For example, several of Burt's (1980) RMAS items are too long and complex and often include several concepts within one item, which makes them difficult to understand and answer unambiguously. This results in further methodological problems, as it threatens the scale's reliability and validity (Hinck and Thomas 1999; Payne *et al.* 1999). Furthermore, the classic scales often feature items whose wording is marked by a heavy usage of colloquialisms and slang terminology (e.g. 'put out', 'necking', 'fair game'). Payne *et al.* (1999) argued that the use of colloquialisms can severely affect the cross-cultural applicability of the scales, since particular culture-specific wordings might not be grasped by persons from a different cultural background.

A more recent RMA measure that avoids many of the pitfalls of item wording discussed above is the *Illinois Rape Myth Acceptance Scale* (IRMA: Payne *et al.* 1999). The IRMA comes in two versions, a 45-item long version and a 20-item short form (IRMA-SF). In factor analyses, Payne and colleagues identified seven factors, but again, research on the differential validity of these seven factors is lacking and the scale is usually treated as measuring a one-dimensional construct. The scale's reliability and construct validity is good, and during the last decade the IRMA has been used in both basic and applied research (e.g. Bohner and Lampridis 2004; Loh *et al.* 2005; Lonsway *et al.* 2001).

More recently, however, Gerger and her colleagues (2007) have noted a problem with the classic RMA scales. Especially in research with college students, these scales often produce floor effects, i.e. highly skewed distributions and means near the low endpoint of the scale. Skewed distributions have disadvantages because statistical tests of correlational or experimental hypotheses usually require a normal distribution of scores or error terms. Also, in applied studies aimed at reducing RMA through appropriate interventions, any beneficial effects of the intervention may be difficult to determine if the means of the target variable are already near the bottom of the scale. Gerger *et al.* point out that the observed low means of self-reported RMA may have two possible causes: (1) that respondents nowadays are more aware of and so comply with socially accepted answers to explicit and blatant RMA items; and (2) that the content of common myths about sexual aggression may have changed. They drew an analogy with similar historical developments that took place in the areas of sexism and racism over the last decades. For example, Swim *et al.* (1995) proposed that sexist beliefs have become more subtle and covert, and distinguish between 'old fashioned' and 'modern' sexism, where the former includes the endorsement of traditional gender roles, discriminatory treatment of women and stereotypes about female competence, whereas the latter includes the denial of present discrimination, antagonistic attitudes toward women and a lack of support for women's needs.

Based on these guiding ideas, Gerger *et al.* (2007) developed a new RMA scale, the 30-item *Acceptance of Modern Myths about Sexual Aggression Scale* (AMMSA). Its items were generated to reflect the content categories as shown in Table 2.1.

Table 2.1 Content categories and exemplar items of the Acceptance of Modern Myths about Sexual Aggression (AMMSA) Scale (Gerger *et al.* 2007)

Content	Example
(a) *Denial of the scope of the problem*	'Many women tend to misinterpret a well-meant gesture as a "sexual assault".'
(b) *Antagonism toward victims' demands*	'Although the victims of armed robbery have to fear for their lives, they receive far less psychological support than do rape victims.'
(c) *Lack of support for policies designed to help alleviate the effects of sexual violence*	'Nowadays, the victims of sexual violence receive sufficient help in the form of women's shelters, therapy offers and support groups.'
(d) *Beliefs that male coercion forms a natural part of sexual relationships*	'When a woman starts a relationship with a man, she must be aware that the man will assert his right to have sex.'
(e) *Beliefs that exonerate male perpetrators by blaming the victim or the circumstances*	'Alcohol is often the culprit when a man rapes a woman.'

Note: English, German and Spanish versions of the scale are available online at http://www.uni-bielefeld.de/psychologie/ae/AE05/AMMSA/index.html.

Empirical studies showed that mean scores on the AMMSA, as intended by its authors, were generally higher than the mean scores on classic scales (for direct comparisons with the IRMA-SF, see Gerger *et al.* 2007). Also, AMMSA scores were symmetrically distributed, approximating a normal distribution. Furthermore, the scale's excellent reliability and construct validity was demonstrated in various studies. The scale is available in English, German and Spanish (Megías *et al.* 2009), and two parallel short versions are currently being developed (Eyssel and Bohner 2009). For a review of the concept of modern rape myths and research using the AMMSA scale, see Eyssel and Bohner (2008a). Additional studies using the AMMSA with UK samples are currently being undertaken (e.g. Calogero *et al.* 2009; Pina and Hallmark 2009).

Functions of rape myths: cognitive, affective, behavioural

Why do people endorse rape myths? It has long been posited that rape myths may serve various psychological functions (e.g. Bohner 1998; Brownmiller 1975; Burt 1980, 1991; Lonsway and Fitzgerald 1994). They may help people to understand and explain events in their social world, to maintain cognitive consistency, to fend off negative affect and threats to self-esteem, and to rationalise problematic behaviour. Here we review research on these cognitive, affective and behavioural functions of RMA, addressing both *general* functions and *gender-related* functions which are typically relevant only to women or only to men.[1]

Rape myth acceptance as a general cognitive schema

Early research focused on external perceivers' responsibility attributions in relation to rape scenarios (e.g. Jones and Aronson 1973; for reviews, see Krahé 1991; Pollard 1992). A central finding was that perceivers with higher RMA attributed greater responsibility to the victim and lesser responsibility to the perpetrator. Furthermore, it was shown that perceivers with high (vs. low) RMA perceived the trauma of the victim to be less severe and were less likely to recommend that the victim report the incident to the police (e.g. Frese *et al.* 2004; Krahé 1988). Attributions of responsibility may also be expressed in subtle linguistic choices: Bohner (2001) showed that students high (vs. low) in RMA who described a rape they had observed in a film scene were more likely to use language that put the perpetrator in the background and the victim in the focus of discourse (e.g. agentless passive: 'she was raped'; nominal phrases: 'then the rape occurred').

RMA may thus be conceived as a general *schema* which guides and organises an individual's interpretation of specific information about rape cases. Generally speaking, cognitive schemas are broad knowledge structures that people use to assist the processing of incoming information (e.g. Neisser 1976). Processing of information becomes selective, with attention being focused on a potential match between incoming information and the schema-related information stored in memory (e.g. Bem 1981). Importantly, schemas allow perceivers to 'go beyond the information given' (Bruner 1957), that is to infer things that were not actually present in the stimulus material.

Applied to rape myths, this means that perceivers high in RMA may readily use a particular piece of information contained in a rape case (e.g. that the complainant had been drinking alcohol), or infer information that was never presented (e.g. that the complainant may have consented because she knew the defendant), with the result of exonerating the defendant. Recent research by Krahé *et al.* (2008) shows that even prospective lawyers fall prey to these schematic influences. In their studies, undergraduate and postgraduate law students rated rape scenarios varying with respect to the defendant–complainant relationship. Those law students who were high in RMA held the defendant less liable and blamed the complainant more, especially when the two had known each other (for related research on rape myths within the criminal justice system, see Andrias 1992; Burt and Albin 1981; Spohn and Horney 1993).

Although the findings we review here pertain to external perceivers, we should note that rape victims often interpret their own experiences in terms of rape myths. This may prevent them from labelling these experiences as rape; it may also cause them to find fault with their own behaviour and, hence, to fail to report an incident to the police (Peterson and Muehlenhard 2004; Warshaw 1988). Some research points to the conclusion, however, that becoming a victim may attenuate the effect that a rape myth schema has on people's processing (for discussion see Bohner 1998: 62–3).

Schematic influences tend to be strong when external facts are uninformative or ambiguous (e.g. Dunning and Sherman 1997; Kunda and Sherman-Williams 1993). In an ongoing research programme, we tested the hypothesis that the influence of RMA on judgments about rape cases would increase when the available information was mixed or uninformative. In one experiment, students received pieces of case-related information in a sequence of five steps: (1) contradicting statements of complainant and defendant; (2) summary of expert witness A's statement; (3) summary of expert witness B's statement; (4) extended version of A's statement, and (5) extended version of B's statement. The expert witnesses' statements were prepared in such a way that one pointed to the defendant's guilt whereas the other suggested his innocence. After reading each piece of information, participants were repeatedly asked to rate the likelihood that the defendant was guilty of rape. In line with our hypothesis, these ratings were not influenced by RMA whenever the weight of the evidence clearly implied either guilt or innocence (i.e. after steps 2 and 4), but were influenced by RMA whenever the evidence was completely balanced (i.e. after steps 1, 3 and 5; Eyssel and Bohner 2008b: Study 1).

In another experiment, participants received either a low amount or a high amount of case-*irrelevant* information about the defendant versus the complainant (e.g. what subject the person studied or where he/she lived). We hypothesised that the effect of participants' RMA on judgments about the defendant's guilt would increase with increasing amounts of case-irrelevant information. As Figure 2.1 shows, the data clearly supported this prediction: high-RMA participants generally perceived lower levels of guilt than did low-RMA participants; more importantly, this effect was particularly pronounced when a lot of irrelevant information had been provided (Eyssel and Bohner 2008b: Study 2).

A third experiment in this series showed that people's reliance on their RMA for making guilt judgments may increase even if people merely believe that they possess case-related evidence when in fact they do not. In their 'social judgeability' approach to stereotyping, Leyens et al. (1992) had shown that people often avoid using stereo-types in person judgments unless they feel 'entitled to judge' because they believe that relevant individuating information was presented to them subliminally. Building on this approach, we set out to create an illusion of being informed in some of our participants. All participants first received minimal case information, consisting only of very brief,

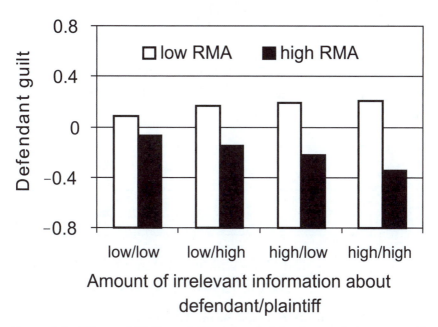

Figure 2.1 Effects of RMA on judgments of defendant guilt increase with the amount of irrelevant information presented (Eyssel and Bohner 2008b)

divergent statements from defendant and complainant. Then they performed a vigilance task, where they had to respond quickly to stimuli appearing on a computer screen. Embedded in the vigilance task was the repeated subliminal presentation of masked strings of non-words that resembled text sentences. We later told half of the participants that these strings (which participants had not been able to recognise) had actually been sentences containing relevant case information; we further told them that 'psychological studies have shown that people are capable of processing information, even if it was not recognised consciously.' The other half of the participants were simply told that the vigilance task had served as a distractor task (control condition). When participants later judged the defendant's guilt, high-RMA participants gave lower guilt ratings than did low-RMA participants. More importantly, as shown in Figure 2.2, the effect of RMA on guilt judgments was stronger, as predicted, for those participants who were under the illusion of having received additional case information (Eyssel and Bohner 2008b: Study 3).

Self-perpetuating aspects of the rape myth schema

That people draw specific conclusions about rape cases which blame the victim and exonerate the perpetrator may be conceived as part

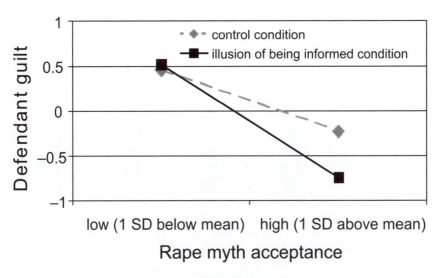

Figure 2.2 Effects of RMA on judgments of defendant guilt increase with the illusion of being informed (simple slopes analysis – Eyssel and Bohner 2008b)

of a more encompassing cognitive motive, the 'belief in a just world'. This construct describes a tendency to perceive the world as a fair place, where people generally get what they deserve and where bad things happen only to bad people (Lerner 1980). Just-world beliefs thus offer reassurance that if all necessary precautions are taken, and if people are good, nothing bad will happen to them. If these beliefs are challenged, for example by encountering information that an innocent person has suffered violence, one way of restoring cognitive consistency is by blaming the victim. In the case of sexual violence, rape myths offer the necessary 'explanations' as to why rape victims 'got what they deserved' (e.g. they did not protect themselves sufficiently or they even provoked their own victimisation). Research has shown that individual differences in the belief in a just world correlate positively with RMA (Bohner 1998; Lonsway and Fitzgerald 1994). By interpreting information in a way that is consistent with rape myths (and thus also with more general just-world beliefs), individuals thus generate 'evidence' that seemingly supports their own myths.

A similar self-perpetuating principle may operate at the societal level when rape myths and jury verdicts influence each other. Sinclair and Bourne (1998) have proposed a 'cycle of blame' framework, suggesting that the same rape myths that limit convictions may in turn be strengthened by not-guilty verdicts. On the one hand, rape myth endorsement by jury members may lead to more restrictive rape definitions and fewer convictions (see Andrias 1992; Burt and Albin 1981; Rhode 1989). On the other hand, not-guilty verdicts may reinforce those very myths that have contributed to the verdicts in the first place. Sinclair and Bourne tested this idea by presenting identical case summaries but telling participants either that the jury's verdict was 'guilty' or that it was 'not guilty'. Later, participants' RMA was assessed as a dependent variable. For male participants, the 'cycle of blame' hypothesis was supported, in that their RMA scores were higher after a not-guilty verdict and lower after a guilty verdict. For women, interestingly, the opposite effect was found, in that a not-guilty verdict lowered RMA and a guilty verdict increased RMA. The authors' explanation for the women's discrepant results invokes the just-world hypothesis: because women generally fear rape victimisation more than men do (see Bohner *et al.* 1993), they may endorse rape myths in order to feel safer ('If it *was* rape, the woman must have contributed to it happening'). Below we will have more to say about the idea that rape myths may fulfil a self-protective function for women.

In sum, there is compelling evidence that RMA serves as a cognitive schema for interpreting information in rape cases. These schematic influences affect both laypersons and legal experts. The effects of RMA are particularly pronounced if the available evidence is mixed or irrelevant, or if people are merely under the false impression of being informed. Cognitive and motivational principles operating at the individual and the societal level contribute to the perpetuation of rape myths.

Gender-related functions for women: affect management and self-esteem protection

Our research suggests that RMA has divergent functions for the two genders. For women specifically, an important aspect of the rape myth schema is that it pertains to their self-categorisation. Their level of RMA determines whether they include the threat of rape in their self-concept or exclude this threat from their self-concept. Specifically, women who reject rape myths would agree that any woman can be raped and, thus, perceive rape as a potential threat to *all women*, including themselves; women who endorse rape myths, by contrast, believe that rape only happens to a *certain type of woman* (e.g. who behaves carelessly or improperly), whom they perceive as dissimilar from themselves (Bohner 1998; Bohner *et al.* 1993).

Based on this proposed relationship between RMA and the cognitive representation of self and rape victims, we tested the hypothesis that women low (vs. high) in RMA would be more likely to use gender spontaneously as a general category when thinking about themselves or others and when solving cognitive tasks. In other words, we predicted that the concept of gender would chronically be more accessible to women low (vs. high) in RMA (Bohner, Siebler *et al.* 1998). This hypothesis was supported in a series of three studies. In Study 1, women were asked to complete ten statements starting with the phrase 'I am ...'. As predicted, low-RMA (compared to high-RMA) women provided self-descriptions in terms of gender (e.g. 'a woman', 'female') or gender-related roles (e.g. 'a daughter', 'a sister') both earlier and more frequently. In Study 2, low-RMA women were more likely to use gender as a discriminating feature when judging the similarity of pairs of target persons, although gender was never mentioned in the task instructions. Finally, in Study 3, women were asked to complete word fragments as quickly as possible with the first solution that came to mind; in critical trials, where both gender-related and neutral solutions existed, low-RMA participants were more likely to generate gender-related solutions, and did so more quickly, than high-RMA participants.

The proposed RMA-linked differences in the accessibility of gender and in self-categorisation have implications for affect management and self-esteem maintenance in situations where rape is salient. A first experimental test of the effect of fear of rape on women's self-related judgments indicated that women who were presented with reminders of rape (in the form of rape scenarios) showed severely impaired self-perceptions, with a particularly negative effect on their self-esteem and trust in others. Furthermore, women faced with reminders of rape also showed an increased acceptance of traditional gender norms (Schwarz and Brand 1983). In follow-up studies, Bohner and his colleagues examined the hypothesis that level of RMA would moderate the effects of rape salience on self-esteem and affect, in line with the assumed RMA-related differences in self-categorisation (Bohner 1998; Bohner and Lampridis 2004; Bohner et al. 1993, 1999). The general result of these studies was that the negative effects of rape salience on women's self-esteem that Schwarz and Brand had observed were limited to women who reject rape myths. Women who endorse rape myths, on the other hand, showed no decrease in self-esteem or affect after exposure to a rape scenario, or even reported somewhat heightened self-esteem (Bohner et al. 1993; Bohner and Lampridis 2004).

To illustrate this line of research, we review in some detail the most recent empirical test of the effect of RMA on women's self-esteem (Bohner and Lampridis 2004). Female students who were either high or low in RMA participated in what they thought was a study about 'getting acquainted'. They expected having a first conversation with another woman about a topic that the other woman had suggested. Participants were randomly assigned to one of three topic conditions which were designed to vary experimentally the salience of rape. In a rape-salient condition, the other woman had apparently been raped and wanted to talk about this experience; in a neutral control condition, the other woman wanted to talk about studying at their university; and in a further control condition, the other woman had apparently been diagnosed with leukemia and wanted to talk about her illness. This latter condition was included to rule out the possibility that any differential reactions of high-RMA and low-RMA participants to the rape-salient versus neutral control conditions might be caused by general differences in emotional reactivity. After participants had read about the alleged conversation topic, they completed scales measuring different facets of self-esteem as well as their affective reactions in anticipation of the upcoming conversation. (After completing these scales, the participants were debriefed, and no conversation took place.) Results indicated that the prospect of meeting a rape victim had a strong impact on women's self-esteem and affect (stronger than the effects of reading information about rape that we had found in previous studies). Again, this negative effect of rape salience was clearly more negative for low-RMA women than for high-RMA women, replicating previous results (e.g. Bohner *et al.* 1993, 1999).

As illustrated in Figure 2.3 for the dependent variable gender-related self-esteem (i.e. self-reported importance and evaluation of being a woman: Bohner and Sturm 1997), the differential effects on low-RMA versus high-RMA women were limited to the rape-salient condition and did not generalise to the leukemia-salient condition. This supports the idea that RMA acts as a specific anxiety buffer related to sexual violence (for an extended discussion, see Bohner and Lampridis 2004).

In sum, RMA was shown to serve as an anxiety buffer that allows women to feel less vulnerable to sexual assault and to protect their self-esteem. The more they endorse rape myths the less threatened and vulnerable they feel about their own possibility of victimisation

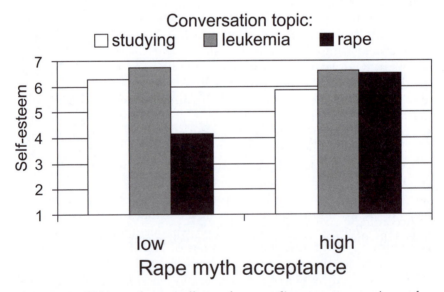

Figure 2.3 RMA moderates effects of rape salience on women's gender-related self-esteem (data from Bohner and Lampridis 2004)

(see also Bohner 1998). However, women who reject rape myths may experience negative effects on their self-esteem because they do not believe that only certain women are at risk of being raped, but rather construe rape as a potential threat to all women, including themselves (Bohner and Schwarz 1996). The beliefs of women low in RMA thus seem to be more realistic, but this greater realism comes at a cost, as the rejection of rape myths makes low-RMA women prone to negative affective reactions when confronted with the topic of sexual violence. Nonetheless, high-RMA women's illusion of invulnerability may be even more problematic, as it seems to prevent these women from learning self-defence strategies and from engaging in protective behaviours that have been shown to be effective in the case of an attack (e.g. shouting, talking to the attacker: Bohner 1998: 66–9). As noted above, women high in RMA who become rape victims may also be less likely to report the incident to the police because they are less likely to label their own experiences as rape (Peterson and Muehlenhard 2004; Warshaw 1988).

Gender-related functions for men: rationalisation of aggressive tendencies

Research conducted with male participants has focused on behavioural functions of RMA. Given the high prevalence of sexual violence, it is plausible to assume that many men harbour aggressive sexual tendencies. The endorsement of rape myths may serve both to rationalise these tendencies and to turn them into actions. From the beginning, feminist writers have noted this rationalising function of rape myths (Brownmiller 1975; Burt 1980). In our own research, we (Bohner, Reinhard et al. 1998) have drawn parallels between the content and functions of rape myths and the 'techniques of neutralisation' which have been proposed to explain juvenile delinquency (Sykes and Matza 1957) and other socially deviant behaviours (e.g. Schahn et al. 1995). Among the neutralising beliefs that Sykes and Matza described are *denial of injury* ('no harm was done'), *denial of responsibility* ('it was not my fault', 'I was provoked'), and *denial of victim* ('they had it coming'). By endorsing these beliefs, an offender may avoid perceiving his own criminal acts as norm violations.

Accordingly, we concluded that the prevalence of rape can be linked to the use of rape myths as mechanisms that neutralise or trivialise rape and sexual violence. In line with this reasoning, several studies have shown RMA to be highly correlated with measures of self-reported rape proclivity (e.g. Abrams et al. 2003; Malamuth 1981; Malamuth and Check 1985; Quackenbush 1989). Going beyond these correlational findings, we conducted an extensive research programme to examine the causal role of men's own RMA and of the perceived RMA of others in predicting rape proclivity.

To assess rape proclivity, we developed an instrument that contains several scenarios in which an acquaintance rape is described (but the word 'rape' is never used). Participants indicate for each scenario whether they would have behaved like the perpetrator and how much they would have enjoyed getting their way in this situation. Averaging participants' responses across scenarios yields a valid measure of rape proclivity that is less affected than earlier measures by tendencies to answer in a socially desirable way (see Bohner, Reinhard et al. 1998; for a recent adaptation addressing more general tendencies toward sexual aggression, see Eyssel et al. 2009; for a laboratory measure of milder forms of sexual aggression, see Siebler et al. 2008). In our initial studies, we manipulated the temporal order in which we assessed men's RMA and rape proclivity to vary their relative salience. Our reasoning was that a causal impact of RMA on rape proclivity should be indicated by higher correlations between the two measures if RMA had been assessed first. If, however, RMA was a result of pre-existing rape proclivity, then the reverse order should yield higher correlations. The results of three studies, two conducted in Germany and one in the UK, were clearly in line with the first alternative: making participants' own RMA accessible to them (by presenting the RMA scale before the rape proclivity measure) consistently yielded a higher correlation than did the reverse order (Bohner, Reinhard et al. 1998; Bohner et al. 2005).

Furthermore, Bohner et al. (2005) found evidence for a chronically high accessibility of RMA in men who had been sexually coercive before. These men generally showed a high correlation between RMA and rape proclivity, and were faster in responding to RMA items than were men who had not been sexually coercive. This indicates that sexually coercive men may use rape myths to justify their actions (Bohner 1998; Burt 1980), and that therefore these myths may become more cognitively accessible to them in future situations, including future sexual encounters. Thus RMA as a cognitive schema in men may indeed facilitate sexual aggression (Bohner et al. 2005).

Another line of our research looked at normative effects of others' perceived RMA on men's rape proclivity (Bohner et al. 2006; Eyssel et al. 2006). Bohner et al. (2006: Study 2) asked male students to complete an RMA scale. Then they provided participants with manipulated feedback about the alleged level of RMA in their peer group. Depending on experimental condition, participants learned that their fellow students had either low, high or very high RMA scores. Later, participants completed our scenario measure of rape proclivity. As shown in Figure 2.4, both participants' own RMA and the level of perceived RMA in their peer group influenced their self-reported rape proclivity. Importantly, the two variables had an interactive effect: higher perceived RMA in participants' peer group increased rape proclivity especially in those students whose RMA was high to begin with.

Additional research confirmed that the effect of others' RMA on men's rape proclivity was quite robust. Eyssel *et al.* (2006) found that the effect was independent of whether the level of peers' RMA was presented to participants as a social norm (as in Bohner *et al.* 2006) or whether participants merely considered that level of RMA as a judgmental anchor ('Do you think the mean response of students at your university is higher or lower than X?'). In two further studies, Bohner *et al.* (2009) showed that the perceived RMA of an outgroup (foreign students or pensioners) can be just as effective in influencing rape proclivity as can the perceived RMA of one's ingroup (native

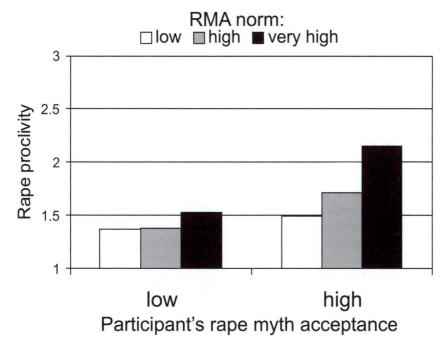

Figure 2.4 Participant's own RMA and perceived RMA norm jointly affect men's rape proclivity (data from Bohner *et al.* 2006)

students). Interestingly, when participants expected the outgroup's level of RMA to be high and then learned that the outgroup's level of RMA was actually low, the effect on reducing rape proclivity was greater than that of learning about the ingroup's low level of RMA (Bohner *et al.* 2009: Study 2). In sum, for men, RMA serves as a means to rationalise and justify their own tendencies to engage in sexual aggression. Furthermore, the perceived RMA of others may provide a social norm for men's sexually aggressive behaviour (Bohner *et al.* 2006; Eyssel *et al.* 2006). These results corroborate Berkowitz's (2002) proposal that men who believe that their peers are using coercive methods to obtain sexual relations are more likely to engage in similar behaviours themselves. They may be seen as the laboratory equivalent of applied work conducted by Berkowitz and his colleagues (Berkowitz 2002; Fabiano *et al.* 2003). Longitudinal research by Loh *et al.* (2005) also, tentatively, indicates that level of RMA in fraternity memberships (in the US) has some influence on actual rape perpetration.

Applications

We have discussed the detrimental effects of rape myths which may nurture false beliefs about a just world, provide women with illusory feelings of safety and offer men ways of rationalising tendencies toward committing sexual violence. Our theoretical analysis and empirical results thus show that RMA is one of the main factors that need to be addressed in order to prevent sexual violence and ameliorate negative attitudes toward victims. Indeed, existing programmes of sex-offender treatment have aimed at correcting distorted beliefs about sexual violence (e.g. Marshall 1999; Seto and Barbaree 1999). In this final section we will focus on the primary prevention of sexual offending, mainly addressing general rape prevention programmes directed toward individuals that have not offended.

A plethora of educational programmes, especially in the US, address sexual violence on college campuses (e.g. Fonow *et al.* 1992; Foubert 2000; Foubert and Marriott 1997; Foubert and McEwen 1998; Gidycz *et al.* 2001; Hanson and Gidycz 1993, Lonsway *et al.* 1998; Lonsway and Kothari 2000; Malamuth and Check 1984; O'Donohue *et al.* 2003). Most of these programmes use various methodologies, including video presentations, seminars on victim empathy or training for involvement in rape victim support, to change false beliefs surrounding rape in order to reduce sexual violence, usually relying on the self-reported likelihood to sexually aggress or on self-reported behaviour as criterion measures.

Although many of these intervention programmes lack a clear theoretical basis, some (e.g. Foubert 2000; Foubert and Marriott 1997; Foubert and McEwen 1998; Gilbert *et al.* 1991; Heppner *et al.* 1995) rely on Petty and Cacioppo's (1986) elaboration likelihood model (ELM), a theory of persuasion that specifies the conditions for lasting attitude change. In numerous studies, Petty and Cacioppo have demonstrated that information perceived to be personally relevant leads to high-effort processing, which in turn may produce attitude change that is resistant to subsequent challenges if the information is of high argument quality. Interventions designed to successfully change attitudes should therefore use well-argued messages and establish high personal relevance of these messages to their target group (Foubert and McEwen 1998).

Other programmes (O'Donohue *et al.* 2003; Schewe and O'Donohue 1993; Yeater and O'Donohue 1999) rely on theoretical models that are widely used in the aetiology of child sexual abuse or adult sexual assault, as well as several cognitive and information processing models, for example Finkelhor's four-factor model (1986) and Bandura's social learning model of aggression (1973). According to these models, rape myths are cognitions that make liable conduct ethically acceptable, minimise the consequences of that behaviour and devalue the victim (O'Donohue *et al.* 2003; see our earlier discussion of rape myths as neutralising cognitions: Bohner, Reinhard *et al.* 1998). Most of these programmes appear to be successful in reducing RMA in college males as well as reducing the likelihood of these males to engage in sexually coercive behaviour (Fonow *et al.* 1992; Foubert 2000; Foubert and McEwen 1998; Foubert and Marriott 1997; Gilbert *et al.* 1991; Hanson and Gidycz 1993, Lonsway *et al.* 1998; Lonsway and Kothari 2000; Malamuth and Check 1984; O'Donohue *et al.* 2003).

Nevertheless, existing programmes have their limitations. The reported effects are often relatively short-term (e.g. Foubert and McEwen 1998), and we lack information on the long-term effectiveness of interventions (e.g. O'Donohue *et al.* 2003). Furthermore, most of the existing programmes are aimed at college males (in particular fraternity members), whereas there is very limited current research addressing the reduction of RMA in females. Moreover, a systematic evaluation of the above programmes has not yet been undertaken, thus making the assessment of the success of such programmes very difficult (for a review, see Lonsway and Kothari 2000).

35

The research we have reviewed in this chapter may provide additional insights that can be used in interventions aimed at reducing RMA in both males and females. Evidence for a causal influence of RMA on rape proclivity (Bohner, Reinhard *et al.* 1998; Bohner *et al.* 2005) is in keeping with most of the aforementioned programmes on rape prevention that show a reduction of RMA followed by a reduction in rape proclivity (e.g. Foubert and McEwen 1998; Gilbert *et al.* 1991; O'Donohue *et al.* 2003). In addition, our work on RMA as a social norm may form the basis for new types of intervention. We have shown that presenting normative information about others' denouncement of rape myths may effectively lower both RMA and rape proclivity in male participants (Bohner *et al.* 2006, 2009). Such normative information about low RMA is effective when it pertains to reference groups that the recipient belongs to (peer group norms), but may even be more effective when it pertains to an outgroup that the recipient expects to be higher in RMA (Bohner *et al.* 2009). Turning these experimental findings into interventions may require some changes of procedure. In an intervention setting, there are ethical constraints against telling recipients that their peer group (or a given outgroup) strongly rejects rape myths unless this is in fact true (although perceptions of peer group norms are often distorted toward seeing norms as more pro-violent than is warranted: Berkowitz 2002). But if a single communicator who is clearly identifiable as a group member strongly argues against rape myths, then the effect of this communication on recipients' attitudes may be as large as feedback about the attitude of the group as a whole. Compared to the feedback of group norms, this approach would provide the advantage that it should always be possible to find individual group members who are willing to endorse an anti-rape myth position and to collaborate in an intervention programme. These assumptions will of course need to be tested and evaluated in future research.

So far, we have focused on the possibility of *changing* RMA as a means of changing problematic behaviour. Might it be possible, alternatively, to keep people from *using* their rape myths, without necessarily changing RMA? Research by Krahé and her associates has examined this possibility with respect to rape-case related judgments. In a study conducted in Germany (Krahé *et al.* 2008: Study 2), prospective lawyers judged various rape scenarios in terms of defendant liability and complainant blame. To examine if information about the legal code might reduce participants' reliance on rape myths, the researchers provided half of the sample with the legal definition of rape from the German Criminal Code prior to reading the case scenarios. These participants were explicitly instructed to 'base [their] assessment of the cases that follow on the definition provided by the law' (p. 472). The other half of the sample was not given the legal definition. Disappointingly, this experimental intervention had no effect whatsoever: participants' judgments of defendant liability and complainant blame as well as their sentencing recommendations were strongly affected by their RMA no matter if they had been reminded of the legal code beforehand or not (see also Schewe 2002). A different type of intervention, however, promises to be more successful: in an earlier study with psychology students (Krahé et al. 2007), the researchers tried to foster greater accuracy by making participants accountable for their judgments. They did so by informing half of the sample at the outset that they might be asked to explain and justify their judgments about a rape case in subsequent mock jury sessions. This experimental intervention significantly reduced the impact of stereotypic beliefs about rape on participants' judgments about an ex-partner rape case.

Further research is again needed to corroborate these findings and determine their long-term effects. Interventions similar to those employed by Krahé et al. (2007, 2008) might also be tested as a means for improving the judgments and behaviour of people involved in victim support (e.g. social workers), of police officers who interact with rape victims and of judges and juries involved in rape cases.

Conclusion

In sum, the research presented in this chapter highlights the wide impact rape myths have on men and women who endorse them (in terms of liable behavioural inclinations and/or self esteem), on attitudes toward victims and perpetrators of sexual violence and on judgments about rape cases. It also emphasises how crucial it is to recognise the implications of RMA as a social norm, and to challenge their apparent normativity by the use of broadly targeted educational campaigns. Such interventions may destroy comfortable illusions but will ultimately help to reduce sexual violence.

Acknowledgments

Preparation of this chapter was facilitated by a grant from the Deutsche Forschungsgemeinschaft to Gerd Bohner and Friederike Eyssel (BO

1248/6-1). The authors would like to thank Philipp Süssenbach for his helpful comments on a previous draft.

Note

1 Many of the studies reviewed in this section used an experimental approach, often including the temporary deception of participants. Such methodology is sometimes necessary in order to test causal hypotheses and to avoid motivated response distortions. It always requires the careful consideration of ethical issues, especially when materials contain sensitive information such as descriptions of sexual violence. In all of our studies we followed applicable ethical guidelines as laid down by the American Psychological Association, the British Psychological Society and the German Society for Psychology (Deutsche Gesellschaft für Psychologie). Participants always gave informed consent to participate, and they were informed that they could terminate participation at any time without giving a reason. When a study involved deception, participants were thoroughly debriefed immediately after the experimental session. The debriefing always included educational information about rape myths and their detrimental consequences. In studies with female participants we employed screening procedures to avoid assigning participants who may have experienced sexual violence themselves to conditions in which they would be exposed to information about rape.

References

Abrams, D., Viki, G. T., Masser, B. and Bohner, G. (2003) 'Perceptions of stranger and acquaintance rape: the role of benevolent and hostile sexism in victim blame and rape proclivity', *Journal of Personality and Social Psychology*, 84: 111–25.

Andrias, R. T. (1992) 'Rape myths: a persistent problem', *Criminal Justice*, 7: 51–3.

Bandura, A. (1973) *Aggression: A Social Learning Analysis*. Englewood Cliffs, NJ: Prentice-Hall.

Bem, S. L. (1981) 'Gender schema theory: a cognitive account of sex typing', *Psychological Review*, 88: 354–64.

Berkowitz, A. D. (2002) 'Fostering men's responsibility for preventing sexual assault', in P. A. Schewe (ed.), *Preventing Violence in Relationships*. Washington, DC: American Psychological Association, pp. 163–96.

Bohner, G. (1998) *Vergewaltigungsmythen* [*Rape Myths*]. Landau, Germany: Verlag Empirische Pädagogik.

Bohner, G. (2001) 'Writing about rape: use of the passive voice and other distancing text features as an expression of perceived responsibility of the victim', *British Journal of Social Psychology*, 40: 515–29.

Bohner, G. and Lampridis, E. (2004) 'Expecting to meet a rape victim affects women's self-esteem: the moderating role of rape myth acceptance', *Group Processes and Intergroup Relations*, 7: 77–88.

Bohner, G. and Schwarz, N. (1996) 'The threat of rape: its psychological impact on nonvictimized women', in D. M. Buss and N. Malamuth (eds), *Sex, Power, Conflict: Evolutionary and Feminist Perspectives*. New York: Oxford University Press, pp.162–75.

Bohner, G. and Sturm, S. (1997) 'Evaluative Aspekte sozialer Identität bei Frauen und Männern: Vorstellung einer Skala des Kollektiven Selbstwerts in bezug auf das Geschlecht (KSW-G) [Evaluative aspects of social identity in women and men: presentation of a German scale of collective self-esteem concerning gender]', *Psychologische Beiträge*, 39: 322–35.

Bohner, G., Siebler, F. and Raaijmakers, Y. (1999) 'Salience of rape affects self-esteem: individual versus collective self-aspects', *Group Processes and Intergroup Relations*, 2: 191–9.

Bohner, G., Siebler, F. and Schmelcher, J. (2006) 'Social norms and the likelihood of raping: perceived rape myth acceptance of others affects men's rape proclivity', *Personality and Social Psychology Bulletin*, 32: 286–97.

Bohner, G., Jarvis, C. I., Eyssel, F. and Siebler, F. (2005) 'The causal impact of rape myth acceptance on men's rape proclivity: comparing sexually coercive and noncoercive men', *European Journal of Social Psychology*, 35: 819–28.

Bohner, G., Siebler, F., Pina, A. and Viki, G. T. (2009) 'Perceived Rape Myth Acceptance of In-group and Out-group Affects Men's Rape Proclivity'. Manuscript under review.

Bohner, G., Weisbrod, C., Raymond, P., Barzvi, A. and Schwarz, N. (1993) 'Salience of rape affects self-esteem: the moderating role of gender and rape myth acceptance', *European Journal of Social Psychology*, 23: 561–79.

Bohner, G., Reinhard, M.-A., Rutz, S., Sturm, S., Kerschbaum, B. and Effler, D. (1998) 'Rape myths as neutralizing cognitions: evidence for a causal impact of anti-victim attitudes on men's self-reported likelihood of raping', *European Journal of Social Psychology*, 28: 257–68.

Bohner, G., Siebler, F., Sturm, S., Effler, D., Litters, M., Reinhard, M.-A. and Rutz, S. (1998) 'Rape myth acceptance and accessibility of the gender category', *Group Processes and Intergroup Relations*, 1: 67–79.

Briere, J., Malamuth, N. M. and Check, J. V. P. (1985) 'Sexuality and rape-supportive beliefs', *International Journal of Women's Studies*, 8: 398–403.

Brown, J. and King, J. (1998) 'Gender differences in police officers' attitudes toward rape: results of an exploratory study', *Psychology, Crime and Law*, 4: 265–79.

Brownmiller, S. (1975) *Against Our Will: Men, Women and Rape*. New York: Simon & Schuster.

Bruner, J. S. (1957) 'Going beyond the information given', in J. S. Bruner, E. Brunswik, L. Festinger, F. Heider, K. F. Muenzinger, C. E. Osgood and D. Rapaport (eds), *Contemporary Approaches to Cognition*. Cambridge, MA: Harvard University Press, pp. 41–69.

Buhi, E. R. (2005) 'Reliability reporting practices in rape myth research', *Journal of School Health*, 75: 63–6.

Burt, M. R. (1980) 'Cultural myths and supports of rape', *Journal of Personality and Social Psychology*, 38: 217–30.

Burt, M. R. (1991) 'Rape myths and acquaintance rape', in A. Parrot and L. Bechhofer (eds), *Acquaintance Rape: The Hidden Crime*. New York: Wiley, pp. 26–40.

Burt, M. R. and Albin, R. S. (1981) 'Rape myths: rape definitions and probability of conviction', *Journal of Applied Psychology*, 11: 212–30.

Calogero, R., Pina, A., Fisher, N. and Thompson, T. (2009) 'Rape Myth Acceptance and Sexual Objectification in College Students'. Manuscript in preparation.

Costin, F. (1985) 'Beliefs about rape and women's social roles', *Archives of Sexual Behavior*, 14: 319–25.

Costin, F. and Schwarz, N. (1987) 'Beliefs about rape and women's social roles: a four nation study', *Journal of Interpersonal Violence*, 2: 46–56.

Dobash, R. E. and Dobash, R. P. (1992) *Women, Violence and Social Change*. London: Routledge.

Donnerstein, E., Berkowitz, L. and Linz, D. (1986) 'Role of Aggressive and Sexual Images in Violent Pornography'. Unpublished manuscript, University of Wisconsin-Madison.

Dunning, D. and Sherman, D. A. (1997) 'Stereotypes and tacit inference', *Journal of Personality and Social Psychology*, 73: 459–71.

Ellis, A. L., O'Sullivan, C. S. and Sowards, B. A. (1992) 'The impact of contemplated exposure to a survivor of rape on attitudes toward rape', *Journal of Applied Social Psychology*, 22: 889–95.

Eyssel, F. and Bohner, G. (2008a) 'Modern rape myths: the Acceptance of Modern Myths about Sexual Aggression (AMMSA) scale', in M. A. Morrison and T. G. Morrison (eds), *The Psychology of Modern Prejudice*. Hauppauge, NY: Nova Science Publishers.

Eyssel, F. and Bohner, G. (2008b) *Rape Myth Acceptance: A Cognitive Schema?* Paper presented at the XIII Workshop Aggression, Potsdam, Germany.

Eyssel, F. and Bohner, G. (2009) 'Measuring Rape Myth Acceptance: The German and English Short Version of the Acceptance of Modern Myths about Sexual Aggression Scale (AMMSA-SV)'. Manuscript in preparation.

Eyssel, F., Bohner, G. and Siebler, F. (2006) 'Perceived rape myth acceptance of others predicts rape proclivity: social norm or judgmental anchoring?', *Swiss Journal of Psychology*, 65: 93–9.

Eyssel, F., Bohner, G., Süssenbach, P. and Schreiber, P. (2009) 'Neuentwicklung und Validierung eines szenariobasierten Verfahrens zur Erfassung der Neigung zu sexueller Aggression [Development and validation of a scenario-based measure of sexual aggression proclivity]', *Diagnostica*, 55: 117–27.

Fabiano, P. M., Perkins, H. W., Berkowitz, A., Linkenbach, J. and Stark, C. (2003) 'Engaging men as social justice allies in ending violence against women: evidence for a social norms approach', *Journal of American College Health*, 52: 105–11.

Feild, H. S. (1978) 'Attitudes toward rape: a comparative analysis of police, rapists, crisis counselors, and citizens', *Journal of Personality and Social Psychology*, 36: 166–79.

Finkelhor, D. (1986) 'Prevention: a review of programs and research', in D. Finkelhor and Associates (eds), *A Sourcebook on Child Sexual Abuse*. Beverly Hills, CA: Sage, pp. 224–54.

Fonow, M. M., Richardson, L. and Wemmerus, V. A. (1992) 'Feminist rape education: does it work?', *Gender and Society*, 6: 108–21.

Foubert, J. D. (2000) 'The longitudinal effects of a rape prevention program on fraternity men's attitudes, behavioral intent, and behavior', *Journal of American College Health*, 48: 158–63.

Foubert, J. D. and McEwen, M. K. (1998) 'An all-male rape prevention peer education program: decreasing fraternity men's behavioral intent to rape', *Journal of College Student Development*, 39: 548–56.

Foubert, J. D. and Marriott, K. A. (1997) 'Effects of a sexual assault peer education program on men's belief in rape myths', *Sex Roles*, 36: 259–68.

Franiuk, R., Seefelt, J. L., Cepress, S. L. and Vandello, J. A. (2008) 'Prevalence and effects of rape myths in the media: the Kobe Bryant case', *Violence Against Women*, 14: 287–309.

Frese, B., Moya, M. and Megías, J. L. (2004) 'Social perception of rape: how rape myth acceptance modulates the influence of situational factors', *Journal of Interpersonal Violence*, 19: 143–61.

Gerger, H., Kley, H., Bohner, G. and Siebler, F. (2007) 'The Acceptance of Modern Myths About Sexual Aggression (AMMSA) Scale: development and validation in German and English', *Aggressive Behavior*, 33: 422–40.

Gidycz, C. A., Layman, M. J., Rich, C. L., Crothers, M., Gylys, J., Matorin, A. and Jacobs, C. D. (2001) 'An evaluation of an acquaintance rape prevention program: impact on attitudes, sexual aggression, and sexual victimization', *Journal of Interpersonal Violence*, 16: 1120–38.

Gilbert, B. J., Heesacker, M. and Gannon, L. J. (1991) 'Changing the sexual aggression-supportive attitudes of men: a psychoeducational intervention', *Journal of Counselling Psychology*, 38: 197–203.

Gordon, M. T., Riger, S., LeBailly, R. K. and Heath, L. (1980) 'Crime, women and the quality of urban life', *Signs: Journal of Women in Culture and Society*, 5 (3): S144–S159.

Hanson, K. A. and Gidycz, C. A. (1993) 'Evaluation of a sexual assault prevention program', *Journal of Consulting and Clinical Psychology*, 61: 1046–52.

Heppner, M. J., Humphrey, C. F., Hillenbrand-Gunn, T. L. and DeBord, K. A. (1995) 'The differential effects of rape prevention programming on attitudes, behavior, and knowledge', *Journal of Counseling Psychology*, 42: 508–18.

Hinck, S. S. and Thomas, R. W. (1999) 'Rape myth acceptance in college students: how far have we come?', *Sex Roles*, 40: 815–32.

Holmes, M. M., Resnick, H. S. and Frampton, D. (1998) 'Follow-up of sexual assault victims. Transactions of the Sixtieth Annual Meeting of the South Atlantic Association of Obstetricians and Gynecologists', *American Journal of Obstetrics and Gynecology*, 179: 336–42.

Jones, C. and Aronson, E. (1973) 'Attribution of fault to a rape victim as a function of respectability of the victim', *Journal of Personality and Social Psychology*, 26: 415–19.

Kelly, L., Lovett, J. and Regan, L. (2005) *A Gap or a Chasm? Attrition in Reported Rape Cases*, Home Office Research Study No. 293. London: HMSO.

Kopper, B. A. (1996) 'Gender, gender identity, rape myth acceptance and time of initial resistance on the perception of acquaintance rape blame and avoidability', *Sex Roles*, 34: 81–93.

Krahé, B. (1988) 'Victim and observer characteristics as determinants of responsibility attributions to victims of rape', *Journal of Applied Social Psychology*, 18: 50–8.

Krahé, B. (1991) 'Social psychological issues in the study of rape', *European Review of Social Psychology*, 2: 279–309.

Krahé, B., Temkin, J. and Bieneck, S. (2007) 'Schema-driven information processing in judgments about rape', *Applied Cognitive Psychology*, 21: 601–19.

Krahé, B., Temkin, J., Bieneck, S. and Berger, A. (2008) 'Prospective lawyers' rape stereotypes and schematic decision making about rape cases', *Psychology, Crime and Law*, 14: 461–79.

Kunda, Z. and Sherman-Williams, B. (1993) 'Stereotypes and the construal of individuating information', *Personality and Social Psychology Bulletin*, 19: 90–9.

Lerner, M. J. (1980) *The Belief in a Just World: A Fundamental Delusion*. New York: Plenum Press.

Leyens, J.-P., Yzerbyt, V. Y. and Schadron, G. (1992) 'The social judgeability approach to stereotypes', *European Review of Social Psychology*, 3: 91–120.

Loh, C., Gidycz, C. A., Lobo, T. R. and Luthra, R. (2005) 'A prospective analysis of sexual assault perpetration: risk factors related to perpetrator characteristics', *Journal of Interpersonal Violence*, 20: 1325–48.

Lonsway, K. A. and Fitzgerald, L. F. (1994) 'Rape myths: in review', *Psychology of Women Quarterly*, 18: 133–64.

Lonsway, K. A. and Fitzgerald, L. F. (1995) 'Attitudinal antecedents of Rape Myth Acceptance: a theoretical and empirical re-examination', *Journal of Personality and Social Psychology*, 68: 704–11.

Lonsway, K. A. and Kothari, C. (2000) 'First year campus acquaintance rape education: evaluating the impact of a mandatory intervention', *Psychology of Women Quarterly*, 24: 220–32.

Lonsway, K. A., Welch, S. and Fitzgerald, L. F. (2001) 'Police training in sexual assault response: process, outcomes, and elements of change', *Criminal Justice and Behavior*, 28: 695–730.

Lonsway, K. A., Klaw, E. L., Berg, D. R., Waldo, C. R., Kothari, C., Mazurek, C. J. and Hegeman, K. E. (1998) 'Beyond "no means no" – outcomes of an intensive program to train peer facilitators for campus acquaintance rape education', *Journal of Interpersonal Violence*, 13: 73–92.

Malamuth, N. M. (1981) 'Rape proclivity among males', *Journal of Social Issues*, 37 (4): 138–57.

Malamuth, N. M. and Check, J. V. P. (1984) 'Debriefing effectiveness following exposure to pornographic rape depictions', *Journal of Sex Research*, 20: 1–23.

Malamuth, N. M. and Check, J. V. P. (1985) 'The effects of aggressive pornography on beliefs in rape myths: individual differences', *Journal of Research in Personality*, 19: 299–320.

Margolin, L., Miller, M. and Moran, P. B. (1989) 'When a kiss is not just a kiss: relating violations of consent to rape myth acceptance', *Sex Roles*, 20: 231–43.

Marshall, W. L. (1999) 'Current status of North American assessment and treatment programs for sexual offenders', *Journal of Interpersonal Violence*, 14: 221–39.

Mergías, J. L., Romero-Sánchez, M., Durán, M., Moya, M. and Bohner, G. (2009) 'Aceptación de mitos sobre las agresiones sexuales; Validación en español y propiedades psicométricas de la escala "acceptance of modern myths about sexual aggression" [Acceptance of modern myths about sexual aggression: Validation and psychometric properties of a Spanish scale]. Manuscript under review.

Mirrlees-Black, C. and Allen, J. (1998) *Concern About Crime: Findings from the 1998 British Crime Survey*, Research Findings No. 83. London: Home Office, Research Development and Statistics Directorate.

Neisser, U. (1976) *Cognition and Reality*. San Francisco: Freeman.

O'Donohue, W., Yeater, E. A. and Fanetti, M. (2003) 'Rape prevention with college males: the roles of rape myth acceptance, victim empathy, and outcome expectancies', *Journal of Interpersonal Violence*, 18: 513–31.

Payne, D. L., Lonsway, K. A. and Fitzgerald, L. F. (1999) 'Rape myth acceptance: exploration of its structure and its measurement using the Illinois Rape Myth Acceptance Scale', *Journal of Research in Personality*, 33: 27–68.

Peterson, Z. D. and Muehlenhard, C. L. (2004) 'Was it rape? The function of women's rape myth acceptance and definitions of sex in labeling their own experiences', *Sex Roles*, 51: 129–44.

Petty, R. E. and Cacioppo, J. T. (1986) 'The elaboration likelihood model of persuasion', *Advances in Experimental Social Psychology*, 19: 124–203.

Pina, A. and Hallmark, K. (2009) 'Rape Myth Acceptance, Sentencing and Conviction Attitudes Towards Alleged Rapists'. Manuscript in preparation.

Pollard, P. (1992) 'Judgements about victims and attackers in depicted rapes: a review', *British Journal of Social Psychology*, 31: 307–26.

Quackenbush, R. L. (1989) 'A comparison of androgynous, masculine sex-typed, and undifferentiated males on dimensions of attitudes toward rape', *Journal of Research in Personality*, 23: 318–42.

Rhode, D. L. (1989) *Justice and Gender*. Cambridge, MA: Harvard University Press.

Schahn, J., Dinger, J. and Bohner, G. (1995) 'Rationalisierungen und Neutralisationen als Rechtfertigungsstrategien: Ein Vergleich zwischen Delinquenz- und Umweltbereich [The role of rationalizations and neutralizations for the justification of environmentally harmful behavior and delinquency: a comparison]', *Zeitschrift für Differentielle und Diagnostische Psychologie*, 16: 177–94.

Schewe, P. A. (2002) 'Guidelines for developing rape prevention and risk reduction interventions', in P. A. Schewe (ed.), *Preventing Violence in Relationships*. Washington, DC: American Psychological Association, pp. 107–36.

Schewe, P. A. and O'Donohue, W. T. (1993) 'Rape prevention: methodological problems and new directions', *Clinical Psychology Review*, 13: 667–82.

Schwarz, N. and Brand, J. F. (1983) 'Effects of salience of rape on sex-role attitudes, trust and self-esteem in non-raped women', *European Journal of Social Psychology*, 13: 71–6.

Schwendiger, J. R. and Schwendiger, H. (1974) 'Rape myths: in legal, theoretical and everyday practice', *Crime and Social Justice*, 1: 18–26.

Seto, M. C. and Barbaree, H. E. (1999) 'Psychopathy, treatment behavior, and sex offender recidivism', *Journal of Interpersonal Violence*, 14: 1235–48.

Siebler, F., Sabelus, S. and Bohner, G. (2008) 'A refined computer harassment paradigm: validation, and test of hypotheses about target characteristics', *Psychology of Women Quarterly*, 32: 22–35.

Sinclair, C. H. and Bourne, L. E. (1998) 'Cycle of blame or just world: effects of legal verdicts on gender patterns in rape-myth acceptance and victim empathy', *Psychology of Women Quarterly*, 22: 575–88.

Spohn, C. and Horney, J. (1993) 'Rape law reform and the effect of victim characteristics on case processing', *Journal of Quantitative Criminology*, 9: 383–409.

Swim, J. K., Aikin, K. J., Hall, W. S. and Hunter, B. A. (1995) 'Sexism and racism: old fashioned and modern prejudices', *Journal of Personality and Social Psychology*, 68: 199–214.

Sykes, G. M. and Matza, D. (1957) 'Techniques of neutralization: a theory of delinquency', *American Sociological Review*, 22: 664–70.

Temkin, J. and Krahé, B. (2008) *Sexual Assault and the Justice Gap: A Question of Attitude*. Oxford: Hart.

United Nations (ed.) (2000) *The World's Women 2000: Trends and Statistics*. New York: United Nations.

United Nations Development Fund for Women (2008) *Violence Against Women: Facts and Figures*. Available at: http://www.unifem.org/attachments/gender_issues/violence_against_women/facts_figures_violence_against_women_2007.pdf (accessed 10 December 2008).

Warshaw, R. (1988) *I Never Called It Rape*. New York: Harper Perennial.

Wilson, M. and Scholes, A. (2008) 'The typical rape: factors affecting victims' decision to report', in J. Wood and T. Gannon (eds), *Public Opinion and Criminal Justice*. Cullompton: Willan, pp. 123–44.

World Bank (1993) *World Development Report: Investing in Health*. New York: Oxford University Press.

Yeater, E. A. and O'Donohue, W. T. (1999) 'Sexual assault prevention programs: current issues, future directions, and the potential efficacy of interventions with women', *Clinical Psychology Review*, 19: 739–71.

Chapter 3

Anger, disgust and sexual crimes

Roger Giner-Sorolla and Pascale S. Russell

Introduction

There should be a law against it ...

It should be no surprise to readers of tabloid newspapers that emotions such as anger, disgust or shock often arise when people disapprove of other people's sexual behaviours. Despite the law's usually more measured tone, it is concerned with the regulation of sexual behaviour just as much as public opinion and tabloid newspapers are. But does this mean that the same emotions of moral outrage that characterise everyday judgments of sexuality also lie behind the framing and enforcement of sexual law? We believe this to be true, particularly for the emotions of anger and disgust. Furthermore, in this chapter we will show that the differences between these two distinct emotions carry implications for the ways in which individuals and the law deal with sexual issues, and in particular rape and sexual violence.

Maroney (2006) summarises a number of reviews of the field of emotions and the law, showing that 'emotion and the law' is a distinct field and has been studied in multiple ways: for example, emotion can appear in the theory of law, emotions of legal actors can be studied or the role of emotions in specific legal doctrines can be analysed. The essential role of emotions in psychological processes related to justice has also been outlined. For example, De Cremer and van den Bos (2007) argue that emotion should be taken into account within numerous aspects of the law and that justice can also be based on intuition. Some of these approaches outline ways in which legal concepts such as hate crime, reasonable provocation or public nuisance depend critically upon psychological models of emotion (Ellis 1984; Posner 2000). Other psychological studies implicate emotions themselves in the practice of the law, documenting their ability to influence reasoning about justice; for example, anger at an unresolved injustice can raise the level of punitive decisions in an unrelated case (Goldberg *et al.* 1999).

These demonstrations have accompanied a lively debate over a parallel question: what is the proper role of emotion in the law? Some express reservations about the primacy of emotion over other aspects of moral judgment and the wisdom of allowing emotion to influence legal decisions (e.g. Karstedt 2002). Others are more accepting of the role of moral passions in justice (e.g. Berman and Bibas 2008; Kahan 2000). Still others draw the distinction that some emotions, such as anger, are compatible with liberal humanistic ideals of justice, while other emotions, such as disgust, are not (Nussbaum 2004). We find this latter point to be most compatible with emerging knowledge about the differences between these two emotions. While anger has irrationalities of its own that must be watched closely, it has greater ability than disgust to fit within a liberal rationale for justice and punishment. The differences between these two emotions will be outlined in more detail when we consider the theoretical background of moral anger and disgust.

While many other emotions are relevant to the law of sexuality – sympathy, fear, remorse and shame among them – our purpose here is to focus on anger and disgust as two emotions that closely inform law-makers, their constituencies and law enforcers. As an instrument of social control (Pound 1942), the law depends most explicitly on external disapproval to regulate behaviour. While fear, shame, regret and remorse are important internal consequences of criminal punishment, they cannot be imposed without the prior impulse to punish, shun and disapprove. In fact, shame and guilt feelings have been said to respectively resemble internalised expressions of disgust and anger (Roseman *et al.* 1996), and Nussbaum (2004) puts these two emotions in parallel with anger and disgust. Therefore, while our argument does not explicitly cover shame or guilt, we can suggest that readers interested in these two distinct emotions might provisionally treat them as inwardly directed examples of disgust and anger.

In the English lexicon, 'anger' and 'disgust' are seen as close synonyms (e.g. Russell and Fehr 1994) and many expressions of moral disapproval include both anger and disgust. However, in other ways

47

the two emotions are distinct; they have different facial expressions (Ekman 1999) and physiological responses (Levenson *et al.* 1990). We think there are four main points of interest separating anger from disgust when people judge the sexual actions of others.

1 *Focus on different **content** elicits anger as opposed to disgust.*
Both anger and disgust can arise through previous experiences of associative and social learning. But in new situations anger is most likely to arise when an act is seen as harming someone or violating his or her rights, whereas sex acts that go against cultural and personal norms have the potential to be seen as disgusting, no matter what the circumstances.

2 *Different thought **processes** precede and modify expressions of anger and disgust.*
We have found that moral anger responds to relatively abstract ideas regarding harm, rights, responsibility and intent. This means that anger can be easily elicited and changed. It also means that people seek to justify their anger using abstract propositional reasoning – and this can be a problem when irrational reasons are invented to justify anger that actually arose through social learning or mere association. By contrast, disgust responds fairly inflexibly to concrete aspects of acts that violate a norm about the use of the body, can only be changed through a fairly slow process of acclimatisation or social learning and is hard to justify with reasons.

3 *Feeling morally angry versus disgusted has different mental **consequences** for thought.*
For example, moral anger influences subsequent judgments by increasing the need to blame but dissipates on learning that justice has been done. Moral disgust, on the other hand, influences subsequent judgments through mere association and contamination, an influence that is not easily dissipated and that can have tragic consequences for blameless victims of a disgusting act.

4 *Anger and disgust prepare a person for different **actions**.*
It is well established that anger prepares people to attack, punish and rebuke verbally, while disgust leads to avoidance and expulsion. While the link between emotion and action is not absolute or automatic, these different tendencies have important implications for action and punishment under the law.

In the next section, we will examine evidence from psychological studies supporting these four points.

Theory of moral anger and disgust

Content

Are emotions reasoning or unreasoning? Our view of emotions recognises two ways in which emotions can arise in a situation: associatively or functionally. Emotions can arise associatively from existing experience of emotion in a recent or superficially similar situation, but they can also arise functionally from a cognitive appraisal of aspects of the current situation. Research in our laboratory supports the view that in appraising novel moral situations, different things elicit anger as opposed to disgust. In new situations, anger is most likely to arise when an act is seen as harming someone or violating his or her rights. However, independently of anger, disgust comes from an appraisal of a bodily action, including sex acts, that breaks cultural and personal norms.

In situations where the sexual acts of others are judged in moral situations, anger depends on quite a different appraisal to the kind of anger that comes when one's computer crashes, for example. In moral situations, people look to concepts such as harm and intent in order to establish whether relationships need to be repaired or if ties need to be broken. If someone else's rights have been violated or if someone has been harmed, this is likely to elicit moral anger rather than disgust (Gutierrez and Giner-Sorolla 2007; Haidt 2003; Rozin *et al.* 1999). It is particularly likely that people will respond with anger when it is believed that the target's actions were intentional and/or unjustified (Goldberg *et al.* 1999; Russell and Giner-Sorolla 2009a). Therefore, in a novel situation, moral anger at another person seems to depend on a sequence of perceptions: the person must be seen as harming another; this harm must be seen as intentional, or at the very least negligent, such that the person is held responsible; and there must be an absence of excuses or justifications for the intentional harm. It should also be added that because sexual contact usually presumes a high level of trust and is related to the basic integrity of the person, there is usually the potential for psychological harm in a sexual interaction; for example, if consent is not given, or if sex is used exploitatively.

Emotion theorists often show wide disagreement about what novel situations or appraisals should elicit disgust. These theorists have often linked disgust with the synonymous concept of distaste and have not provided a clear definition of an appraisal that elicits moral disgust. For example, Rozin *et al.* (1993) have argued that disgust originates as a biological adaptation to avoid ingestion of contaminating substances through the mouth. This core disgust has then extended itself to include interpersonal and moral domains, in which persons seek to avoid contact with undesirable others. Disgust at this level functions to determine which persons are either fit or unfit for social contact, thus this emotion is used as a form of social control to preserve the social order. According to this formulation, persons can be deemed as disgusting when they are perceived to have character flaws; however, it has not been empirically proven what exactly makes these persons disgusting and if this domain elicits the same reaction as physical disgust.

In a broad interpretation of Rozin *et al.'s* theory, people can be deemed as disgusting from most norm violations. Experiments have shown that a number of different cues related to contamination elicit physical disgust; for example, bodily secretions are strong and near-universal elicitors of disgust (Curtis and Biran 2001). However, equivalent results have not clearly shown the existence of moral or social disgust as defined by Rozin's theory. Often, scenarios that are taken to show purely moral disgust also involve elements of physical disgust (e.g. Davey and Marzillier 2004; Rozin *et al.* 1999), while social disgust seems to be most strongly expressed towards violators of bodily norms (e.g. the male homosexuals in Cottrell and Neuberg 2005). Further confusing matters is the tendency to use disgust synonyms to refer to the emotion of anger in English and other languages (Nabi 2002).

We argue specifically that moral disgust, as distinct from anger, is concerned with whether or not a concrete bodily norm has been violated. A society maintains many of these norms governing the appropriate uses of the body, some of which are merely conventional or hygienic ('wipe your nose') but others of which are moralised more strongly ('sex should be between people of opposite gender'; 'married people should only have sex with each other'). This distinction has recently been supported by findings of differences in brain systems between violations of conventional, sexual and non-sexual moral norms (Schaich Borg *et al.* 2008). While sexual acts can be physically messy and involve core disgust, we think that moral disgust felt at the violation of sexual norms goes beyond mere revulsion at secretions, responding to general notions of what is not an acceptable use of the human body per se. At the same time, we emphasise that bodily norms only concern themselves with what is literally done with the body; they are not sensitive to more general norms and principles such as intentionality, consent or harm, which are more related to anger. For example, a heterosexual who subscribes to a sexually conservative morality may feel revulsion at the mere fact of a homosexual act just because it is seen as abnormal, even if it is harmless, consensual and has positive consequences.

A number of studies within our lab group support this view of the factors governing moral disgust and anger in moral violations of bodily norms. For example, in one recent study we manipulated harm, intent and bodily norm violation in a story describing the eating of cloned meat (Russell and Giner-Sorolla 2009a). Harm occurred when a scientist fed the meat to friends without their knowing what it was, as opposed to eating the meat herself. Intent was manipulated by the scientist either knowing what the meat was, or not knowing due to an assistant's lab error. Crucially, we manipulated norm violation by having the meat either being cloned from the scientist's own healthy cells (violating the norm against cannibalism, even when no humans were harmed), or from those of a sheep. Within this study it was found that disgust was always higher when a taboo violation had occurred. In contrast, anger was influenced by combinations of harm and intent, in addition to being influenced by the norm violation. As in previous research (Gutierrez and Giner-Sorolla 2007), this may reflect previously formed associations between cannibalism and moral anger. From this research, it appears that disgust is not responsive to contextual cues, such as harm and intentionality, but rather to the simple categorisation of whether a behaviour regarding the body is normal or otherwise.

Thought processes

The appraisals that elicit new instances of anger and disgust thus appear to differ in their level of abstraction and flexibility. Unlike disgust, anger responds to abstract ideas that are more malleable than the basic fact of having committed a bodily norm violation. This makes it important to examine other evidence on how cognitively flexible these emotional responses are. In this task it is useful to keep in mind the distinction made by Kahan and Nussbaum (1996) between mechanistic and evaluative models of emotion in the law. A mechanistic view sees emotion as an automatic process outside the control of the individual, while an evaluative view sees emotion as potentially modifiable by the will of the individual. In our opinion, both views are justified; some emotions, in some circumstances, follow mechanistic processes, while others are more able to be modified evaluatively.

Our research has also examined the extent to which people can and will give reasons after feeling emotions of moral disapproval. In arguing for the greater appropriateness of anger than disgust in influencing law and legal procedures, Nussbaum (2004) supports the assumption that anger is an emotion that is associated with reasons such as harm and often needs to be justified socially with explicitly given reasons because it regulates the rights of individuals when they come into conflict. Because disgust is often shared among the members of a culture, there are fewer suitable reasons to convince other people of one's disgust.

As we have seen, disgust is responsive to the simple categorisation of whether or not a certain stimulus is present – in the case of moral disgust, whether or not a bodily norm violation has occurred. This superficial, inflexible and concrete nature of disgust elicitation is appreciated by the toy and novelty industry, who rely on plastic replicas of bugs or bodily mess to elicit amusing disgust reactions – amusing, because disgust at such objects remains even though one knows rationally that the plastic object is perfectly sterile (Rozin *et al.* 1986; Woody and Tolin 2002). Also, it appears that once an association with disgust has been formed, it is hard to change. It may be that the only way to make something *not* disgusting is through a lengthy process in which the previous association is unlearned. For example, Rozin (2008) has recently found a disgust habituation effect, in which medical students became more accustomed to cold dead bodies but not warm bodies after a few months in medical school. This shows that even when disgust feelings are changed by habituation, the effects are very stimulus-specific and do not generalise.

We have also recently found across two studies that people have trouble giving reasons for why they are disgusted towards groups that violate sexual norms compared to reasons given for their anger. Participants were asked to explain why they felt either angry or disgusted toward various groups that violated either a non-sexual or a sexual norm (Russell and Giner-Sorolla 2009b). Explanations or justifications of their emotional response (e.g. 'they harm innocent children') were coded as true reasons as opposed to subjective responses (e.g. 'I don't like them') which just reiterated a basic negative evaluation. The first study found that people gave fewer true reasons when explaining the disgust, as opposed to anger, they felt toward paedophiles. In the second study we used a wider variety of groups and found that people were especially likely to resist giving reasons when explaining any disgust they felt toward a group that violated a sexual norm, for example prostitutes or voyeurs. Frequently, within both studies we found that when people were explaining their disgust they sometimes responded using tautological statements, such as 'Paedophiles are disgusting because they are gross'; tautology was almost never used in explaining anger. Thus people cannot articulate the reasons for moral disgust as well as the reasons for their moral anger.

This finding may suggest that these emotions can be changed using different mechanisms. Since people are aware of their reasons for feeling angry, it may be enough to convince them that their reasons are not justified within a given situation. However, such arguments are less likely to work for disgust; it may be necessary to unlearn the actual emotional response through such means as desensitisation or vicarious observation, since people are less aware of their reasons for feeling disgust in the first place. This finding may also have a broader implication, as suggested by Nussbaum (2004). Because it is not responsive to reasoning, disgust should be considered to be an inadmissible emotion within criminal court cases, while anger may be admissible as a more reasonable emotion.

While anger responds to reasons, the need to justify moral anger sometimes results in people using inaccurate justifications in order to explain their irrationally produced emotion. Although moral anger is mostly predicted by harm and rights violation, there is also some indication from research that people can become irrationally angry at an act that in the past has been associated with harm and anger, even when its current instance is described as completely harmless (Gutierrez and Giner-Sorolla 2007; see also Parkinson 1999). In such a situation, people will make a *presumption of harm* – especially when a bodily violation has occurred – and this presumption is explained by anger, not disgust (Gutierrez and Giner-Sorolla 2007; Haidt and Hersh 2001; Horvath and Giner-Sorolla 2007). Ironically, anger appears to be such a reasoned emotion that when it arises irrationally or automatically, the need to provide justifications still exists. Thus this emotion encourages the person experiencing anger to search for relevant reasons when in fact they are not always valid in doing so. According to Nussbaum (2004), because harm is central to reasonable anger, people feel socially accountable which results in the need for them to articulate their reasons. Thus people want to explain why they feel angry even if their anger is not reasonable in the first place.

Consequences for thought

The emotional states of disgust and anger, once activated, also have different influences on thought. Research has indicated that angry individuals are more likely to have optimistic beliefs about future life events (e.g. strokes and floods) than do fearful people (Lerner and Keltner 2000). Lerner and Keltner (2001) have also found that angry people showed a different pattern to fearful people in estimates of risk and choice. Specifically, angry people showed a more optimistic strategy and were able to surpass current gains for long-term goals. Also, findings more relevant to our focus have shown that anger impacts people's mindsets when judging criminal cases. For example, Goldberg et al. (1999) found that people would become 'intuitive prosecutors' after being primed with anger if injustice has occurred. Thus these people lowered their threshold for accepting blame attributions, and their anger also influenced subsequent judgments. In contrast, if participants learned that justice had been done, they would not adopt this 'intuitive prosecutor' mindset and their anger would not influence subsequent judgments.

Disgust also has mental consequences different from those of anger and other emotions. For example, Lerner et al. (2004) found that previously induced disgust and sadness carried over to impact unrelated economic decisions; however, these emotions had differential effects. Disgust reduced both selling and buying prices, while sadness reduced selling prices and increased choice prices. Therefore disgust encouraged people to get rid of current objects and to avoid buying anything new in contrast to the more sanguine approach to risk encouraged by anger.

Disgust also has been shown to spread itself by mere association or contamination. Rozin et al. (1986) have found that disgusting qualities can be transferred between objects through magical thinking, through the 'laws of sympathetic magic', which includes the laws of similarity and contagion. In these studies it was found that people engaged in avoidance and purification behaviours when disgusting qualities had been transferred onto a previously neutral object; however, when asked to explain these behaviours people admitted that they could not come up with reasons and could not deny that their behaviours were based on irrational thoughts. For example, people refused to drink orange juice that had come into contact with a sterilised plastic cockroach (law of contagion). These results imply unfortunate social consequences of disgust. According to these 'laws' people can be labelled as disgusting by mere association when in fact the targeted person has done nothing wrong or harmful. For example, someone who is found innocent of a particularly disgusting sexual crime may still be judged negatively despite the acquittal because of the association to the crime. An even more disturbing example of the tarnishing nature of disgust would be that a victim of incest would be likely to be viewed as disgusting despite doing nothing wrong because of association between the victim and the mere act of incest. And, out of concern for being likewise tarred with the disgusting act, other people might also avoid association with the victim.

Disgust also can influence judgments irrationally and without awareness beyond its contagious nature. Wheatley and Haidt (2005) have found that when priming disgust using hypnosis this resulted in participants making more severe moral judgments, which indicates that disgust can influence our judgments unconsciously. Disgust has also been theoretically and empirically related to phobias (Davey *et al.* 2006; Olatunji *et al.* 2005), supporting the notion that disgust may be elicited and maintained in the same way that phobias are, by mere association. Moreover, disgust has also been found to have a negative impact on the person being labelled as disgusting, in that he or she is automatically labelled as disgusting without an evaluation of whether or not they have done something wrong or harmful. For example, Park *et al.* (2003) have found that people automatically react with disgust and avoidance to a person with a disability, even if the person cannot help their disability and/or is not contagious. Such reactions often came out through implicit and non-verbal responses. Therefore, even though people with disabilities are harmless, others will still automatically react with revulsion and avoidance.

Cumulatively, research evidence indicates that disgust qualities can be transferred thoughtlessly, often without an evaluation of who is to blame, and this automatic transference of disgustingness can have tragic consequences for a targeted individual, often acting as a permanent marker. This fits well with other theoretical perspectives maintaining that in social judgment, disgust reflects a global negative judgment of the whole individual, while anger reflects a negative judgment of a specific behaviour and is compatible with a positive view of the person (Fischer and Roseman 2007).

Action tendencies

A final point of difference between anger and disgust is that they lead to different action tendencies. Anger in general motivates people to approach the cause of their anger in a hostile way. Numerous studies have highlighted verbal and/or physical aggression as an outcome of anger (Izard 1977). In many instances people are motivated to attack, humiliate or otherwise get back at the person who has offended them (Haidt 2003). Anger also encourages the person experiencing the emotion to either punish or rebuke verbally the person who has done them wrong (Haidt 2003; Nussbaum 2004), although, when a friend or other close person is the object of anger, it has sometimes also been found that anger promotes people to engage in reparative behaviours such as talking things over (Fischer and Roseman 2007; Weber 2004). An angry individual may also be concerned with how their behaviour will impact others (Averill 1983) and whether they feel they have the appropriate resources to respond to their anger (Mackie *et al.* 2000). When an individual feels that they have the ability and resources to respond to the situation they are then more likely to react with approach behaviours. Therefore anger is often associated with approach behaviours, but due to the flexible nature of this emotion, there is often encouragement to evaluate the appropriateness of one's reaction within a given situation.

In contrast to anger, it appears as if there is only one route to take after becoming disgusted, which is avoidance. People normally respond to their disgust with avoidance and/or purification strategies (Haidt 2003). However, the most common behavioural tendency is avoidance: the motivation to either expel or break off contact with the offender (Haidt 2003). The need to break off contact can also extend to actions such as purifying one's self, that is trying to remove any residue of contact (Rozin and Nemeroff 2002). In theory people should seek to establish whether or not this response is warranted; however, it appears as if the disgust response is fairly automatic. Theory and evidence points to the disgust reaction arising more because of who a person is than because of what they have done (Fischer and Roseman 2007; Haidt 2003; Nussbaum 2004). Hence, people can feel disgust toward a person just for who they are, instead of engaging in rational thought processes as to whether or not the person did something wrong or harmful. In particular, a disgusting act may automatically and irrevocably lead to an inference about the nature of the person regardless of mitigating circumstances.

Overall, it can be concluded that disgust motivates the person experiencing the emotion to avoid the source of their disgust. In contrast, anger, while its outcomes are more flexible, generally encourages the person experiencing anger to approach the source of their anger. Gutierrez and Giner-Sorolla (2007) have successfully shown that moral anger and disgust differ in their behavioural tendencies; it was found across studies that anger had more of an effect on desire to punish than desire to avoid, while disgust had a greater influence on avoidance. From this research it can be argued that these emotions promote different types of behaviours.

These tendencies have important implications for action and punishment under the law. Anger encourages people to be active and do something about their emotion, normally causing the angry individual to evaluate the source of the emotion and to call for punishment when appropriate. However, disgust encourages people to stigmatise and avoid others, without stopping to think what they have done wrong or if their actions are actually harmful or wrong. It is this distinction between anger and disgust that underlies the objections raised by Nussbaum (2004) and Abrams (2002) to Kahan's (2000) proposal that moral disgust be used by progressives as an element of justice. This evidence leads to a critical view of disgust's place in law, because it encourages people to make irrational judgments and to rely on a limited behavioural repertoire of avoidance and exclusion.

This difference between anger and disgust can influence many different people involved in a sexual offence, and it can also play a role at different stages. First, if a rape arouses strong feelings of anger in the victim, this may make it more likely that the victim will think about the injustice and report the case to the police, whereas disgust might lead to more avoidant behaviour. Second, jurors who are evaluating a sexual crime will be more or less likely to pay attention to situational factors depending on how much they feel anger or disgust. If the circumstances surrounding the court case are likely to elicit strong feelings of revulsion, then jurors may be less likely to take into account factors surrounding the case and punish the defendant irrationally. Even though anger is an emotion that encourages a search for blame and often leads to punishment, it is more likely that factors such as intentionality, harm and consent will also be taken into account. These are just two examples of how anger and disgust can influence people involved in the legal proceedings surrounding sexual crimes; however, these emotions can have other influences as well.

Moral emotions and rape

The preceding review of the psychological literature, and of our own research, yields further insights into the intersection of moral emotions with the law. The different precursors of anger and disgust lead to a deeper understanding of why people from different cultures, historical eras and ideologies have considered certain sexual acts to be moral and immoral, and, furthermore, the extent to which an immoral act is regarded as falling under the purview of the law. To take an example, recent years have seen the repeal of state laws in the US prohibiting consensual non-vaginal intercourse ('sodomy laws': *Lawrence* v. *Texas* 2003), and the updating in Britain of the Sexual Offences Act 2003 to eliminate the more restrictive treatment of sex between men. These changes are indicative of a shift from disgust- to anger-based morality. Also, the feminist movement has transformed the nature of opposition to prostitution, infusing anger-morality concerns about abuse and trafficking into an argument originally founded on disgust-morality objections to loose sexual activity (e.g. Cotton *et al.* 2002).

Beyond this, the different flexibility of the cognitive processes underlying anger and disgust has something to say about the acceptability of each of these emotions in the courtroom and in society in general. Most troubling is the potential of disgust to generate inflexible negative reactions that ignore several considerations that are important to justice – such as agency, intentionality and harm. Moral anger, however, is not without its own problems. As an emotion, it can become associated with a person or act for reasons that have little to do with justice, as shown by the finding of irrational anger towards people who violate a sexual norm. As we have seen in our studies, and as statistics on violence against sexual minorities attest (e.g. Dick 2008), even harmless sexual acts or identities can arouse anger that has become associated with them through social learning, defensive processes or past associations with harm. In these instances, anger's status as a 'reasonable' emotion can motivate people to support it with spurious reasons, such as making presumptions of harm about the sexual acts in question or claiming that same-sex marriage is a threat to existing heterosexual marriages.

After this general overview, we now bring our analysis to bear on the issue of rape and related crimes such as the violation of the age of sexual consent.

Autonomy and divinity ethics in sexual law

Sexual activity has been regulated by law since the Code of Hammurabi (the earliest known written law code, believed to be created around 1760 BC in Babylon), which includes characteristically drastic punishments for such crimes as incest and adultery. In law-making cultures ever since that time, a number of different principles of morality and pragmatism have governed legal views of sexuality. These can largely be understood with reference to a theory of cultural differences in moral codes proposed by Shweder *et al.* (1997). In this scheme, cultures differ in their emphasis on autonomy ethics (e.g. prevention of harm and promotion of rights), community ethics (e.g. the cohesion of the family and state) and divinity ethics (e.g. beliefs about what is pure or polluting and the proper use of the body).

Sexual behaviour touches upon all three realms. Most obviously, it involves the divinity ethic through its intimate connection with the body, and also involves the community ethic through its involvement in creating and maintaining families. The role of autonomy is intertwined with notions of the positive right to sexual expression; more negatively, sexual acts can potentially infringe upon the rights of the body as one's own property, and autonomy ethics can also explain moral outrage at sexual acts in which unfairness, inequality or coercion are seen to occur.

Each one of these moral orientations has also been linked to a specific emotion of condemnation for those who violate it, with a serendipitous coincidence of initials that has led to the label 'CAD hypothesis' (Rozin *et al.* 1999). The violation of autonomy ethics has been linked to anger, the violation of divinity ethics has been linked to disgust and the violation of community ethics to contempt. This linkage is generally corroborated by our research findings on the content that elicits moral anger and moral disgust. However, recent research improving on the method of the Rozin *et al.* (1999) study has found contempt to be only weakly related to community violations, which instead evoked a mixture of lesser anger and disgust responses (Guerra 2008). Because of this, and the clearer status of anger and disgust as entirely separate basic emotions, our research has focused only on those two emotions and the moral code violations that evoke them.

By this account, cultural differences in moral codes will give rise to different concerns in sexual morality. Research into these codes has found that while middle-class people in western cultures generally value the autonomy ethic over the other two, other populations have a more balanced valuation of community and divinity concerns, seeing these as moral and not just conventional areas (Guerra 2008; Guerra and Giner-Sorolla in press; Haidt *et al.* 1993). Even within western cultures, conservatives take into account community and divinity concerns to a greater degree than liberals do (Haidt and Graham 2007; Haidt and Hersh 2001). This suggests a greater role for anger versus disgust in more liberal sexual discourses, which fits neatly with Nussbaum's (2004) analysis of disgust as an emotion incompatible with liberal jurisprudence – whereas anger fares somewhat better in her estimation.

If the recent revolution in the emotional basis of morality and law (De Cremer and van den Bos 2007; Haidt 2001; Maroney 2006) can be extended to consider the effects of distinct emotions in those fields, then, based on our theoretical analysis of anger and disgust, we can now sketch out tentative images of one sexual morality based on anger and another based on disgust. Anger-based sexual morality is based on autonomy ethics, and in line with research on moral anger, considers an act wrong if it harms a person or violates his or her rights. Acts seen as causing no literal harm are generally approved of (even if grudgingly), unless they violate a more abstract notion of rights, such as consent – as in sex with children – or trust – as in the case of a clandestine, adulterous affair. Because of the flexible nature of anger, its disapproval can be intensified or diminished by beliefs that are later brought to bear relevant to harm, intentionality or justification. Also, the impulse to action from anger supports punishment rather than avoidance.

By contrast, a disgust-based morality sees certain acts, such as incest or homosexuality, as categorically wrong in and of themselves even if they are consensual and enjoyable for those involved. The inflexible nature of disgust means that information about harm, intent or justification plays little role in these reactions. Additionally, the merely associative and strongly contagious nature of disgust means that any kind of association between a sexual violation and an individual is enough to create some degree of negative reaction. At the most trivial level, this can mean that repeated protestations of non-involvement in repulsive acts can backfire. The emotional impact of association with disgusting acts bypasses the more logical statement of negation (cf. Wegner *et al.* 1981, in which headlines such as 'Bob Talbert Not Linked to Mafia' still created negative impressions of the target person). More disturbingly, this may also mean that the negative associations from disgust do not care about basic concepts in jurisprudence, such as agency or responsibility; all are tarred with the same brush of disgust. The existence of disgust reactions beyond the reach of reasoning also means that they are more resistant to reasoning than anger reactions, and thus more problematic to liberal judicial values, as Nussbaum (2004) argues.

If the scheme of anger- and disgust-based morality presented above showed a pure separation between the two emotions, then those motivated by disgust-based morality should make their judgments known only by withdrawing from the objects of their disgust, as disgust's characteristic action tendencies would predict. However, it is indisputable that those who offend merely on grounds of divinity or community ethics (e.g. gay men and lesbians, political protesters burning the national flag) often attract angry as well as disgusted reactions from those who hold such ethics, and that attack as well as avoidance can result. How can we explain these angry outbursts?

First, violations of community or divinity norms might be seen by those who hold those ethics as symbolically harming an abstract entity – God, nature, the family or the nation – in much the way as some harm-free violations are seen by autonomy ethics proponents as symbolically harming a person's abstract rights. Indeed, as we have mentioned, presumption of harm has been shown to arise in such scenarios even where harm is not described, or where direct physical or psychological harm is explicitly ruled out (Haidt and Hersh 2001; Haidt et al. 1993; Horvath and Giner-Sorolla 2007). In fact, Kahan (2007) proposes that people are biased toward finding harmful consequences for any act they consider immoral on whatever grounds. However, there are both theoretical (Haidt 2001) and empirical (Gutierrez and Giner-Sorolla 2007) reasons to accept a more specific account: that presumption of harm arises post hoc, as a justification of automatic moral anger – but, importantly, not of automatic moral disgust (Gutierrez and Giner-Sorolla 2007).

Social learning provides one explanation of how anger comes to be associated with sexual minorities or flag burners in the first place. A person sees other people outraged by those examples of immorality, or hears stories in which those social groups cause actual harm, and comes to associate them with anger. A more motivational explanation is that anger becomes associated with moral violators for ego-defensive reasons; that shame or anger at the self is transformed into anger at others (Tangney et al. 1992). From a legal point of view, then, these irrational features of anger urge liberal jurisprudence to be as sceptical of anger as of disgust. While disgust is a subjective, often irrational emotion that encourages avoidance and disengagement rather than proactive behaviour, anger can also be applied without reason (Berkowitz and Harmon-Jones 2004; Parkinson 1999). Once felt, anger leads people to generate post hoc reasons to cover its tracks, and provokes the more potentially harmful actions of rebuke and attack. Therefore, in making legal and policy judgments, the source and justification of anger should be subjected to the same scrutiny as the source and justification of any judgment. Anger may provide the motivation to pursue justice, but it needs to be applied accurately.

Moral emotions: applications to the crime and law of rape

As Rozée (1993) demonstrates with a random sample of 35 world cultures, rape of women by men is a nearly universal practice, and sexual acts not chosen by the woman are in more cultures socially normative (e.g. marital rape or punitive rape) than non-normative (i.e. seen as a crime). The question, then, is not whether rape exists in any given society, but in which contexts it is condemned or condoned, and the moral systems and emotions underlying its condemnation.

Anger and rape

In her landmark study of rape, Brownmiller (1975) traces differences across cultures and historical periods in the ethical basis for legal codes governing rape. In traditional patriarchal societies, rape of a woman has been seen primarily as a crime against the property of a man – an anger-arousing offence under our scheme. Under modern liberal and feminist conceptions, by contrast, ownership of a woman's body is shifted to the woman herself, expanding the crime of rape to any sexual contact not freely chosen – again, an offence under autonomy ethics likely to arouse anger. As we have seen, appropriately for the moral emotion of anger, the circumstances rather than the mere fact of sexual activity are critical in considering whether a sexual act is rape. Under patriarchal morality, the critical fact is whether a sexual act violates the rights of a woman's 'owner', while under liberal or feminist morality, the critical fact is whether it is approved of by the woman herself. If sex is seen to violate these standards of autonomy ethics, anger at the perpetrator and sympathy for the victim should follow.

Unlike the feminist position, however, the liberal position also makes available a counter-narrative of infringed rights in which the accused rapist is potentially the victim of an unstable or vindictive woman who initially consented to sex. In the legal system, this narrative has been sustained by biased interpretations of statistics, for example assuming all withdrawn rape accusations to have been false

(Rumney 2006). It has been characterised as a prevalent rape myth that can often turn moral scrutiny onto the victim of rape (Bohner *et al.* this volume; Lonsway and Fitzgerald 1994). Thus, while free-floating anger or a propensity to experience moral outrage could result in willingness to convict and punish the accused rapist, it could backfire against the complainant if her veracity is called into question.

Although little research exists to examine this possibility, we might speculate that anger might cut both ways in a case of rape that imports unresolved, irrational anger from another related issue. For example, the context of the case might bring up racial or class frustrations in a way irrelevant to the judgments of guilt at hand, but nonetheless influencing the jurors or jurists as 'intuitive prosecutors' (Goldberg *et al.* 1999). However, depending on perceptions of who is to blame, anger might swing a person in the favour of the complainant or the defendant. The flexibility of anger is not always going to be helpful to those who defend the rights of women.

Disgust and rape

Stevenson (2000), characterising the state of British law in the nineteenth century, writes: 'A societal mystification remained about whether rape was a property crime infringing another man's right in relation to a woman's sexuality, a physical crime of violation, or a "moral" crime of defilement undermining feminine sexual chastity' (p. 351). While anger, as we have seen, regulates the first of these two grounds for moral objection to rape, the third is regulated by disgust, which, as we have argued, responds to acts that violate norms about the use of the body. Although an act of rape always involves the body, whether and in what way it violates norms can vary. As shown by Rozée's (1993) analysis, rape is often allowed by a culture's sexual norms. Even when legally prohibited, some kinds of rape that were formerly allowed under law may still register as normative, rather than repulsive, in the public mind – for example, when a husband rapes his wife.

We think that disgust exerts a subtle influence on contemporary rape cases in a number of ways. For one, the anger–disgust distinction can help explain some issues that arise when a sex act is itself non-normative but also violates consent. As an example, we can take the critique by Taylor (2004) of the media and legal use of the term 'incest' to refer to father–daughter rape. In Taylor's argument, using 'incest' serves to exonerate rapist fathers, because incest can also have a consensual basis. In our scheme, 'incest' is a term that evokes disgust morality whereas 'rape' evokes anger as well as disgust, bringing to the fore the notions of harm and rights violation. With this in mind, we can identify another possible consequence of using 'incest' to describe intrafamilial rape: because disgust at incest is contagious and inflexible, it will taint a daughter as well as a father, regardless of culpability or consent.

Likewise, the rape of men by men is often minimised by giving it the label of 'homosexual' rape, as noted by Sivakumaran (2005). In our analysis this term implies that both men are homosexuals, therefore shifting the reason for moral disapproval from the violation of one man's rights by another to a stigmatised social identity which neither man may necessarily identify with, and opening the counter-narrative possibility that the raped man consented because he was a 'homosexual'. Again, the action tendency of disgust is to ostracise all parties involved, not to differentially punish the violator and help the victim. When people feel that some moral outrage should be expressed, then, there are real consequences to whether the specific emotion has cognitive action tendencies that are empowering (anger) or not empowering (disgust) under law.

Disgust logic, too, underlies beliefs about a victim's chastity which explicitly informed western rape law in the nineteenth century, continue to inform deliberations on rape cases today via widespread rape myths, and are explicitly endorsed in many non-western cultures. Of course, if virginity is seen as an element of a woman's social value, then under patriarchal concepts of woman as property, rape detracts from her value (Brownmiller 1975) and like a property crime would lead to anger. However, many cultures also value chastity as a moral aspect of a woman's pure character. In these contexts, chastity is the responsibility of the woman to maintain, as well as of her male guardian to protect; women who have sexual relations outside the norms of marriage are viewed with moral disgust. This has a number of implications for rape.

Most seriously, societies who endorse the value of chastity often apply the inflexible logic of disgust to women who have had any kind of extramarital sexual contact – condemning, often violently, women who are thought to have been involved in wilful adultery or premarital sex, but also women who have been raped (Welchman and Hossain 2006). Although in theory disgust should adhere to both people in the sexual act, this is set against biased standards that make a woman's activity more disgusting than a man's because it is set against a more absolute standard of purity. The extreme expression of such attitudes is the honour killing or ostracism of rape victims in societies where strong codes of family honour prevail (e.g. Ruggi 1998). However, irrational stigmatisation by disgust, in particular from loved ones, is a problem that rape victims also face in modern western societies (Holmstrom and Burgess 1979) – in addition to the inwardly turned disgust and shame they often feel toward their own victimisation (Russell 1975).

Chastity standards have also historically held implications for the definition of what is considered a sexual crime. Oberman (1994) traces the evolution of the underpinning of Anglo-American laws of age of sexual consent from the protection of young girls' chastity to the protection of young people from harm – in our terms, from disgust- to anger-based rationales. This shift has had several important implications. For example, it was once true in many jurisdictions that a man could not be convicted for having had sex with a sexually experienced underage girl because she had already been 'spoiled'. This bias has now largely been written out of the law, reflecting similar changes in popular attitudes (Horvath and Giner-Sorolla 2007). Likewise, whereas traditional age-of-consent laws covered only girls because of beliefs about the special importance of their chastity, modern law-makers seek to protect girls and boys alike. However, norms about chastity are not entirely absent from contemporary judgments of whether rape is a crime. For example, prostitutes are routinely judged as 'unrapeable' and not harmed by rape (Coy this volume; Miller and Schwartz 1995).

Finally, because moral disgust carries implications about a person's character, it has the potential to influence judgment in rape cases through a more indirect process of casting doubt upon the credibility of the complainant. Assumptions about the chastity of a complainant were a major part of argumentation in Victorian-era adult rape trials (Stevenson 2000). Showing the arbitrary nature of modern rape myths, the *un*attractiveness, rather than attractiveness, of a complainant was sometimes held as proof of a low and sexually loose character in the nineteenth century. Prior sexual experience of a woman not only invalidated the claim that something of value (virginity) had been taken away from her, but invalidated her testimony, as liberal sexual morals were taken to signify general untrustworthiness. Such attitudes were not entirely left behind in the Victorian era. They have survived to form part of modern rape myths that hinder the prosecution of rape. Taslitz (2000) argues that they impact judges and jurors in two ways: by casting doubt on the question of consent, holding women to a standard by which they must never consent to sex in order to be given the benefit of the doubt when raped; and by casting doubt on the veracity of the woman herself.

It is tempting, but impossible, to insist that each case be judged entirely on the evidence directly bearing on the incident. As Taslitz (2000) argues, coming to conclusions about the character of the defendant and witnesses is an important part of criminal justice. It is in this task that the irrational nature of disgust can exert a biasing influence. Based on findings about blame in rape scenarios, this is especially likely to be true when judging complainants from such stigmatised groups as gay men and lesbians (White and Kurpius 2002) or, more generally, when judging those who violate norms of sexual behaviour (Viki and Abrams 2002).

Conclusions

The emotions of anger and disgust, and their accompanying moral systems, offer a number of ways to understand contemporary rape trials, historical or cultural differences in the law of rape and popular attitudes toward morality that supplement and inform the enforcement of the law. Although much of the evidence of the involvement of anger and disgust in legal matters is indirect, we hope that interested researchers will take this as a challenge to document the role of these emotions in legal contexts. However, the more important problem is to address current failures in the prosecution and definition of rape cases. It is clear that, descriptively, emotion has consequences for the application of the law. In a prescriptive sense, too, legal scholars and practitioners are still trying to establish the proper role of emotion in legal proceedings. What pointers to action emerge from our analysis of the moral emotions, anger and disgust?

Emotions can influence rape trials and the people involved in their investigation in both a rational and an irrational way. Establishing the agency and responsibility of a rapist, seeing that there is nothing to exculpate him and finding that the victim's rights have been violated are all judgments that can lead to moral anger. Anger is an important motivation for justice seeking. On a small scale it can motivate punishment of wrongdoers even at significant costs for the punishing individual (Cosmides and Tooby 1992), which can have practical benefits in terms of social deterrence. Retributive punishment, too, has been shown to be the principal factor in public satisfaction with justice (Carlsmith *et al.* 2002). Purely in terms of increasing rape convictions, then, it would seem that anger could be enlisted by directing it at double standards for male and female sexuality, at the situation of raped women who face unjust disbelief and dismissal from many in the criminal justice system, and at the rapist himself.

But as rhetoricians since Aristotle have noted, anger can be applied unreasonably as well as reasonably. Most seriously, anger is equally appropriate to the defendant's counter-narrative of an innocent man unjustly accused. Because the emotion of anger can be transferred irrationally from one situation to another, it seems that trying to involve raw anger in the prosecution of rape – for example, by favouring anger-prone jurors in jurisdictions that use *voir dire* or by using anger-enhancing rhetoric – could have side effects favourable to the defendant as well as the complainant. (See also Chapter 13 by Barbara Krahé and Jennifer Temkin this volume that discusses in more detail the implication of voir dire procedures). Also, anger can become associated with people or social groups for reasons irrelevant to justice; for example, Tapias *et al.* (2007) found reciprocal implicit associations between African-Americans and anger among Whites in the United States. The relationship of such a stigma to historical miscarriages of justice under lynch law has been extensively documented. However, it is also true that anger associations can feed into judgments against complainants who belong to the stigmatised groups (Taslitz 2000). In our opinion, such prejudices have no place in the process of justice.

Perhaps the most relevant question is whether moral anger is necessary to render justice. On the positive side, moral anger can be satisfying to spectators of justice and motivating to those who pursue it. In fact, we think that one possible application of moral anger is to encourage it as an alternative emotion to shame, disgust, guilt or doubt among rape victims and justice officers involved in their cases. Given that rape arouses strong emotions, it is important to acknowledge that anger is a better motivation for prosecuting rape than other feelings.

However, in a trial's truth-finding process, many of the factors that lead to moral anger can directly influence judgment without emotion. For example, the different standard of sexual behaviour for men and women exerts a major influence on judgment in rape trials, especially in acquaintance rape. To change one's expectation about male sexual behaviour shifts the burden of negligence from the woman's non-resistance to the man's insensitivity, as Taslitz (2000) suggests, and therefore tells us who has violated a norm or a right of the other. The question is whether anger is needed for blame to work; that is, whether a justice-making robot could properly assess who has committed a crime without feeling anger. The concept of a completely emotionless judge gives pause. After all, such a creature would perhaps lack other attributes we find useful in justice, such as compassion and common sense. However, it is only reasonable to insist that a judge's emotions respond to the facts and not the other way around. Indeed, one of the troubling characteristics of anger that emerges from our research is that, when irrationally based, it can encourage people to create superficially plausible reasons that support it, for example a presumption of harm or of the violation of rights.

Despite the strong tendency to view rapists and other sexual violators with disgust and the arguments of some that disgust can be recruited to serve social justice (Kahan 2000), we see disgust as a definite obstacle to the prosecution of rapists. Disgust at human sexuality is historically linked to sex-negative attitudes, especially those regulating female chastity. The divinity ethic it underpins is today prevalent in many patriarchal societies and among conservatives in Europe and North America. Because of the contagious and inflexible nature of disgust, such attitudes are likely to adhere to both parties in a sexual act for the mere fact of having committed it, regardless of agency or consent. This is especially likely when the sex act itself or its circumstances are socially abnormal.

Moreover, disgust in its cognitive origins and action tendencies does not lend itself to creating the narrative of unjust action, victimisation and retributive punishment that modern law requires. Instead, it is associated with a narrative of general repulsion and disengagement. Specifically, rapes in which the sex act or victim violates social norms, such as incestuous rape, rape of sex workers or rape between men, run the risk of being assimilated to disgust instead of anger and thus of being taken less seriously as a crime between people. The law's move toward greater acceptance of activities previously outlawed because they offended divinity concerns (e.g. the repeal of 'sodomy' laws) thus presents some ironic side effects. If violations of divinity norms are seen as victimless, then the reinterpretation of rape in divinity and not autonomy terms is just as problematic; instead of both people being condemned as criminals under disgust morality, neither person is condemned. Thus, while it is tempting to enlist the outrage and repulsion of disgust in condemning rape, our theoretical perspective and empirical evidence suggests that a disgust-based strategy will be counterproductive in bringing justice to rape's victims.

References

Abrams, K. (2002) "Fighting fire with fire:' Rethinking the role of disgust in the crimes', *California Law Review,* 90: 1423–1464.

Alicke, M.D. (2000) 'Culpable control and the psychology of blame', *Psychological Bulletin,* 126, 556–574.

Averill, J. (1983) 'Studies on anger and aggression: Implications for theories of emotion', *American Psychologist,* 38: 1145–1160.

Berkowitz, L. and Harmon–Jones, E. (2004) 'Toward an understanding of the determinants of anger', *Emotion,* 4: 107–130.

Berman, D.A. and Bibas, S. (2008) 'Engaging capital emotions', *Northwestern University Law Review Colloquy,* 102, 355–364.

Brownmiller, S. (1975) *Against Our Will: Men, Women and Rape.* New York: Simon and Schuster.

Carlsmith, K.M., Darley, J.M. and Robinson, P.H. (2002) 'Why do we punish? Deterrence and just deserts as motives for punishment', *Journal of Personality and Social Psychology,* 83 (2): 284–299.

Cosmides, L. and Tooby, J. (1992) 'Cognitive adaptations for social exchange' in J.H. Barkow, L. Cosmides & J. Tooby (eds.), *The Adapted Mind: Evolutionary Psychology and the Generation of Culture.* New York: Oxford University Press, 163–228.

Cotton, A., Farley, M. and Baron, R. (2002) 'Attitudes toward prostitution and acceptance of rape myths', *Journal of Applied Social Psychology,* 32: 1790–1796.

Cottrell, C.A. and Neuberg, S.L. (2005) 'Different emotional reactions to different groups: A sociofunctional threat-based approach to prejudice', *Journal of Personality and Social Psychology,* 88: 770–789.

Curtis, V. and Biran, A. (2001) 'Dirt, disgust, and disease – is hygiene in our genes?', *Perspectives in Biology and Medicine,* 44: 17–31.

Davey, G.C.L., Bickerstaffe, S. and MacDonald, B.A. (2006) 'Experienced disgust causes a negative interpretation bias: A causal role for disgust in anxious psychopathology', *Behaviour Research and Therapy,* 44: 1375–1384.

Davey, M. and Marzillier, S. (2004) 'The emotion profiling of disgust-eliciting stimuli: Evidence of primary and complex disgusts', *Cognition and Emotion,* 18, 313–336.

De Cremer, D. and van den Bos, K. (2007) 'Justice and feelings: towards a new era in justice research', *Social Justice Research,* 20: 1–9.

Dick, S. (2008) *Homophobic Hate Crime: The Gay British Crime Survey 2008.* Available online at http://www.stonewall.org.uk/documents/homophobic_hate_crime_final_report.pdf (accessed 31 December 2009).

Ekman, P. (1999) 'Basic emotions' in T. Dalgeish and M. Power (eds.), *Handbook of Cognition and Emotion.* New York: John Wiley & Sons, 45–60.

Ellis, A. (1984) 'Offense and the liberal conception of the law', *Philosophy and Public Affairs,* 13, 3–23.

Fischer, A.H. and Roseman, I.J. (2007) 'Beat them or ban them: The characteristics and social functions of anger and contempt', *Journal of Personality and Social Psychology*, 93 (1): 103–115.

Goldberg, J.H., Lerner, J.S. and Tetlock, P.E. (1999) 'Rage and reason: the psychology of the intuitive prosecutor', *European Journal of Social Psychology*, 29, 781–795.

Guerra, V. M. (2008) 'The CADS as a Predictor of Moral Emotions', Unpublished manuscript, University of Kent.

Guerra, V.M. and Giner-Sorolla, R. (in press) 'Community, Autonomy, and Divinity Scale (CADS): development of a theory-based moral codes scale for research across and within cultures', *Journal of Cross-Cultural Psychology*.

Gutierrez, R. and Giner-Sorolla, R. (2007) 'Anger, disgust, and presumption of harm as reactions to taboo-breaking behaviours', *Emotion*, 74, 853–68.

Haidt, J. (2001) 'The emotional dog and its rational tail: A social intuitionist approach to moral judgment', *Psychological Review*, 4, 814–34.

Haidt, J. (2003) 'The moral emotions' in R.J Davidson, K.R. Scherer, and H.H Goldsmith, *Handbook of Affective Sciences*. Oxford: Oxford University Press, 852–70.

Haidt, J. and Graham, J. (2007) 'When morality opposes justice: conservatives have moral intuitions that liberals may not recognize', *Social Justice Research*, 20, 98–116.

Haidt, J. and Hersh, M.A. (2001) 'Sexual morality: The cultures and emotions of conservatives and liberals', *Journal of Applied Social Psychology*, 31: 191–221.

Haidt, J., Koller, S.H. and Dias, M.G. (1993) 'Affect, culture and morality, or is it wrong to eat your dog?', *Journal of Personality and Social Psychology*, 65, 613–28.

Haidt, J., Rozin, P., McCauley, C. and Imada, S. (1997) 'Body, psyche, and culture: the relationship between disgust and morality', *Psychology and Developing Societies*, 9: 107–31.

Holmstrom, L.L. and Burgess, A.W. (1979) 'Rape: The husband's and boyfriend's initial reactions', *The Family Coordinator*, 28: 321–30.

Horvath, M.A.H. and Giner-Sorolla, R. (2007) 'Below the age of consent: Influences on moral and legal judgements of adult–adolescent sexual relationships', *Journal of Applied Social Psychology*, 37, 2980–3009.

Izard, C.E. (1977) *Anger, Disgust, and Contempt and Their Relationship to Hostility and Aggression*. London: Plenum Press.

Johnson-Laird, P.N. and Oatley, K. (1989) 'The language of emotions', *Cognition and Emotion*, 1: 29–50.

Kahan, D.M. (2000) 'The progressive appropriation of disgust' in S. Bandes (ed.), *The Passions of Law*. New York: New York University Press, 63–79.

Kahan, D.M. (2007) 'The cognitively illiberal state', *Stanford Law Review*, 60: 115–154.

Kahan, D.M. and Nussbaum, M.C. (1996) 'Two conceptions of emotion in criminal law', *Columbia Law Review*, 96: 269–374.

Karstedt, S. (2002) 'Emotions and criminal justice', *Theoretical Criminology,* 6: 299–317.

Lawrence v. Texas (2003) 539 US 558.

Lerner, J.S. and Keltner, D. (2000) 'Beyond valence: toward a model of emotion-specific influences on judgment and choice', *Cognition and Emotion,* 14: 473–93.

Lerner, J.S. and Keltner, D. (2001) 'Fear, anger, and risk', *Journal of Personality and Social Psychology,* 81: 146–59.

Lerner, J.S., Small, D.A. and Loewenstein, G. (2004) 'Heart strings and purse strings: effects of emotions on economic transactions', *Psychological Science,* 15, 337–41.

Levenson, R.W., Ekman, P. and Friesen, W.V. (1990) 'Voluntary facial action generates emotion specific autonomic nervous system activity', *Psychophysiology,* 27, 363–84.

Lonsway, K.A. and Fitzgerald, L.F. (1994) 'Rape myths', *Psychology of Women Quarterly,* 18: 133–64.

Mackie, D.M., Devos, T. and Smith, E. (2000) 'Intergroup emotions: Explaining offensive action tendencies in an intergroup context', *Journal of Personality and Social Psychology,* 79: 602–16.

Maroney, T.A. (2006) 'Law and emotion: A proposed taxonomy of an emerging field', *Law and Human Behavior,* 30: 119–42.

Miller, J. and Schwartz, M.D. (1995) 'Rape myths and violence against street prostitutes', *Deviant Behavior,* 16: 1–23.

Nabi, R.L. (2002) 'The theoretical versus the lay meaning of disgust: Implications for emotion research', *Cognition and Emotion,* 16, 695–703.

Nussbaum, C.M. (2004) *Hiding from Humanity: Disgust, Shame, and the Law.* Oxford: Princeton University Press.

Oberman, M. (1994) 'Turning girls into women: re-evaluating modern statutory rape law', *The Journal of Criminal Law & Criminology,* 85: 15–79.

Olatunji, B.O., Lohr, J.M., Sawchuk, C.N. and Westendorf, D.H. (2005) 'Using facial expressions as CSs and fearsome and disgusting pictures as UCSs: affective responding and evaluative learning of fear and disgust in blood-injection injury phobia', *Anxiety Disorders,* 19: 539–55.

Park, J.H., Faulkner, J. and Schaller, M. (2003) 'Evolved disease avoidance processes and contemporary anti-social behaviour: Prejudicial attitudes and avoidance of people with physical disabilities', *Journal of Nonverbal Behaviour,* 27: 65–87.

Parkinson, B. (1999) 'Relations and dissociations between appraisal and emotion ratings of reasonable and unreasonable anger and guilt', *Cognition and Emotion,* 13 (4): 347–85.

Posner, E.A. (2000) *Law and Social Norms.* Cambridge, MA: Harvard University Press.

Pound, R. (1942) *Social Control Through Law.* New Haven, CT: Yale University Press.

Roseman, I.J., Antoniou, A.A. and Jose, P.E. (1996) 'Appraisal determinants of emotions: constructing a more accurate and comprehensive theory', *Cognition and Emotion*, 10: 241–77.

Rozée, P.D. (1993) 'Forbidden or forgiven? Rape in cross-cultural perspective', *Psychology of Women Quarterly*, 17: 499–514.

Rozin, P. (2008) 'Hedonic adaptation: Specific habituation to disgust/death elicitors as a result of dissecting a cadaver', *Judgment and Decision Making*, 3 (2): 191–4.

Rozin, P. and Nemeroff, C. (2002) *Sympathetic Magical Thinking: The Contagion and Similarity 'Heuristics'*. Cambridge: Cambridge Press.

Rozin, P., Haidt, J. and McCauley, C.R. (1993) 'Disgust' in M. Lewis and J.M. Haviland (eds.), *Handbook of Emotions*. London: Guildford Press, 579–94.

Rozin, P., Millman, L. and Nemeroff, C. (1986) 'Operation of the laws of sympathetic magic in disgust and other domains', *Journal of Personality and Social Psychology*, 50: 703–12.

Rozin, P., Lowery, L., Imada, S. and Haidt, J. (1999) 'The CAD hypothesis: a mapping between three moral emotions (contempt, anger, disgust) and three moral codes (community, autonomy, divinity)', *Journal of Personality and Social Psychology*, 4: 574–86.

Ruggi, S. (1998) 'Commodifying honor in female sexuality: honor killings in Palestine', *Middle East Report*, 206: 12–15.

Rumney, P. (2006) 'False allegations of rape', *Cambridge Law Journal*, 65: 128–158.

Russell, D.E.H. (1975) *The Politics of Rape*. New York: Stein and Day.

Russell, J.A. and Fehr, B. (1994) 'Fuzzy concepts in a fuzzy hierarchy: varieties of anger', *Journal of Personality and Social Psychology*, 67: 186–205.

Russell, P.S. and Giner-Sorolla, R. (2009a) 'Moral Anger, But Not Moral Disgust, Responds to Intentionality', Unpublished manuscript, University of Kent.

Russell, P.S. and Giner-Sorolla, R. (2009b) 'Disgust does not require reasons', Unpublished manuscript, University of Kent.

Schaich Borg, J., Lieberman, D. and Kiehl, K.A. (2008) 'Infection, incest, and iniquity: investigating the neural correlates of disgust and morality', *Journal of Cognitive Neuroscience*, 20: 1529–46.

Shweder, R.A., Much, N.C., Mahapatra, M. and Park, L. (1997) 'The "big three" of morality (autonomy, community, and divinity) and the "big three" explanations of suffering', in A. Brandt and P. Rozin (Eds.), *Morality and Health*. New York: Routledge, 119–69.

Sivarkumaran, S. (2005) 'Male/male rape and the "taint" of homosexuality', *Human Rights Quarterly*, 27: 1274–306.

Stevenson, K. (2000) 'Unequivocal victims: The historical roots of the mystification of the female complainant in rape cases', *Feminist Legal Studies*, 8, 343–66.

Tangney, J.P., Wagner, P., Fletcher, C. and Gramzow, R. (1992) 'Shamed into anger? The relation of shame and guilt to anger and self-reported aggression', *Journal of Personality and Social Psychology*, 62: 669–75.

Tapias, M.P., Glaser, J., Keltner, D., Vasquez, K. and Wickens, T. (2007) 'Emotion and prejudice: Specific emotions toward outgroups', *Group Processes and Intergroup Relations*, 10, 27–39.

Taslitz, A.E. (2000) 'Race and two concepts of the emotions in date rape', *Wisconsin Women's Law Journal*, 15: 3–76.

Taylor, S.C. (2004) *Court Licensed Abuse: Patriarchal Lore and the Legal Response to Intrafamilial Sexual Abuse of Children*. New York: Peter Lang.

Viki, G.T. and Abrams, D. (2002) 'But she was unfaithful: Benevolent sexism and reactions to rape victims who violate traditional gender role expectations', *Sex Roles: A Journal of Research*, 47: 289–93.

Weber, H. (2004) 'Explorations in the social construction of anger', *Motivation and Emotion*, 28: 197–19.

Wegner, D.M, Wenzlaff, R., Kerker, R.M. and Beattie, A.E. (1981) 'Incrimination through innuendo: Can media questions become public answers?', *Journal of Personality and Social Psychology*, 40: 822–32.

Welchman, L. and Hossain, S. (eds.) (2006) *'Honour': Crimes, Paradigms and Violence Against Women*. London: Zed Books.

Wheatley, T. and Haidt, J. (2005) 'Hypnotic disgust makes moral judgements more severe', *Psychological Science*, 16: 780–4.

White, B.H. and Kurpius, S.E. (2002) 'Effects of victim sex and sexual orientation on perceptions of rape', *Sex Roles: A Journal of Research*, 46: 191–200.

Woody, S.R. and Tolin, D.F. (2002) 'The relationship between disgust sensitivity and avoidant behavior: Studies of clinical and nonclinical samples', *Journal of Anxiety Disorders*, 16: 543–59.

Chapter 4

Rape in the media[1]

Jenny Kitzinger

The media are a key arena in which rape is defined. Television reports, newspaper articles, films and other media help to shape understandings of what counts as rape, who perpetrates it and why. Such representations also influence perceptions about the victim and the likely consequences of sexual violence. Yet the media present a highly partial view of this crime, and often promote a series of unhelpful stereotypes and myths (see Bohner *et al.* this volume; Franiuk *et al.* 2008). Such representations are informed by dominant social attitudes and external factors such as police and court procedures and thus reflect many of the problems discussed in this volume. But media representations are also framed by *internal* media dynamics including institutional racism and sexism within the media industries, news values (such as the search for the sensational) and journalistic practices (such as the impact of tight deadlines).

This chapter reviews research into how rape has been represented in the news media in the UK and the US from the 1970s to the early years of the twenty-first century.[2] I outline feminist challenges to traditional understandings of sexual violence and the ways in which these have helped to transform discourse and representation. I then review the ongoing problems with media reporting and track controversial developments such as the emergence of new discourses of disbelief.

Read all about it! Sexual violence as media fodder: a brief historical introduction

The sexual exploitation of women and children has played a key role in the history of the news media. In 1885 scandal shook London when William Stead, editor of the *Pall Mall Gazette*, undertook a groundbreaking piece of investigative journalism. In the context of widespread debate about child prostitution and with the initial prompting of women's rights campaigners, he bought a 13-year-old local girl for 'immoral purposes'. He had the girl, Eliza Armstrong, medically examined to confirm that she was a virgin and then packed her off to Paris. Stead wrote up descriptions of his adventure in a series of articles with headings such as 'Delivered for seduction', 'The violation of virgins', 'Strapping girls down' and 'The forcing of unwilling maidens'. The newspaper was banned by major newsagents but sold out on the streets. The *Gazette* reports attracted national notoriety, provoked massive public demonstrations and are credited with helping to raise the age of consent for girls from 12 to 16 (Barry 1979). Just three years later, sexual violence was again the focus of intense media interest with the tale of 'Jack the Ripper.' A serial sex-killer loose in London was perfect fodder for the 13 national dailies in hot competition at this time. Gory details, descriptions of 'fallen women' and reports of foreign-looking suspects or that the victims were ritually murdered by orthodox Jews ensured good circulation figures for the burgeoning newspaper industry. Such was the success of this story that one suggestion was that the Ripper was an enterprising newspaper man who killed in order to create 'good copy' for his newspaper (Curtis 2001).

Over a hundred years later sexual violence still makes 'good copy'. Instead of virginal Eliza Armstrong or the spectre of 'Jack the Ripper' the UK now has figures such as the iconic 'Yorkshire Ripper' (modelled on his nineteenth-century counterpart), who raped and murdered at least 13 women before he was caught in 1980, and Fred and Rosemary West, who assaulted an unknown number of women and children over decades and were finally arrested in 1994. High-profile events in the USA include the 1984 'Big Dan' trial (involving the gang rape of a woman in a tavern, which inspired the film *The Accused*) and the 1989 brutal assault on a jogger in Central Park. There were also televised celebrity rape trials during the 1990s such as that of William Kennedy-Smith (a member of the prominent Kennedy family). Other notorious cases involved fraternity groups such as the Delta Chi case, in which the contested rape was videoed and later circulated on the internet (Horeck 2004). The early twenty-first century also included a series of headline grabbing scandals involving contested allegations against athletes including Kobe Bryant (2003) and the Duke lacrosse trial (2006) (Leonard 2007; Markovitz 2006).

The issues raised by newspaper reports about Eliza Armstrong or Jack the Ripper over a hundred years ago still capture many of the tensions in more recent media representations of sexual violence. Media exposure is important to inform and provoke public awareness, debate and policy responses. Journalists, though, are highly selective in what they report and can be guilty of voyeurism and sensationalism. Coverage can decontextualise abuse, encourage racism, promote stereotypes of women (as virgins or whores), blame victims and excuse assailants. Increasingly in the late twentieth and early twenty-first centuries there has also been a tendency to focus on the issue of false allegations.

The (re)discovery of sexual violence: the rise in media attention during the 1970s and 1980s and the role of the Women's Liberation Movement

It is a truism to declare that sexual violence makes 'good copy'. However, precisely which forms of sexual violence attract the media and *how* it is defined vary across time and across cultures. Prior to developments in the 1970s, the mainstream UK and US media paid very little attention to rape: journalists even avoided the word, preferring phrases such as 'carnal knowledge'. In 1971, for example, there were just 31 reports of rape cases in the British newspapers the *Sun*, the *Daily Mirror* and *The Times*. However, coverage more than doubled in 1978 and had almost doubled again by 1985 (Soothill and Walby 1991: 18). A similar (slightly earlier) increase in attention to sexual assault is evident in the American press with a 250 per cent increase in coverage of this issue in the *New York Times* between 1972 and 1974 (Byerly 1999) while a similar expansion in media coverage of sexual violence against children emerged from the 1980s onwards (Kitzinger 1996).

The Women's Liberation Movement played a key part in this increasing recognition of sexual violence. In the early 1970s, women began to organise to campaign for the equal treatment of women. This movement is often called 'second-wave' feminism, the first wave having peaked with the Suffragette movement and feminist campaigns at the end of the nineteenth and in the early twentieth centuries. Second-wave feminism identified violence against women as a top priority, along with issues such as equal pay, access to childcare, abortion rights and sexual self-determination. The seventh demand of the Women's Liberation Movement (WLM) is reproduced in Figure 4.1.

Freedom from intimidation by threat or use of violence or sexual coercion, regardless of marital status. An end to the laws, assumptions and institutions that perpetuate male dominance and men's aggression toward women.

Figure 4.1 The seventh demand of the Women's Liberation Movement

Feminists shared experiences in consciousness-raising groups and documented and exposed sexual violence through research, fiction and autobiography (for instance, Angelou 1969; Armstrong 1978). Activists established crisis lines and opened refuges so that women and girls who were being abused by men they lived with could escape their assailants. They also fought to put these issues on the public agenda and to transform the way sexual violence was represented in the media and understood by the public (see Donat and D'emilio 1992; Smart and Smart 1978). Alongside this, feminists worked to reform criminal justice practice and legislation. Campaigns included challenging the unsympathetic way in which police treated rape complainants, the routine use of women's previous sexual history to discredit them in court and the fact that a man could not be charged with raping his wife.

Feminist analysis re-envisaged rape and sexual abuse as a symptom of a culture of violence against and disrespect for women, which should be viewed as a form of sexist hate crime (rather than an impulsive act of sexual need).[3] Solutions had to include radical social change. Refusing to accept that such violence should be taken for granted feminists criticised strategies which put the onus purely on women to be 'sensible' (such as avoiding public parks, locking car doors, crossing the street to avoid groups of men or carrying rape alarms). The tongue-in-cheek advice about 'how to avoid rape' reproduced in Figure 4.2 sums up some of the feminist arguments at this time. The parody highlights the unrealistic nature of most advice. It also challenges the ways in which women were expected to behave, such as being careful not to dress 'provocatively' and obeying an unofficial curfew.

How to Avoid Rape

Don't go out without clothes – that encourages some men.
Don't go out with clothes – any clothes encourage some men.
Don't go out alone at night – that encourages men.
Don't go out with a female friend – some men are encouraged by numbers.
Don't go out with a male friend – some male friends are capable of rape.
Don't stay at home – intruders and relatives can both rape.
Avoid childhood – some men are 'turned on' by little girls.
Avoid old age – some rapists 'prefer' aged women.
Don't have a father, grandfather, uncle or brother – these are the relatives who most often rape young women.
Don't marry – rape is legal within marriage.
To be quite sure – don't exist.
(War on Rape Collective 1977, cited in London Rape Crisis Centre 1984: 2–3)

Figure 4.2 How to avoid rape

The WLM was very successful in achieving some reforms, even if its seventh demand is far from realised even in these so-called post-feminist days. Rape in marriage has been made a crime, a change achieved in some American states in the late 1970s and early 1980s but not realised in England and Wales until 1991. There are now some local and central government feminist-inspired initiatives to challenge sexual violence (Kitzinger 1994). More and more women now talk openly about their experiences, and the number prepared to try to seek justice has increased – although most rapes still go unreported and most brought to trial still fail to secure a conviction.

The WLM also had a profound impact on media representations. Most journalists now recognise sexual violence as a serious social issue. It is less likely to be treated simply as a titillating, salacious and bizarre story to be juxtaposed with pictures of half-naked women, and there has been a decrease in sensationalism and overt sexism (Soothill and Walby 1991). Certain myths, such as women 'enjoy' rape, that used to be routinely invoked have all but disappeared (Los and Chamard 1997: 315). Feminist ideas and the experiences of raped women are increasingly articulated (Cuklanz 1996: 116). Many researchers also point to some excellent coverage of sexual violence issues, especially by women reporters (Mills 1997; Soothill and Walby 1991).

In fact, the media not only responded to feminist critiques but were sometimes an ally in achieving feminist goals. Specific media events were vital to some campaigns for reform. In 1982, for example, a savvy female reporter from a major Seattle television station included footage of a veteran senator standing on the Senate floor asking: 'Well, if you can't rape your wife, who you can rape?' This caused a public outcry and helped to finally remove the marital exclusion from the Washington state rape law, an exclusion now lifted in nearly all US states (Byerly 1994: 60). It was similarly a televisual event which helped to prompt outrage the same year in the UK. Police handling of rape complaints was revealed in a fly-on-the-wall documentary on Thames Television. Millions of viewers saw the vicious and bullying interrogation of a woman who had gone to the police saying she was raped. The programme provoked widespread protest and helped to fuel demands for improvements in the treatment of rape complainants (Soothill and Walby 1991: 9).

In addition to the importance of such events, the impact of media recognition in itself should not be underestimated. The rapid expansion in media attention to sexual violence (across both fact and fiction) both reflected, and had a dramatic impact upon, changing understandings of everyday life. My own interviews and focus group discussions around incest conducted from the early 1980s through to the mid-1990s highlight the crucial interplay between media attention, public awareness and survivors' abilities to identify their experiences of sexual assault, discuss them with other people and protest against such abuse (see Kitzinger 2001). The 11-year time span of this research highlights the media's special role, quite distinct (but not independent) from other cultural resources, in helping to confront and name sexual abuse, particularly assaults by known men. Prior to this children and adult survivors often lacked the conceptual tools to make sense of their experiences in the first place. The crime was not only unspeakable, it was literally 'inconceivable'. One 16-year-old, for example, explained that she could not define what her father and other men had done to her since childhood as rape. This was because she felt that she displayed insufficient resistance: 'I let them do it.' In any case, she saw rape as an encounter in a dark alleyway with 'a man with a knife'. This young woman argued that, in fact, she could *never* be raped by anyone because 'I would just lie down and take it, to get it over with' (Kitzinger 2001: 95, 2004).

Media recognition and representation became (and continue to be) a vital part of women's process of naming and making sense of their memories and communication about the experience. Media coverage made a crucial contribution to a spiral of recognition helping to fundamentally transform private and public thinking and discussion. It encouraged the formation and expression of personal identities around this very fragmented and silenced experience and helped sexual violence, including rape by one's own father or stepfather, to enter public discourse (Kitzinger 2001, 2004).

Any account of how the media represent sexual violence should remember quite how new and crucial such media attention has been and continues to be. This includes recent moves to address rape linked to sex trafficking, rape in prison and rape as a systematic weapon of genocide and war (Houge 2008).

However, this does not mean that media coverage gives cause for uncritical celebration. Although there have clearly been highly significant changes in the extent of attention, and some reform in the nature of coverage, many of the criticisms feminists were making in the 1970s still applied in the 1980s and 1990s and have remained valid into the new millennium. New problems have also emerged. It is these criticisms that are the focus of the next section of this chapter.

New and ongoing criticisms of media coverage

The following subsections highlight a range of interrelated areas in which the media in general, or certain segments of the media, are open to criticism. These are:

- the 'events-based' emphasis of news reporting;
- media 'fatigue' and declining interest in routine abuse;
- the focus on controversial allegations;
- objectifying victims;
- reflecting court-based discourse: excusing perpetrators and perpetuating stereotypes about victims and victimisation;
- stereotyping rape and obscuring the complexity of dominance and submission;
- the 'symbolic expulsion' of sexual violence from mainstream society;
- the emphasis on stranger-danger;

- evasion or misrepresentation of social analysis;
- positioning sex attackers as 'other';
- selective cultural explanations of rape;
- positioning victims as 'other';
- promoting a law-and-order agenda or appropriating disgust against rape to justify foreign policy interventions;
- racism, the white gaze and selective 'colour blindness'.

The 'events-based' emphasis of news reporting

Many media critics have noted that the news as a format tends to be led by *events* rather than *issues*. This is certainly true of news reporting about sexual violence. One study, for example, found that coverage of particular cases accounted for 71 per cent of UK press reports about child sexual abuse (Kitzinger and Skidmore 1995). This leaves little space for in-depth exploration of theoretical issues or any thorough debate about the underlying causes of, or solutions to, the problem. Indeed, the above study located just four articles that focused on the causes of child sexual abuse (out of a total sample of 1,668 items). Similar observations have been made about the reporting of the rape and abuse of adult women (Bathla 1998: 107; Cuklanz 1996: 84). The news media's bias toward focusing on events rather than issues implicitly presents sexual violence as a taken-for-granted fact of life, with the emphasis placed on intervention and judgment in *particular* accusations rather than broader social solutions. The facts that sexual violence often fits within a traditional crime beat and that much reporting relies on individual court cases also prioritise the justice system as the primary avenue of intervention.

Media 'fatigue' and declining interest in routine abuse

In addition to being events-based the news media also have a notoriously short attention span. Peak interest in the 1970s and 1980s soon gave way to media ennui. Journalists interviewed in the 1990s recorded their sense that their editors and their audiences had become 'fatigued' with stories about rape and abuse (Benedict 1992: 251; Kitzinger and Skidmore 1995; Skidmore 1998). If routine abuse quickly ceased to be news, however, that does not mean that certain 'angles' on the story do not gain a hearing. A new angle has often been provided by controversial allegations and the rise of a new form of scepticism.

The focus on controversial allegations

Statistics about the prevalence of sexual violence no longer make for new, exciting stories or attract sustained reporting. Controversial cases in which allegations are disputed can, however, fit very well into the media's news values and routine journalistic practices. Even where such cases do not conform to standard 'hard' news values (for example, having clear news 'events' and high-status sources), there has been a successful backlash against women's and children's testimony. This backlash has hooked into other media and cultural values, including the 'human interest story' (portraying the distressed men being 'victimised' by false allegations), long-standing prejudice against the veracity of women and children and the low status of those who intervene in suspected abuse cases. The media now often pay more attention to supposedly false allegations than they do to established facts about sexual violence. 'Date rape', 'false memory syndrome' and contested allegations against celebrities have all fed into a new (or revitalised) discourse of scepticism.[4] Studies of media reporting of supposedly false allegations highlight how such reporting follows problematic fault lines. There is, for example, a striking asymmetry in how the credibility of each side in such cases is often assessed. The emotions of the accused are used to underline their innocence; the 'hysteria' of those making the accusations is used to undermine their credibility (Kitzinger 1998).

Efforts to address the attrition rate in rape cases are dismissed and ridiculed, For example, in 2005 the then Metropolitan Police Commissioner Sir Ian Blair ordered a top-level inquiry into the growing discrepancy between the number of rapes that are alleged to have taken place and the number of convictions that result. This was condemned by some journalists. The right-wing columnist Melanie Phillips attacked this effort to address the problem by highlighting false allegations and cases of women too drunk to recall what had happened to them. In an article entitled 'Q: When is a person guilty until proven innocent? A: When he's a man who is accused of rape', she concluded that 'Sir Ian's initiative reflects nothing other than the politically correct obsession with proving that men are intrinsically violent and predatory and women are always their victims' (*Daily Mail*, 6 June 2005).

The rapid rise and nature of media attention to false allegations also speak volumes about gendered power and media practices. Men may have greater authority and practical/cultural resources as media sources. Men also hold more positions of power within media organisations and interviews with some male journalists have shown how some clearly identify with the (falsely) accused – (Kitzinger 1998). However, as Melanie Phillips' article illustrates, the focus on false allegations is not restricted to male journalists – some of the stiffest critics are women. However, perhaps more significant is the way in which a 'masculine' ethos permeates newsroom culture. Media coverage can be informed by subtle processes such as the selective privileging of 'masculine' over 'feminine' discourses and 'ways of knowing' and the gendered operation of media formats and genres (Kitzinger 1998, 2004).

Objectifying victims

Reporting has also been criticised for silently objectifying rape victims in news reports. Even those factual outlets which might give more 'voice' to victims – such as the talk show genre – can be problematic: objectifying the survivor, employing facial close ups to highlight emotion and intrusive questions to prompt details of an attack. This approach can turn the woman (or man) into a media commodity and obscure any analysis beyond the personal (see Alcoff and Gray 1993: 278; Haug 2001: 55).

Reflecting court-based discourse: excusing perpetrators and perpetuating stereotypes about victims and victimisation

The reliance of journalists on controversial care or court proceedings for many of their stories means that the ideas about causes of sexual violence that slip into reports are often unreflective reiterations of common-sense assumptions. Alternatively they may simply echo courtroom discourse. The latter is particularly problematic because courtrooms are places where traditional patriarchal understandings of rape are reified.

Media reporting of court cases often reflects, and sometimes amplifies, this patriarchal discourse. The victim is often invisible and silent, the anonymous object of competing discourses. She 'is constantly spoken of but herself remains inaudible or inexpressible; she is displayed as a spectacle but remains unrepresentable' (Moorti 2002: 110). In the courtroom and in the media, victims are often also routinely cast either as 'innocent' or as 'guilty' – a dichotomy that is oppressive regardless of which category particular women and children are allowed to occupy and often follows racialised fault lines reflecting myths about the innocent white woman and the black

Jezebel (Meyers 2004: 97). Children who are raped are usually cast as inherently 'innocent' but this can be equally oppressive (see Kitzinger 1988, 1990). Similar criticisms apply to the framing of adultvictims/ survivors of sexual violence, a category usually more 'up for grabs' for adult women than for children (Benedict 1992; Kitzinger 1988).

Innocence or guilt may also depend on a woman's behaviour. The woman raped by the American boxer Mike Tyson was subtly smeared in the media for driving too fast, partying and social climbing (Benedict 1992: 257). Claims of rape against William Kennedy-Smith were challenged by declarations by the defence council, reiterated in the media, that the rape charge was made 'after a night of drinking in several Palm Beach bars' (Moorti 2002: 95).

While women's behaviour is subject to intense scrutiny, the men charged with their assault may have their actions obscured. Journalists often use the passive tense to describe assaults in ways which remove agency from the perpetrator and fail to hold him accountable for his violence (Henley *et al.* 1995; Meyers 2004: 106–7). Journalists may give prominence to the defendant's claims, such as that he misread the signals or that he was provoked by the woman's behaviour or by uncontrollable lust (Lees 1995). Analyses of particular cases also show how reports may obscure the nature of assaults. Some newspapers used terms such as 'fondling' and 'having sex' to describe the gang rape of a victim bashed in the face with a rock (Benedict 1992). An NCB news report described a rape charge against William Kennedy-Smith as a 'whiff of sexual misconduct' (Moorti 2002: 91).

Such reports excuse assailants and discredit individual women. More generally they reinforce ideas about how sexual violence should be considered (as not real violence) or how consent should be deduced (for example, accepting an invitation to a hotel room). The responsibility is placed on women to avoid 'provocative dress', 'immodest behaviour', being too assertive or not assertive enough, or simply going out for a drink with a man. The media are guilty of reinforcing myths such as women often lie about rape or that they provoke it through lewd dress and behaviour (see Aplat 2006: 310; Meyers 2004: 106–7, 110). The 1977 parody of advice to women reproduced above (in Figure 4.2) is, unfortunately, just as recognisable today as it was all those decades ago.

Stereotyping rape, obscuring the complexity of dominance and submission

Alongside the problems noted above the media often fail to engage with the complexity of power in rape cases. Anything short of stabbing or murder may not be recognised as force, and the glamourisation of overwhelming sexual desire in popular culture, combined with the trivialisation of rape, can make a rape and 'normal sex' appear easily confused. This was graphically illustrated in the 'Delta Chi' case. This involved allegations of rape by Lisa Gier King against members of the Delta Chi fraternity, much of which was filmed by the men themselves. The footage, now circulating on the Internet, was interpreted by the judge as evidence of the men's innocence and this interpretation is shared by some public audiences. This is in spite of the fact that during the filming the men themselves can clearly be heard repeatedly referring to rape and making statements such as: 'One of the most exciting evenings in the history of Delta Chi ... the raping of a white trash crackhead bitch' (Horeck 2004: 1519). For Lisa Gier King, the footage represents her victimisation made available for mass consumption. In a very telling comment she notes: 'The general public don't understand [that] rape doesn't always look the way it does in the movies.' The irony now is, perhaps, that many people judge the credibility of rape allegations against the narratives supplied by pornography or by the dramatic images in fiction (Horeck 2004: 149).[5]

The 'symbolic expulsion' of sexual violence from mainstream society

The final set of major issues I wish to highlight here are connected to what I shall call the 'symbolic expulsion' of sexual violence. I use the phrase to highlight the fact that mainstream representations of sexual violence fail to address radical strategies for expelling this from society (involving, for example, fundamental challenges to gender and sexual norms and power inequalities). Instead, these representations often market a kind of token solution to the problem. This involves very distorted reflections of the nature of sexual violence, with an emphasis on stranger-danger and a tendency to attribute sexual violence to only a certain type of 'person' ('the other'). This then sets the scene for promoting a law-and-order-agenda that tackles sexual violence purely by identifying and controlling these individuals. I will illustrate each of these themes and their interrelation below.

The emphasis on stranger-danger

Although media representations of sexual violence no longer exclusively focus on attacks by pathological strangers, this form of assault still receives disproportionate attention. An analysis of UK news reporting in 2006 found that attacks by strangers accounted for over half of the press reports about rape, despite the fact that less than 17 per cent of rapes in the UK are stranger rapes; over half of the reports also concerned rapes that took place in public places, in spite of the fact that this only accounts for 13 per cent of attacks. The report also noted that 'the majority – 56% – of rapes are perpetrated by a current or former partner, but these cases were almost invisible in the press, accounting for only 2% of stories about rape' (Marhia 2008: 4). The media are much more drawn to spectacular and unusual cases of serial attacks than the boring routine of ordinary sexual violence endemic in everyday life. The stranger-attack fits with traditional ideas about the nature of 'newsworthiness' and the search for a serial sex-attacker, for example, has its own momentum and rationale that attract intense and prolonged coverage (Kitzinger and Skidmore 1995; Meyers 1997: 93; Soothill and Walby 1991: 145, 157). The 'Jack the Ripper' type of approach to telling stories about sexual violence has its own narrative power which evades important social questions. Analysing an episode of Fox TV's *America's Most Wanted* about the disappearances of 31 women in Vancouver, Pitman, for example, argues that the imposition of a Jack-the-Ripper 'media template' had very problematic consequences. It 'displaced local and highly politicized explanations related to prostitution laws, community policing practices, and dangerous urban spaces' (Pitman 2002: 167). The 'real crime' genre fascination with rape accounts and the way in which such programmes frame sexual violence can also have the effect of imprisoning women in a network of fear. Weaver's analysis of a TV programme called *Crimewatch*, for example, shows how the programme mediates messages to women about the need for self-regulation if they are to avoid becoming victims and how it reinforces women's fear of public spaces (Weaver 1998; see also Dowler 2006).

Evasion or misrepresentation of social analysis

At the same time as highlighting the spectacular and evading social implications, the media also actually often trash any research that highlights the widespread nature of sexual violence – especially if the research is identified with feminism (Soothill and Walby 1991: 145). Often the authority of such points of view is undermined by their being portrayed as biased, emotional or incoherent (Los and Chamard 1997: 302, 322). Official statistics released by government or state bodies are harder to discredit. Such figures are more likely to be reported respectfully, but are often treated as one-off or isolated items of information that have no implications for broader media reporting strategies.

Positioning sex attackers as 'other'

In addition to sidelining analysis about the widespread nature of sexual violence and locating sexual threat in 'the stranger', journalists also often position abusers as outsiders via a variety of other rhetorical tricks. They may portray an abuser as a 'beast', an 'animal' or a distinct type of person, almost a separate species. The very fact that there is a special noun, 'paedophile', to describe those who rape and sexually abuse children implies that those who commit such acts constitute a breed apart (Hebenton and Thomas 1996; Kelly 1996: 45). The concept of the paedophile also, of course, singles out the sexual abuse of children, as if there were no connection between abuse perpetrated against boys and girls and that perpetrated against adults.[6]

Where feminists highlight the links between a wide range of forms of sexual violence, masculinity and normal heterosexuality, the mass media often take the opposite tack. Just as the concept of the paedophile is part of the ring-fencing of the rape of children so the label 'homosexual rape' serves to fragment different forms of violence and deny their connection. It also dissociates rape from heterosexuality. The rape of women or girls is not treated as a 'heterosexual' crime; however, attacks on men and boys are often labelled 'homosexual'. One study found that most cases of sexual assaults on children reported in the national UK press involved allegations of men assaulting girls, there was not a single example of an assault or assailant being described as heterosexual. By contrast, there were 50 reports explicitly identifying the assault or the assailants as 'gay' or 'homosexual' (Kitzinger 2004).[7]

Selective cultural explanations of rape

Feminist criticisms of how mainstream culture validates sexually violent behaviour are usually ignored by the mainstream media. When journalists do connect sexual violence to endemic cultural attitudes about normal sex or masculinity, it is often in considering 'sub-' or 'foreign' cultures rather than taking on board the feminist critique of dominant patriarchal values. News coverage of the 'Big Dan' case in 1983, for example, suggested that only the Portuguese-American community held the sort of attitudes which led to rape (Moorti 2002: 82–3). Accusations against a group of young black men for the rape of the Central Park jogger in 1989 were used to discuss 'inner-city youth culture' as the problem (Cuklanz 1996: 83).[8] The trials of 'Muslim youth' on gang rape charges in Sydney between 2000 and 2003 quickly became culturally inflected as a problem linked to being 'Muslim' and 'Lebanese' by media reporting (Humphrey 2007).[9] The media may mobilise accounts of attacks on Muslim women to justify 'saving' them from Muslim men (Mishra 2007) or promote an image of the 'foreign rapist'. A study of UK media, for example, found that reports of rape by non-nationals could be used as a vehicle for mobilising xenophobia (Marhia 2008: 4).

This type of 'cultural' explanation, combined with racism and nationalism, can be even more evident in reporting sexual violence from abroad, especially from the so-called underdeveloped countries. The US media reporting of the 1991 mass rape case in a Kenyan school, for example, associated the abuse of women with 'tribal tradition' and collapsed all Kenyan women into the one-dimensional category of 'the oppressed' (Hirsch 1994: 1043, 1045). Sometimes the media seem happier to focus on 'exotic' violence against women, so that 'dowry burning', 'foot binding', 'female genital mutilation' or the mistreatment of women under 'alien' fundamentalist regimes are treated as evidence of those countries' backwardness. In the case of Afghanistan, the denial of women's rights was even used as one of the justifications to invade by the 'liberating' American and British forces in 2001.

Positioning victims as 'other'

It is not only the perpetrators who are presented as 'other', outside society. The *victims* of sexual exploitation and rape can also be 'othered' as if the damage done to them does not really touch society as a whole. This was exemplified most explicitly when the serial killer 'the Yorkshire Ripper' was terrorising women in northern England in the late 1970s: the media distinguished between prostitutes and 'innocent' victims. The Attorney General declared that 'perhaps the saddest part of this case is that ... [t]he last six attacks were on totally respectable women', and, after one of the murders, the police warned that the next victim could be 'somebody's daughter', as if the murdered prostitutes were not part of anybody's family (Lopez-Jones 1999).

Promoting a law-and-order agenda or appropriating disgust against rape to justify foreign policy interventions

The tendencies outlined above allow a 'law-and-order' solution to be proposed as the only way forward. It can be used to justify a disproportionate application of the law to certain populations (such as gay men or black inner-city youth). It can also support a refusal to consider how 'policing sex' can actually make some women more at risk (for example, kerb-crawling laws which make it harder to assess punters or the use of condom-possession as evidence against sex workers) (Lopez-Jones 1999). Radical social solutions are ignored and rape prevention initiatives are trivialised – the media seem to prefer to orchestrate outrage about sentencing rather than looking at wider causes (Soothill and Walby 1991: 145). Some feminists have also argued that feminist campaigns against sexual violence have become problematically allied with the neo-liberal state and that this, and the accompanying media framing of rape through this lens, can harm impoverished women and support punitive and racially based crime control interventions (Bumiller 2008). It is also clear that protecting women from rape has become a powerful rhetorical strategy selectively applied to justify certain foreign policy interventions – where a chivalrous western masculinity is transposed against the barbaric and primitive 'other' masculinity (Stables 2003). The final theme I wish to draw out in this review of criticisms is that of racism. This cross-cuts many of the themes discussed above.

Racism, the white gaze and selective 'colour blindness'

Reporting about Jack the Ripper in nineteenth-century London suggested he was a 'foreigner' or a Jew. Had the sex-murderer been active in America at the same time he undoubtedly would have been cast as a 'Negro'. The history of media coverage of sexual violence is also a history of racism. In America stories of 'black beasts' attacking white women and the lynching of the alleged perpetrators were the main vehicle through which sexual violence was mentioned throughout the first part of the twentieth century. Such reporting served to keep both black men and white women in their place (Benedict 1992: 30). At the same time as black men were being persecuted for the alleged sexual threat they posed to white women, black women (especially under slavery) were routinely sexually victimised by white men. This sexual violence was taken for granted, legitimised or obscured

(Moorti 2002: 55). Black women's position in the anti-rape movement thus has diverse historical roots, including involvement in the late nineteenth-/early twentieth-century anti-lynching movement as well as the investigative journalism of pioneering reporters such as Ida B. Wells (Moorti 2002: 54–7).

Although a white-dominated feminist movement has often prioritised gender as a category of analysis, critics have pointed out that the intersections of gender and race make for specific experiences that cannot be subsumed under the category of 'universal woman' as if all women were the same, living under the same conditions. These critics warn against 'raceless talk of gender subordination' (Crenshaw 1992; Pitman 2002). The enduring legacy of the myth of the all-pervasive black predator was illustrated in the false allegations against an imaginary group of four, tall black men conjured up in the Katie Robb case at Iowa State University (see Patton and Snyder-Yuly 2007: 3). At the same time the inadequacies of any 'colour-blind' approach were clearly evident in the 1990s controversies surrounding accusations against black men such as Mike Tyson, the boxer, or Clarence Thomas, the nominee for the Supreme Court (Morrison 1992; see also Meyers 2004). The importance of analysis which takes into account the intersecting experiences of gender, race and class has been highlighted by scholars writing about this issue in general (e.g. Davis 1982) and about rape in particular (e.g. Meyers 2004; Projansky 2001).

Moorti's study of rape on television in the US between 1989 and 1993 provides a thorough and incisive study of the problems of racism and 'colour blindness'. She highlights, for example, the racism in the reporting of the rape trial of Mike Tyson. Before the rape allegations surfaced, the boxer was, she argues, presented as an athlete who partially transcended his race. However, once the trial was underway, news workers emphasised his racial identity. 'The press offered two visions of Tyson, both informed by stereotypes of African Americans. He was a crude, sex obsessed, violent savage who could barely control his animal instincts; or he was a victim of terrible social circumstances, almost saved from the streets by a kindly overseer, who finally faltered and fell to the connivance of others' (Moorti 2002: 101).

Black women are subject to a different form of racism as it intersects with sexism. The rape of black women may receive less press attention, their allegations may be given less credibility and the fact that this may be a racist as well as a sexist crime may be ignored (Benedict 1992: 251; Meyers 1997: 66). If the media cast a black woman as a credible and worthy rape victim then this may be achieved by erasing her race. Thus, for example, Tyson's accuser, a black beauty queen, was characterised during his trial as the all-American girl, effectively positioning her as the 'white', virginal woman (Moorti, 2002: 104–5). This honorary whiteness is precarious, however: after the trial her privileges were withdrawn and she was recast in the mould of the 'temptress Jezebel' (Moorti 2002: 104–5).[10]

Moorti's study identifies how 'gender, race and class shape who speaks about rape in the public arena and how they speak about it' (Moorti 2002: 14). She highlights the 'white gaze' assumed in news reporting and the ways in which the audience is positioned as white, for instance by the use of the word 'we' and assumptions that viewers need to be introduced to the language and culture of 'them' – inner-city youth (a code for blackness). Programmes 'rarely show how race and gender work together to shape individual experience of sexual violence … [They] either address rape as it affects (white) women or as an effect of black masculinity, rarely as a site where gender and racial discourse intersect in problematic ways' (Moorti 2002: 13–14). Thus although, for example, racial difference may be used in prime-time entertainment programmes to provide dramatic tension, 'when the story lines focus on race, rape tends to slide out of view. Racial oppression and gender oppression are rarely shown simultaneously' (Moorti 2002: 215).

Conclusion

In sum, the media coverage of rape has been transformed since the early 1970s. The degree of recognition of sexual violence and the nature of reporting have in many cases improved. The media have been a vital conduit contributing to a radical reshaping of the public profile of sexual violence. Parts of the media continue to do an excellent job of raising awareness of this issue and helping to challenge myths. However, problems persist. Sometimes all that has happened is that the racism or sexism, for example, has become more subtle; a 'white male gaze' is still dominant. In addition, while appearing to adopt feminist perspectives, most of the media have consistently failed to take on the more radical critiques of how society supports and perpetuates sexual violence. Instead they opt for the purely 'symbolic expulsion' of sexual violence from our midst or adopt a glib 'post-feminist' analysis in which anti-rape collective activism is rendered unnecessary (see Projansky 2001). New problems have also emerged. These include the ambivalence of reporting around issues such as 'date rape', which reawakens old myths about sexual assault, and the focus on disputed allegations. Analysts of recent media coverage point to a growing media ennui with the issue of routine sexual violence, which is now seen as old news, as well as a backlash against women's testimony and a shift of focus whereby accused men become the real victims.

It would be wrong simply to blame journalists. The media are often reflecting popular assumptions and sometimes may even be echoing problems from within parts of feminist analysis. The 'colour-blind' approach which appeals to the notion of some universal women (as if all women shared a common experience), for example, is a problem in some strands of feminist analysis as well as in the media. Efforts to understand media coverage need to take into account the source organisations and events and other production processes which feed into reporting. I have highlighted the way court discourses are reflected in the news media and the implications of an 'events-based' approach. Other factors that impact on reporting include deadlines, news values and issues such as format constraints. One clear problem is also the lack in newsrooms of sexual violence specialists who are experienced in the complexities of the issue. (For discussion of such constraints see Benedict 1992; Kitzinger and Skidmore 1995; Meyers 1997.)

This chapter has tried to give an overall picture of media coverage, often focusing on news reporting. However, there are limitations to generalising about the media without attention to diversity and to genre. Some journalists are at the forefront of challenging sexual violence and many theorists argue that media formats such as one-off dramas, soap opera and talk shows present new challenges but also open up new possibilities for addressing sexual violence in innovative ways. (For a discussion see Cuklanz 1996, 2000; Henderson 2007; Kilby 2007; Moorti 2002.) Finally, a full understanding of the role of the media in representing sexual violence would also need to analyse audience reception ... but that, of course, is another story.

Notes

1 An earlier version of this review appeared in K. Ross and C. Byerly (eds) (2004) *Media and Women*. Blackwell. Thanks to Wiley-Blackwell for permission to reprint.
2 Media coverage has played different roles in different countries, and the form of sexual violence around which women have campaigned also varies. This chapter focuses on the US and the UK context. Other issues have become important in other countries. For example, the media have played a crucial, and controversial, role in campaigns against military sexual slavery when Korean women, for example, sought to sue the Japanese government (Yoon, n.d.).
3 For examples of radical feminist analysis of sexual violence during the 1970s see the classic books: *Against Our Wills* (Brownmiller 1977) and *Female Sexual Slavery* (Barry 1979).
4 For critical reflections about false memories and the construction of sexual abuse experience through a feminist lens see Reavey and Warner (2003) and Haaken and Reavey (2009).
5 This chapter focuses on factual reporting, however it is important to recognise the role of fiction including the way in which sexual force may be glamourised in internet games and in both Hollywood and other films (for an analysis of Hindi film see Ramasubramanian and Oliver 2006). Several recent books offer insightful analysis of fiction (e.g. see Cuklanz 2000; Horeck 2004) and locate this in relation to cultural shifts of the late twentieth and early twenty first century. One example of such work is Projansky (2001) who examines how post-feminist discourses in popular culture assumes collective anti-rape activism is no longer necessary, incorporates an unproblematised whiteness and present a colour-blind view of the world. She explores how black women are displaced by contemporary representations of both blackness and post-feminism in film and TV drama. She highlights, for example, how film and drama often present rape as if it were only a specifically racialised experience for African American women in the *past* (e.g. under slavery); or how they address race by focusing on evil white men or the trauma for black men, 'African American women may be highly visible, their rapes are necessary to instigate the narrative', she argues, 'but their voices, perspectives and experiences are silenced' (p. 193).
6 Many of the most notorious 'paedophiles' have no compunction about extending their violence against children to adults too. The internationally notorious Austrian, Josef Fritzl, kept his daughter locked in a dungeon for 24 years, repeatedly raping her, and fathering her seven children. The Belgian man, Marc Dutroux, attacked both children and adults. Similarly, the British couple, the Wests, raped and murdered with little regard for the age of their victims.

7 This figure underestimates the extent of the asymmetry because it does not include the more subtle coded reference to assailants who were unmarried or 'effeminate' or still lived with their mothers – common ways of implying homosexuality (Kitzinger 1999).

8 This case is further complicated by the fact that the convictions of the accused boys/men were overturned in 2002 (Saulny 2002).

9 For a discussion about how cultural 'tradition' versus 'Islam' are implicated in news discussions of rape in newspapers in Islamic, Middle Eastern countries see Anon. (in press).

10 Diverse stereotypes apply to different categories of 'non-white' and/or 'foreigners'. Asian women, for example, may be stereotyped as exotic and sensual, and/or passive and subordinate and Marhia (2008) analyses the reporting of an Indian man's sexual assault of a Swedish woman and highlights the cultural assumptions that were mobilised in this case. 'The attack is directly linked with the perpetrator's 'otherness' in an extraordinarily patronising way', she notes. Statements within the report implicitly assert the supposed 'superiority', sophistication and self-mastery of the 'Western' male over the infantilised figure of the unsophisticated Indian who cannot master his bodily urges (Marhia 2008: 38).

References

Alcoff, L. and Gray, L. (1993) 'Survivor discourse: transgression or recuperation', *Signs: Journal of Women in Culture and Society*, 18 (2): 260–90.

Angelou, M. (1969) *I Know Why the Caged Bird Sings*. New York: Random House.

Aplat, Z. (2006) 'News coverage of violence against women', *Feminist Media Studies*, 6 (3): 295–314.

Armstrong, L. (1978) *Kiss Daddy Goodnight: A Speakout on Incest*. New York: Pocket Books.

Barry, K. (1979) *Female Sexual Slavery*. New York: Avon.

Bathla, S. (1998) *Women, Democracy and the Media*. London: Sage.

Benedict, H. (1992) *Virgin or Vamp: How the Press Cover Sex Crimes*. Oxford: Oxford University Press.

Brownmiller, S. (1977) *Against Our Will*. New York: Penguin Books.

Bumiller, K. (2008) *In an Abusive State: How Neoliberalism Appropriated the Feminist Movement Against Sexual Violence*. Durham, NC: Duke University Press.

Byerly, C. (1994) 'An agenda for teaching news coverage of rape', *Journalism Education*, Spring, 59–69.

Byerly, C. (1999) 'News, feminism and the dialectics of gender relations', in M. Meyers (ed.), *Mediated Women: Representations in Popular Culture*. Cresskill, NJ: Hampton Press, 383–403.

Crenshaw, K. (1992) 'Whose story is it anyway? Feminists and anti-racist appropriations of Anita Hill', in T. Morrison (ed.), *Race-ing Justice, En-Gendering Power: Essays on Anita Hill, Clarence Thomas and the Social Construction of Reality.* New York: Pantheon, 402–41.

Cuklanz, L. (1996) *Rape on Trial.* Philadelphia: University of Pennsylvania Press.

Cuklanz, L. (2000) *Rape on Prime-Time: Television, Masculinity and Sexual Violence.* Philadelphia: University of Pennsylvania Press.

Curtis, L. P. (2001) *Jack the Ripper and the London Press.* New Haven, CT: Yale University Press.

Davis, A. (1982) *Women, Race and Class.* London: Women's Press.

Donat, P. and D'emilio, J. (1992) 'A feminist redefinition of rape and sexual assault: historical foundations and change', *Journal of Social Issues,* 48 (1): 9–22.

Dowler, K. (2006) 'Sex, lies, and videotape: the presentation of sex crime in local television news', *Journal of Criminal Justice,* 34 (4): 383–92.

Franiuk, R., Seefelt, J., Cepress, S. and Vandello, J (2008) 'Prevalence and effects of rape myths in print journalism', *Violence Against Women,* 14 (3): 287–309.

Haaken, J. and Reavey, P. (2009) *Memory Matters: Contexts for Understanding Sexual Abuse Recollections.* London: Routledge.

Haug, F. (2001) 'Sexual deregulation, or, the child abuser as hero in neoliberalism' *Feminist Theory,* 2 (1): 55–78.

Hebenton, B. and Thomas, T. (1996) 'Tracking sex offenders', *Howard Journal,* 35 (2): 97–112.

Henderson, L. (2007) *Social Issues in Television Fiction.* Edinburgh: Edinburgh University Press.

Henley, N., Miller, M. and Beazley, J. (1995) 'Syntax, semantics and sexual violence: agency and the passive voice', *Journal of Language and Social Psychology,* 14 (1): 60–84.

Hirsch, S. (1994) 'Interpreting media representations of a "night of madness": law and culture in the construction of rape identities', *Law and Social Review,* 19 (4): 1023–56.

Horeck, T. (2004) *Public Rape: Representing Violation in Fiction and Film.* London: Routledge.

Houge, A. (2008) 'Subversive victims? The (non)reporting of sexual violence against male victims during the war in Bosnia-Herzegovina', *Nordicom Review,* 29 (1): 63–78.

Humphrey, M. (2007) 'Culturalising the abject: Islam, law and moral panic in the West', *Australian Journal of Social Issues,* 42 (1): 9–25.

Kelly, L. (1996) 'Weasel words: paedophiles and the cycle of abuse', *Trouble and Strife,* 33: 44–9.

Kilby, J. (2007) *Violence and the Cultural Politics of Trauma.* Edinburgh: Edinburgh University Press.

Kitzinger, J. (1988) 'Defending innocence: ideologies of childhood', *Feminist Review*, 28: 77–87.

Kitzinger, J. (1990) 'Who are you kidding? Children, power and the struggle against sexual abuse', in A. James and A. Prout (eds), *Constructing and Reconstructing Childhood*. London: Falmer Press, pp. 157–83.

Kitzinger, J. (1994) 'Challenging sexual violence against girls: a public awareness approach to preventing sexual abuse', *Child Abuse Review*, 3 (4): 246–8.

Kitzinger, J. (1996) 'Media representations of sexual abuse risks', *Child Abuse Review*, 5 (5): 319–33.

Kitzinger, J. (1998) 'The gender-politics of news production: silenced voices and false memories', in C. Carter, G. Branston and S. Allan (eds), *News, Gender and Power*. London: Routledge, pp. 186–203.

Kitzinger, J. (1999) 'The ultimate neighbour from hell: stranger danger and the media representation of paedophilia', in B. Franklin (ed.), *Social Policy, the Media and Misrepresentation*. London: Routledge, pp. 207–1.

Kitzinger, J. (2001) 'Transformations of public and private knowledge: audience reception, feminism and the experience of childhood sexual abuse', *Feminist Media Studies*, 1 (1): 91–104.

Kitzinger, J. (2004) *Framing Abuse: Media Coverage and Public Understanding of Sexual Violence Against Children*. London: Pluto.

Kitzinger, J. and Skidmore, P. (1995) 'Playing safe: media coverage of the prevention of child sexual abuse', *Child Abuse Review*, 4 (1): 47–56.

Lees, S. (1995) 'The media reporting of rape: the 1993 British "Date Rape" controversy', in D. Kidd-Hewitt and R. Osborne (eds), *Crime and the Media: The Post-Modern Spectacle*. London: Pluto Press, pp. 107–30.

Leonard, D. (2007) 'Innocent until proven innocent – in Defense Duke lacrosse and White power (and against menacing Black student-athletes, a Black stripper, activists, and the Jewish media)', *Journal of Sport and Social Issues*, 31 (1): 25–44.

London Rape Crisis Centre (1984) *Sexual Violence: The Reality for Women*. London: Women's Press.

Lopez-Jones, N. (ed.) (1999) *Some Mother's Daughter: The Hidden Movement of Prostitute Women Against Violence*. London: International Prostitutes Collective/Crossroads Books.

Los, M. and Chamard, S. (1997) 'Selling newspapers or educating the public? Sexual violence in the media', *Canadian Journal of Criminology*, 39 (3): 293–328.

Marhia, N. (2008) *Just Representation? Press Reporting and the Reality of Rape*. London: Eaves. Available online at: http://www.eaves4women.co.uk/Lilith_Project/Documents/Reports/Just%20Representation_press_reporting_the_reality_of_rape.pdfRepresentation (accessed 15 January 2009).

Markovitz, J. (2006) 'Anatomy of a spectacle: race, gender, and memory in the Kobe Bryant rape case', *Sociology of Sport Journal*, 23 (4): 396–418.

Mayers, M. and Halim, S. (in press, 2010) 'News coverage of violence against Muslim women: a view from the Arabian Gulf', *Communication, Culture and Critique*, Vol 3, Issue 1, due March 2010.

Meyers, M. (1997) *News Coverage of Violence Against Women: Engendering Blame*. London and Newbury Park, CA: Sage.

Meyers, M. (2004) 'African American women and violence: gender, race and class in the news', *Critical Studies in Media Communication*, 21 (2): 95–118.

Mills, K. (1997) 'What difference do women journalists make?', in P. Norris (ed.), *Women, Media and Politics*. Oxford: Oxford University Press, pp. 41–56.

Mishra, S. (2007) '"Saving" Muslim women and fighting Muslim men: analysis of representations in the New York Times', *Global Media Journal*, 6 (11). Available online at: http://lass.calumet.purdue.edu/cca/gmj/fa07/gmj-fa07-mishra.htm (accessed 20 November 2008).

Moorti, S. (2002) *Color of Rape: Gender and Rape in Television's Public Spheres*. New York: State University of New York Press.

Morrison, T. (ed.) (1992) *Race-ing Justice, En-Gendering Power: Essays on Anita Hill, Clarence Thomas and the Social Construction of Reality*. New York: Pantheon.

Patton, T. and Snyder-Yuly, J. (2007) 'Any four black men will do – rape, race, and the ultimate scapegoat', *Journal of Black Studies*, 37 (6): 859–95.

Pitman, B. (2002) 'Re-mediating the spaces of reality television: *America's Most Wanted* and the case of Vancouver's missing women', *Environment and Planning*, 34 (1): 167–84.

Projansky, S. (2001) *Watching Rape: Film and Television in Postfeminist Culture*. New York: New York University Press.

Ramasubramanian, S. and Oliver, M. (2006) 'Portrayals of sexual violence in popular hindi films', in K. Weaver and C. Carter (eds), *Criticial Readings: Violence and the Media*. Maidenhead: Open University Press, pp. 210–25.

Reavey, P. and Warner, S. (2003) *New Feminist Stories of Child Sexual Abuse: Sexual Scripts and Dangerous Dialogues*. London: Routledge.

Saulny, S. (2002) 'Convictions and charges voided in '89 Central Park Jogger Attack', New York Times 20 December 2002. Available at http://www.nytimes.com/2002/12/20/nyregion/convictions-and-charges-voided-in-89-central-park-jogger-attack.html.

Skidmore, P. (1998) 'Gender and the agenda: news reporting of child sexual abuse', in C. Carter, G. Branston and S. Allan (eds), *News, Gender and Power*. London: Routledge, pp. 204–21.

Smart, C. and Smart, B. (1978) 'Accounting for rape: reality and myth in press reporting', in C. Smart and B. Smart (eds), *Women, Sexuality and Social Control*. London: Routledge & Kegan Paul, pp. 89–103.

Soothill, K. and Walby, S. (1991) *Sex Crimes in the News*. London: Routledge.

Stables, G. (2003) 'Justifying Kosovo: representations of gendered violence and US military intervention', *Critical Studies in Media Communication*, 20 (1): 92–115.

War on Rape Collective (1977) *War on Rape*. Melbourne: WRC.

Weaver, K. (1998) '*Crimewatch UK*: keeping women off the streets', in C. Carter, G. Branston and S. Allan (eds), *News, Gender and Power*. London: Routledge, pp. 248–62.

Yoon, B. (n.d.) *Military Sexual Slavery: Political Agenda for Feminist Scholarship and Activism*. Available online at: http://witness.peacenet.or.kr/kindex. htm.

Chapter 5

Sexual scripts, sexual refusals and rape

Hannah Frith

The construction of sexual violence between heterosexual partners as a problem of communication (a misunderstanding in which consent or non-consent is poorly communicated or inaccurately understood) has been at the heart of debates about the nature of sexual negotiation, what 'counts' as rape, and how to eradicate sexual violence. But womens' refusals are often not heard, ignored or overruled, and establishing women's right to refuse sexual activities (of any kind, with any one and under any circumstances) and to have these refusals recognised has been central to campaigns asserting that 'No Means No'. This chapter explores the 'problem' of sexual negotiation and communication – often simplistically characterised as saying 'yes' or 'no' – as represented in both academic and lay discourse.[1] In lay discourse, women often report that they fail to say 'no' clearly or effectively, or that their behaviour is misperceived as indicating sexual interest, while men report difficulty understanding women's communications about sex. The 'problem' of communication also underpins two of the most popular explanations for rape (especially acquaintance rape) in academic discourse – sexual script theory and miscommunication theory. Script theory asserts that culturally prescribed 'scripts' for sexual interactions ascribe the role of sexual initiator and pursuer to men and sexual gatekeeper to women. So, women are responsible for limiting and saying 'no' during sexual interactions which follow cultural patterns of activities in a preset order. Miscommunication theory suggests that 'acquaintance rape' results from poor communication between men and women, in which women fail to say no clearly and effectively while men fail to understand or act upon women's refusals.[2] This chapter explores the interplay between lay explanations for difficulties in sexual negotiations and these academic theories. Drawing on discursive psychology and conversation analysis, the chapter highlights some of the limitations of sexual script and sexual miscommunication theories for understanding rape and sexual aggression, but also seeks to account for their prevalence in young heterosexuals' everyday talk about sexual interactions.

Sexual scripts and miscommunication

Sexual 'scripts' refer to cultural messages which define what counts as sex, how to recognise sexual situations and what to do during sexual encounters. Commonly used within (feminist) writing on sexuality and rape, the term has two different theoretical origins, one based in sociology (Gagnon and Simon 1973) and one in cognitive psychology (Schank and Abelson 1977), which are often used interchangeably (e.g. Popovitch *et al.* 1995). Presenting a radical departure from mainstream biologically orientated sexology, Gagnon and Simon's (1973) notion that sexual interactions follow culturally produced, predictable and *learned* scripts proved very popular. Although they were interested in how culturally available scripts became internalised, it is the cognitive version of this theory which focuses on these internal mental representations. Here, scripts are 'cognitive models that people use to guide and evaluate social and sexual interactions' (Rose and Frieze 1993: 499), or 'sexual blueprints that guide behaviours and cognitions, both our own and those of others' (Kurth *et al.* 2000: 329). Scripts dictate the kinds of activities that typically take place within heterosexual sexual interactions and, importantly, the order in which these are expected to occur. While both versions of the theory focus on identifying socially shared patterns of behaving, those drawing on the cognitive version of script theory have focused on identifying the patterning of different kinds of sexual interactions, while those drawing on Gagnon and Simon's approach have been more concerned with identifying the gendered nature of scripts.

One key aspect of heterosexual scripts identified in this research is that sexual activities are seen as progressing through a series of predictable stages from kissing to 'heavy petting' and culminating in intercourse. To identify scripts participants generate a list of sexual activities which they would typically expect in a given situation (a first date, a one-night-stand, an established relationship, etc.) and put these activities in the order in which they would expect them to occur (Edgar and Fitzpatrick 1993; Geer and Broussard 1990; Rose and Frieze 1993). In addition, different roles for men and women are written into these scripts (Gagnon and Simon 1973, 1987). For men, the traditional sexual script includes actively seeking out multiple sexual partners, uncontrollable sexuality once aroused, seeking sex as a source of pleasure for its own sake and actively initiating sexual activity. In contrast, women's scripts include a desire for love or affection rather than sex, passively waiting to be chosen rather than actively seeking sexual partners, belief in the importance of male pleasure above their own and acting as sexual gatekeepers by restricting or resisting sexual activities (Byers 1996; LaPlante *et al.* 1980). Despite significant changes in the sexual landscape over the last 20 years, especially for young women (e.g. decreasing age of first sex, increasing numbers of sexual partners, heterosexual activity equal to that of men), this sexual double standard remains resilient, although there is some evidence that it may be accepted as a societal norm while being resisted at a personal level (Jackson and Cram 2003; Milhausen and Herold 1999). Similarly, there is also evidence to suggest that although men still practise male-dominated patterns of sexual initiation, some express a desire for more egalitarian modes of interaction (Dworkin and O'Sullivan 2005).

The belief that sexual encounters follow a predictable sequence ending inevitably in sexual intercourse, coupled with the idea that men should initiate sexual activity and should overcome women's reluctance, has been used to account for why some men may feel justified in using verbal coercion and physical force to obtain sex. As such, these scripts are argued to form part of a rape supportive culture (Jackson 1995; Kahn and Mathie 2000; Laws and Schwartz 1977). For example, research with young people suggests that both men and women believe that 'having led a man on' or having 'gone too far' means that a woman has forfeited her right to say 'no' (Quinn *et al.* 1991), and over half of the men in one study said that it was 'okay for a guy to hold down a girl and force her to have sexual intercourse' if she 'says she's going to have sex with him and then changes her mind', or if 'she's led him on', or if she 'gets him sexually excited' (Goodchilds *et al.* 1988: 254–5). Disrupting the script by saying 'no' or changing your mind is apparently unacceptable. Women's role in restricting men's persistent sexual advances and limiting sexual behaviours, coupled with the sexual double-standard in which women should avoid actively seeking out sexual contact, are used to account for why women say 'no' when they really want to have sex – referred to as 'token' or 'scripted' refusals of sex (Muehlenhard and McCoy 1991). Moreover, script theory also accounts for why men may feel that they should interpret these refusals as 'only' token and ignore them (Muehlenhard 1988a). Scripts are also used to account for why women might say 'yes' when they really mean 'no' or consent to unwanted sex[3] – because they want to maintain a relationship, because they feel they should satisfy the man or because they feel his sexuality is unstoppable (Walker 1997). Finally, researchers have been concerned to identify the similarities and differences between scripts for consensual and non-consensual sexual interactions (Krahé *et al.* 2007a, 2007b). For example, Littleton and Axsom (2003) found that scripts for a typical rape and a typical seduction both often mentioned at least one manipulative tactic on the part of the man (e.g. trying to persuade the woman to have sex with him), and both involved a minimal relationship between the man and the woman. However, more male violence, more female resistance and more negative emotions for the woman (such as feeling ashamed or guilty afterwards) were apparent in the rape script, while there were more positive emotions and behaviours displaying sexual interest for women in the seduction script. Littleton and Axsom conclude that their data illustrate 'the areas of overlap between rape and seduction scripts that could lead to confusion about how to label certain incidents of unwanted, forced sex' (p. 473). Supporting this, others have found that compared to unacknowledged rape victims whose rape scripts are more likely to involve a violent attack by a stranger, acknowledged victims are more likely to have rape scripts which are less violent and involve an acquaintance (Kahn *et al.* 1994; Kahn and Mathie 2000).[4] Although they focus on the 'confusion' of rape victims, in summarising a range of research in this area Ryan (2004) argues that rapists too may see themselves as following a seduction script rather than a rape script such that these rapists 'may be genuinely surprised when confronted later with the information that they raped someone' (p. 592).

It is perhaps easy to see, then, the connections between script theory and miscommunication theory. When applied to acquaintance rape, this theory can be described in the following way: 'Rape and other forms of sexual abuse are often the outcome of "miscommunication" between partners: he misinterprets her verbal and nonverbal communication falsely believing that she wants sex; she fails to say "no" clearly and effectively' (Frith and Kitzinger 1997: 518). Sex role socialisation and gendered sexual scripts are widely used to explain why these misunderstandings occur. Research which focuses on men's misunderstanding typically argue either that men see a more sexually orientated world than do women, or that they misperceive women's refusals as 'token'. For example, a survey of over 1,000 US college graduates found that women were more likely to have their friendliness 'misperceived' as sexual interest because men interpreted a broader range of behaviours as indicative of sexual interest (Abbey 1991). Abbey concluded that these differences 'may cause some men to force sexual relations on dating partners, mistaking their partners' true lack of interest for flirtatious repartee' (p. 103). Consequently, when women drink alcohol (Morr and Mongeau 2004), wear revealing clothes (Whatley 1996) or when the man has paid for the date (Muehlenhard *et al.* 1985), men are more likely to see this as indicative of sexual interest and to hold the women responsible if they are then raped. Moreover, if a woman then rejects a potential partner by refusing to engage in sexual activities which he perceives her to have desired, a further discrepancy arises. According to some, 'this discrepancy could cause some men to feel led on if they thought a woman was acting as if she wanted sex more than she actually did, and some men regard being led on as a justification for rape' (Muehlenhard 1988b: 31).

Alternatively, researchers who focus on women's apparent poor communication skills claim that women often fail to say no clearly and unambiguously. Women themselves often report difficulty in refusing unwanted sex (Warzak and Page 1990) and researchers attribute this to gender role socialisation (focusing on passivity, submissiveness, acquiescence to male needs, etc.) in which women are 'trained to be ineffective communicators' (Murnen *et al.* 1989: 102). This is further complicated by the use of 'token resistance' or the 'scripted refusal' mentioned earlier, where women reportedly say 'no' when they really mean 'yes' (Muehlenhard and Hollabaugh 1988; Muehlenhard and McCoy 1991). Finally, alcohol consumption is said to impair women's ability to recognise sexual aggression and high-risk cues and, by reducing their cognitive and motor functioning, limits their ability to either verbally or physically resist rape (Abbey *et al.* 2004). Miscommunication theory has been criticised for obscuring the fact that men are responsible for rape and placing responsibility onto women for improving their communication skills to avoid sexual victimisation (Crawford 1995; Frith and Kitzinger 1997). Nonetheless, the notion of sexual miscommunication is prevalent among social science research and is also a popular (as in often used) explanation for acquaintance rape among young men and women alike (Corcoran

1992; Frith and Kitzinger 1997; O'Byrne *et al.* 2008). For example, only 27 per cent of women whose sexual assault met the legal definition of rape believed that they had been raped: 49 per cent said it was 'miscommunication' (Koss 1988). Consequently, the teaching of 'refusal skills' is common to many acquaintance rape prevention programmes which aim to provide women with the skills to avoid sexual victimisation by learning to say 'no' effectively (Kidder *et al.* 1983: 159). Such programmes 'emphasize to young teenagers that they have the right to say "no"' and 'reinforce the idea that they do not have to give a reason or explanation; they should just say "no" and keep repeating it' (Howard 1985: 82 and 87).

So, both script theory and miscommunication theory have been used to explain men's and women's sexual behaviour, including instances of non-consensual sex such as rape. Both theories draw on self-reports to provide evidence in support of their theories and assume that when talking about sexual interactions in research settings individuals are faithfully and neutrally reporting on what sexual interactions are really like. In contrast, a discursive approach sees language as constitutive of social reality and as actively constructing 'what sex is like'. One way to reconceptualise sexual scripts would be as post-structuralist 'discourses' which shape our understanding of sexual interactions and offer up (or close down) particular subject positions or 'ways of being' for people to embody (see Gavey 2005 for a description of this approach in relation to sexuality). While useful, this approach does not attend to the linguistic mechanisms through which sexual interactions are constructed *as* scripted, or explore the ways in which coercive sexual behaviour is accomplished, justified and 'explained away'. This is a key area where discourse analysis can make a contribution. The following sections outline a discursive psychology approach to understanding talk about sexual activities as if they were scripted and as if they were based on miscommunication.

Script formulations

Rather than seeing scripts as cognitive structures governing behaviour and waiting to be exposed during research, a focus on script *formulations* explores the ways in which the regularity and scripted nature of experience is worked up and constituted through talk and the interactional functions this serves. Edwards (1997) describes script formulations as 'kinds of talk which describe events as following a routine and predictable pattern' (1997: 21; see also 1994, 1995).

Drawing on Edwards' reworking of script theory from a discursive perspective, Celia Kitzinger and I set out to explore the ways in which young women describe sexual interactions *as if* they were scripted and some of the consequences of so doing (see Frith and Kitzinger 2001). We drew on data collected as part of a larger project in which young, white, heterosexual female school and university students participated in focus groups about sexual refusals and unwanted sex. Although these young women were not explicitly asked to produce scripts (as is typically the case in research on this area), they did talk about sexual activities *as if* they were scripted and discussed some of the consequences of this for negotiating sexual refusals. The extract below provides an example of the kind of talk which young women produced which, as script theory would predict, indicated that sexual activities follow a predictable sequence and that this makes sexual refusals difficult to accomplish:

Jill: It gets more difficult as the things are considered less far, if you know what I mean, because –

Deb: Well, it's not like you don't ... if you are ... I don't know, you don't really feel like you have to ask permission to, whereas sex ...

Karen: Yeah, it's naturally assumed.

Deb: Yeah, yeah, it's just like carry on.

Karen: Yeah, you go really ...

Deb: and then you go more and more into it

Karen: It's like a natural progression

Jill: And then if you pull their hand away then,

Karen: I think a lot of blokes would be so surprised if you stopped them at things like that, I think a lot of people ... because they just naturally assume.

(From Frith and Kitzinger 2001: 217; pseudonyms have been used to protect anonymity)

In this extract, the three young women are discussing at what 'stage' in this apparently predictable sequence of sexual activities it is easiest to say 'no'. They agree that 'sex' (by which they presumably mean intercourse) is the easiest stage. Activities which are considered 'less far' into the sequence are more difficult to refuse because people assume that there is a 'natural progression' towards sex, consequently men would not be expected to 'ask permission' to engage in these activities. One could claim that young women describe sexual encounters in this way because that is (more or less) what their sexual encounters are like. This kind of data could be used as supportive evidence for the idea that existing sexual scripts make it difficult for women to say 'no', and this is how some researchers using the concept of 'scripts' would be likely to interpret our data. Rather than seeing this talk as a neutral description of sexual interactions, we were interested in exploring the linguistic and discursive mechanisms through which sexual interactions are described *as if* they were predictable and routine and the functions this serves. We examined how the 'scripted' quality of sexual interaction is actively produced as part of speakers' orientation to issues of accountability.

In this work, Kitzinger and I identified five devices used to construct sexual encounters as scripted. First, young women described sexual interactions as following a series of *predictable stages* that followed a 'natural progression' starting with 'kissing and hugging', followed by other activities (such as 'heavy petting) 'in the middle' or 'half way through', and leading 'all the way to sex'. Second, there are references to *common knowledge* where ideas about sexual encounters are constructed as widely shared through references to what 'most' people 'usually' believe, 'often' think or 'generally' assume. In the extract above, Karen outlines how she thinks 'a lot of blokes' would react and the assumptions that 'a lot of people' would make. In presenting people as having a shared, predictable set of ideas about what sex involves, and about what can reasonably be expected of a sexual partner at any given 'stage' of sexual interaction, these young women construct sex as if it were following a script. The idea that processes of sexual interaction are 'common knowledge' is further reinforced by the use of the generalised 'you', which constructs a version of sexual negotiation as shared by all the group participants. Third, there is *the production of consensus through seamless turn-taking and collaborative talk*. We noted that these young women virtually always accepted each other's version of what sex is like (although they may disagree and challenge each other in other areas) and collaborate in presenting an apparently consensual view of the difficulties involved in saying no to sex. When completing each other's talk, for example, they construct a sense of having such a completely shared view of the world that they are able to know what the other would have said. The repeated use of agreement tokens (such as 'yeah') reinforces the idea that the interjections are appropriate and further supports the impression of consensus. Fourth is the *use of hypothetical and general instances*. Rather than reporting on actual experiences, the vast majority of the women talked about 'typical' incidents, 'the sort of thing that usually happens' or to what they (or a generalised 'you') would do, or might do, in possible future incidents. In other words, young women are making statements about a general class of activities, rather than providing accounts specific to any one sexual encounter. Claims made about sexual encounters *in general* are part of what constitutes sexual encounters as scripted. The 'hypothetical' nature of young women's accounts is often formulated in terms of 'if–then' structures that blur the distinction between what is real and what hypothetical: '*if* you pull their hand away *then*, [...] a lot of blokes would be so surprised'. Finally, we also identified the use of *active voicing* where women illustrate their claims with snatches of dialogue that interpolate male voices (and thoughts), as well as their own, into their talk (Wooffitt 1992). Active voicing constructs sexual negotiations as scripted because the sorts of things men say (or think) during sexual interactions are displayed as easily mimicked and as unproblematically recognisable *instances* of the general category of 'the sorts of things men say'. These are not intended as faithful renditions of actual conversations in their own lives, but rather to represent the *kinds of things* men and women *typically* say (and think): that is, to represent sexual scripts.

Having identified the mechanisms by which young women work up accounts of sexual interactions as if they are scripted, we then wanted to explore the functions of this kind of talk. Why, especially when much of the (largely feminist) work on sexual scripts suggested that these scripts were not in women's best interests, did women account for their experiences in this way? In order to answer this, discursive psychology argues that we need to pay attention to the local interactional context in which this account is produced. For the young women taking part in our focus groups, this context is one in which they are being asked to account for saying (or not saying) no to unwanted sex and to account for their difficulty in making a sexual refusal. Accounts are never neutral but are rhetorically organised to rebut potential alternatives and to manage accountability and identity. The following extract (taken from the same focus group) offers a good illustration of the intricacy and detail of script formulations in managing personal accountability. Here, the young women are talking about what happens after you say 'no'.

Deb: But then you'll often get these kind of 'oh you're a tease', or 'you led me on'. I mean, you don't actually get it like that, but you know that's what they mean. 'Well, if you didn't want it you shouldn't have flirted',

Karen: '– led me on –'
Deb: '– that way.' Exactly. So they put that on to you, and
        sometimes you feel, 'oh god, maybe I'm a real tart or
        whatever, and I have led him on', and that makes you
        feel really shitty.
Jill: But that's just their way of –
Deb: – yeah –
Jill: – making you do something you don't want to do.

(From Frith and Kitzinger 2001: 218)

Deb describes how men might 'put on to you' undesirable
dispositional or moral qualities – such as being a 'tease', 'flirt', or 'a
real tart' – when attempting to say no to sex. At the same time as
accounting for the *difficulty* of saying no to sex, Deb and the others
attempt to counter these negative inferences. Jill, Deb and Karen
jointly produce a scripted version of 'the sorts of things men say'
and a commentary upon it. According to them, men's descriptions
of women as 'prick teasers' and 'tarts' are not reasonable inferences
drawn from observing how women act, but false accusations driven
by men's stake in obtaining sex. These false accusations (evoked
through active voicing, e.g. using what are presented as snatches of
male dialogue), they say, are part and parcel of the normal (scripted)
process of sexual interaction, so it is unsurprising that women find
it difficult to say no to sex. By offering a script formulation, saying
'no' is presented as difficult for them because saying no *is* difficult
– for everyone, always – because it breaches a taken-for-granted,
socially shared sexual script. If accusations such as having 'gone
too far' or 'led someone on' are entirely predictable features of
sexual encounters that do not culminate in intercourse, then these
accusations are undermined: they are not *genuine* complaints from
particular men upset by the decisions of *particular* women; rather,
they are accusations that *all* men will *routinely* make, regardless of
the individual actions of women. Instead of apportioning blame to
particular young women who do not know the right time to say 'no'
to intercourse, this formulation makes clear that there is never a right
time to say no – women's actions are always open to the accusation
of having 'gone too far' from men with a vested interest in going
further. Script formulations were constructed to avoid individualised
explanations of women's difficulties in refusing sex, such as those
prevalent in social scientific literature which positions women who

find it difficult to say no as too inexperienced, lacking in self-esteem, cultural dupes, or are robotically regurgitating pre-learned scripts or are poor communicators (see later discussion of sexual miscommunication). Scripted talk about sex thus enables young women to address the accountability of their actions or inactions in refusing unwanted sex, and to engage in reputation management by using the ordinariness of their difficulties to refute potentially negative dispositional attributions. Moreover, in describing the reactions of young men as scripted, routine and predictable, they present themselves as able easily to identify and negotiate the manipulative strategies of young men. Script formulations simultaneously present young men as routine manipulators who readily invoke verbal strategies to attempt to persuade or coerce women into unwanted sexual activities, while at the same time presenting these attempts as transparent, easily identifiable and even a little clumsy. Paradoxically, this positions women as knowledgeable and competent sexual actors able to recognise these coercive moves and able to dismiss them as 'typical' and not to be taken seriously. Avoiding holding individual men as responsible for sexual coercion (by positioning coercive behaviours as ordinary and expected features of sexual interactions) may be advantageous for heterosexual women waiting to maintain relationships with men.

In sum, adopting a discursive approach to script formulations allows consideration of the ways in which sexual activities are worked up as scripted in subtle and routine ways to construct a shared reality of what sexual interactions are typically like. This allows for an examination of the construction of cultural scripts *in action*. Rather than seeing young women as drawing on pre-existing cognitive scripts, attention to the ways in which these ideas are constituted through everyday talk demonstrates how these discourses are produced at the local, micro level. In addition, a focus on the local interactional context also allows an exploration of the ways in which such explanations may paradoxically have 'advantages' for young women in the context of local interactions (such as presenting themselves as knowledgeable and competent sexual actors, presenting men as hapless in their attempts at coercion, etc.), even though – as analysts – we might recognise the pernicious consequences of constructing sexual activities as scripted (i.e. as presenting women's no's as inappropriate, as justifying sexual coercion, etc.). I revisit these issues at the end of the chapter.

Communicating sexual refusals

In critiquing sexual miscommunication theory, Celia Kitzinger and I (1997) again drew on discursive psychology to argue that accounting for coercive sexual interactions in terms of 'miscommunication' might be popular for young women because it serves a number of functions. Firstly, it obscures the fact that men are responsible for rape by presenting men not as manipulative and abusive coercers but as well-intentioned sexual partners who are confused by women's signals. This opens up the possibility of continuing a relationship with a man on the understanding that coercive sex was a 'mistake' which they can get right next time. Secondly, ironically miscommunication theory may give women an illusory sense of control. If women are at least partly to blame for acquaintance rape, then miscommunication theory offers them the opportunity to prevent it happening again by giving them ways of protecting themselves (by communicating assertively) which women may experience as empowering (even if this takes place within a broader context which analysts may argue is profoundly disempowering). Finally, miscommunication theory obscures institutionalised power relations which means that women can avoid the possibility that men are abusing their power in heterosexual relationships and that this is linked to the unequal distribution of power in patriarchal societies. Next, using conversation analysis (CA) we went on to demonstrate that despite their use of miscommunication theory as a resource to explain sexual coercion, rape and unwanted sex, the same women could demonstrate sophisticated knowledge of the conversational 'rules' for negotiating saying 'no'.

CA is concerned with providing a detailed and systematic account of the structural organisation of naturally occurring conversation. Conversation analysts have studied talk across a wide variety of different settings including helplines, courtrooms, medical settings and therapy sessions as well as ordinary telephone conversations or dinner-table talk. In addition, CA has built up a considerable body of knowledge about the structure of refusals in everyday conversations. This body of work relies on careful attention to the small details of talk such as pauses, hesitations, false starts and self-corrections. This work consistently demonstrates that speakers and hearers are very finely tuned to these small details of talk and are able to respond to them. This work shows that acceptances and refusals are typically managed in very different ways – while acceptances typically involve 'just saying yes', refusals rarely involve 'just saying no'. Acceptances are immediate and direct, there is no pause and the acceptance itself is often very short and simple (e.g. 'I would love to'). In contrast, refusals typically involve the following: (1) delays, (2) prefaces, (3) palliatives and (4) accounts (Atkinson and Drew 1979). We demonstrated that there was a great deal of overlap between the ways in which young women talk about how sexual refusals should be done and the way that conversation analysis says that refusals are typically done.

Whereas acquaintance rape prevention programmes insist that women should give a direct and straightforward 'no' in relation to unwanted sex, young women display their understanding of the cultural rules by describing how direct refusals would make them feel rude, foolish or wrong. Liz says that 'It just doesn't seem right to say no when you're up there in the situation' and Sara agrees, 'It's not rude, but it's the same sort of feeling'. A direct 'no' was also seen as having negative consequences for the young women who would 'feel like a right prat' or 'a right Charlie'. In line with their understanding that refusals require some delicate interactional work, young women also insist (counter to acquaintance rape prevention advice) that it is necessary to offer an account (reason, excuse or justification) for a refusal. As Jan says, 'I think it's better if you try and be nice and explain why', and Wendy agrees, 'just saying no is not good enough if you're in a relationship'. In line with conversational analytic research, young women report the advantages of using accounts which focus on their *inability* to engage in sexual interactions rather than their *unwillingness*. Accounts such as feeling ill, tired, scared, worried about becoming pregnant and not feeling 'ready' to engage in intercourse were all offered not as genuine explanations for a sexual refusal, but as an account which could reasonably be offered. Such explanations were preferred because, as Jill explains, just saying no to a boyfriend might lead to him being 'really upset about it'. Using a plausible excuse – such as pretending to be menstruating – was more acceptable according to Jill because it would 'stop the boy from blaming you'. Another strategy was to present a 'delayed acceptance' – 'just say that you're not ready yet, or you want to keep it for a special time', or 'I'm not ready yet, can we wait awhile?' Although the women did discuss some of the problems with this strategy, they nonetheless agreed that this was preferable to a stark 'no'. Finally, the women in this study were clear that it was advisable to offer (what conversation analysts would call) a palliative when refusing sex: 'look you're a really nice guy and I do like you, but that's it' or 'well, it's very flattering of you to ask'. These attempts to 'soften the blow' were seen as an attempt to refuse sex 'without hurting his feelings' (see also Frith and Kitzinger 1998).

So, despite drawing on 'miscommunication' as an explanation for acquaintance rape and sexual coercion, these young women were able to articulate some of the culturally shared rules for doing refusals that have been identified by conversation analysts. Young women's concerns about the appropriate ways in which to do refusals contrasts sharply with the advice given in sexual refusal skills training and acquaintance rape prevention programmes to 'just say no'. However, although women may demonstrate a clear understanding of socially shared ways of communicating refusals, proponents of miscommunication theory might argue that men may misperceive these signals and/or may not share an understanding of these cultural 'rules'.

Follow-up work by O'Byrne *et al.* (2006) used focus groups with Australian men aged 19–34 to explore men's understanding of sexual refusals. What they found was that men too show a sophisticated understanding of the subtle verbal and non-verbal ways in which sexual refusals are done – including refusals which do not contain the word 'no'. Like women, these men said that refusals were difficult to achieve – they have to be hearable *as* a refusal, but also have to be done in a way which avoids negative consequences for the person producing the refusal and the person receiving it. These men described doing sexual refusals as something which had to be handled with 'kid gloves', an issue that 'you gotta be sort of delicate around', and one in which you 'test the waters without making yourself too vulnerable' (pp. 137–8). Unlike women who treated the expectation that they might be engaged in regularly producing sexual refusals as unproblematic, these men repeatedly worked to present saying 'no' as initially unthinkable for men in general, and for the speakers themselves, despite also being able to go on to give detailed descriptions of how a 'no' would have to be delivered. So, men appear to perform refusals in the same ways that women do. As well as *performing* refusals, to examine their *understanding* of women's refusals these men were asked to think about a situation in which a woman might refuse sex and to indicate how they thought she would go about it. Men are able to provide examples of things that women say which are hearable as refusals, including recognition of some of the clichéd 'excuses'. For example, one of their participants – John – provides three such illustrations (again invoked through active voicing): 'It's getting late', 'I just remembered I'm working early in the morning' and 'I've just uh changed my mind'. As John says, 'there's always a little hint' which can be read as a refusal (O'Byrne *et al.* 2008: 177). The word 'no' is noticeably absent from these examples.

However, despite demonstrating their awareness and understanding of the subtle cultural rules which govern sexual refusals, the same men overwhelmingly drew on 'miscommunication' to account for the issue of rape (O'Byrne *et al.* 2008). Not only was 'miscommunication' used to undermine women's indirect refusals, but it was also used to present a direct 'no' as being insufficiently explicit for men to be able effectively to make sense of women's refusals. The version of miscommunication theory being drawn on was not a 'different but equal' approach; rather men were accorded the status of naive mis-hearers left the impossible task of making sense of women's baffling messages, while women were accorded the status of culpable and accountable deficient communicators. The authors conclude that men's claims to 'not know' how to interpret women's communications should not necessarily be taken as evidence of insufficient knowledge since such claims may be strategically employed to achieve specific rhetorical aims – such as managing accountability for rape.

Collectively, this research suggests that seeking to 'improve communication' is not a necessary goal for rape prevention since evidence suggests that both men and women are capable of understanding and communicating refusals in ways which are hearable as refusals.

Concluding remarks

This work has significant theoretical and methodological implications for the study of rape and sexual consent and can inform the development of rape prevention programmes.

Methodologically, this research urges caution in taking men's and women's self-reported beliefs about rape and sexual interactions as transparent evidence in support of social scientific theories. Such an approach risks providing supportive evidence for theories which are politically problematic in that they engage in victim-blaming and deny men's culpability for rape. By taking what people say as evidence of how sexual interactions 'really are' such theories contribute to, and further institutionalise, the discursive resources which buttress a rape-supportive culture (Doherty and Anderson 1998). In contrast, a discursive approach seeks to examine men's and women's talk about sexual scripts and about miscommunication as local instantiations of the production of rape-supportive culture *in action*. Much feminist discursive work on rape focuses on unpacking the talk of young men (Anderson 1999), convicted rapists (Lea and Auburn 2001) or courtroom talk (Coates and Wade 2004; Ehrlich 1998) in order to examine the function of this talk for the operation of gendered power relations. For example, Lea and Auburn's (2001) analysis of the talk of a convicted rapist undergoing the Sexual Offences Treatment Programme (SOTP) demonstrates how 'Nathan' describes the behaviours of his accomplice 'Michael' in ways which embody many of the features of the stereotypical rape script (i.e. as being perpetrated by a violent, pathologically motivated man) in order to 'excuse' and manage accountability for his own actions of rape. Similarly, Ehrlich (1998) demonstrated that miscommunication – and in particular the deficient efforts of women to communicate their non-consent – is often used by defendants in sexual assault tribunals to reframe rape as consensual sex. Feminists have been more reluctant to explore and deconstruct the talk of women in these contexts – fearing that this might fail to pay attention to the 'lived experience of sexual coercion' or depict women as self-serving (Gavey 2005: 100–1). However, failing to critically engage with the ways in which women commonly talk about their experiences and ignoring the local functions of this talk does women a disservice. As Kitzinger and Wilkinson (1997) have argued, there are real problems in taking everything women say as literally true in order to 'validate' women's experience. They ask, for example, what it would mean to 'validate' the experience of a woman who says that her breast cancer is a punishment for past sins. Similarly, if women describe interactions which fit the legal definition of rape as a problem of miscommunication (as Koss 1988 indicates they do), should we really take this as evidence that it was indeed a problem of communication? Theoretically, discursive psychology invites researchers to attend to the local interactional functions served by accounting for events and experiences in particular ways, specifically to examine how such accounts serve to legitimise or de-legitimise behaviour, including rape. Attending to the functions that these rape-supportive 'explanations' provide for young women themselves may help to explain their 'popularity' and account for women's resistance to rape-prevention campaigns designed to provide alternative explanations. In so doing, this approach avoids assuming that women are cultural dupes passively enacting cognitive scripts or mindlessly adopting the dominant 'miscommunication' model. Instead, it allows an exploration of why women might value such apparently women-blaming explanations and how, paradoxically, they may experience them as empowering even as theorists perceive them to be profoundly disempowering to women as a whole.

A discursive approach may also help to explain women's resistance to some of the acquaintance rape prevention education programmes which have been developed, and perhaps open new avenues for rape prevention research. Some educators have proposed that, insofar as acquaintance rape and other forms of unwanted sexual activity depend upon the fact that sexual activities are scripted in such a way that refusing sex is difficult for women, the problem can be solved by interrupting or rewriting these scripts. For example, the highly publicised sexual offences policy introduced by Antioch College in the USA aimed to redefine the normalised version of sexual activity as a seamless 'natural progression' from kissing to petting to genital contact to intercourse, requiring instead that sexual partners obtain explicit verbal consent for each and every sexual act.[5] Although some Antioch students were enthusiastic about the new policy, there was also fierce resistance from both men's and women's groups. Discursive psychology's focus on the social function of talk as a basis for accountability and identity management enables us to explore the investments women might have in talking about sexual interaction in the conventionally 'scripted' way. While the young women in our focus groups constructed themselves as knowledgeable and competent sexual actors, familiar with the ways in which sexual interactions normatively progress and canny about male attempts at persuasion and coercion, the Antioch policy has been seen as infantilising women (Roiphe 1993). It is not too difficult to see which version they might tend to prefer.

In the UK, legislative reform (see the Sexual Offences Act 2003) similarly attempts to shift the onus away from women having to prove non-consent by saying 'no' towards establishing the responsibility of men to obtain a clear 'yes'. The Act aims to give a clear definition of consent and outlines new responsibilities surrounding consent such that 'it is up to everyone to ensure that their partner agrees to sexual activity' (Home Office 2004: 3). The Act also attempts to set down circumstances where the courts will start from the presumption that the victim did not consent – such as when someone is drugged, unconscious or asleep. The accompanying information campaign featured the slogan 'Have sex with someone who hasn't said yes to it, and the next place you enter could be prison [...] If you don't get a yes don't have sex' (Home Office 2004). Though this may be a positive move in shifting responsibility away from women having to prove the absence of consent, it is still too early to say whether this has been effective in making changes in public attitudes or within the criminal justice system. Previously if defendants who wanted to claim that the activity was consensual needed only to demonstrate that they believed (however unreasonable this belief was) that their partner had consented, now 'if a defendant in court wants to claim they believed the other person was consenting, they will have to show they have reasonable grounds for that belief' (Home Office 2004: 2). However, given the lack of specificity with which 'reasonableness' is defined within the law, some have argued that this may simply result in the proliferation of a new set of legal tests and unpredictable legal outcomes (Finch and Munro 2006). While the Act may go some way towards changing cultural understandings of sex to centre on obtaining consent (the success of which remain to be seen), the focus on establishing a 'yes' reinforces the idea of sexual assault as a problem of communication.

Rape prevention educational programmes which attempt to improve women's communication skills or to tackle the social and cultural ideologies or rape myths which support a culture of sexual violence operate on the assumption that changing attitudes will also lead to a change in behaviour. Unfortunately, such studies rarely show long-term success in changing attitudes (Lonsway 1996; Schewe 2002) and a 'rebound effect' has been noted in some studies where attitudes actually become more entrenched following intervention (see Carmody and Carrington 2000 for an overview). Cowling (2004) is critical of rape avoidance strategies that focus on an idealised form of communicative sexuality, and argues that sex education aimed at avoiding rape should take account of the student's existing knowledge and experiences and consider the process of consent. O'Byrne et al. (2008) have suggested that drawing attention to shared commonsensical knowledge about how sexual refusals are normatively done and how this knowledge is discounted in the discourse of mis-communication may be a powerful classroom strategy for exploring how sexual consent and refusal is actually negotiated and prevent this rebound effect. A sexual education programme for culturally diverse inner-city youth based on these ideas is currently being piloted in London (Keeling et al. 2008). Perhaps only by treating young women as culturally aware social actors and recognising the advantages which young women gain from speaking in the ways that they do, and by making them aware of how this sustains the very situation with which they are dissatisfied, can we create a climate in which other initiatives will be welcomed.

Notes

1 This chapter deals exclusively with sexual communication within heterosexual couples. Researchers exploring sexual interactions between homosexual couples have also drawn on the notion of scripts and miscommunication – see, for example, Beres *et al.* (2004), Klinkenberg and Rose (1994) and Mutchler (2000).

2 This chapter uses the term acquaintance rape to describe instances of rape by a partner, date or acquaintance. The term 'date rape' is commonly used in the predominantly US-based literature in this area. However, the term 'date rape' is not without its difficulties, particularly when used in a UK context which does not have the same kind of 'dating' culture as the US. Date rape is sometimes described as a subset of acquaintance rape where the victim and perpetrator are in a romantic relationship together, while 'acquaintance rape' is used to refer to situations where victim and perpetrator are known to each other. Both are contrasted with 'stranger rape' in which both victim and perpetrator are not known to each other prior to the rape.

3 Walker argues that consent to unwanted sex is a 'grey area' in the spectrum of sexual violence in which individuals may consent to sexual activity that they do not really want. Although this activity may not be defined as rape in the legal sense, it may have negative effects on women's emotional and psychological well-being. Recently, Peterson and Muehlenhard (2007) argued that conceptualising sexual activity dichotomously as either wanted and consensual or unwanted and non-consensual risks conflating wanting and consenting. They reiterate that rape is about the absence of consent, not the absence of desire – this, they argue, may be liberating to many rape victims.

4 Unacknowledged rape victims is the term often used to describe women who report experiences which would meet the legal definition of rape but who do not themselves label their experience as rape. In contrast, acknowledged rape victims report experiences which meet the legal definition of rape and also label their experiences *as* rape.

5 Unlike the UK, in the USA the federal government insists that college campuses which receive federal funds have rape prevention programmes, therefore much of the research evidence relates to US-based programmes. However, US sexual culture is different from that in the UK, particularly among the young where there is no comparable 'dating' culture or fraternity culture in the UK.

References

Abbey, A. (1991) 'Misperceptions as an antecedent of acquaintance rape: a consequence of ambiguity in communication between women and men', in A. Parrot and L. Bechhofer (eds) *Acquaintance Rape: The Hidden Crime*. New York: John Wiley & Sons, pp. 96–111.

Abbey, A., Zawacki, T., Buck, P. O., Clinton, A. M. and McAuslan, P. (2004) 'Sexual assault and alcohol consumption: what do we know about their relationship and what types of research are still needed?', *Aggression and Violent Behavior*, 9 (3): 271–303.

Anderson, I. (1999) 'Characterological and behavioural blame in conversations about male and female rape', *Journal of Language and Social Psychology*, 18: 377–94.

Atkinson, J. M and Drew, P. (1979) *Order in Court: The Organization of Verbal Interaction in Judicial Settings*. London: Social Sciences Research Council.

Beres, M. A., Herold, E. and Maitland, S. B. (2004) 'Sexual consent behaviours in same-sex relationships', *Archives of Sexual Behaviour*, 33 (5): 475–86.

Byers, E. S. (1996) 'How well does the traditional sexual script explain sexual coercion? Review of a program of research', in E. S. Byers and L. F. O'Sullivan (eds), *Sexual Coercion in Dating Relationships*. New York: Howarth Press.

Carmody, M. and Carrington, K. (2000) 'Preventing sexual violence?', *Australian and New Zealand Journal of Criminology*, 33 (3): 341–61.

Coates, L. and Wade, A. (2004) 'Telling it like it isn't: obscuring perpetrator responsibility for violent crime', *Discourse and Society*, 15: 499–526.

Corcoran, C. B. (1992) 'From victim control to social change: a feminist perspective on campus rape prevention programs', in J. C. Chrisler and D. Howard (eds), *New Directions in Feminist Psychology: Practice, Theory and Research*. New York: Springer, pp. 130–40.

Cowling, M. (2004) 'Rape, communicative sexuality and sex education', in M. Cowling and P. Reynolds (eds), *Making Sense of Consent*. Aldershot: Ashgate, pp. 17–28.

Crawford, M. (1995) *Talking Difference: On Gender and Language*. London: Sage.

Doherty, K. and Anderson, I. (1998) 'Talking about rape', *The Psychologist*, 11 (12): 583–6.

Dworkin, S. L. and O'Sullivan, L. (2005) 'Actual versus desired initiation patterns among a sample of college men: tapping disjunctures within traditional male sexual scripts', *Journal of Sex Research*, 42 (2): 150–8.

Edgar, T. and Fitzpatrick, M. A. (1993) 'Expectations for sexual interaction: a cognitive test of the sequencing of sexual communication behaviors', *Health Communication*, 5: 239–61.

Edwards, D. (1994) 'Script formulations: a study of event descriptions in conversation', *Journal of Language and Social Psychology*, 13: 211–47.

Edwards, D. (1995) 'Two to tango: script formulations, dispositions, and rhetorical symmetry in relationship troubles talk', *Research on Language and Social Interaction*, 28: 319–50.

Edwards, D. (1997) *Discourse and Cognition*. London: Sage.

Ehrlich, S. (1998) 'The discursive reconstruction of sexual consent', *Discourse and Society*, 9 (2): 149–71.

Finch, E. and Munro, V. E. (2006) 'Breaking boundaries? Sexual consent in the jury room', *Legal Studies*, 26: 303–20.

Frith, H. and Kitzinger, C. (1997) 'Talk about sexual miscommunication', *Women's Studies International Forum*, 20: 517–28.

Frith, H. and Kitzinger, C. (1998) '"Emotion work" as a participant resource: a feminist analysis of young women's talk-in-interaction', *Sociology*, 32: 299–320.

Frith, H. and Kitzinger, C. (2001) 'Reformulating sexual script theory: developing a discursive psychology of sexual negotiation', *Theory and Psychology*, 11 (2): 209–32.

Gagnon, J. H. and Simon, W. (1973) *Sexual Conduct: The Social Sources of Human Sexuality*. Chicago: Aldine.

Gagnon, J. H. and Simon, W. (1987) 'The scripting of oral–genital sexual conduct', *Archives of Sexual Behavior*, 16: 1–25.

Gavey, N. (2005) *Just Sex? The Cultural Scaffolding of Rape*. London: Routledge.

Geer, J. H. and Broussard, D. B. (1990) 'Scaling heterosexual behavior and arousal: consistency and sex differences', *Journal of Personality and Social Psychology*, 58: 664–71.

Goodchilds, J. G., Zellman, G. L., Johnson, P. B. and Giarrusso, R. (1988) 'Adolescents and their perceptions of sexual interactions', in A. W. Burgess (ed.), *Rape and Sexual Assault*. New York: Garland, pp. 245–70.

Home Office (2004) *Adults: Safer from Sexual Crime: The Sexual Offences Act 2003*. London: Home Office Communications Directorate.

Howard, M. (1985) 'How the family physician can help young teenagers postpone sexual involvement', *Medical Aspects of Human Sexuality*, 19: 76–87.

Jackson, S. (1995) 'The social context of rape: sexual scripts and motivation', in P. Searles and R. J. Berger (eds), *Rape and Society: Readings on Sexual Assault*. Boulder, CO: Westview Press, pp. 16–27; originally published in *Women's Studies International Quarterly*, 1978, 1: 27–38.

Jackson, S. M. and Cram, F. (2003) 'Disrupting the sexual double standard: young women's talk about heterosexuality', *British Journal of Social Psychology*, 42: 113–27.

Kahn, A. S. and Mathie, V. (2000) 'Understanding the unacknowledged rape victim', in C. B. Travis and J. W. White (eds), *Sexuality, Society, and Feminism*. Washington, DC: American Psychological Association, pp. 370–403.

Kahn, A. S., Mathie, V. and Torgler, C. (1994) 'Rape scripts and rape acknowledgement', *Psychology of Women Quarterly*, 18: 53–66.

Keeling, S., Rapley, M. and Hansen, S. (2008) *What Do Young People Know About Rape?* Paper presented at the Annual Conference of the Society for Reproductive and Infant Psychology, London, September.

Kidder, L. H., Boell, J. L. and Moyer, M. M. (1983) 'Rights consciousness and victimization prevention: personal defence and assertiveness training', *Journal of Social Issues*, 39: 155–70.

Kitzinger, C. and Frith, H. (1999) 'Just say no? The use of conversation analysis in developing a feminist perspective on sexual refusal', *Discourse and Society*, 10: 293–316.

Kitzinger, C. and Wilkinson, S. (1997) 'Validating women's experience? Dilemmas in feminist research', *Feminism and Psychology*, 7 (4): 566–74.

Klinkenberg, D. and Rose, S. (1994) 'Dating scripts of gay men and lesbians', *Journal of Homosexuality*, 26 (4): 23–35.

Koss, M. (1988) 'Hidden rape: sexual aggression and victimization in a national sample of students in higher education', in A. W. Burgess (ed.), *Rape and Sexual Assault*. New York: Garland, pp. 3–25.

Krahé, B., Bieneck, S. and Scheinberger-Olwig, R. (2007a) 'Adolescents' sexual scripts: schematic representations of consensual and non-consensual heterosexual interactions', *Journal of Sex Research*, 44 (4): 316–27.

Krahé, B., Bieneck, S. and Scheinberger-Olwig, R. (2007b) 'The role of sexual scripts in sexual aggression and victimisation', *Archives of Sexual Behavior*, 36 (5): 687–701.

Kurth, S. B., Spiller, B. B. and Travis, C. B. (2000) 'Consent, power and sexual scripts: deconstructing sexual harassment', in C. B. Travis and J. W. White (eds), *Sexuality, Society, and Feminism*. Washington, DC: American Psychological Association, pp. 323–54.

LaPlante, N. M., McCormick, N. and Brannigan, G. G. (1980) 'Living the sexual script: college students' views of influence in sexual encounters', *Journal of Sex Research*, 16: 338–55.

Laws, J. L. and Schwartz, P. (1977) *Sexual Scripts: The Social Construction of Female Sexuality*. Washington, DC: University Press of America.

Lea, S. and Auburn, T. (2001) 'The social construction of rape in the talk of a convicted rapist', *Feminism and Psychology*, 11 (1): 11–33.

Littleton, H. L. and Axsom, D. (2003) 'Rape and seduction scripts of university students: implications for rape attributions and unacknowledged rape', *Sex Roles*, 49 (9/10): 465–75.

Lonsway, K. A. (1996) 'Preventing acquaintance rape through education: what do we know?', *Psychology of Women Quarterly*, 20: 229–65.

Milhausen, R. R. and Herold, E. S. (1999) 'Does the sexual double standard still exist? perceptions of university women', *Journal of Sex Research*, 36 (4): 361–8.

Morr, M. C. and Mongeau, P. A. (2004) 'First-date expectations: the impact of sex of initiator, alcohol consumption, and relationship type', *Communication Research*, 31 (1): 3–35.

Muehlenhard, C. L. (1988a) '"Nice women" don't say yes and "real men" don't say no: how miscommunication and the double standard can cause sexual problems', *Women and Therapy*, 7: 95–108.

Muehlenhard, C. L. (1988b) 'Misinterpreted dating behaviours and the risk of date rape', *Psychology of Women Quarterly*, 6: 20–37.

Muehlenhard, C. L. and Hollabaugh, L. C. (1988) 'Do women sometimes say no when they mean yes? The prevalence and correlates of women's token resistance to sex', *Journal of Personality and Social Psychology*, 54: 872–9.

Muehlenhard, C. L. and McCoy, M. L. (1991) 'Double standard/double bind: the sexual double standard and women's communication about sex', *Psychology of Women Quarterly*, 15: 447–61.

Muehlenhard, C. L., Friedman, D. E. and Thomas, C. M. (1985) 'Is date rape justifiable? The effects of dating activity, who initiated, who paid, and men's attitudes toward women', *Psychology of Women Quarterly*, 9: 297–309.

Murnen, S. K., Perot, A. and Byrne, D. (1989) 'Coping with unwanted sexual activity: normative responses, situational determinants, and individual differences', *Journal of Sex Research*, 26: 85–106.

Mutchler, M. G. (2000) 'Young gay men's stories in the States: scripts, sex and safety in the time of AIDS', *Sexualities*, 3 (1): 31–54.

O'Byrne, R., Hansen, S. and Rapley, M. (2008) '"If a girl doesn't say 'no' …": young men, rape and claims of "insufficient knowledge"', *Journal of Community and Applied Social Psychology*, 18 (3): 168–93.

O'Byrne, R., Rapley, M. and Hansen, S. (2006) '"You couldn't say 'no', could you?": young men's understandings of sexual refusal', *Feminism and Psychology*, 16: 133–54.

Peterson, Z. and Muehlenhard, C. L. (2007) 'Conceptualizing the "wantedness" of women's consensual and non-consensual sexual experiences: implications for how women label their experiences with rape', *Journal of Sex Research*, 44 (1): 72–88.

Popovich, P. M., Jolton, J. A., Mastrangelo, P. M., Everton, W. J., Somers, J. M. and Gehlaug, D. N. (1995) 'Sexual harassment scripts: a means to understanding a phenomenon', *Sex Roles*, 32: 315–25.

Quinn, K., Sanchez-Hucles, J., Coates, G. and Gillen, B. (1991) 'Men's compliance with a woman's resistance to unwanted sexual advances', *Journal of Offender Rehabilitation*, 17: 13–31.

Roiphe, K. (1993) *The Morning After: Sex, Fear and Feminism*. London: Hamish Hamilton.

Rose, S. and Frieze, I. (1993) 'Young singles' contemporary dating scripts', *Sex Roles*, 24: 499–509.

Ryan, K. M. (2004) 'Further evidence for a cognitive component of rape', *Aggression and Violent Behaviour*, 9: 579–604.

Schank, R. C. and Abelson, R. P. (1977) *Scripts, Plans, Goals, and Understanding*. Hillsdale, NJ: Erlbaum.

Schewe, P. A. (2002) *Preventing Violence in Relationships: Interventions Across the Lifespan*. Washington DC: American Psychological Association.

Walker, S. J. (1997) 'When "no" becomes "yes": why girls and women consent to sex', *Applied and Preventive Psychology*, 6: 157–66.

Warzak, W. J. and Page, T. J. (1990) 'Teaching refusal skills to sexually active adolescents', *Journal of Behavioral Therapy and Experimental Psychiatry*, 21: 133–9.

Whatley, M. A. (1996) 'Victim characteristics influencing attributions of responsibility to rape victims: a meta-analysis', *Aggression and Violent Behavior*, 1 (2): 81–95.

Wooffitt, R. C. (1992) *Telling Tales of the Unexpected: The Organization of Factual Discourse*. Hemel Hempstead: Harvester Wheatsheaf.

Part 2

Victim Vulnerabilities

Chapter 6

Alcohol and drugs in rape and sexual assault

Jo Lovett and Miranda A. H. Horvath

Introduction

What do we know?

The links between alcohol and sexual assault are now well established and have been documented in both UK and international research (Abbey *et al.* 2001; Horvath and Brown 2006, 2007; Kelly *et al.* 2005; Ullman *et al.* 1999; Walby and Allen 2004). Although research has identified that administration of alcohol and drugs as means of obtaining illicit sex is not a new phenomenon, it has been argued that the techniques for using alcohol and drugs to facilitate rape have changed and this issue is therefore worthy of renewed interest (Foote *et al.* 2004). This chapter brings together and compares findings from two large independent studies which collected data on the involvement of alcohol and drugs in cases of rape and sexual assault reported to the police and/or sexual assault referral centres. We seek to explore the complexities of alcohol-related sexual assault by outlining a common methodological approach which generates findings that take greater account of the role of the perpetrator, the broader assault context (e.g. the location and relationship between the parties) and other situational characteristics (e.g. the type of intoxicants consumed and the nature of consumption).

The aims of our chapter are to:

- promote a broader and more nuanced understanding of the realities of alcohol-related rape, which, we argue, are commonly oversimplified in both academic and popular representations of this crime;

- advance the view, based on research evidence, that alcohol is the drug most commonly associated with rape; and

- move beyond the tendency to focus solely on the role and characteristics of victims of alcohol-related sexual assault and incorporate perpetrator characteristics.

Our purpose is to dispel some persistent myths about alcohol and drugs in rape in relation to types of substances consumed and the nature of consumption, context, victims and perpetrators. We will present findings from two datasets side by side which although is not commonly done will allow for direct comparison and the generation of new hypotheses.

Myths about alcohol and drugs in rape

Several reviews and meta-analyses (Abbey *et al.* 2004; Finney 2004; Ullman 2003) reveal that few studies address the involvement of both alcohol and drugs[1] in sexual assault, either concurrently or comparatively, and almost all draw on North American data (exceptions include Scott-Hamm and Burton 2005). Despite strong associations, a causal relationship between alcohol and sexual assault has not been demonstrated (Abbey *et al.* 2004). Existing findings suggest that, in contrast with rape and sexual assault generally, alcohol is more commonly involved when parties do not know each other well and in the context of bars and parties (Ullman 2003).

While the term 'drug rape' has become common parlance, particularly in the media, and has prompted high-profile anti-spiking campaigns and products, it appears that alcohol is most likely to be a perpetrator's substance of choice. Research conducted by toxicologists on the incidence of alcohol and drugs in alleged drug-assisted rape cases in the USA, Canada and the UK has consistently found that sedative drugs that could not be attributed to voluntary use by the complainant were detected in only very few cases (Hindmarch and Brinkmann 1999; Seifert 1999; Slaughter 2000). In the recent Scott-Ham and Burton (2005) research in the UK, which analysed samples of (n = 1,014) suspected cases of drug-assisted rape, alcohol was found to be the most common substance, being detected in 46 per cent of cases. Illicit drugs were detected in 34 per cent of cases, but in only 2 per cent was a sedative or disinhibiting drug detected which could be deemed the result of deliberate drugging by the offender (commonly referred to as 'spiking'). This low level of 'spiking' in rape cases confirms findings from the USA and Canada that alcohol is the most common substance associated with sexual assault and thus challenges the media representation of this offence (Hindmarch *et al.* 2001; Seifert 1999; Slaughter 2000). Moreover, a recent study in America found that only 12.6 per cent of 406 college students surveyed were aware that alcohol is the most common substance associated with sexual assault (Crawford *et al.* 2008).

Has there been a rise in binge drinking?

We contest the claim made frequently in the media – that 'binge drinking' by young women has increased notably (see Measham and Brain 2005 for an account of the rise and fall and rise again of political, press and public concerns about excessive drinking in the UK). Figures from the 2007 General Household Survey reveal that while alcohol is a common feature in the lives of British adults, gender differences persist. Over half of women (57 per cent) and three-quarters of men (72 per cent) surveyed had drunk alcohol at least once in the previous week, but men were more likely to have drunk frequently (22 per cent of men compared with 12 per cent of women drank on at least five days) and a higher proportion of men reported heavy drinking than women (24 per cent of men compared with 15 per cent of women). Further, men were much more likely to have drunk alcohol every day during the previous week than women (13 per cent vs. 7 per cent) (Office for National Statistics 2008). Contrary to popular perception, drinking levels among adults and young people have remained relatively stable over the past five years (Department of Health 2008; Office for National Statistics 2008), and men who have been drinking are far more likely to be both victims and perpetrators of physical assault and mugging (Budd 2003). While these figures suggest that alcohol consumption presents a relatively constant risk factor for negative experiences in both men and women, the predominant focus on women appears unwarranted, since their consumption is lower and less frequent than men's on all measures.

Alcohol and behaviour: influences and impacts

Alcohol is known to have a variety of effects on individuals. It impairs cognitive and motor skills and people's ability to engage in higher-order cognitive processes such as abstraction and problem-solving (Hindmarch *et al.* 1991; Peterson *et al.* 1990). Based on limited research conducted in the USA, it has been suggested that alcohol is also thought, especially in men, to enhance sexual behaviour and aggressiveness (Abbey *et al.* 1999), although it should be noted that many drinking occasions do not result in violence (Zimmerman *et al.* 2007). It has also been found that when intoxicated, people tend to focus on the most salient cues in a situation and ignore more peripheral information (Steele and Josephs 1990; Taylor and Leonard 1983). As a result, it is possible that women may pay less attention to cues which would normally alert them to a dangerous situation, while men may focus on their immediate feelings of sexual arousal and entitlement rather than a woman's discomfort or the potential for later punishment (Abbey *et al.* 2001; Nurius and Norris 1996; Parks and Miller 1997).

The inhibiting response to unpleasant stimuli caused by alcohol in intoxicated women may lead them to give only a mild response to an aggressive act. The intoxication may reduce the likelihood of resistance and diminish the ability to try and alter the situation (Strizke *et al.* 1995; Testa and Parks 1996). This noted, it is important to acknowledge that while a woman's ability to spot the warning signs or indeed resist an assault may be impaired when she is intoxicated, this does not imply that if women were to remain sober they would necessarily avoid the risk of sexual assault. The responsibility for the act remains with the perpetrator (Testa and Parks 1996). Indeed, it has been argued that consumption of alcohol may be employed as a justification for committing violent behaviour, especially if it is seen as decreasing the chance of facing penalties (Markowitz 2005). All of these factors are likely to be of relevance in the context of sexual assaults.

Stereotypes, rape myth acceptance and the responses of the public and criminal justice system

Studies suggest that stereotypical notions about female sexuality, including those in relation to drinking, are factors not only in the behaviour of perpetrators but also in the responses of criminal justice agencies and the general public to sexual offences (Cameron and Strizke 2003; Finch and Munro 2005; Lees 2002). This was demonstrated in an opinion poll in which around one-third of respondents agreed that women who act flirtatiously or are drunk should be held partly or fully responsible if they were sexually assaulted (ICM 2005). The public view has also been reflected in the courts. For example, in *R* v. *Dougal* (2005, Swansea Crown Court) an alleged rapist was cleared despite the fact that the woman could not remember if she had consented to sex because of the amount of alcohol she had consumed. The judge, Mr Justice Roderick Evans, directed the jury to reach a not guilty verdict after the prosecution claimed it was unable to prove that the complainant had not given consent because of her level of intoxication. The prosecuting counsel's statement included the remark that 'drunken consent is still consent' (*The Times* 2005). The emphasis throughout the case and the subsequent media reportage focused on the fact that the victim was heavily intoxicated and could not remember giving consent rather than on whether the suspect's belief in consent was reasonable and whether he had taken the appropriate steps to ensure the victim had consented (Gibb *et al.* 2005), as specified by the law in England and Wales.[2] Whether the victim's degree of intoxication and subsequent lack of consciousness at various points during the course of events could be seen to have impinged on her ability to give true or meaningful consent was also not seriously addressed.

We postulate that these perceived norms about women and drinking, coupled with limited public and criminal justice system understanding about the potential effects of alcohol can lead to unrealistic expectations about the steps women should take to protect themselves from rape and, in turn, how responsible they are for male behaviour (as highlighted by the ICM poll). Men's illegal and coercive behaviour often seems, conversely, to be perceived as understandable and excusable. In a study involving focus groups and trial simulations with mock jurors, men accused of rape while drunk tended to be seen as less blameworthy, while the victims' responsibility remained paramount even in scenarios where men had deliberately taken advantage of the victim's intoxication or deliberately targeted them through spiking (Finch and Munro 2005).

Concepts and terminology

Debate continues in both the academic literature and popular press between the terms 'date rape' and 'drug-assisted (or facilitated) rape'. While a date rape can also be a drug-assisted rape and vice versa, the two are often mistakenly conflated and used interchangeably. Date rape was originally defined by Koss and Cook (1993) as 'a specific type of acquaintance rape that involves a victim and a perpetrator who have some level of romantic relationship between them' (p. 105). Indeed, we would propose that the term should only be used to refer to rapes that occur between people at the initial stages of forging a romantic or sexual relationship. It is not a prerequisite of a date rape that the victim and/or perpetrator has consumed alcohol/drugs and, equally, for a drug-assisted rape to occur the victim and perpetrator do not have to be on a date. Further misunderstanding arises from the conflation of date and intimate/acquaintance rape, which means that 'date rape' is often used to refer to assaults that do not occur on dates. In short 'date rape' is a frequently misused and, arguably, a misleading term (Temkin 2002) which can be employed in ways that trivialise and downplay the impacts of rapes occurring in these circumstances.

Methods

Much research to date on the relationship between alcohol/drugs and sexual assault has concentrated on the correlation of certain victim attributes with the presence or absence of one or other substance, and has been restricted to examining consumption by the victim (e.g. Operation Matisse 2006 and Scott-Hamm and Burton 2005).[3] Although this provides useful information about the prevalence of sexual assaults where alcohol/drugs are involved and who is more likely to be victimised in this specific type of assault, it suggests that the determining factors in why such assaults occur are related primarily to the victim and/or the alcohol. In such an analysis, the perpetrator – the actual agent of the assault – remains a hidden and unexplored quantity. This can feed into a culture of victim blame, and lead to personal safety and prevention approaches that prioritise avoidance strategies aimed at women as potential victims. There is also a failure to investigate whether certain contexts are conducive to the targeting of intoxicated victims by men or are seen as situations in which consent to sex will be forthcoming.

To move beyond the prevailing 'victim focus' in the literature on alcohol and sexual assault we also look in this chapter at perpetrator characteristics, though we note the inherent difficulties in obtaining as detailed information on perpetrators as on victims. For example, a proportion of rape suspects are never caught or apprehended, so information on their alcohol/drug consumption and socio-demographic status is limited to what the victim has been able to tell police and may be vague or inaccurate. In some of these cases, the perpetrator will have been a stranger so many of these details will not be known. We also address the overall sexual assault context, including the assault location and the relationship between perpetrator and victim in order to understand the dynamics of alcohol-related sexual assault holistically, and seek to locate both the victim and perpetrator(s) within it.

The two studies reported on here originated from separate research projects and were conducted independently. However, since they recorded whether alcohol/drugs had been consumed by both the victim and the perpetrator, they offered the potential to explore the involvement of alcohol and drugs in relation to two large samples of rape and sexual assault cases. If similar results were found to arise in not one but two studies, this would also strengthen the validity of findings. Because of the differing original aims and methodologies employed, for the analysis reported in this chapter a decision was made to use the two datasets comparatively rather than in combination so that any differences clearly deriving from these would remain apparent. Although both studies had coded data for the involvement of alcohol and drugs, a more detailed shared methodology, including new variables, was developed jointly across the two projects for this specific aspect. The original methods used to collect each dataset will be described separately first and then the shared methodology and process used to develop this will be outlined before the findings are presented.

The Lovett project[4]

The first project, conducted under the Crime Reduction Programme Violence Against Women Initiative (CRP VAWI), involved victims reporting rape or sexual assault to sexual assault referral centres (SARCs) and police in six areas in England and Wales, and resulted in a dataset of 3,527 cases. The original aim was to assess the role of SARCs and the issue of attrition (see Kelly *et al.* 2005; Lovett *et al.* 2004; Regan *et al.* 2004). The sample included female and male victims, single and multiple perpetrator assaults, reported and unreported cases and adult victims (two of the six sites saw victims under the age of 16 as well).[5] Information was gathered on the victim, the perpetrator, the assault, the forensic examination, the take-up of support services and the legal proceedings and outcomes. Data were gathered through a combination of agency records and police pro formas, where officers recorded a series of relevant details relating to the legal case. No direct access to police records was agreed, so the quality and extent of the information provided both within and between research sites is variable.

The Horvath project

The second project involved rape cases reported to two police forces in the South of England. One force was medium-sized and covered a mix of urban and rural areas; the other was a large urban force. The project had three broad aims: firstly, to clarify the definition of drug-assisted rape; secondly, to extend and refine the phenomenology of drug-assisted rape; and finally, to propose and explore some explanatory theoretical concepts (Horvath and Brown 2005, 2006, 2007; Horvath 2006). This project initially focused on collecting a comparable sample from the medium-sized police force over a five-year period of sexual assaults where the victim had and had not consumed alcohol and/or drugs before being assaulted. In the second phase of the project, data was collected from a large police force for cases where the victim had consumed alcohol and/or drugs. The combination of data from the two forces resulted in a dataset of 483 cases. The parameters of this project limited data collection (apart from a very small number of exceptions) to cases involving a single male perpetrator and single female victim. The limitation was a result of time constraints but is also justified from the work of Greenfield (1997), who identified that more than 91 per cent of rape victims are female and nearly 99 per cent of perpetrators are male.

Retrospective application of a shared methodology to the two datasets

In view of convergence between the two studies in terms of a higher than anticipated level of alcohol and a lower than anticipated level of drugs we decided to collaborate on and pilot a shared methodology which was to be applied retrospectively to each dataset. The datasets were kept separate partly because of the differences in the initial aims and methodologies used but also to allow us to identify the similarities that nonetheless emerged. The shared methodology involved subjecting primarily qualitative data held within the existing datasets to new coding and analysis, with a specific focus on alcohol/ drugs and context. New fields were added on: whether alcohol/ drug consumption was consensual or non-consensual; if consensual, whether consumption was chosen by the victim independently or in conjunction with the perpetrator; drug type; how intoxicated the victim was at the time of the assault; and whether the victim was asleep. In relation to the sexual assault context two further fields were also developed. Firstly, detailed analysis was undertaken of the context of the initial approach or contact between the victim and perpetrator. This was undertaken for all cases, whether involving alcohol/drugs or not, and revealed a wide variety of situations, from meeting in a bar or club to being accosted in a public place to more closed settings such as schools or residential homes. Secondly, particular contexts were grouped under six analytic 'arenas' – broader areas corresponding to routine spheres of daily life (personal, social, public space, residential, institutional and contacts with authority). A key aim of analysis here was to ascertain whether alcohol was more commonly a feature of certain sexual assault contexts compared to others.

The lack of a common project design from the outset presents issues in that some data are not available across both projects or are more limited in one compared to the other. This is due to differences in the original research aims and questions. However, there are sufficient comparable data to present a robust array of findings.

Findings

Prevalence of alcohol and drugs

Across both datasets alcohol was the most frequently consumed substance for both victims and perpetrators, while rates of drug consumption and combined alcohol and drug consumption were similarly low (see Table 6.1). The differences between the datasets in the numbers of victims consuming either just alcohol or neither substance can be explained because a significant proportion of the Horvath data were collected selecting only cases where victims had consumed alcohol and/or drugs.

Both studies also found that, while perpetrators had consumed alcohol/drugs in a substantial number of cases, these rates were consistently lower than among victims, with the difference especially marked in the Horvath sample in relation to alcohol.

In order to explore the nature of victims' consumption of alcohol/ drugs a series of drinking modes were developed. These were designed to test how common scenarios involving victims' consensual consumption were compared with those involving surreptitious or overt encouragement of intoxication by perpetrators (coded as 'pressured' and 'non-consensual' in Table 6.2 and non-consensual and mixed in Table 6.3). Consensual consumption was graded according to whether it was purely initiated by the victim, by both the victim and the perpetrator or purely the perpetrator. Tables 6.2 and 6.3 show the mode of alcohol and drug consumption in the cases where either or both substances were consumed by the victim.

Table 6.1 Prevalence of alcohol/drug-related rape and sexual assault

| | Victim | | | | Perpetrator | | | |
| | Lovett | | Horvath | | Lovett | | Horvath | |
	N	%	N	%	N	%	N	%
Alcohol only	768	36.3	301	62.8	189	35.1	202	48
Drugs only	129	6.1	31	6.5	18	3.3	23	5.5
Both	262	12.4	59	12.3	49	9.1	31	7.4
Neither	956	45.2	88	18.4	282	52.4	165	39.2
Total	2,115	100	479	100	538	100	421	100

NB: Across both datasets there were a number of cases where victim and/or perpetrator consumption was unknown. This is particularly a problem in the Lovett data, where it was not possible to look directly at police records: In the Lovett dataset victim consumption of alcohol and/or drugs was unknown in 1,412 cases and for perpetrators in 2,989 cases. In the Horvath dataset victim consumption was unknown in 4 cases and perpetrator in 62 cases.

Table 6.2 Method and type of victim's alcohol consumption

| | Alcohol | |
	Lovett %	Horvath %
Consensual – victim only	90.3	48.6
Consensual – victim and perpetrator	8.5	39.4
Consensual – perpetrator only	0	8.9
Pressured	0.2	2.8
Non-consensual – victim drink spiked with alcohol	0	0
Unknown	1	0.3
Total	100 (n=1,030)	100 (n= 360)

Across both datasets almost all victims' alcohol and drug consumption was consensual, although there were some differences between the two in terms of who initiated the consensual consumption. Table 6.3 shows that victims who were made to take drugs, either by being forced to or as a result of having their drink spiked, represent

Table 6.3 Method and type of victim's drug consumption

	Drugs	
	Lovett %	Horvath %
Consensual – victim only	33.8	32.2
Consensual – victim and perpetrator	5.4	25.6
Consensual – perpetrator only	1.3	20
Non-consensual – victim drink spiked with drugs	28.4	4.4
Non-consensual – victim forced to take drugs	2.3	5.6
Mixed – drugs voluntarily and drink spiked with drugs	2.6	1.1
Unknown	26.3	4.4
Other	0	6.7
Total	100 (n=391)	100 (n=90)

less than one third of the cases. This is in direct contradiction to the media portrayal of a large number of victims having their drinks spiked with drugs like Rohypnol and then being sexually assaulted. The proportion of cases where the victim believed s/he had been spiked was considerably higher in the Lovett sample, although still lower than the 40 per cent rate of consensual consumption.

Where details were known, across both datasets the most frequently consumed drug was cannabis (Horvath n = 29, Lovett n = 40). In the Horvath dataset cocaine was the next most frequently consumed drug (n = 16) whereas in the Lovett dataset it was heroin/methadone (n = 23). The third most frequently consumed in both datasets were prescription drugs (Horvath n = 13, Lovett n = 20). These findings directly contradict the media portrayal of the dynamics and types of drugs involved in 'drug rape'.

Victim's state of intoxication when assaulted

Figure 6.1 shows the state of intoxication when assaulted across both datasets of those victims who had consumed alcohol, drugs or both. In view of the absence of consistent toxicological data on alcohol/drug consumption or other reliable objective measures, victims' level of intoxication is based on a combination of descriptions provided in accounts from victims, police and forensic examiners consulted

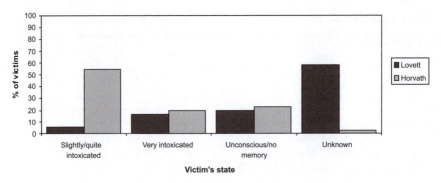

Figure 6.1   Victim's state when assaulted across both datasets

during the original data collection. Although these measures are by nature subjective, they represent the only means available to quantify the victim's state of intoxication when assaulted. This is important, as mere consumption of alcohol/drugs should not be assumed to equate to extreme, or even moderate, intoxication. Contrary to media representation, in fewer than one quarter of cases in both datasets was the victim unconscious or had no memory of being assaulted. In fact, the victim was very intoxicated in less than one fifth of cases across both the datasets. Although in the Lovett sample the lowest proportion of cases fell into the category of slightly/quite intoxicated, the high proportion where information was missing suggests that where the level and/or effects of substance consumption was minimal, no reference may have been made.

In just over one quarter (Lovett = 27.8 per cent, n = 322; Horvath = 27.2 per cent, n = 106) of cases in both of the datasets, victims who had consumed alcohol, drugs or a combination of the two were asleep at the time of the assault.

Comparative profile of cases involving alcohol/drugs and neither

In order to explore the interaction of alcohol with a range of variables such as age, gender and assault characteristics both samples were divided into cases where the victim had consumed just alcohol, just drugs, a combination of the two or neither substance. Table 6.4 summarises the socio-demographic profiles of the victims and the perpetrators across these four subsets and the two datasets.

The most common profile for victims consuming alcohol within both samples was females aged 16–20, although there was a fairly similar prevalence across all age groups, with the second most common age group in the Lovett sample being 31–40. It should be noted that, although lower than for female, not insignificant proportions of male victims also consumed alcohol. This suggests that alcohol-related rape is not a phenomenon affecting young women exclusively. Findings in relation to ethnicity were less clear, with white victims by far the most affected in the Lovett sample, compared with black victims in the Horvath sample and a high prevalence among all other ethnic groups. This may relate to local trends in the areas where the two study samples were drawn from.

The profile of perpetrators assaulting victims who had been drinking indicated a broad age range, with the highest prevalence found in men older than the majority age of affected victims – 21–50 in the Lovett sample and 16–40 in the Horvath sample.[6] Interestingly, in both samples the highest rates of rapes where victims had consumed alcohol were registered among Asian perpetrators, while those among white and black perpetrators were lower and of identical proportions. Recent acquaintances were by far the most common perpetrators of these rapes, including among multiple perpetrators in the Lovett sample. In very few instances were these recent acquaintances in the capacity of 'dates', being more commonly men with whom victims had come into contact in the hours immediately preceding the assault. This was followed by friends and acquaintances in the Lovett sample and strangers and friends in the Horvath sample. This indicates that a substantial proportion of assaults occur involving alcohol/drugs where both parties know each other relatively well and where there is a degree of trust between them. This departs further from the concepts of 'date rape' and binge-drinking women making themselves vulnerable to attacks by predatory strangers.

Pubs/clubs/discos, vehicles and other homes[7] were among the most common assault locations where victims had consumed alcohol. Although the high representation of friends and acquaintances points to slightly different dynamics in some cases, on the whole this profile suggests older men befriending victims they have little or no prior knowledge of in the context of commonly frequented social environments where alcohol is readily available and consumed.

No significant trends were highlighted among cases where the victim had consumed drugs and both drugs and alcohol, although findings were strikingly similar across both samples for the majority of categories, despite the wider variations between the two in relation to the 'alcohol' and 'neither' groups.

Table 6.5 shows the number of vulnerabilities victims had according to what substances they had consumed. Vulnerabilities

Table 6.4 Socio-demographic profiles of victims and perpetrators according to victim consumption

| | Victim consumption | | | | | | | | | |
| | Alcohol | | Drugs | | Both | | Neither | | Total[a] | |
	Lovett %	Horvath %	Lovett %	Horvath %	Lovett %	Horvath %	Lovett %	Horvath %	Lovett n	Horvath n
Victim sex										
Female	36.8	63	6.1	6.6	12.4	12	44.7	18.4	1,970	468
Male	29.7	54.5	5.5	0	12.4	27.3	52.4	18.2	145	11
Perpetrator sex										
Male	36.3	63	5.9	6.3	12.4	12.3	45.3	18.4	2,105	478
Female	20	0	60	100	0	0	20	0	5	1
Male and female (if multiple perps)	20	n/a	20	n/a	40	n/a	20	n/a	5	n/a
Victim age										
Under-16	36.7	20	3.3	40	5.8	40	54.2	0	240	5
16–20	39.3	68.3	6.3	4.9	15.5	7.7	39	19	575	142
21–30	34.7	64.7	8.2	5.9	15.7	15.3	41.4	14.1	648	170
31–40	37.4	55.2	4.3	7.6	10.6	12.4	47.7	24.8	398	105
41–50	32.1	62.5	6.1	10	9.1	12.5	52.7	15	165	40
51 and over	32.4	62.5	1.5	0	0	12.5	66.2	25	68	16
Unknown	23.8	0	19	0	0	0	57.1	100	21	1
Perpetrator age										
Under-16	25	75	0	0	0	0	75	25	40	4
16–20	30.9	68.8	5.3	4.2	10.5	10.4	53.3	16.7	152	48
21–30	38.9	66.7	4	5.4	9.9	10.7	47.2	17.3	324	168
31–40	34.9	68.4	5.3	7.9	8.5	12.5	51.2	11.2	281	152

41–50	34.4	54	5.6	7.9	8	11.1	52	27	125	63
31–50 (multiple perps)[b]	38.5	n/a	15.4	n/a	15.4	n/a	30.8	n/a	13	n/a
51 and over	24.1	30.3	2.4	3	10.8	24.2	62.7	42.4	83	33
Mixed ages (multiple perps)	35.3	n/a	0	n/a	11.8	n/a	52.9	n/a	17	n/a
Unknown	38.2	45.5	7.6	18.2	15.5	18.2	38.7	18.2	1,080	11
Victim ethnicity										
White	39.5	61.2	5.7	6	12.9	12.9	41.9	19.9	1,709	402
Black	13.7	76	6.8	12.	7.7	8	71.8	4	117	50
Asian	12.9	55.6	4.8	5.6	3.2	5.6	79	33.3	62	18
Other	3.8	100	7.7	0	0	0	88.5	0	26	4
Unknown	33.8	60	9	0	15.4	40	41.8	0	201	5
Perpetrator ethnicity										
White	38.8	61.2	5.1	3.3	12.7	12.1	43.4	23.5	670	307
Black	36.8	61.9	4.4	13.6	10.3	16.1	48.5	8.5	68	118
Asian	50	87	4.2	0	10.8	0	35	13	120	23
Other	37.3	80	9.8	13.3	5.9	6.7	47	0	51	15
Unknown	33.5	50	6.8	18.8	12.8	12.5	46.9	18.8	1,206	16
Assault location										
Victim's home	38.1	54.1	4.1	4.5	7.3	15.3	50	26.1	341	111
Perpetrator's home	38	68.1	7.7	8.7	18.2	15.2	36.1	8	379	138
Shared home	21.5	50	3.2	0	1.1	0	74.1	50	93	44
Other home[c]	44.9	75.6	6.3	11.1	22.2	11.1	26.6	2.2	158	45
Pub/club/disco	64.6	100	4.6	0	20	0	10.8	0	65	12
Public place	39.2	65.2	4.3	3	7	12.1	49.5	19.7	558	66
Vehicle	50.5	85.7	3.2	0	7.5	7.1	38.7	7.1	93	28

Table 6.4 continues overleaf

Table 6.4 continued

| | Victim consumption | | | | | | | | | |
| | Alcohol | | Drugs | | Both | | Neither | | Total[a] | |
	Lovett %	Horvath %	Lovett %	Horvath %	Lovett %	Horvath %	Lovett %	Horvath %	Lovett n	Horvath n
Hotel	55.6	23.1	3.7	7.7	29.6	23.1	11.1	46.2	27	13
Education/care/ medical facility	14.2	0	3.6	50	3.6	0	78.6	50	28	2
Abroad	6.1	0	12.1	0	21.2	0	60.6	0	33	0
Workplace	5.6	33.3	11.1	33.3	0	0	83.3	33.3	18	6
Other	31	40	13.8	40	3.4	0	51.7	20	29	5
Unknown	21.8	55.6	10.6	11.1	19.1	33.3	48.5	0	293	9
Number of perpetrators										
1	36.5	62.8	6	6.5	11.5	12.3	46.1	18.4	1,901	479
2 or more	35	n/a	7	n/a	20.6	n/a	37.4	n/a	214	n/a
Perpetrator–victim relationship (single perp)										
Current/ex-partner	27.1	47.4	4.6	5.3	4.6	4.2	63.6	43.2	280	95
Family member	20.6	43.8	3.1	0	3.1	12.5	73.2	43.8	97	16
Friend	36.9	63.4	7.0	3.4	15	18.6	41.2	14.5	187	145
Acquaintance	35.3	61.9	8.4	19	13.2	14.3	43.1	4.8	371	42
Professional	11.6	62.5	9.3	18.8	0	0	79.1	18.8	43	16
Recent acquaintance	54.5	78	4.1	4.6	19.4	14.7	21.9	2.8	242	109
Stranger	26.5	66.7	5.3	6.7	6.7	4.4	51.6	22.2	510	45
Unknown	43.3	54.5	7.6	18.2	25.7	18.2	23.4	9.1	171	11

Perpetrator–victim relationship (multi perps)[d]									
At least one known	27.8		11.1		16.7		44.4		18
At least one acquaintance	34.5		8.6		29.3		27.6		58
All recent acquaintance	40		6.7		33.3		20		15
All stranger	38.4		6.1		12.1		43.4		99
Unknown	25		4.2		29.2		4.17		24
Victim vulnerabilities									
Substance misuse	30.8	40	46.2	32	17.9	28	5.1	0	39	25
Insecure housing	29.5	0	11.6	0	8.4	100	50.5	0	95	1
Asylum seeker/refugee	100	80	0	0	0	20	0	0	22	5
Previous victimisation	20.3	56.3	4.7	6.3	7.8	0	67.2	37.5	64	16
Disability	30.2	34.8	4.8	17.4	7.1	8.7	57.9	39.1	126	23
Prostitution	5.4	0	40.5	0	13.5	0	40.5	0	37	0

a   All percentages equal 100.

b   The ages of multiple perpetrators were only coded as 31–50, not the two categories 31–40 and 41–50, hence another category has been created.

c   A sub-category of 'other home' is 'social gathering' – parties and collective events involving friends/other groups. This was coded separately in the Lovett but not the Horvath data, so the two categories have been combined here for reasons of comparability. When treated as a separate category, however, assaults occurring at social gatherings saw far higher rates of involvement of alcohol (63.4 per cent, n = 18), which is, in fact, the second highest among all assault locations in the Lovett dataset. The elevated presence of alcohol is not surprising here, although the small numbers in this group may affect the results.

d   The Horvath data does not include any multiple perpetrator cases; only Lovett data are presented.

Table 6.5 Number of victim vulnerabilities according to their consumption of alcohol/drugs

| | Victim consumption | | | | | | | | | |
| | Alcohol | | Drugs | | Both | | Neither | | Total[a] | |
	Lovett %	Horvath %	Lovett %	Horvath %	Lovett %	Horvath %	Lovett %	Horvath %	Lovett n	Horvath n
No vulnerabilities	38.3	65.5	5.3	5	13.1	12	43.3	17.5	1,788	417
One vulnerability	26.5	46.3	6.9	13	8	13	58.5	27.8	275	54
Multiple vulnerabilities	19.2	37.5	28.8	37.5	11.5	25	40.4	0	52	8

a All percentages equal 100.

are characteristics of the victim that may make them more likely to be targeted for sexual assault, such as mental health problems, previous victimisation and young age (under 16) (see Campbell *et al.* 2007; Cybulska 2007; Stanko *et al.* 2007). Across both datasets the majority of victims had none or one vulnerability. For those who had consumed alcohol, the rates of consumption decrease as the number of vulnerabilities increases whereas for drugs the opposite trend can be observed, with drugs consumed by around a third of those who had multiple vulnerabilities. At the same time, it is noteworthy that between one quarter and one half of those with one disability and between one fifth and one third of those with multiple disabilities consumed alcohol before being assaulted, as it suggests that these original vulnerabilities may be compounded by its consumption.

As can be seen in Table 6.6, the profile of victims assaulted when the perpetrator has consumed alcohol/drugs differs from the profile where victims have in that, while notable proportions of female victims are affected, male victims appear more likely to be victimised. This is particularly evident in the Horvath sample in relation to perpetrator alcohol consumption and in the Lovett sample in relation to consumption of both alcohol and drugs. Perpetrator consumption also relates most closely to younger victims (aged 16–30 in the Horvath sample and 20 or under in the Lovett sample) and to older victims (aged 51 and over) in the Horvath sample. It also appears more prevalent among very young (16–20) and slightly older (31–40) perpetrators.

In both samples, the assault locations most correlated with perpetrator consumption tended to be casual meeting places in a social context, such as 'other homes'[8] and pubs or clubs. Rates of perpetrator consumption were particularly low where the assault occurred in a vehicle. This is understandable from the perpetrator perspective as consumption here would constitute a drink-driving issue. However, vehicles were particularly high-risk for victims who had been drinking. This suggests that they represent assault locations in which there is a high disparity between levels of victim and perpetrator intoxication. Where perpetrators had consumed alcohol, the victim was most likely to be a recent acquaintance or friend in the Lovett sample and a friend, recent acquaintance or professional in the Horvath sample. The inclusion of professionals is slightly anomalous and only relates to a small number of cases. However, this profile is otherwise aligned with that relating to victim consumption in that a combination of relationships involving recent acquaintances and friends is apparent. This fits with the finding alcohol-related assaults are more prevalent

Table 6.6 Socio-demographic profiles of victims and perpetrators according to perpetrator consumption

| | Perpetrator consumption | | | | | | | | | |
| | Alcohol | | Drugs | | Both | | Neither | | Total[a] | |
	Lovett %	Horvath %	Lovett %	Horvath %	Lovett %	Horvath %	Lovett %	Horvath %	Lovett n	Horvath n
Victim sex										
Female	35	47.6	3.3	5.6	8.8	7.5	52.9	39.3	514	412
Male	37.5	66.7	4.2	0	16.7	0	41.7	33.3	24	9
Perpetrator sex										
Male	35.2	48.1	3.2	5.5	9.1	7.1	52.5	39.3	537	420
Female	0	0	100	0	0	100	0	0	1	0
Victim age										
Under-16	50	0	1.6	66.7	17.7	33.3	30.6	0	62	3
16–20	46	51.2	5.6	6.5	10.5	4.1	37.9	38.2	124	123
21–30	26.4	50.3	4.3	2	7.4	11.3	62	36.4	163	151
31–40	28	42.9	1.6	5.5	8	7.7	62.4	44	125	91
41–50	39.5	38.9	0	11.1	4.7	0	55.8	50	43	36
51 and over	27.8	56.3	5.6	6.3	5.6	6.3	61.1	31.3	18	16
Unknown	33.3	100	0	0	0	0	66.7	0	3	1
Perpetrator age[b]										
Under-16		33.3		0		0		66.7		3
16–20		50		4.8		9.5		35.7		42
21–30		45.8		5.6		8.3		40.3		144
31–40		55.8		3.6		8		32.6		138
41–50		47.3		10.9		0		41.8		55

31–50 (multiple perps)[c]										
51 and over	n/a	n/a	n/a	n/a	n/a	n/a	n/a	n/a	n/a	n/a
Mixed ages (multiple perps)[c]										
Unknown	44.4	23.3	0	6.7	22.2	6.7	33.3	63.3	9	30
Victim ethnicity										
White	40.8	47.2	3.6	5.1	10.1	7.3	45.5	40.4	385	354
Black	9.2	53.3	0	8.9	4.6	6.7	86.2	31.1	65	45
Asian	25.8	42.9	0	7.1	3.2	7.1	71	42.9	31	14
Other	0	100	0	0	0	0	100	0	13	3
Unknown	40.9	40	9.1	0	13.6	20	36.4	40	44	5
Perpetrator ethnicity										
White	60.1	48.9	4.9	3.7	17.5	7	17.5	40.4	183	272
Black	47.4	46.2	10.5	11.3	5.3	9.4	36.8	33	19	106
Asian	45.8	44.4	4.2	0	8.3	0	41.7	55.6	24	18
Other	75	46.2	5	0	10	0	10	53.8	20	13
Unknown	15.1	50	1.7	8.3	4.1	16.7	79.1	25	292	12
Assault location										
Victim's home	48.1	52.6	41.7	5.2	2.8	7.2	7.4	35.1	108	97
Perpetrator's home	41.3	52.1	6.4	7.4	17.4	11.6	34.9	28.9	109	121
Shared home[c]	36.7	40.5	6.7	0	6.7	0	50	59.5	30	42
Other home[c]	51.1	64.9	2.2	2.7	11.1	13.5	35.6	18.9	45	37
Pub/club/disco	50	70	0	0	37.5	0	12.5	30	8	10
Public place	23.8	40	2.7	8.3	2.7	3.3	70.7	48.3	147	60
Vehicle	26.7	33.3	0	0	0	0	73.3	66.7	15	24

Table 6.6 continues overleaf

Table 6.6 continued

| | Perpetrator consumption | | | | | | | | | |
| | Alcohol | | Drugs | | Both | | Neither | | Total[a] | |
	Lovett %	Horvath %	Lovett %	Horvath %	Lovett %	Horvath %	Lovett %	Horvath %	Lovett n	Horvath n
Hotel	50	25	0	8.3	0	8.3	50	58.3	4	12
Education/care/ medical facility	14.3	0	0	0	0	0	85.7	100	7	1
Abroad	100	0	0	0	0	0	0	0	2	0
Workplace	0	16.7	0	0	0	0	100	83.3	7	6
Other	28.6	20	0	20	0	20	71.4	40	7	5
Unknown	26.5	50	2	16.7	16.3	16.7	55.1	16.7	49	6
Number of perpetrators										
1	36.4	n/a	3.1	n/a	8.4	n/a	52.1	n/a	489	n/a
2 or more	22.4	n/a	6.1	n/a	16.3	n/a	55.1	n/a	49	n/a
Perpetrator–victim relationship (single perp)										
Current/ex-partner	36.3	40.5	2.2	3.6	13.2	3.6	48.4	52.4	91	84
Family member	36.8	40	0	0	5.3	0	57.9	60	19	15
Friend	46	58	6.3	2.3	7.9	13.7	39.7	26	63	131
Acquaintance	41.1	50	4.2	19.4	5.3	8.3	49.5	22.2	95	36
Professional	15.4	53.3	15.4	0	0	0	69.2	46.7	13	15
Recent acquaintance	61.8	53.3	3.6	5.4	16.4	6.5	18.2	34.8	55	92
Stranger	20.5	20.5	0.8	10.3	2.5	2.6	76.2	66.7	122	39
Unknown	29	33.3	0	11.1	19.4	0	51.6	55.6	31	9

Perpetrator–victim relationship (multi perps)[e]										
At least one known	20	n/a	0	n/a	0	n/a	80	n/a	5	n/a
At least one acquaintance	15.4	n/a	7.7	n/a	23.1	n/a	46.2	n/a	13	n/a
All recent acquaintance	0	n/a	100	n/a	0	n/a	0	n/a	1	n/a
All stranger	30.4	n/a	4.3	n/a	17.4	n/a	47.8	n/a	23	n/a
Unknown	14.3	n/a	0	n/a	0	n/a	85.7	n/a	7	n/a
Victim vulnerabilities										
Substance misuse	27.3	23.8	18.2	23.8	9.1	14.3	45.5	38.1	11	21
Insecure housing	33.3	0	4.2	0	16.7	0	45.8	0	24	0
Asylum seeker/refugee	0	60	0	0	0	20	100	20	1	5
Previous victimisation	43.8	26.7	0	6.7	6.3	0	50	66.7	16	15
Disability	20	15	0	15	6.7	5	73.3	65	30	20
Prostitution	33.3	0	16.7	0	0	0	50	0	12	0

a   All percentages equal 100.

b   This data was not available for the Lovett sample.

c   The ages of multiple perpetrators were only coded as 31–50, not the two categories 31–40 and 41–50, hence another category has been created.

d   A sub-category of 'other home' is 'social gathering' – parties and collective events involving friends/other groups. This was coded separately in the Lovett but not the Horvath data, so the two categories have been combined here for reasons of comparability. When treated as a separate category, however, assaults occurring at social gatherings saw far higher rates of involvement of alcohol (63.4 per cent, n = 18), which is, in fact, the second highest among all assault locations in the Lovett dataset. The elevated presence of alcohol is not surprising here, although the small numbers in this group may affect the results.

e   The Horvath data does not include any multiple perpetrator cases; only Lovett data are presented.

in circumstances of casual acquaintanceship and lesser degrees of intimacy than in a partnership or familial relationship, although the presence of friends points to slightly different dynamics. It is also notable that it was very unlikely for assaults perpetrated by strangers and in public places to occur following perpetrator consumption of either alcohol or drugs. This may indicate a greater need to be sober in order to commit 'blitz' attacks.

Contexts and arenas

In order to assess, not only whether either victim or perpetrator had consumed alcohol/drugs, but whether this occurred in particular settings, a further line of analysis was conducted focusing on the relationship between victim and perpetrator consumption and the assault context. The aim was to conduct a more holistic examination of the interrelationship between substance consumption and the circumstances surrounding the assault.

As described previously, each case was assigned to one of a series of 'contexts' based on the available qualitative material describing the assault. These contexts combined the aspects of assault location, perpetrator–victim relationship and the circumstances in which the assault occurred. The full list of contexts was generated from the two datasets themselves through close analysis of the individual case material. Due to the large number of contexts which resulted, assaults occurring in similar circumstances, but with slightly varying locations or actors, were grouped together within broader 'arenas', each denoting a fundamental aspect of daily life. Table 6.7 demonstrates how the contexts were combined in order to create the arenas.

This schema provides a useful template for understanding and illustrating the range of situations in which all forms of sexual assault occur, covering, in fact, most social and physical environments an individual is likely to come into contact with. In addition, cross-tabulation with the presence or absence of alcohol and/or drugs indicates whether or not certain contexts and arenas were associated with sexual assault following their consumption.

Within both samples overall, the arenas comprising the most cases were personal (Horvath n = 174; Lovett n = 733), social (Horvath n = 177; Lovett n = 749), and public (Horvath n = 71; Lovett n = 600). Figures 6.2(a) and (b) show the distribution of cases among the different arenas according to the victims' consumption of alcohol/drugs.

Table 6.7 Contexts and arenas

Context	Arena
Family event Friends hanging out Relationship (current) Relationship (former) Family member Friend/relative/partner of known other	Personal
On a date Bar/pub Club Party/social gathering Asleep at/after social event	Social
Journey home Followed/jumped/accosted Offered lift/walk home Taxi	Public
Break-in Flatmate/guest Neighbour	Residential
Work/school Residential care home	Institutional
Contacts with authority	Authority
Other	Other

In arenas where there is likely to be less prior contact/acquaintance between the victim and perpetrator (public, social) a greater proportion of victims consumed alcohol than drugs or neither, which suggests that alcohol may act as a facilitator in these environments. In arenas where there is a greater degree of acquaintance (personal, authority) equal or smaller proportions of victims consumed alcohol than drugs or neither, indicating that other facilitating elements, such as trust, access, intimacy, authority and so on may come into play here. Harrington Cleveland *et al.* (1999) have described factors such as these as 'rape tactics', which the perpetrator employs both to increase the chances of achieving rape and to decrease the chances that the victim will report it. They define alcohol and drugs as specific tactics within this model.

(a) Horvath

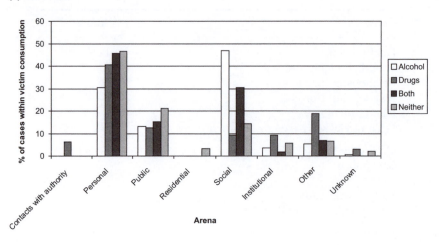

(b) Lovett

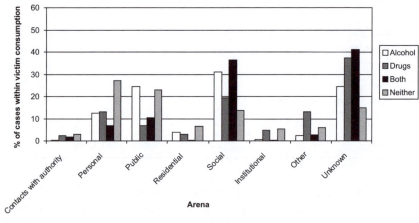

Figure 6.2 Distribution of cases in arenas according to victim consumption

Figures 6.3(a) and (b) show the distribution of cases among the different arenas according to the perpetrators' consumption of alcohol/drugs.

Figures 6.2(a) and (b) show that in 'contacts with authority', 'residential', 'institutional' and 'other' arenas victim substance consumption is low. This may be because there are other tactics available to perpetrators to facilitate the assault so that substance consumption by either is unnecessary. These are not arenas where substance consumption is socially acceptable whereas high levels

(a) Horvath

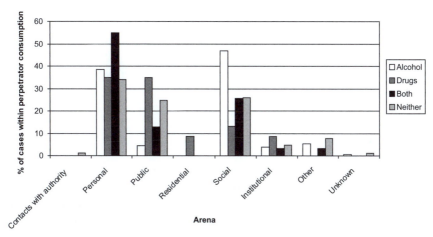

(b) Lovett

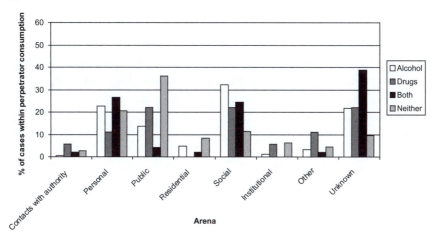

Figure 6.3 Distribution of cases in arenas according to perpetrator consumption

are identifiable in the social arena for both victims and perpetrators, where it is widely acceptable. Comparison of Figures 6.2 and 6.3 shows that in the public arena victims are more likely to have consumed substances while perpetrators appear more sober (apart from a small number in both samples who have consumed drugs: Lovett n = 4; Horvath n = 8). It is possible that in this arena, in addition to being isolated or exposed, the perpetrator also needs the victim to be identifiably vulnerable as a result of intoxication in order to gain access to her. The reverse is the case in the personal arena, where victims consumed relatively low amounts of substances and perpetrators somewhat higher amounts. This suggests that in the personal arena the perpetrator does not require the victim to be intoxicated as he already has access to her or a relationship of trust, but that his own intoxication may act to facilitate or excuse the assault.

Discussion

The findings that have emerged in this chapter from combining the Lovett and Horvath datasets have demonstrated that many of the popular myths surrounding the role of alcohol and drugs in rape are unsupportable. In this discussion section we aim to use our data to challenge and discuss the four areas where myths are prevalent: types of substances and the nature of consumption; context; perpetrators; and victims.

Myths about types of substances and nature of consumption

Despite considerable research evidence to the contrary (see, for example, Hindmarch and Brinkmann 1999; Seifert 1999), the myth still remains that drugs such as Rohypnol are being widely used by men seeking to incapacitate women and sexually assault them. Whilst we do not wish to deny that a small proportion of men are drugging women and sexually assaulting them, independent and voluntary alcohol consumption by the victim was associated with a substantially higher proportion of sexual assaults while drugs were present in a consistent minority, and consensual consumption of drugs by victims accounted for a large degree of cases where drugs were involved. This strong association with alcohol reflects findings from other studies (e.g. Hindmarch *et al.* 2001; Scott-Ham and Burton 2005; Slaughter 2000) but, equally importantly, it does not demonstrate a causal relationship between consuming alcohol and subsequent victimisation. Rather, it indicates that victim intoxication is one of a number of vulnerabilities that can be identified and exploited to facilitate sexual assault by predatory men, particularly where there is little or no prior acquaintance or relationship.

Where alcohol consumption and rape have been linked, a common assertion has tended to be that this is a result of the increased prevalence of alcohol consumption among women and particularly due to the rise in the phenomenon of 'binge drinking'. An analysis of drinking levels among the general population has shown that this assertion is contestable. In addition, although neither the Horvath nor the Lovett study had access to consistent clinical data on the precise amounts of alcohol consumed and the levels of intoxication among victims, available qualitative data indicated a range of physiological states among victims who had consumed either alcohol or drugs, and a degree of intoxication that led to unconsciousness in only one-fifth of cases overall.

An additional explanation exists for the high proportions of alcohol and low proportions of drugs in both samples, which is that it may simply be a reflection of the greater acceptability and more widespread consumption of alcohol compared to drugs within society generally. As mentioned in the introduction, over half of those people surveyed (irrelevant of gender) had consumed alcohol in the previous week (Office for National Statistics 2008), while the figures for drug consumption were much lower – just 5 per cent of people had used drugs in the past month and across all age groups levels among women were even lower than for men[9] (Hoare and Flately 2008). These figures are not highly dissimilar from the proportions consuming alcohol and drugs in both the Horvath and Lovett samples of rape and sexual assault victims. Equally, this widespread acceptability coupled with public awareness that a victim is less likely to be believed if they have been sexually assaulted after having consumed alcohol (Jordan 2004; Lopez 1992) means a situation exists which provides perpetrators with relatively low-risk opportunities to assault intoxicated victims.

Myths about context

One of the most prevalent myths about the context of alcohol/drug-related sexual assault is that it occurs when people are on dates and is hence often labelled as 'date rape'. Across the two datasets there were very few cases which involved two people on a date,[10] so the overall proportion of 'date rapes' was very low. This supports findings from the British Crime Survey that only 4 per cent of rapes and 6 per cent of serious sexual assaults occurred in the context of 'dates' (Walby and Allen 2004). In fact, our analysis reveals that sexual assaults occur in many different contexts whether alcohol is involved or not.

We argue that in certain environments consumption of alcohol/drugs can act as a facilitator of sexual assault. The pattern that emerged was that alcohol seems to be more prevalent in social and public arenas where there is minimal prior contact between the victim and perpetrator. So alcohol is most likely used to initially facilitate interaction between them and then provide an opportunity for the perpetrator to commit the assault. Alcohol is commonly and legitimately consumed in these contexts, which were typically the customary sites of social interaction and recreation – pubs and clubs, friends' homes – or public spaces occupied between social events or while travelling home, including in taxis and other vehicles. This may be because such environments provide easy access to potential victims who are drinking voluntarily and independently, where social interactions commonly involve shared drinking and/or drug taking and where there may be expectations that sexual encounters can be initiated. In the case of taxis and vehicles, it was notable that while victims assaulted in these locations had commonly consumed alcohol, perpetrators were unlikely to have.

Myths about perpetrators

A common myth about why men commit rape, originating from evolutionary psychology, is that they are driven by physiological impulses and are simply responding to/misreading women's cues (see Frith this volume and, for an overview of this literature, see Buss and Malamuth 1996; George et al. 1995 and Holloway 1984). Where alcohol is involved, this means that they are mistakenly assuming that women who are drinking in public/social locations are available for sex. The findings above do show a correlation between cases where victims and perpetrators have consumed alcohol and sexual assault occurring in locations such as pubs, clubs, bars and parties. However, it is also evident that there are situations in which there is a clear disparity between the victim's and perpetrator's levels of consciousness, which negates the possibility for consent to be negotiated or given. For example, where victims were asleep, unconscious or highly intoxicated there is little or no possibility for any interaction between victim and perpetrator that would enable consent to be conveyed. The commission of sexual assaults in these circumstances suggests a clear disregard for the victim as an equal party to sexual activity and a sense of entitlement on the part of the perpetrator to achieve sexual gratification at any cost. It also provides evidence that there are situations in which men knowingly take advantage of women who have been drinking and may even see them as legitimate targets for sexual assault.

Myths about victims

Three main myths in relation to rape victims and alcohol exist: firstly, that women are always capable of saying no, no matter how drunk they are; secondly, that by drinking women are asking to be raped; and, finally, that women who say they were raped when drunk are lying/regret having sex/just had bad sex. With regard to the first, if a victim is asleep or unconscious they cannot say no or resist, and where they are very drunk it is questionable whether they can give meaningful consent. Further, media portrayal of victims of sexual assault when alcohol or drugs are involved frequently focuses on women who cannot remember anything (see, for example, O'Kane 2004; Weathers 2005). As the data in this chapter have shown, these cases represent a small though significant minority (less than a quarter) of the cases in both datasets. We propose that more awareness is needed about the degrees of intoxication that victims can experience. In everyday conversation distinctions are made between being 'tipsy', 'merry', 'blind drunk' and 'wasted' and yet these are not applied to victims of sexual assault. Further, regardless of where on a continuum from sober to unconscious a victim may fall, the belief that women who are drinking are asking to be raped needs to be challenged.

Confronting the myths that surround victims could be achieved in a number of ways. Initially, in response to the claim that women indulging in excessive drinking are contributing to sexual assault, we draw attention to the evidence presented in this chapter which shows that both female and male victims are affected. The fundamental issue remains, however, that it is the perpetrator who decides to commit a sexual assault regardless of the victim's behaviours and the responsibility must remain with them; all victims are deserving of protection from the law.

Conclusions

In this chapter we have challenged persistent myths about the prevalence of drug-assisted rape, showing that alcohol is far more common than drugs in sexual assault. We have also shown that rape and sexual assault occur in a variety of contexts and arenas spanning those in the daily lives of individuals, and that those in which alcohol/drug consumption and sexual assault co-occur are particularly linked to a variety of locations and situations within social, public and personal arenas. This analysis has especially exposed the misleading nature of the notion of 'date rape' and its common conflation with drug-assisted rape, since very few cases in either sample occurred in such circumstances. In addition, the data presented have clearly demonstrated that the vulnerability created by the consumption of alcohol is being exploited by perpetrators to facilitate sexual assaults, findings which are supported by Stanko and Williams in Chapter 9 of this volume. Thus is appears that women (and some men) who are drinking and/or consuming drugs are seen as legitimate targets for sexual exploitation and victimisation.

The exploration of both victim and perpetrator consumption has highlighted the need to reframe approaches to researching and understanding this offence. We have shown that the prevalence of consumption among victims and perpetrators and correlations with certain assault contexts shifts depending on whose perspective is taken, and that there is not necessarily a match between contexts involving both victim and perpetrator consumption. While broadening the range of circumstances with which we perceive alcohol and drug-related sexual assault to be associated, this also calls for a move away from an exclusive focus on the drinking and personal safety behaviours of women as the most likely potential victims of sexual assault and greater emphasis on both the drinking and targeting behaviours of potential perpetrators. More research is needed that takes a more holistic approach to understanding offending, considering all of the actors and situational factors and their interconnections. Ultimately, public education needs to focus, not only on the risks of alcohol/drug consumption in relation to long-term health and the possibilities of victimisation for women and men, but also on men's attitudes towards women who are drinking and the limits of consent in situations where one or both parties are intoxicated.

Acknowledgments

Miranda would like to thank Darren Hollett and Jess Fielding for their assistance with coding the data and Jennifer Brown for her collaboration on the initial project. Jo would like to thank Liz Kelly and Linda Regan for their collaboration on the initial project and ongoing dialogue and advice about the dataset. Miranda and Jo would also like to thank Maddy Coy for her very helpful comments on an earlier version of this chapter.

Notes

1 Drugs include those that are illegal and over-the-counter and prescription medicines.
2 Sexual Offences Act 2003, sections 1(1) and 1(2).
3 Some research has been conducted into perpetrator consumption in the US (see Brecklin and Ullman 2001), although this is rarely presented in conjunction with data on victim consumption.
4 Original research was conducted by Kelly, Lovett and Regan 2005.
5 These are included in the data presented here.
6 In the Horvath sample, the highest prevalence was found in perpetrators aged under 16, but the fact that this group only comprised three out of a total of four individuals means it does not constitute a robust finding.
7 Note that this includes parties and other social gatherings in both samples.
8 This category included social gatherings.
9 Among 16–59 year olds surveyed for the 2007/08 British Crime Survey.
10 For example, in the Lovett data there were 12 in the whole sample of 3,527 and in 10 of the 2,115 cases where details of victim consumption were known the victim and perpetrator were on a date.

References

Abbey, A., McAuslan, P., Ross, L. T. and Zawacki, T. (1999) 'Alcohol expectancies regarding sex, aggression, and sexual vulnerability: reliability and validity assessment', *Psychology of Addictive Behaviour*, 13: 174–82.

Abbey, A., Zawacki, T., Buck, P. O., Clinton, A. M. and McAuslan, P. (2001) 'Alcohol and sexual assault', *Alcohol Research and Health*, 25 (1): 43–51.

Abbey, A., Zawacki, T., Buck, P. O., Clinton, A. M. and McAuslan, P. (2004) 'Sexual assault and alcohol consumption: what do we know about their relationship and what types of research are still needed?', *Aggression and Violent Behaviour*, 9: 271–303.

Brecklin, L. and Ullman, S. (2001) 'The role of offender alcohol use in rape attacks', *Journal of Interpersonal Violence*, 16 (1): 3–21.

Budd, T. (2003) *Alcohol-related Assault: Findings from the British Crime Survey.* Home Office Online Report 35/03. Available online at: http://www. homeoffice.gov.uk/rds/pdfs2/rdsolr3503.pdf (accesssed 12 March 2009).

Buss, D. M. and Malamuth, N. (eds) (1996) *Sex, Power, Conflict: Evolutionary and Feminist Perspectives.* New York: Oxford University Press.

Cameron, C. A. and Strizke, W. G. K. (2003) 'Alcohol and acquaintance rape in Australia: testing the presupposition model of attributions about responsibility and blame', *Journal of Applied Social Psychology*, 33 (5): 983–1008.

Campbell, L., Keegan, A., Cybulska, B. and Forster, G. (2007) 'Prevalence of mental health problems and deliberate self-harm in complainants of sexual violence', *Journal of Clinical Forensic Medicine*, 14: 75–8.

Crawford, E., O'Dougherty Wright, M. and Birchmeier, Z. (2008) 'Drug-facilitated sexual assault: college women's risk perception and behavioural choices', *Journal of American College Health*, 57 (3): 261–72.

Cybulska, B. (2007) 'Sexual assault: key issues', *Journal of the Royal Society of Medicine*, 100: 321–4.

Department of Health (2008) *Smoking, Drinking and Drug Use among Young People in England in 2007*. Leeds: Information Centre.

Finch, E. and Munro, V. (2005) 'Juror stereotypes and blame attribution in rape cases involving intoxicants', *British Journal of Criminology*, 45: 25–38.

Finney, A. (2004) *Alcohol and Sexual Violence: Key Findings from the Research*, Home Office Findings No. 215. London: Home Office.

Foote, W., Wangmann, J. and Braaf, R. (2004) *Old Crime, New Modus Operandi: Preventing Drug and Alcohol Assisted Sexual Assaults*. Available online at: http://www.lawlink.nsw.gov.au/lawlink/vaw/ll_vaw.nsf/pages/vaw_resources_vawreports (accessed 12 January 2009).

George, W. H., Cue, K. L., Lopez, P. A., Crowe, L. C. and Norris, J. (1995) 'Self-reported alcohol expectancies and postdrinking sexual inferences about women', *Journal of Applied Social Psychology*, 25: 164–86.

Gibb, F., De Bruxelles, S. and Coates, S. (2005) 'Binge drinking women may lose right to rape claim', *The Times*, 24 November. http://www.timesonline.co.uk/article/0,,2-1888035-1,00.html

Greenfield, L. A. (1997) 'Sex offences and offenders: an analysis of data on rape and sexual assault', cited in E. F. Avakame (1999) 'Females' labour force participation and rape: an empirical test of the Backlash Hypothesis', *Violence Against Women*, 5: 926–49.

Harrington Cleveland, H., Koss, M. and Lyons, J. (1999) 'Rape tactics from the survivor's perspective: contextual dependent and within-event independence', *Journal of Interpersonal Violence*, 14 (5): 532–47.

Hindmarch, I. and Brinkmann, R. (1999) 'Trends in the use of alcohol and other drugs in cases of sexual assault', *Human Psychopharmacology: Clinical and Experimental*, 14: 225–31.

Hindmarch, I., Kerr, J. and Sherwood, N. (1991) 'The effects of alcohol and other drugs on psychomotor performance and cognitive function', *Alcohol*, 26: 71–9.

Hindmarch, I., ElSohly, M., Gambles, J. and Salamone, S. (2001) 'Forensic urinalysis of drug use in cases of alleged sexual assault', *Journal of Clinical Forensic Medicine*, 8: 197–205.

Hoare, J. and Flatley, K. (2008) *Drug Misuse Declared: Findings from the 2007/08 British Crime Survey England and Wales*, Home Office Statistical Bulletin 13/08. London: Home Office.

Holloway, W. (1984) 'Women's power in heterosexual sex', *Women's Studies International Forum*, 7 (1): 63–8.

Horvath, M. A. H. (2006) 'Drug-assisted Rape: An Investigation'. Unpublished PhD, University of Surrey.

Horvath, M. A. H. and Brown, J. (2005) 'Drug-assisted rape and sexual assault: definitional, conceptual and methodological developments', *Journal of Investigative Psychology and Offender Profiling*, 2 (3): 203–10.

Horvath, M. A. H. and Brown, J. (2006) 'The role of alcohol and drugs in rape', *Medicine, Science and the Law*, 46 (3): 219–28.

Horvath, M. A. H. and Brown, J. (2007) 'Alcohol as drug of choice: is drug-assisted rape a misnomer?', *Psychology, Crime and Law*, 13 (5): 417–29.

ICM (2005) *Sexual Assault Research Summary Report*. Prepared for Amnesty International UK.

Jordan, J. (2004) 'Beyond belief? Police, rape and women's credibility', *Criminal Justice*, 4: 29–59.

Kelly, L., Lovett, J. and Regan, L. (2005) *A Gap or a Chasm? Attrition in Reported Rape Cases*, Home Office Research Study No. 293. London: Home Office.

Koss, M. P. and Cook, S. L. (1993) 'Facing the facts: date and acquaintance rape are significant problems for women', in R. J. Gelles and D. R. Loseke (eds), *Current Controversies on Family Violence*. Newbury Park, CA: Sage.

Lees, S. (2002) *Carnal Knowledge: Rape on Trial*. London: Women's Press.

Lopez, P. (1992) 'He said ... she said ... an overview of date rape from commission through prosecution through verdict', *Criminal Justice*, 13: 275–302.

Lovett, J., Regan, L. and Kelly, L. (2004) *Sexual Assault Referral Centres: Developing Good Practice and Maximising Potentials*, Home Office Research Study No. 285. London: Home Office.

Markowitz, S. (2005) 'Alcohol, drugs and violence', *International Review of Law and Economics*, 25: 20–44.

Measham, F. and Brain, K. (2005) '"Binge" drinking, British alcohol policy and the new culture of intoxication', *Crime Media Culture*, 1 (3): 262–83.

Nurius, P. S. and Norris, T. (1996) 'A cognitive ecological model of women's response to male sexual coercion in dating', *Journal of Psychology and Human Sexuality*, 8: 117–39.

O'Kane, M. (2004) 'I got the feeling from his words that they'd done it before', *The Guardian*, 9 September.

Office for National Statistics (2008) *General Household Survey 2007*. Available online at: http://www.statistics.gov.uk/Statbase/Product.asp?vlnk=5756 (accessed 4 February 2009).

Operation Matisse (2006) *Investigating Drug Facilitated Sexual Assault*. London: Association of Chief Police Officers.

Parks, K. A. and Miller, B. A. (1997) 'Bar victimisation of women', *Psychology of Women Quarterly*, 21: 509–25.

Peterson, J. B., Rothfleisch, J., Zelazo, P. D. and Pihl, R. O. (1990) 'Acute alcohol intoxication and cognitive functioning', *Journal of Studies in Alcohol*, 51: 114–22.

Regan, L., Lovett, J. and Kelly, L. (2004) *Forensic Nursing: An Option for Improving Responses to Reported Rape and Sexual Assault*, Home Office On-line Research Report 28/04. Available online at: http://www.homeoffice.gov.uk/rds/pdfs04/rdsolr2804.pdf (accessed 4 February 2009).

Scott-Hamm, M. and Burton, F. C. (2005) 'Toxicological findings in cases of alleged drug-facilitated sexual assault in the United Kingdom over a 3-year period', *Journal of Clinical Forensic Medicine*, 12: 175–86.

Seifert, S. A. (1999) 'Substance use and sexual assault', *Substance Use and Misuse*, 34: 935–45.

Slaughter, L. (2000) 'Involvement of drugs in sexual assault', *Journal of Reproductive Medicine*, 45: 425–30.

Stanko, B., Norman, J. and Wunsch, D. (2007) *The Attrition of Rape Allegations in London: A Review*. London: Metropolitan Police Service.

Steele, C. M. and Josephs, R. A. (1990) 'Alcohol myopia: its prized and dangerous effects', *American Psychologist*, 45: 921–33.

Strizke, W. G. K., Patrick, C. J. and Lang, A. R. (1995) 'Alcohol and human emotion: a multidimensional analysis incorporating startle-probe methodology', *Journal of Abnormal Psychology*, 104: 114–22.

Taylor, S. E. and Leonard, K. E. (1983) 'Alcohol, drugs, and human physical aggression', *Journal of Studies in Alcohol*, 11: 78–88.

Temkin, J. (2002) 'Digging the dirt: disclosure of records in sexual assault cases', *Cambridge Law Journal*, 61: 126–45.

Testa, M. and Parks, K. A. (1996) 'The role of women's alcohol consumption in sexual victimisation', *Aggressive and Violent Behaviour*, 1: 217–34.

The Times (2005) 'Binge-drink women may lose right to rape claim', 24 November. Available online at: www.timesonline.co.uk/article/0,,2-1888035,00.html (accessed 4 February 2009).

Ullman, S. E. (2003) 'A critical review of field studies on the link of alcohol and adult sexual assault in women', *Aggression and Violent Behaviour*, 8: 471–86.

Ullman, S. E., Karabastsos, G. and Koss, M. (1999) 'Alcohol and sexual assault in a national sample of college women', *Journal of Interpersonal Violence*, 14 (6): 603–25.

Walby, S. and Allen, J. (2004) *Domestic Violence, Sexual Assault and Stalking: Findings from the British Crime Survey*, Home Office Research Study No. 276. London: Home Office.

Weathers, H. (2005) 'Drug-rape – the disturbing facts', *Daily Mail*, 8 August.

Zimmerman, P. R. and Benson, B. L. (2007) 'Alcohol and rape: an "economics-of-crime" perspective', *International Review of Law and Economics*, 27: 442–73.

Chapter 7

Narratives of survival: South Asian women's experience of rape

Aisha Gill

Introduction

According to the women's movement, rape (along with gender-based violence) is one of the most frequently committed crimes in the UK, if likely incidence rather than reported cases are considered. Often such crimes are conceptualised in terms of the male desire to have dominance over women (Brownmiller 1975; Derne 1994; Kelly 1996; Naffine 2003). Recent feminist research has emphasised the threat of violence confronting all women (Chakravarti 2009; Volpp 2000), demonstrating that such violence often stems directly from women's lower social status. Bunch and Carrillo (1998) argue that violence against women is 'an extension of the ideology that gives men the right to control women's behaviour, mobility, access to material resources, and their labour, both productive and reproductive' (Bunch and Carrillo 1998: 60).

Since the 1970s, those working to combat rape and other forms of violence against women (VAW) have attempted to reduce the impact of these crimes by creating rape crisis centres: safe places where women of all backgrounds can go to discuss their abuse. These centres were also intended to change the criminal justice system's response to rape, and to challenge social myths and stereotypes concerning this crime (Rape Crisis 2008). The centres' interventions were thus intended to be simultaneously spatial and discursive: they represented places where women could recover from past rapes and work to prevent future ones. As such, they addressed the issue as both an individual and cultural crisis. Through the centres' interventions it was possible to re-conceptualise rape (and the threat of rape) as a tool used by men to control women and confine them within 'proper' gendered spaces. Rape therefore serves a pivotal role in the feminist critique of the patriarchal construction and enforcement of women's roles as naturalised victims who are inherently vulnerable to male power.

The situation is particularly complex in South Asian communities. Since rape and sexual violence are rarely discussed in these communities, incidence data are difficult to obtain: in many cases crimes go unreported, or are reported long after the event, when victims have often suffered repeat victimisation. Research examining why women from South Asian communities, in particular, tend not to disclose rape or sexual abuse has revealed three key explanatory factors.[1] The first suggests that the women tend to feel 'betrayed' by the male perpetrators of these acts; often these men are well known to their victims as members of the same community (Gupta 2003; Siddique *et al.* 2008; Thiara 2003; Uberoi 1996). The second key factor is that these women often fear that they will not be believed, especially since the criminal justice system does not usually prosecute in cases where the only evidence is the victim's testimony (Gill 2008; Patel 2008; Wilson 2006). The third key finding suggests that some women do not report sexual violence because they believe that the assault is not violent enough to constitute rape (Gangoli 2007; Haven 2008; Rape Crisis 2008). Professionals working in the field report that South Asian female victims experience a higher degree of shame than their white counterparts and that they are often less inclined to reveal abuse for fear that they will not be believed and will, instead, be punished. Negative reactions from mainstream public service providers also contribute to this problem.

These issues have prompted professionals to question whether existing outreach services in the UK adequately address cases of rape and/or sexual abuse involving South Asian women. First-hand accounts reveal that family and community responses play a key role in allowing these women to publicly discuss their rape and sexual abuse. This has far-reaching implications for policy, practice and the need for further research. Although theoretical studies have made a significant contribution to understanding rape within South Asian communities, issues regarding the individual experience of female victims are largely undocumented (Ahmed *et al.* 2009; Dasgupta 1996). The voices of these women need to be heard. At the same time, such accounts must be examined critically via a nuanced analytical approach that recognises the diverse realities of these women's lives. In order to evaluate and understand these women's experience of sexual violence, it is important to consider the socio-cultural context in which such violence occurs.

Socio-cultural context

Over the last three decades, violence against women (VAW) has become a matter of major public and academic interest (Gangoli *et al.* 2006; Hester *et al.* 1995; Thiara and Gill 2009). Recent research has revealed the global scale and varied extent of these crimes, which range from domestic violence to sexual violence, and from culturally sanctioned forced marriages[2] to female genital mutilation (FGM) (Horvath and Kelly 2007). Although there has been considerable progress in understanding VAW, there is still much work to be done, especially in terms of addressing its causes and consequences. Although policymakers have looked at the legal issues surrounding rape and sexual violence, especially since the implementation of the Domestic Violence, Crime and Victims Act 2004, they have failed to take into account the range of personal and cultural experiences of the women who experience these crimes.

Perhaps the most significant facet of South Asian culture in this context concerns 'honour' (*izzat* in Urdu). In 'honour'-based societies, the man is defined as the head of the family and the defender of its 'honour'; the man is expected to protect his family (including womenfolk, who are viewed as his property) against any behaviour that might be seen as shameful or humiliating by the community. Female family members are valued as a resource and as symbols of 'honour'. For this reason, although a women's honour is considered to be of paramount importance for the family, the status of women themselves is relatively low: this situation creates conditions which foster the perpetuation of VAW in such societies (Welchman and Hossain 2005).

A family's 'honour', and thus prestige, is achieved through the conduct, actions and social performances of its women; consequently, family interests take precedence over individual interests (Derne 1994). More significantly, since *izzat* relies on the behaviour of women, safeguarding the family *izzat* can also be viewed as a means of exercising social control over women's bodies and behaviour. Thus there is a tendency to commodify women as vessels of honour that men own and defend, hence the reason that male members of a family often view themselves as protectors of their womenfolk's *izzat*. This gives rise to a variety of social norms concerning women's sexuality and sexual practices (e.g. a woman must remain a virgin until marriage, then must maintain fidelity to her husband). Female consent to the patriarchal norms of religion, culture and class is strongly encouraged, and the degree to which each woman conforms to the value systems embedded in these institutions determines the way she is perceived by her marital and blood family (Ortner 1978).

In such patriarchal societies, women are invested with immense negative power, since any misbehaviour on their part can bring shame and dishonour to the male members of an entire community or lineage (Kandiyoti 1988). This produces the conditions in which a particular form of VAW flourishes – so-called 'honour'-based violence. This form of VAW functions as a cornerstone of patriarchal order: it is, effectively, a method of controlling women in order to maintain the patriarchal status quo (Kandiyoti 1988). 'Honour'-based violence – violence that has the patina of social respectability – paves the way for other forms of gender-based violence: putting aside notions of 'honour', men perpetuate the abuse of women largely to sustain their own social dominance. Thus 'honour', far from being a celebration of women's dignity and social importance, actually leads to their victimisation and abuse.

This chapter considers how notions of 'honour' intersect with South Asian women's sexuality by examining interview data collected during the author's doctoral research (Gill 2004) and presenting a narrative analysis of the rape of five women survivors[3] (from a total number of 18). This analysis focuses on: (1) the ways in which these women draw from, revise and construct scripts of 'coping' with regard to the coercive nature of the violence they continue to experience in their ongoing relationships with their partners, and (2) how these women interpret their lived experiences of violence and abuse. Ultimately, this analysis reveals the culturally defined nature of their responses to sexual violence. As such, the chapter illuminates the personal and social issues surrounding rape and sexual abuse within South Asian communities. It should be remembered, however, that these crimes are simply subtypes of VAW and must be understood within a context of the diversity of violence experienced by women. However, sexual abuse and rape throw a particularly interesting light on VAW in South Asian communities because of the very nature of the social and cultural norms and practices which give rise to VAW in these communities: the issue of women's sexuality is at the heart of VAW and, thus, exploring sexual acts of violence contributes to the debate on VAW as a whole.

Language and terminology

The UK legal definition of rape has been substantially changed by the Sexual Offences Act 2003, which came into force on 1 May 2004. Under the Sexual Offences Act 1956 statutory definition, any act of non-consensual intercourse (vaginal or anal) by a man with another person (male or female) was considered rape; non-consensual oral sex was excluded from the definition. Consent was given its ordinary meaning, and lack of consent was considered to be inferred from the surrounding circumstances, such as submission through fear. The Sexual Offences Act 2003 extended the definition of rape to include the penetration by a penis of the vagina, anus or mouth of another person. The Act also changed the law about consent and belief in consent. According to the new statutory definition, a defendant is guilty of rape if he intentionally penetrates the vagina, anus or mouth of another person with his penis, and the victim does not consent to the penetration or could not reasonably be believed to consent: 'a person consents if he [or she] agrees by choice, and has the freedom and capacity to make that choice' (Crown Prosecution Service 2004).

However, cultural background is an important factor, not only in how individual women define and respond to sexual violence, but how it is defined and discussed in different cultural/ethnic groups. In South Asian Hindi/Urdu-speaking communities, the most common term for talking about rape is *meri izzat looti gayi/meri izzat lut gayi* (I could not prevent them from stealing my honour). This euphemistic discourse subverts the experiences of rape victims by reaffirming the patriarchal values and attitudes about honour and shame that shape the power structures of South Asian communities. Note that, linguistically speaking, a man *lut* (loots) a women's *izzat* (honour) by committing rape instead of surrendering his own.

Message board discussions examining the use of these terms in films question why such language is tolerated, given that it implicitly lays the blame for tarnished honour on the women. The most commonly used euphemism for rape in such films (*izzat lut gaye*) linguistically suggests that honour is housed in female reproductive organs and is, thus, physically susceptible to violent sexual assault; moreover, the wording implies that the victim is at fault for losing her *izzat* in this way – literally, for 'not being able to hold on to it'. Thus the victim is disgraced and not the perpetrator. In South Asian communities when a woman 'loses her *izzat*' as a result of rape she is likely to be socially ostracised and, in extreme cases, she may be murdered.

The complexities of language offer insights into how sexual abuse is perceived in these communities: this perception plays a major role in both the personal and social effects of rape on victims and their families, as well as having important consequences for the social status of acknowledged perpetrators. There is a particular need for sensitivity to the disclosure of such experiences within South Asian communities because of the real danger of a backlash against the victim. Understanding and combating lack of disclosure must recognise the key role that this potential backlash plays with respect to women's willingness to report sexual violence and how it limits their ability to speak of rape and sexual violence.

Analysis of narratives

Although analysing victim accounts is the foundation of this chapter, it is important to stress that such stories, like all autobiographical discourses, are always incomplete, partial and open to challenge (Denzin 1989). Moreover, Denzin (1989) contends that 'each teller speaks from a biographical position that is unique and, in a sense, unshareable. Each hearer of a story hears from a similarly unshareable position'. Both the speaker and listener's subjectivities must be considered in analysing such accounts. Kvale (1996) reminds researchers of the danger of viewing written interview transcripts as representing the full content of the interview:

> Although produced as an oral discourse, the interview appears in the form of a written text. The transcript is a bastard, a hybrid between an oral discourse unfolding over time, face to face, in a lived situation – what is said is addressed to a specific listener present – and a written text created for a general, distant, public. (p. 5)

True communication involves listening to and participating in the creation of the story: the storytelling relationship. In a research setting, stories emerge as a result of the interaction between interviewer and participant (Rosenthal 1993). The transcript, therefore, acts as an 'artificial construct' of a lived oral conversation (Kvale 1996). Analysis must examine this relationship, acknowledging the fact that the interview transcript is jointly constructed: it is a negotiated product of social interaction, not a 'pure' and objective document that represents a definite account of the interviewee's experiences of sexual violence.

Thus the transcripts examined in this study are authentic, though subjective tellings of the interviewees' experiences.

Giving participants a chance to voice their own stories serves to validate their experiences. The 'denial' of the participant's voice is a common criticism of interview-based research: often, instead of 'giving voice to' participants, the researcher's interpretations and analysis hold sole authority in the text and, where these conflict with the participant's views, this authority nullifies them. Even feminist research has been criticised for annihilating the speech of the participants by denying their voices, as bell hooks (1991) powerfully asserts:

> [N]o need to hear your voice when I can talk about you better than you can speak about yourself. No need to hear your voice. Only tell me about your pain. I want to know your story. And then I will tell it back to you in a new way. Tell it back to you in such a way that it has become mine, my own. Re-writing you, I write myself anew. I am still author, authority. I am still the colonizer, the speak subject, and you are now at the centre of my talk. (pp. 151–2)

Similarly, it is not enough to listen to a single voice: for this reason, the chapter considers the stories of five different women and gives them room to 'speak for themselves'. Through their stories, the chapter attempts to address the following questions: How do South Asian women interpret their experiences of rape and sexual violence? How do women conceptualise their own experiences in the stories they tell? What can be learnt from these stories to strengthen attempts to address rape in these communities?

Interpretation becomes vastly more difficult when socio-cultural norms render situations ambiguous: it is often hard to define the point at which marital intimacy becomes rape. In her study of domestic violence, Pagelow (1984) notes that, even though some of the women she interviewed had been choked to the point of unconsciousness during sexual intercourse, they did not define themselves as victims of sexual violence since they did not consider choking to be sexual in nature; they also believed that intercourse was a husband's natural right. Not surprisingly, victims were confused about the distinction between marital sex and rape, especially when society in general had, until recently, offered few clear guidelines on the matter. Differing perceptions about the appropriateness of an act, along with the prevalent belief in South Asian communities that husbands have the right to deal with their wives as they see fit (because they are 'property'), often leads to misattribution of violence by South Asian women. This, in turn, leads to understatement of the abuse they have suffered: understatement is endemic in their narratives of sexual abuse and rape partly because VAW is interpreted as the norm in these communities (Ahmed *et al.* 2009; Gill 2004).

This problem is exacerbated by the fact that, traditionally, society has offered more protection to the perpetrators of sexual violence than the victims, especially in relation to marital rape and physical assaults on wives (Browne 1993). Studies that demonstrate the level of under-reporting of sexual VAW, demonstrate that victims often refuse to describe their abuse altogether (Hayden and McCarthy 1994). This is not simply because of the ubiquity of violence: Wood and Rennie's (1994) examination of rape victims reveals that retelling the experience is traumatic for the victim, since it involves not only recalling the act itself, but also constructing oneself as a victim. The only non-passive position available is one in which the narrator accepts blame; thus women must choose to remain silent or accept responsibility for the crimes committed against them if they are unwilling to accept the role of victim. Analysing stories of violence is therefore extremely difficult because such stories are 'wrapped up in agency and positioning'; consequently, instances of failure to name 'the acts of violence or deflections of discourse and the silences surrounding coercive acts must also be examined' (O'Connor 1995: 309): in other words, silence and omission are as important as spoken content in such interviews.

Listening to the accounts of South Asian women exposes significant variations in individual conceptions of identity, reflexivity and power: variations which underlie their presentation of self through narrative (Kelly 1988). It is only possible to understand these differences by providing a space in which women can voice their experiences: silencing, shaping or constraining their stories (common practices in research interviewing) would be an additional level of abuse. Giving women the opportunity to articulate their experiences illuminates how they live with gender-based violence (Kelly 1988). Above all, it is important to recognise that a strategy of valorising disparate and heterogeneous female voices is an important aspect of efforts to combat VAW. Partial and even contradictory these stories may be, but they are, nevertheless, a record of patriarchal violence. Moreover, these stories suggest promising avenues for combating rape and sexual abuse, offering alternatives to the narrow path of state-sponsored legislation which is demonstrably ineffective as a method for reducing, let alone preventing, VAW. Through exploring these accounts, it is possible to educate and train agencies to ensure that specialist services meet the diverse and particular needs of South Asian women facing violence and abuse. By examining individual stories, research can give voice to the voiceless and provide an impassioned advocacy for those whose experiences are typically ignored: ultimately, large-scale change must derive from learning more about the experiences of individual survivors.

Narratives of sexual abuse and 'unwanted sex'

Although the women interviewed are South Asian, their experiences are not homogenous (Collins 1992): their narratives reveal the uniqueness of their lives as well as reaffirming that there are important common themes in South Asian women's experiences of sexual violence. The stories do not fit traditional narrative patterns because they are spoken from a position of powerlessness: from within communities in which women have little autonomy. The act of telling a story becomes, for these women, a process of sharing survival strategies and presenting the self as a good, or at least morally justified, survivor. As such, their involvement in the research can be said to have therapeutic value.

All five of the narratives deal with the emotional impact that woman suffer after surviving sexual abuse, assault or rape. The women offer very little detail about the actual nature of the sexual violence they suffered, focusing instead on the impact of the assault on themselves and their families. The women all mentioned that they were unable to escape the violence, and that they were compelled to 'take it' since they 'deserved it': testimony that demonstrated their sense of powerlessness as well as their internalisation of patriarchal values. Special care was taken not to use the term 'rape' during the interviews, primarily because the term is not usually spoken in the context of VAW in South Asian communities, as such crimes are usually shrouded in silence. Occasionally probing questions were asked, using the terms that the interviewees themselves employed, such as 'unwanted sex'.

Enabling the women to tell their own stories in this way meant that they were also able to reveal their awareness, both of the violence done to them and the fact that it resulted from the patriarchal values to which they were subjected. The stories' lack of narrative structure is illustrated through the absence of temporal framing, itself a consequence of the nature of the abuse: the unspeakable character of these offences generates a sense of the experience continuing beyond the act itself.

Cultural attitudes towards rape can impact upon a victim's response to this crime, influencing whether or not she seeks help at a refuge or rape crisis centre, for instance, or whether she turns to friends, family, other community members or the state for protection. The concept that most defined the women's responses to rape in this study, and which also dictated how they dealt with the assault, was the notion of 'honour'. One interviewee, Taj Kaur[4] said that she was too frightened to tell her female family members of her abuse because of the question of *izzat*: her socio-cultural background effectively ensured her silence. She feared that disclosure would cause a hostile reaction from her mother and sisters which would ultimately mean that she would be cut off from her family's support. She stated that:

> He literally used to tie me down, my face in the pillow, and he had anal sex with me – he forced me, and there was no way to get out of it. I do not know why he did that. He just wanted to have sex anywhere, and it got to a point where I could not cope with it … I began to hate this person. I used to try to stop him from doing it, but he was just too strong for me. I did not know how to deal with it and I could not tell anyone. What I did know was that my culture did not accept women who left their marriages.
>
> I found it very hard to deal with this violence in my marriage. When it's somebody you make love to and you share every part of your being with him, and that person turns around and hits you, abuses you, it's the most shocking thing. And you know you have to go, logically, but you know that when it's good he makes you feel great and you love him. So you stay 'cause you just want things to be normal. And then he hits you again, and it starts tearing you apart bit by bit. (Taj Kaur)

Although Taj Kaur did not initially used the term 'rape', she did view herself as having suffered acts of 'violence': despite recounting these experiences as instances of physical and mental abuse, Taj Kaur did not initially see this 'forced sex' as marital rape:

> I did not see it that way: I thought it was his right, as I am his wife. But when I spoke to a friend of mine about it and she helped me to see it as rape. You don't think about it until someone tells you that your husband is raping you. (Taj Kaur)

Here the culture of shame and honour – a patriarchal discourse – threatens to overwhelm Taj's own subjective experience of rape. However, it is the speaking of 'rape' that leads to eventual empowerment of women survivors. Women's voices are rarely sanctioned; however, when women are empowered to speak, their stories reveal the scale of VAW.

Another survivor, Zenab, was 'persuaded' to have an 'arranged' marriage at the age of 21 so that her parents could retire to Pakistan. She had been married for only three months when her husband began to abuse her; eventually, this led to her being raped:

> My husband pinned me against the bedroom wall after he'd come back from drinking with friends. I was asleep and wasn't interested in having sex. He dragged me out of bed, pulled my nightdress and put his hands on my neck, beating my head against the wall. He did his stuff and I passed out ... (Zenab)

The physical violence that Zenab endured was frequent and severe. Although her husband, Osman, never beat her in front of his family, they admitted to Zenab that they knew that the assaults were taking place. Like Taj Kaur, Zenab found it hard to see the abuse for what it was, believing that her husband did not mean to hurt her, that he was sorry and that he would never do it again. Despite the severity of the assaults, she was too afraid to report her experiences; perhaps more significantly, she was too *ashamed* to do so. When asked if she had ever considered calling the police, she replied:

> Calling the police to an Asian home – what will the neighbours say? I think I'd have died first. I had this idea of what an Asian wife should be, and being beaten did not fit in. It started to get worse and worse, and I always took him back and accepted the violence as what happens in marriage. But when I couldn't get out of bed 'cause of the violence, that was it: I had to do something ... He beat me at least twice a day. I was constantly covered in bruises from head to toe; always making excuses for my appearance if I had to leave the house. He never gave me a day's peace. And in the end, I just got tired of it and had to get out. (Zenab)

Zenab left her husband after years of sustained physical and sexual abuse, but she did not turn to the authorities for help.

As Zenab's testimony attests, rape victims experience the stigma of shame and dishonour as so threatening that this often hinders their attempts to seek help. South Asian societies have developed ideologies of rape that discredit victims, causing them to be seen as blameworthy (Abraham 1999). There are numerous other cultural influences affecting South Asian women's ability to seek help in response to VAW, including state policies (particularly official immigration policies), the international status of their country of origin and their own diasporic experience, as well as their social class, level of education, employment status and their position within community networks in the UK (Gill and Sharma 2006).

South Asian women's groups have thus long criticised the designation of black, minority and ethnic (BME) communities as 'faith communities', objecting to the state's privileging of male religious figureheads as 'community spokespersons': a practice which reinforces prevailing hierarchies within these communities and ignores the wider range of cultural forces that define the position of women, such as socio-cultural mores that require them to stay in violent marriages (Gupta 2003; Wilson 2006). Recent policies that stress community cohesion have resulted in the closing of specialist domestic violence services for BME women, removing the only accessible route for many South Asian women to seek support to resist coercion and violence within their families and communities (Imkaan 2008).

Research indicates that South Asian women face shared challenges which centre on their function as the 'bearer' of the family's honour. It is this ascribed role which most serves to reinforce existing patriarchal codes and provides justification for the policing of female behaviour (Gill 2004). Socially and culturally constructed notions like shame often make women feel as though they have no choice but to stay in a violent marriage in order to avoid stigmatising their family; more importantly, they must stay in these marriages in order to preserve their own sense of self (Gangoli *et al.* 2006: 11). Such constraints prevent many South Asian women from articulating their experiences of violence and seeking help.

However, although 'honour'-related norms do not always go unchallenged by women in these communities, they are hard to escape. Indeed, women who have left their families because of sexual violence continue to struggle against these norms, often in contradictory and conflicting ways. Women who consistently challenge these dominant societal norms serve as examples for others in their attempts to rebuild their lives (Ahmed *et al.* 2009).

Nevertheless, for some women the struggle is too demanding: many women find it too difficult to leave an abusive relationship and, in so doing, turn their backs on their own society. This reluctance ultimately prevents them from speaking out: they are trapped between their desire to end the violence they experience and their need to preserve the network of support they have built up, and have come to rely upon, in their communities. Take, for example, the case of Rashpal, a 54-year-old woman who lives with her two grown sons and her husband. Despite being abused for over twenty years by her second husband, she feels unable to leave her marriage due to a lack of support. Her words demonstrate her pervading sense of powerlessness:

I was doomed to have a bad life; it was my kismet to be miserable. I am coping with the karma bestowed upon me, the actions of my last life, and I must learn to do things properly so that I don't suffer in the next life. To be a victim of your husband's violence is more than bearable. I have put my faith in God to rid me of my pain I suffer, but he is slow in answering my prayers. (Rashpal)

Though her husband, Darshan, was 'cooperative' at the beginning of their marriage, after they moved to the south of England he began abusing her. She described one event which resulted in her, and her two children, becoming homeless:

When we were living in Manchester, my husband was very violent. I remember one particular night when he came home drunk and started swearing and shouting. He dragged me out of bed by my hair and started kicking and punching me. The next thing I knew he was pouring petrol around the bedroom. I begged him to think of the children. I tried to fight with him and managed to escape out of the bedroom. It was four o'clock in the morning and the house was on fire. We were all very frightened. It was an awful experience. (Rashpal)

I asked Rashpal why her husband tried to burn the house down, and she said: 'Insurance. He wanted money. He did not care about his sons or us. Money ...' She reported that, although her family and friends were fully aware of her predicament, they contended that the violence stemmed from the attitudes of her in-laws and from her own inadequacies as a wife and mother. What might, in other circumstances, be called her support network – her friends and family – even suggested to her son that he should remarry to escape the family home. Rashpal reported that her 'friends and family hide behind clichés' (e.g. 'All Asian men are like this') to justify their inaction, implying that Rashpal was at fault for not being more understanding and tolerant. She also described instances in which they refused to believe her when she spoke out against her abuse, accusing her of exaggeration and advising her 'not to be so sensitive'. As a result, she reported feeling 'mad', 'crazy' and incredibly alone, especially when her family advised her to pray for a mild-tempered husband. Towards the end of the interview, Rashpal said:

> I have lost the will to live. He is so very violent, to the point where he would leave scars on my body. He would kick me in the face or knock me out. When he would hit me, he would say that it was because I started arguing with him. I believed him when he said it was my fault: that I asked for it ... I did not know it was sexual abuse ... But I remember how it made me feel inside: not good – empty and alone. Afterwards he would blame me and say 'you made me do it. If you weren't so mad I would not do this to you.' I believed him. I was hurt by the way he treated me and the words he used to say: 'no one will have you if you leave me. No one loves you as much as me ... You would never be allowed to live in the UK if it was not for me supporting you.' (Rashpal)

Perhaps the most destructive part of this abuse was the emotional hold Rashpal's husband had over her. When she threatened to go to the police, her husband told her that they would send her back to the Punjab:

> He threatened to tell the police that I was illegal. I knew I was not, because I had a British passport, but he told me it could be taken away from me if I questioned his authority. (Rashpal)

A major theme which emerged from the interviews was the concern the women had regarding how disclosing their abuse would affect their families and, particularly, their male relatives. In the case of Daljit, constant abuse led her to contemplate suicide: she could see no way to escape her marriage, especially as she believed that her family would be ruined if she sought a divorce. She stated:

I did not want to do it and my husband wanted and forced me to. And I let him, because I thought, 'well, if I don't, he's going to beat me.' I blame myself for letting it happen to me. I don't know if I should call it sexual abuse or rape. I don't know. It's like there was a time when we were in the first year of marriage and he wanted sex all the time. Just to keep him quiet, I would do what he asked me. I had no choice. I know its rape but I just blank it out of my mind. I didn't want to verbalise what was happening to me because that would make it real. The transformation you go through is so subtle, and so progressive. As a teenager I vowed to myself that I would never let a man hit me. And then, when it happens, you kind of rationalise it, justify it, because you don't want it to be so. I really lost myself, cut myself off from the world outside. I guess I never really, honestly saw myself as a victim. I was so ashamed of my marriage, and suicide was a way out. That is how I saw it at the time. And I still kind of wear the shame that comes with accepting the violence. (Daljit)

She attributed her suicidal inclinations to feelings of being trapped and the concomitant desire to find a way out. She described various ways in which her husband monitored her movements and communication with others, making it virtually impossible for her to confide in anyone and causing her to become severely depressed. She cited fear, shame and self-blame as the main motives for her silence.

Although all of the women interviewed spoke of being forced to have sex by their husbands, their experiences of the assaults themselves were quite diverse. While Rashpal described her assault as being quick in duration and involving little physical force, both Zenab and Taj Kaur's rape experiences were torturous and lasted for hours. Two types of rape were identified: one consisting of non-consensual sex without any form of violence, and the other consisting of non-consensual sex accompanied by violence sustained over a prolonged period. While Rashpal experienced non-consensual sex and 'non-violent' rapes on more than one occasion, she reported that she feared that resistance would lead to violent reprisals by her husband. Zenab, Taj Kaur and Daljit all experienced violence while being raped, resulting in broken bones and bruises. Taj Kaur also remembers violence during her pregnancy:

He punched me in the stomach when I was five months pregnant and I just couldn't believe it. I hadn't done anything to provoke such violence. It was terrible – I actually passed out and my in-laws had to call for an ambulance. (Taj Kaur)

However, Taj Kaur did not tell her in-laws about her husband's abuse, because she did not want to challenge their view of her as a dutiful daughter-in-law. She subordinated her own feelings to the needs of the dominant social order. She was afraid of bringing shame, not only to herself, but also to her relatives. The honour code is so effective in defining social opinion and moral force that women are left with few opportunities to speak about the oppression and violence they experience (Bradby 1999). Taj Kaur summarised the personal and cultural complexities of this situation when she said:

I have never really talked about the violence I have experienced. In our culture you keep these things to yourself. If you get married then it's for life, and you have to take whatever is dished out to you. (Taj Kaur)

The women found different ways to negotiate their experiences, but all of their accounts testified to their resilience. For instance, another interviewee, Harpreet, revealed that she was subjected to a forced marriage[5] within three weeks of her family discovering that she had an 'unsuitable' boyfriend. Although she thought she could cope with the coercive aspect of her parents' involvement in her marriage, the sudden responsibility of looking after a husband she did not love and his family, coupled with the fact that she soon missed her independence and her boyfriend, soon made life intolerable. Within a year of marriage, Harpreet was pregnant, during which time Jeet's temper often exploded into fury. He began throwing food at her when he thought it had not been properly prepared or was not to his taste. He broke dishes and spilled food on the floor and walls, leaving it for her to clean up. He also began to slap her when she defended herself or exercised any independence of thought. Sometimes he would kick or slap her in the stomach when she walked past. When Harpreet went into labour with her first child, Jeet refused to drive her to the hospital, complaining that there was something really important on television, thus forcing her to take a taxi.

The abuse did not stop there, but Harpreet did not report the violence to anyone, nor did she seek outside help of any kind for fear of her life. Although she tried to leave her husband on two occasions, each time he persuaded her to come back:

When I fell pregnant, my husband kicked the crap out of me. Yep, because I should have been 'careful'. I did not know he could be so violent. I did not know he was like this. When he raped me, I just did not know what was going on. Why? I thought becoming a family would make him really happy – it didn't. I tried leaving, but was too scared to go it alone. He was desperate to have me back, so he asked his parents to move out and they did. I still do not know the full story, but it temporarily saved my marriage! But after the birth of my child he became more violent. I was in and out of hospital for months because he forced things inside of me. It messed up my insides. After the final attempt at my life I left: the violence was just getting really bad. (Harpreet)

Societal norms also work to define the abuser as all-powerful and immune to outside intervention (Anitha *et al.* 2008; Chakravarti 2009; Siddique *et al.* 2008). The abuser becomes untouchable, and thus women believe that reporting their abuse only puts them at greater risk. Victims may also be economically and personally dependent on their abusers. In such cases, the victims' need for continued financial support from their abusive spouses makes the risk of disclosure seem too great (Dasgupta 1996). This is especially true for South Asian communities.

Seeking help is a complex process for South Asian women facing gender-based violence (Thiara and Gill 2009). Kelly (2006) argues that it is the quality, consistency and reliability of the responses that abused women receive which has the greatest influence on whether or not they achieve effective outcomes for themselves as well as their families. In practical terms, achieving this requires providing resources for preventative measures and financially securing victim-centred specialist service provisions, many of which are currently under threat from a lack of funding. A more victim-centred approach to supporting South Asian women would avoid treating these women as passive victims and, instead, facilitate their agency. To be effective, such an approach must include processes to:

- establish victim safety, including offering women (and their children) access to specialist support and safe spaces in which to discuss their experiences and express the impact of the violence they have suffered in their own words (Thiara and Gill 2009);

- create support structures and robust multi-agency responses which recognise women's agency (allowing them to make their own choices) and treat them as individuals, thus helping them to address their individual difficulties and to seek a solution fitted to their particular circumstances;

- give women from BME communities the right to citizenship in cases of gender-based violence and recourse to public funds (which are currently denied to women seeking asylum); and

- set up outreach services to implement preventative measures in South Asian communities (Coy *et al.* 2009).

It is vital that efforts to address VAW, especially in South Asian communities, move beyond criminal justice solutions in order to more fully engage with social justice approaches for combating gender-based violence and preventing sexual abuse.

Conclusion

By exploring the intersection between sexual abuse and the rights of women in Britain's South Asian communities, this chapter explores the ways in which survivors cope with the violence in their lives. Socio-cultural expectations, reinforced by conservative religious and patriarchal values, often cause women from these communities to feel unable to challenge these norms: silencing women's voices, and denying them opportunities to speak about their experiences in their own words, denies them opportunities for resisting their subjugation. Disclosure will only increase if condemnation from victims' communities can be reduced or circumvented.

The complexities of the language used to describe rape also offer insights into how sexual abuse is perceived in these communities: this perception plays a major role in both the personal and social effects of rape on victims and their families. The act of speaking about their experiences of sexual violence provides an opportunity for reinterpreting these experiences, allowing survivors to come to terms with their own past powerlessness as a way of gaining power and agency in the present. More flexible and more diverse support systems must be put in place to respond to the needs both of victims/survivors and of those working with vulnerable women. For instance, better screening by hospital/social workers when signs of gender-based violence first become evident is needed; however, enabling women to speak about sexual violence requires specialist training, focused on sensitivity to the nuances of language. Victims/survivors must have access to therapeutic interventions which acknowledge their experiences and listen to the ways in which they name the violence in their lives; these interventions must also respond to those who continue to live with rape and sexual abuse. It is especially important that support services recognise how discourses focused around gender, culture and coercion create a culture of silence, especially in South Asian communities, locking women into violent relationships and hindering their ability to access support services. Increased gender and cultural awareness is needed in order to combat the conditions in which sexual violence originates and to facilitate the provision of aid to victims.

There is limited funding available to help women who choose to remain within their communities when faced with such violence (Imkaan 2008; Southall Black Sisters 2008); in fact, research shows that these women are effectively excluded from current help systems altogether (Horvath and Kelly 2007). If women were offered multiple avenues to access help, public services (such as the NHS and police) might be more effective in supporting minority women across the continuum of need, including those who return to violent relationships. Horvath and Kelly (2007) also suggest that attempts to end VAW by treating it solely as a crime (for instance, by promoting the narrow strategy of a woman's 'right to exit') need to be reconsidered and replaced by a combined criminal and non-criminal judicial response that would support women who are unable or unwilling to leave violent relationships.

The issue of rape and sexual abuse in South Asian communities must be addressed at multiple levels, including via education, a more victim-focused judicial response and institutional change in the health services. According to Heise (1996: 25) 'the most important shift the antiviolence groups could make to improve their effectiveness is to place greater emphasis on primary prevention', which requires changing 'social norms and behaviours that promote violence against women'.

It seems fitting to end with the survivors' own accounts of what needs to be done to address rape and sexual violence in South Asian communities:

Our community needs to know this shit goes on … and something needs to happen to protect women – fast. (Zenab)

There needs to be more awareness, so that we can step out in confidence and say 'it's happening to me' … it hurts me to keep silent about this kind of thing (Taj Kaur).

179

I want to talk about it, but there is no place for me to put it. I can't keep it inside of me anymore, and I need a place to go where I can get support. I want people to hear me. (Rashpal)

I think we need to teach young people that violent abuse is wrong. (Daljit)

If it happens, it is not your fault and you should not be ashamed to ask for support and speak up against the way in which women are treated. (Harpreet)

Notes

1 The term 'South Asian' refers to people born in the Asian subcontinent (i.e. India and Pakistan) and those of South Asian heritage born in Britain. Despite the diversity within the category, it is useful to highlight those aspects of cultural ideology and practice that are predominantly shared among (im)migrant communities originating from the Indian subcontinent, which also share commonalities of political and social history as a result of imperialism, racism, globalisation and the diasporic experience.

2 Research indicates that, within the UK, forced marriage is a problem that affects women originating from the Indian subcontinent, Iran, Afghanistan, Turkey, Armenia, Somalia, Eritrea and Sudan, and also women from Irish traveller communities (Hester *et al.* 2008).

3 These women victims are referred to as 'survivors' in accordance with their own wishes. However, although all the women interviewed identified with this term, some expressed discomfort at being seen exclusively as 'survivors'; for example, one woman felt that the term was problematic as it implied that she had totally recovered from her past victimisation. The terms 'victim' and 'survivor' do not define mutually exclusive categories as recovery from sexual abuse is often a non-linear process (Martin 2005).

4 Pseudonyms were chosen by the interviewees to afford them anonymity.

5 In the context of South Asian communities, early marriage or forced marriage may be regarded as 'normal' given cultural expectations that girls 'should marry young'.

References

Abraham, M. (1999) 'Sexual abuse in South Asian immigrant marriages', *Violence Against Women*, 5 (6): 591–618.

Ahmed, B., Reavey, P. and Majumdar A. (2009) 'Constructions of "culture" in accounts of South Asian women survivors of sexual violence', *Feminism and Psychology*, 19 (1): 7–28.

Anitha, S., Chopra, P., Farouk, W., Haq, Q. and Khan, S. (2008) *Forgotten Women: Domestic Violence, Poverty and South Asian Women with No Recourse to Public Funds*. Manchester: Saheli.

Bradby, H. (1999) 'Negotiating marriage: young Punjabi women's assessment of their individual and family interests', in R. Barot, H. Bradley and S. Fenton (eds), *Ethnicity, Gender, and Social Change*. Basingstoke: Macmillan, pp. 152–66.

Browne, A. (1993) 'Violence against women by male partners: prevalence, outcomes, and policy implications', *American Psychologist*, 48: 1077–87.

Brownmiller, S. (1975) *Against Our Will: Men, Women and Rape*. London: Penguin.

Bunch, C. and Carrillo, R. (1998) 'Violence against women', in N. P. Stromquist (ed.), *Women in the Third World: An Encyclopaedia of Contemporary Issues*. New York and London: Garland, pp. 59–68.

Chakravarti, U. (2009) *The Law as a Horizon: Challenging Impunity, Pursuing Justice*. Paper presented to LASSNET Conference, JNU University, India.

Collins, P. (1992) *Black Feminist Thought*. London: Routledge.

Coy, M., Kelly, L. and Foord, J. (2009) *Map of Gaps: The Postcode Lottery of Violence Against Women Services in Britain*. London: End Violence Against Women.

Crown Prosecution Service (2004) *Policy for Prosecuting Cases of Rape*. London: CPS. Available at http://www.cps.gov.uk/publications/docs/prosecuting_rape.pdf (accessed 4 April 2009).

Dasgupta, S. (1996) 'Private face, private space: Asian Indian women and sexuality', in N. B. Maglin and D. Perry (eds), *Bad Girls, Good Girls: Women, Sex, and Power in the Nineties*. New Brunswick, NJ: Rutgers University Press, pp. 226–47.

Denzin, N. (1989) *Interpretive Interactionism*. Newbury Park, CA: Sage.

Derne, S. (1994) 'Hindu men talk about controlling women: cultural ideas as a tool of the powerful', *Sociological Perspectives*, 37: 203–27.

Gangoli, G. (2007) *Indian Feminisms. Campaigns Against Violence and Multiple Patriarchies*. Aldershot: Ashgate.

Gangoli, G., Razack, A. and McCarry, M. (2006) *Forced Marriage and Domestic Violence Among South Asian Communities in North East England*. Bristol: University of Bristol.

Gill, A. (2004) 'Voicing the silent fear: South Asian women's experiences of domestic violence', *Howard Journal of Criminal Justice*, 43 (5): 465–83.

Gill, A. (2008) '"Crimes of honour" and violence against women in the UK', *International Journal of Comparative and Applied Criminal Justice*, 32 (2): 243–65.

Gill, A. and Sharma, K. (2006) 'Marriage migration in the UK: response and responsibility', in S. Walsum and T. Spijkerboer (eds), *Women and*

Immigration Law: New Variations on Classical Feminist Themes. London: Glass House Press, pp. 183–203.

Gupta, R. (ed.) (2003) *From Homebreakers to Jailbreakers: Southall Black Sisters*. London: Zed Books.

Haven (2008) *Annual Report*. London: Haven.

Hayden, M. and McCarthy, I. (1994) 'Women battering and father–daughter incest disclosure: discourses of denial and acknowledgement', *Discourse and Society*, 5 (4): 543–65.

Heise, L. (1996) 'Health workers: potential allies in the battle against women abuse in developing countries', *Journal of the American Medical Women's Association*, 51 (3): 120–2.

Hester, M., Chantler, K. and Gangoli, G. (2008) *Forced Marriage: The Risk Factors and the Effect of Raising the Minimum Age for a Sponsor, and of Leave to Enter the UK as a Spouse or Fiancé(e)*. Bristol: University of Bristol.

Hester, M., Kelly, L. and Radford, J. (1995) *Women, Violence and Male Power*. Buckingham: Open University Press.

hooks, b. (1991) *Yearning: Race, Gender and Cultural Politics*. London: Turnaround.

Horvath, M. A. H. and Kelly, L. (2007) *From the Outset: Why Violence Should Be a Core Cross-Strand Priority Theme for the Commission for Equality and Human Rights*. London: End Violence Against Women Campaign.

Imkaan (2008) *Celebrating 'Herstory'*. London: Imkaan.

Kandiyoti, D. (1988) 'Bargaining with patriarchy', *Gender and Society*, 2: 274–90.

Kelly, L. (1988) *Surviving Sexual Violence*. Cambridge: Polity Press.

Kelly, L. (1996) 'When does the speaking profit us? Reflections on the challenges of developing feminist perspectives on the use and abuse of violence by women', in M. Hester, L. Kelly and J. Radford (eds), *Women, Violence and Male Power*. Buckingham: Open University Press, pp. 34–49.

Kelly, L. (2006) *Association of London Government: Why Violence Against Women is an Equalities Issue*, Keynote Speech, London, December.

Kvale, S. (1996) *Interviews*. London: Sage.

Martin, P. (2005) *Rape Work: Victims, Gender, and Emotions in Organization and Community Context*. New York: Routledge.

Naffine, N. (2003) 'Who are law's persons? From Cheshire Cats to responsible subjects', *Modern Law Review*, 66 (3): 346–67.

O'Connor, P. (1995) 'Discourse of violence', *Discourse and Society*, 6: 309–14.

Ortner, S. (1978) 'The virgin and the state', *Feminist Studies*, 4: 19–35.

Pagelow, M. (1984) *Family Violence*. New York: Praeger.

Patel, P. (2008) 'Faith in the state? Asian women's struggles for human rights in the UK', *Feminist Legal Studies*, 16: 9–36.

Rape Crisis (2008) *The Crisis in Rape Crisis Report*. England and Wales: Rape Crisis.

Rosenthal, G. (1993) 'Reconstruction of life stories: principles of selection in generating stories for narrative biographical interviews', in R. Josselson and A. Lieblich (eds), *The Narrative Study of Lives*. London: Sage, pp. 113–29.

Siddique, N., Ismail, S. and Allen, M. (2008) *Safe to Return: Pakistani Women, Domestic Violence and Access to Refugee Protection – A Report on a Transnational Research Project Conducted in the UK and Pakistan*. Manchester: South Manchester Law Centre.

Southall Black Sisters (2008) *Stop Ealing Council: Save Southall Black Sisters*. London: Southall Black Sisters.

Thiara, R. (2003) 'South Asian women and collective action in Britain', in J. Andall (ed.), *Gender and Ethnicity in Contemporary Europe*. London: Berg, pp. 79–95.

Thiara, R. and Gill, A. (2009) *Gendered Violence in South Asian Communities in the UK: Issues for Policy and Practice*. London: Jessica Kingsley.

Uberoi, P. (1996) *Social Reform, Sexuality, and the State*. New Delhi: Sage.

Volpp, L. (2000) 'Blaming culture for bad behaviour', *Yale Journal of Law and Humanities*, 12: 89–116.

Welchman, L. and Hossain, S. (eds) (2005) *'Honor' Crimes, Paradigms and Violence Against Women*. London: Zed Press.

Wilson, A. (2006) *Dreams, Questions, Struggles: South Asian Women in Britain*. London: Pluto.

Wood, L. and Rennie, H. (1994) 'Formulating rape: the discursive construction of victims and villains', *Discourse and Society*, 5(1): 125–148.

Chapter 8

Invaded spaces and feeling dirty: women's narratives of violation in prostitution and sexual violence

Maddy Coy

In the act of rape the rapist seizes control of the victim's body, violating the victim's sense of autonomy. The sense of disempowerment is immense. Another person has taken charge of one's body, manipulating it like a puppet, reducing the victim to an object, a prop in that man's world. (Jordan 2008: 180)

In prostitution, the body of the woman, and sexual access to that body, is the subject of the contract. (Pateman 1988: 203)

Introduction

This chapter explores women's accounts of prostitution and sexual violence to highlight how the ontology of selling sex, even without violence, is often experienced as violating and harmful. Material is drawn from life-story interviews and arts workshops with women in prostitution, conducted as part of the author's research on routes into prostitution from local authority care. Key themes that emerged from the interview narratives centred around sense of self and relationship with the body, and the arts workshops were developed in conjunction with a local youth arts team to explore issues such as rape, selling sex, self-harm, unsafe drug practices, shame, guilt and worthlessness in the context of corporeal ontology and an internalised lack of self-value. The two strands of research are pulled together here with a focus on the ontology of violation – on how women experience and interpret their relationships with their bodies with respect both to sexual violence and the sex industry.

While research studies document the prevalence of sexual assault experienced by women who sell sex, intellectual and policy debates continue as to whether prostitution itself constitutes a form of violence (O'Connell Davidson 2002; O'Neill 2001). It is not quite accurate to say that both are distinguished from consensual sex,[1] since women often perceive that they are entering into each commercial sex transaction with some degree of voluntarism even where their overall involvement in prostitution is framed by coercion and desperation. However, the discursive norms of heterosexuality, particularly the masculine sexual 'need' imperative, exert powerful constraints on women's capacity for agency in sexual encounters (Gavey 2005).

At the core both prostitution and sexual violence crystallise struggles for control over the body in women's lived experience, a main concern of feminist theory and research (Arthurs and Grimshaw 1999; Davis 1997). Capacity to maintain control and ownership over the body is embedded in socio-cultural norms and heterosexual hegemony reinforced at multiple levels, such as visual imagery in pornography, the prevalence of sexual violence and a male prerogative to define aesthetically 'desirable' female bodies (Wesely 2002). Prostitution and sexual violence are manifestations of male entitlement to women's bodies and the 'narrow range of possibilities that are culturally weighted toward sex on men's terms' (Gavey 2005: 153). For instance, selling access to the body to strangers allows sex buyers to temporarily own the areas women specify for use (O'Connell Davidson 1998). This disrupted ability to negotiate ownership of the body is framed here as (dis)embodiment and a form of harm (see also Coy 2009). Activities that are associated with prostitution – such as drug use and self-harm – appear only to further undermine corporeal ownership and therefore accentuate (dis)embodiment.

Empirical evidence of links between prostitution and sexual violence

In this chapter sexual violence is defined using Liz Kelly's (1987) notion of a continuum in order to capture the range of experiences that women describe as sexually abusive and invasive. The continuum of sexual violence refers to events that have a common underpinning of male power and entitlement, and are experienced by women in terms of graduation of harm rather than discrete categories (Kelly 1987). Here these events include: childhood sexual abuse; rape in adulthood by family members, partners, pimps, sex buyers and strangers; coercive and unwanted sex in intimate relationships; and sexual harassment by sex buyers and strangers. For some women, commercial sex encounters themselves were defined as ontologically abusive. All who participated in the life-story interviews were under the age of 18 when they began selling sex and therefore, according to statutory definitions, victims of abuse (Department of Health 2000), and all retrospectively framed their entry into prostitution as abusive.

Prostitution is defined following Lee and O'Brien (1995), encompassing the informal transactions women often undertake that may have the same ontological meaning as those based on cash. 'An activity where sexual acts are exchanged for payment. However, payment need not be a monetary transaction but could be a place to stay, something to eat, drugs or other payments in kind' (p. 4).

Childhood sexual abuse as an antecedent to prostitution is globally well-documented (Bagley and Young 1987; Farley *et al.* 2003; O'Neill *et al.* 1995; Silbert and Pines 1981) and features in the lives of women who participated in research reported in this chapter. Such connections between childhood abuse and selling sex are both material and psychosocial: young women may be coerced into selling sex by perpetrators, run away to escape abuse which then renders them vulnerable to exploitation or engage in survival sex that is framed as volition. Thus to draw a straightforward correlation between childhood sexual abuse and subsequent adolescent and/or adult prostitution oversimplifies the complex ways in which abuse and sexualisation embed 'the exchange value of the female sexed body' (Wesely 2002: 1186) in young women's psychological terms of reference.

Research evidence consistently demonstrates the 'common, frequent and pervasive' violence and risk of bodily trauma faced by women who sell sex, from pimps, sex buyers and the general public (Williamson and Folaron 2001: 457; see also Farley *et al.* 2003; Hoigard and Finstad 1992; McKeganey and Barnard 1996; O'Connell Davidson 1998; O'Neill 2001; Phoenix 1999).

One study of 854 women in prostitution in nine countries found that 63 per cent had been raped since entering prostitution. Of particular note is that 63 per cent reported sexual abuse as children (Farley *et al.* 2003). The same proportions of women therefore experienced sexual violence before entry into and during prostitution. Almost a fifth (17 per cent) described severe emotional problems, including suicidal ideation, anxiety, depression and flashbacks (Farley *et al.* 2003). A UK survey of 240 women in three cities found that one in five reported vaginal rape (22 per cent), over a quarter attempted rape (28 per cent), 5 per cent anal rape and 17 per cent forced oral sex from buyers (Church *et al.* 2001). The majority (81 per cent of women) had experienced some form of assault, including physical assault, suggesting that violence is a routine rather than exceptional event (Church *et al.* 2001). There are indications that women selling sex on the streets are more likely to experience physical violence and women indoors sexual violence (Church *et al.* 2001; Raphael and Shapiro 2004). More nuanced research aiming to explore the range of different contexts in which violence against women in prostitution occurs found one in five (21 per cent) of women selling sex on the streets, in their own homes and as escorts had been raped more than ten times (Raphael and Shapiro 2004). For women ever having experienced sexual violence, proportions range from a quarter (23.8 per cent) for exotic dancers, to over two-thirds (66.7 per cent) for women selling sex in drug houses, with an average of almost half (44.9 per cent) across all seven settings (Raphael and Shapiro 2004). Perpetrators included most commonly sex buyers, but also partners, pimps and police, while surveys of men arrested for soliciting offences in the US suggest a higher endorsement of rape myth acceptance among men who regularly paid for sex (Monto and Hotaling 2001). Finally, a study with women selling sex in the Spanish–Portuguese frontier region found similar high levels of violence experienced outside of 'working hours' that significantly contributed to the psychological harm of prostitution (Nixon *et al.* 2002; Ribeiro and Sacramento 2005).

While discussion here focuses on the psychosocial ontology of selling sex itself – the transactional exchange of commercial sex – the mundane prevalence of sexual violence in prostitution forms a critical backdrop to understanding the nature of violation. Sexual (and physical) violence committed against women in prostitution is typically justified by a coding of women who sell sex as inferior and a threat to gendered social norms, a stigma based on transgressing socio-culturally prescribed codes of women's sexual behaviour – as Gail Pheterson notes, the source of disapprobation is the 'many' and the 'money' (Pheterson 1993). Notions of sexual 'deviancy' and 'loose morality' are amplified by myths of women as reservoirs of infection and (in many policy regimes) ambiguous legal status. Yet such violence is often also similarly rationalised in commonsense discourse by its very prevalence, as its sheer likelihood – the clichéd occupational hazard – also 'renders victimisation marginal ... on the basis of their behavioural responsibility' (Richardson and May 2001: 309).[2] Women who sell sex are therefore still too often regarded as legitimate targets of sexual violence because of 'who they are' and 'what they do'. Thus the lived experience of prostitution is for many women typified by a sense of potential and experience of actual harm.

Simple conflation of men who rape and men who buy sex is not the aim of this chapter; rather the intention is to interrogate the meaning of the commercial sex encounter itself for women (Brewis and Linstead 2000) at a psychosocial level. The ways in which the ontology of selling sex is conceptualised and described by women as violation are discussed alongside experiences of sexual violence in order to link similar themes.

How the ontological reality of selling access to the body results in emotional and/or psychological damage is documented in empirical research by Evelina Giobbe (1991), Cecile Hoigard and Liv Finstad (1992), and Melissa Farley (2005) and also explored by Kathleen Barry (1995) and Sheila Jeffreys (1997). Here women's accounts of prostitution highlight high levels of emotional distress, disruption to relationships with the body and intimate sexual relations despite the use of dissociative techniques to manage commercial sex encounters. Farley concludes that 'although the physical violence of prostitution is brutal and pervasive, it pales into comparison to the emotional trauma' (2005: 960). Evelina Giobbe (1991) draws direct parallels between selling sex and being raped, as described by one woman in her oral history project: 'Prostitution is like rape. It's like when I was 15 years old and I was raped. I used to experience leaving my body ... And while I was a prostitute I used to do that all the time ... I don't know how else to explain it except that it felt like rape. It was rape to me.' (Giobbe 1991: 144).

A recent study also suggests experiential links between prostitution and sexual violence – Campbell et al. (2003), who interviewed 102 women raped as adults, found three-quarters of those involved in prostitution (n = 24) directly attributed this to the rape. Reclaiming control over access to the body was frequently cited as a motivation for beginning to sell sex post the rape experience (Campbell et al. 2003). The same study found higher levels of psychological harm experienced by adult rape survivors who had engaged in prostitution following the rape than those who had not engaged in prostitution (Campbell et al. 2003).

Legacies of sexual violence and prostitution are also inflected by differences in occurrence. While sexual abuse in childhood is often an ongoing sequence of events, sexual violence in adulthood may also refer to single or repeated incidents and varying types of assaults. The cumulative impact may therefore compound levels of violation or alternatively normalise it. As a result of multiple experiences of assault, women may develop coping mechanisms that enable them to survive both further abuse and selling sex. I draw on women's accounts of violence preceding entry into and during prostitution, both single and systematic experiences, with the aim of unpicking some of the psychosocial commonalities that indicate levels of harm. Commonalities are evident in women's accounts, cutting across frequency of incidents perceived to be sexually violating. In this context, conceptualising rape as a single event limits understanding of the impact (Jordan 2008; Kelly 1988; Wasco 2003). As Wasco (2003: 313) suggests: 'For some victims, rape may confirm assumptions that violence is a routine part of their lives or that they do not have sexual control over their lives. The damage to these survivors may be more pervasive than a single act of rape.'

Where women experienced selling sex itself to be abusive, the damage to their sense of self and relationship with the body was clearly more pervasive than a single act, since all who participated in the research were involved in 'full-time' prostitution and thus engaging in several commercial transactions per day.

Understanding legacies of abuse beyond the impact of the actual events enables another factor that negatively affects psycho-social welfare to be explored – stigmatisation and being marked as 'different' – also invoked by childhood sexual abuse (Finkelhor and Browne 1985, cited in Gilfus 1999), rape (Jordan 2008) and, as noted earlier, prostitution (O'Neill 2001; Pheterson 1993). Although the focus of this chapter is primarily on the body, women's narratives show that poor self-image and/or a sense of social inferiority contribute to their capacity to maintain a healthy relationship with their embodied identity.

Tracing women's experiences

This chapter draws on a study carried out from 2002 to 2006 that explored routes into prostitution from local authority care, and in doing so highlighted a sense of ownership of the body as both precursor and central to experiences of selling sex. Methodologically the research used a combination of life-story interviews and participatory arts workshops, building on the extensive and pioneering work of Maggie O'Neill (2001; O'Neill and Campbell 2001; O'Neill *et al.* 2002) in this respect. This feminist participatory action approach offers multiple accessible ways for women to represent their lived experiences (O'Neill 2001; O'Neill *et al.* 2002), and aimed to facilitate understandings of the connections between material circumstances and psychosocial lived experience: 'As a "renewed methodology", combining life stories and artistic representation can transgress conventional or traditional ways of analysing and representing research data' (O'Neill *et al.* 2002: 69).

During the period of the research I was employed at a specialised outreach project for women in the sex industry, and as such the findings also reflect my privileged ethnographic role in the everyday lives of women in prostitution (see also Coy 2006). Combining narratives and ethnography allows researchers to see patterns in the narratives and observe the details that cannot be articulated verbally. As Pink (2001: 45) notes: 'Ethnography may be part of researcher's everyday interactions. There may be a continuous flow of information and objects between the ethnographer and informants. This might include the exchange of images, of ideas, emotional and practical exchanges and support, each of which is valued in different ways.'

My observation and interpretation of the women's actions surrounding drug use and accompanying bodily deterioration, self-harm, poor self-care and injuries (Epele 2001), allowed insights into the women's relationships with their selves and bodies that were fundamental to the development of analytic frameworks.

Over 40 women with diverse experiences of sexual violence and selling sex participated in arts workshops on the theme of 'MyBody MySelf', developed in conjunction with a local youth arts team and facilitated by an arts worker who had similar experience with women in the sex industry (see O'Neill and Campbell 2001). Women were recruited through my outreach contact and through a specialised project for sexually exploited young women, and workshops took place at a range of venues including flats, saunas, the mobile outreach vehicle and drop-ins in the street soliciting area. Some women worked individually with the arts worker for a number of sessions to finalise their image. The images were created using digital photography that was overlaid with text written either by the women (i.e. their own poetry) or evoked by discussions with women during production. The theme of relationship with body and self emerged from the life-story interviews; although eight women ultimately produced the final 11 images in conjunction with the local arts team, some drew on ideas and experiences expressed by several women in interviews and arts workshops, lending richness to all the images. 'MyBody MySelf: Getting Under the Skin' ran as an exhibition in the Midlands during early 2004, to critical local acclaim.

Fourteen women aged between 17 and 33 participated in the life-story interviews.[3] All had histories of local authority care and were selling sex on the streets by 16 years of age, although at the time of the research three women had moved to indoor prostitution. Half the women were initially coerced into prostitution by pimps and peers, while half drifted into selling sex through association within the 'prostitution subculture' (Häkkinen 1999). Most had had multiple experiences of disadvantage and vulnerability – using drugs and/ or alcohol; homelessness; domestic violence; physical abuse, neglect, abandonment by parents/carers. Ten women disclosed experiences of sexual violence. Two were raped by their stepfathers during adolescence, three were abused from infancy by family members or friends and three women described rape in adulthood. Another two referred to sexual abuse without giving further details. In terms of experiences of prostitution, of the women who were identified as solely involved in street prostitution, there was some variation between older women who drifted between escort work, working from home and street work to top up their income, and younger women who were particularly chaotic in terms of drug use and accommodation and found themselves confined to the ghettos of street soliciting areas. While acknowledging that the women who participated represent extreme vulnerability, their experiences resonate with national and international research on the backgrounds of women in prostitution (Farley *et al.* 2003; Hoigard and Finstad 1992; O'Neill 2001; Phoenix 1999).

All interviews were taped and transcribed (with permission) and analysed using Doucet and Mauthner's (1998) voice-centred relational ontology technique. This employs several readings of narratives to identify the story, including key events and researcher responses, for finding the voice of the 'I', how women use personal pronouns and see themselves, giving insights into their perception of agency and social positioning, for relationships and finally for structural and social factors. This method of data analysis reflected the theoretical and epistemological approach of the research, to hear women's accounts embedded in their own terms of references and relational contexts (Doucet and Mauthner 1998).

Templates of (dis)embodiment

Collectively, women's accounts reveal a wide range of experiences of violence and abuse. Elsewhere I have identified that women develop an experiential template of the body from abuse and applied phenomenologist Merleau-Ponty's (1962) notion of the 'habit body' as an explanatory framework (Coy 2009). The 'habit body' enables exploration of the ways in which women absorb messages about their autonomy of the body and develop a corporeal knowledge that forms the basis of their sense of self and embodied behaviours. For most of the women who participated, the habit body was constituted by a regime of violence that afforded them a minimal sense of ownership of their bodies (Coy 2009). Two women (JC and Christina) said that seeking to overcome this lack of ownership, aiming to reinstate autonomy over who had access to their body, was part of the reason they began to sell sex. Campbell *et al.* (2003) also identify that half of the women in their study who entered prostitution after being raped in adulthood (n = 10) cited a need to control access to the body as motivation. Another four described prostitution as an activity that confirmed their sense of worthlessness. For JC and Christina, selling sex was perceived as a source of personal and social power, while they also revealed ambivalence about maintaining control with respect to the threat of violence. An image created by Julie and Helen, both selling sex in a massage parlour, shows the words 'I have strong limits and boundaries – it's my body and I'm in control' yet goes on 'some days you feel guilty and dirty'. These contradictory paths between vulnerability and empowerment can also be traced throughout women's narratives here.

Some of the discussion and division between perspectives on prostitution rests on whether women are selling access to their body or parts of their body or simply selling (dis)embodied sexual services (Chapkis 1997). For instance, sexual acts such as masturbation do not rely on entry to the body which is simplistically taken to represent the corporeal violation of prostitution. However, despite this less invasive aspect, women's bodies (hands and possibly breasts as visual stimulation) are still serving as instruments for men's sexual satisfaction. This instrumentality can still be an element of objectification (Nussbaum 1995) and was not differentiated from penetration by women in either autobiographical narratives or arts workshops. The notion that women sell only sexual services also implies a disembodied self where selling access to parts of the body does not compromise this selfhood (Pateman 1988) and is central to perspectives that regard selling sex as a form of employment like any other (Brewis and Linstead 2000; see also O'Connell Davidson 2002). However, the narratives here demonstrate that despite strategies to distance the self from the 'bought body', women across various prostitution settings experience the commercial sex encounter as inherently dependent on the use of their bodies, specifically how buyers demand that their bodies be in terms of positioning and, for some, shape and size. Discourses of male entitlement to women's bodies underpin this; as Gavey (2005: 141) notes, 'their bodies/their selves became objectified as they acted under a sense of obligation – to be the body/the woman that they understood their partner [here sex buyers] wanted and expected'.

In terms of sexual violence, extensive research highlights complex psychosocial legacies, including depression, anxiety, self-harm and alienation from the body (Church 1997; Herman 1997; Jordan 2008; Kelly 1988). The diagnostic category of post-traumatic stress disorder (PTSD) has been widely used to capture the range of mental health consequences. The Farley *et al.* (2003) study, mentioned earlier, found 68 per cent of women in prostitution in nine countries met the diagnostic criteria for PTSD. While useful to shift blame from victim-survivors and acknowledge the severity of impact, PTSD has been critiqued for limiting understandings to narrow individual medical symptoms and thus obscuring the gendered social context of violence against women (Gilfus 1999; Herman 1997; Wasco 2003). A broader conceptualisation encompasses the often intangible emotional and psychological consequences, including impacts on relationships with others, sense of safety in the world and recovery processes following the actual assault that enable victim-survivors to rebuild their lives (see Jordan 2008). The experiences of women reported here demonstrate that an additional key consequence is (dis)embodiment – a lack of ownership and belonging both of and in the body.

In the women's narratives, the ontology of violation can be traced through the themes of intrusion, corporeal dissociation and ownership of the body. The following sections explore each in turn.

Intrusion

The notion of intrusion into the body features in accounts of women's experiences of sexual violence prominently, but is more nuanced – not less present – in women's narratives of selling sex. Rarely discussed in analyses of commercial sex transactions are the kinaesthetic realities for women. The artificial intimacy (often deliberately created in indoor settings[4]) means not just a stranger's penis/fingers entering the vagina, anus or mouth, but a stranger's fingers/tongue touching, stroking the skin, a stranger looking, judging, perhaps commenting on the curves of the body, a stranger's flesh brushing against and weighing upon the body, the smell and sounds of a stranger lingering along with invisible, indelible fingerprints. Exercises of dissociation, skills to ensure brevity of the sexual act or substances to numb the mind cannot always erase the sensitivity or memory of the skin. The regularity of this multifaceted penetration for women who sell sex was used as justification in a notorious 1991 Australian rape case where the judge decreed that 'chaste' women would be more distressed by forced sex than women accustomed to multiple sexual partners, including many strangers (Scutt 1994). This edict was based on the false assumption that rape would be less frightening or intrusive for women in prostitution. However, in the research reported in this chapter, women's accounts of selling sex were characterised by fear and corporeal management of invasion and shame:

> It made me feel cheap and dirty ... you just can't bear anyone to touch you, but you just have to. (Lisa, 21)

> ... you're lying there naked so you're totally exposed to this person who's on top of you ... and they touch you in a sensitive way and it'll just make you feel sick ... And then you're there cringing. (Dee, 26)

These excerpts mirror women's accounts of sexual abuse and violence, but in the latter intrusion was more immediate and visceral. One young woman created an image in the arts workshops that (re)presented reporting rape to the police. The image depicts underwear sealed in police evidence bags, labelled with anonymous descriptions of each item, superimposed with a speculum – the instrument of medical vaginal examinations. Across the bottom Lynn says:

> When I was raped, I had to give my clothes to the police and they put them into plastic bags. I felt dirty and ashamed. I scrubbed myself raw in the bath afterwards.

She highlights both feeling dirty and violated, and becoming an object, where her own identity is lost in being a vessel of sexual release and, later, a source of potential evidence.[5] Intrusion is multilayered.

Another account of abusive sexual experiences reveals:

> [The first time] it was horrible. It was the first time I'd ever had like proper sex. I'd been raped and that, so I'd lost my virginity, but it was the first time I'd ever willingly gone and had sex, with a punter. (Becky, 17)

What is interesting about Becky's narrative is that she distinguishes between her experiences of being raped as evidence that she is no longer a 'virgin' but she identified her first commercial sex encounter as 'willingly gone and had "proper" sex', despite that fact that she was coerced into this act by her pimp. Becky is unable to recognise the abusive dimension of her initial involvement in prostitution, but is aware of the discourses that conflate selling sex with consent (Ayre and Barrett 2000) and also demonstrates an awareness of the ways in which women who have been sexually abused are regarded as 'impure' and 'fallen' (Lees 1993). In this way, the foundation for her sexual experience and embodied sex object identity was formed by the lack of control over how her body is used by others and her concomitant lack of ownership. In her conceptualisation, Becky's body becomes a sex object that is socioculturally othered by transgression from feminine norms of monogamy (Lees 1993). However, by framing selling sex as voluntary – and later in her narrative as rewarding albeit only financially – she demonstrates that she moved from viewing her body as an object to 'something it can do' (Budgeon 2003). Her body becomes useful, fulfilling a function that fits with her perceived 'habit body' of sexualisation. Similar themes featured in accounts of women interviewed by Campbell *et al.* (2003) to conceptualise their entry into prostitution following rape. That selling sex was enabled to seem meaningful as a consequence of sexual violence indicates that both perpetuate objectification and violation (Coy 2008).

Another young woman, Jessica, created images depicting nightmares about feeling that sex buyers' bodies were crushing her and drowning her in pools of blood representing corporeal and psychological intrusion. In her words:

> thinking it's real ... hearing ... breathing ... getting in a car ... dreaming of men's faces ... on top ... menacing ... too scared to sleep ... crying ... men's faces ... men's faces ... dreaming ... nightmares ... drowning ... crying ... men's faces ... bad dreams ... drowning ... breathing in a pool of blood ... bad dreams ... IT WILL STICK IN YOUR MIND FOREVER (Jessica, 17)

This description mirrors those by women following rape (see Jordan 2008), yet Jessica regarded herself as selling sex from her own volition and in control of each encounter. However, the arts workshops prompted her to explore the impact on her psycho-social welfare, ultimately leading her to reflect on the abusive dimension of her involvement in prostitution that she had previously minimised.[6]

Finally, one woman described her foster father as having made sexually inappropriate advances towards her when she was 15 years old, and linked this to a sense of invasion that she struggled to name as abusive.

> Don't forget I was 15, basically I've the body I've got now, but younger and more oomph [pause] and the husband was kind of – I don't know. Yeah, I do know actually, now that I'm older I do. He wasn't touching me, but he was sexually [pause while thinking] invading my space without touching me if you know what I mean. Making kind of comments and this that and the other and kind of things. (Dee, 26)

This sense of sexual intrusion represents a colonisation of personal space well documented in experiences and fear of violence (Jordan 2008; Kelly 1988; Valentine 1989), and was also perceived by many women to be integral to selling sex. Although women developed strategies to minimise space invasion (such as not kissing on the grounds of intimacy), managing corporeal closeness during commercial sex encounters and the vigilance required to monitor threats of assault featured strongly in the narratives, as expressed above by Jessica, Lisa and Dee. The constancy of intrusion and invasion led to women developing dissociative techniques, many originating in sexually abusive experiences and/or enabling women to survive sexual violence in prostitution.

Dissociation

An overwhelming feature of the women's accounts of selling sex was the separation of self from body and the need to distance the thinking, feeling self from the physical body. As a coping mechanism, this enabled women to remain calm throughout each commercial sex encounter. Hatty (1992) notes that dissociation functions as 'an enabling attitude, an adaptive device which allows prostitute women to engage in intimate activities without risking the disintegration of the self' (p. 79). Here, as women talked about 'pretending that it wasn't happening' to describe both physical and sexual violence, the processes of distancing from the body became an automatic response, fully integrated into the 'habit body' (Merleau-Ponty 1962).

For several women dissociative mechanisms developed to manage childhood sexual abuse were also reflected in their corporeal management in prostitution. For instance, Stacey describes herself as 'pretending it weren't happening to me, like I was somewhere else' during abuse in childhood. Stacey's first sexual experience was perceived as consensual intercourse at 10 years old and she was raped by a stranger when she was 12. She subsequently describes her coercion into selling sex and the process of normalisation:

After a couple of weeks I'd just got used to it. (Stacey 25)

It seems surprising to Stacey that she adjusted to the reality of selling sex so quickly, but the years of abuse she experienced had created within her the psychological landscape that normalised physical and sexual use of her body through the appropriation by others and caused her to dissociate from her body. Dissociation is well documented in research literature as a response to sexual violence (Herman 1997; Jordan 2008; Kelly 1988; Wasco 2003). As Scott (2001: 177) notes: 'Survivors of sexual abuse often describe a disconnection or dissociation such that the "true" self can describe incidents of abuse from a physical and emotional distance. The child's sense of believing "this isn't happening to me" may go on to develop into a profound alienation from the life of the body.'

The formative events of some women's lives led to the development of what Maria Epele (2001: 165) has termed 'estrangement of bodily experiences'. This separation of the body from the self leads to women defining their bodies as beyond their control, as a site where things 'are done to' them.

Techniques to negotiate this ranged from substance misuse to differentiating the work- self/home-self using a range of techniques such as bodily zoning[7] – pseudonyms, wearing costumes, the use of condoms, not allowing kissing or certain sexual acts which are retained for intimate, personal sex (Edwards 1993; Sanders 2005). The prevalence of illicit drug use among the women who participated (all 14 used heroin and/or crack cocaine) suggests that they were seeking ways to dissociate beyond psychological processes in favour of sensory deprivation and consciousness alteration.

> My first punter, I drank a whole bottle of vodka. It's ridiculous really, the things you do to push it out. At one stage I was taking cocaine that bad, you wouldn't believe, just to get me through the night ... I was just doing it every day to keep my mind off what I was doing ... It's ridiculous really, the things you do to push it out. (Jackie, 19)

> At first it made me feel degraded but now I just switch off. Pretend I'm not there. (Christina, 21)

Thirteen women reported that they began using drugs as a means to manage the ontology of selling sex, enabling them to 'block out' commercial sex encounters but simultaneously trapping them in prostitution to generate income to pay for the drugs.

Self-harm was also a prominent feature of women's narratives, manifested by diverse means such as cutting, repeated (but not life-threatening) overdoses and attempted asphyxiation by hanging. In terms of relationships with their bodies, women explicitly linked self-harm to abusive experiences, including prostitution itself (see also Coy 2009; Jordan 2008). Self-harm therefore operated as an embodied narrative of violation (Shaw 2002), and indicates that dissociative strategies (drug use, segmenting the body to sell access to parts of the body, or separating the emotional self from the physical in the commercial exchange) were rarely successful. The chapter turns now to exploring how dissociation segues into a lack of ownership over the body.

Ownership

Parallels between selling sex and experiences of sexual violence are particularly acute in terms of women's sense of ownership of their bodies. Exploring this is an essential element of a psychosocial landscape of women's involvement in prostitution since selling sex requires allowing strangers access to the 'power of command' over the body (O'Connell Davidson 1998). This physical power of command operates in different ways: purchasing specific sexual acts means that the buyer defines the acts that women's bodies perform and defining the use of the body enables buyers to exercise manipulation of the body. At a symbolic level, the command of ownership can represent to the women that they are commodities, objects to be bought and exchanged: 'To make a living from prostitution, it is necessary to surrender control over whom to have sex with, and how and when' (O'Connell Davidson 1996: 193).

Carole Pateman (1988) also observed that prostitution is unique in the investment of the self that is required due to the dynamic between sexuality, the body and sense of self. The experiences of women drawn on in this chapter support Pateman's analysis, as they talked of every part of their bodies being bought many times a day, day after day, and struggling to retain a sense of sovereignty. Women who participated in both arts workshops and life story narratives viewed their bodies as commodities. In a similar vein, accounts from men who pay for sex demonstrate they locate women as objects in the commercial sex exchange through viewing women as instruments for their sexual release, interchangeable and without individual selfhood (Coy 2009). Margaret Radin's (1996) notion of 'contested commodities', where certain attributes are defined as commodities in conditions of subordination and inequality, meaning that the basis of the exchange is oppressive, is useful here. Radin notes that 'objectification comes about through commodification when our cultural rhetoric conceives of certain attributes of the persons as commodities that can be bought and sold' (1996: 156). Developing this to explore women's narratives of corporeal commodification, the location of the sex industry in the wider gender inequality renders such objectification harmful by framing women and women's bodies 'as means of lesser personhood' (1996: 157). One woman created an arts image that reflected her awareness of this, highlighting how stigmatisation led to others affording her little sovereignty over her body or respect for its boundaries:

I am fragile, I am a person too, when you touch me it hurts, I am breakable. (Gemma, 31)

Pain and harm here are located not just in violence, but also in the very touch of strangers who are paying for the sexual use of her body.

For many women objectification and a lack of ownership appear to be both preconditions of the 'habit body' to selling sex and (dis)embodied realities. Sense of ownership of the body depended on experiential knowledge of how the body became understood as under or out of women's control (Budgeon 2003). Dee commented that following a serious attack she learned that she was 'never in control'. Events that deny women's boundaries of the body – rape and other forms of physical and sexual assault – destroy coherent corporeal ownership. Women's descriptions of the incidents and regimes of abuse they survived as children form their experiential templates of (dis)embodiment (Coy 2009).

For instance, Wendy, a 19-year-old young woman talked about the psychosocial impact of childhood sexual abuse in terms of rejecting her body:

> I hate my body ... He liked my body and so I cover it up with jumpers and trousers ... I deserved it.

Michelle's narrative contained detail about behaviours of shame in her own adolescent self when she expressed concern over a female relative that was in contact with her abuser:

> I'm worried cos she's started covering up her body, hiding her body, just like I did. (Michelle 22)

Hannah, who had become involved in a sexual relationship with a much older man at 13 and began selling on the streets at 15, described the impact of sexual violence explicitly in terms of a contested bodily tenure:

> My body's not special anymore, not since everyone got their fingers all over it. (Hannah 21)

Thus their psychosocial landscapes at the time of their entry into selling sex were inflected by a lack of ownership of their bodies. This was also reflected in depictions of commercial sex. One woman, who had been involved in the sex industry for twenty years, described her sense of (dis)embodiment thus:

> Sometimes I feel I am just a hole for men to use. (Tammy, 35)

At the time of the arts project, she was selling sex indoors, in a stable relationship and considered prostitution to be the only source of income that enabled her to have a standard of living that included designer clothes and luxury holidays. Tammy would, to all outward appearances, be described as making a choice to sell sex without any coercive pressures. This provides a starting point to explore the interlinked psychosocial dimensions of selling sex that are narrated by women who describe capacity to 'choose' and those at the most acute end of vulnerability with multiple needs compounding the actuality of each commercial sex encounter. Even as the embodiment of 'agency', Tammy's ontology of prostitution is characterised by ambivalence about her sense of self and clear negativity about her body, in short a disruption to her integrated embodied identity. She identifies herself as reduced to 'just a hole', a powerful message about how the ontology of prostitution is harmful to women's bodies, minds and relationships.

Conclusion

Strategies that women develop and adopt to manage commercial sex encounters and sexual violence, discussed throughout this chapter, demonstrate coexistent manifestations of harm and resilience (see also Jordan 2008; Kelly 1988). However, accounts of both sexual violence and prostitution reveal that psychological landscapes of self-identity are damaged by the intrusive reduction of their personhood to a vagina, anus and mouth. The practice of dissociation reflects this absence of self – I am only my body; my body does not belong to me; I do not belong to myself. The ontological reality of selling sex appears, for the women who participated in the research reported here, to have correlations with trauma caused by experiences of rape and sexual abuse. Emotional and psychosocial responses associated with sexual violence – shame, guilt, hating the body, blame and alienation – were identical to those women revealed when discussing the ontology of commercial sex encounters. Thus women's accounts demonstrate that selling sex is experienced as harm even without violence and coercion, characterised by a sense of intrusion, dissociation and (dis)embodiment.

Notes

1 Julia O'Connell Davidson (2005) argues that demarcation between commercialised sex and intimate heterosex obscures the economic and emotional exchanges in relationships in contexts of social inequality. Here I make the point that women's experiences within (predominantly) street prostitution and of abuse/violence are, at least in their narratives, distinguished from their intimate relationships in terms of psycho-social ontology. This does not imply that women did not also experience coercion and abuse in personal relationships – a significant number did – but that their narratives frame regimes and/or incidents of violence and the commercial sex encounter as qualitatively different from their

intimate relationships. This may not be the case in other samples of women in prostitution.

2 Locations such as street soliciting areas are spatially determined as dangerous and contribute to this sense of women's culpability (O'Connell Davidson 2005).

3 For various reasons, none of the women who participated in the life-story interviews also created the final images, although some of the women participated in early stages of the arts project. There is, however, considerable overlap in experiential terms between how women describe the self and the body in the interviews and the images.

4 For instance, women talked about the performance of sex and romance in indoor settings, creating a 'mock date' scenario that required them to be both intimate and impersonal. As Bernstein (2001) notes, 'the fact that street prostitution now constitutes a marginal and declining sector of the sex trade means that a transaction that has been associated with quick, impersonal "sexual release" is increasingly being superseded by one which is configured to encourage the fantasy of sensuous reciprocity' (p. 402).

5 In the investigating protocol, Lynn's body is not attached to her sense of self and subjectivity, but is the repository of forensic and physical evidence whose quality is judged on the ability to secure a conviction (Lees 2002).

6 Through participation in the arts project, Jessica acknowledged an abusive dimension to selling sex that she consistently denied when engaging with the various professionals who were attempting to support her. Instead she had always focused on the empowering and necessary aspects of prostitution, and this rendered it difficult for the adults around her to address the physical and emotional damage she was experiencing or encourage her to withdraw from prostitution. This points to the potential benefits of arts work to enable women to both represent their lived experience and as a therapeutic intervention.

7 This refers to the demarcation of various zones of the body as available for use in the commercial sex encounter, i.e. allowing genital touching but not breasts/face (Sanders 2005).

References

Arthurs, J. and Grimshaw, J. (1999) 'Introduction', in J. Arthurs and J. Grimshaw (eds), *Women's Bodies: Discipline and Transgression*. London: Cassell, pp. 1–16.

Ayre, P. and Barrett, D. (2000) 'Young people and prostitution: an end to the beginning', *Children and Society*, 14: 48–59.

Bagley, C. and Young, L. (1987) 'Juvenile prostitution and child sexual abuse: a controlled study', *Canadian Journal of Community Mental Health*, 6: 5–26.

Barry, K. (1995) *The Prostitution of Sexuality*. New York: University Press.

Bernstein, E. (2001) 'The meaning of the purchase: desire, demand and the commerce of sex', *Ethnography*, 2 (3): 389–420.

Brewis, J. and Linstead, S. (2000) '"The worst thing is the screwing": (1) consumption and the management of identity in sex work', *Gender, Work and Organization*, 7 (2): 84–97.

Budgeon, S. (2003) 'Identity as an embodied event', *Body and Society*, 9 (1): 37–57.

Campbell, R., Ahrens, C., Sefl, T. and Clark, M. (2003) 'The relationship between adult sexual assault and prostitution: an exploratory analysis', *Violence and Victims*, 15 (3): 299–317.

Chapkis, W. (1997) *Live Sex Acts: Women and Commercial Sex*. London: Routledge.

Church, S. (1997) 'Ownership and the body', in D. Tietjens Meyers (ed.), *Feminists Rethink the Self*. Oxford: Westview Press, pp. 85–103.

Church, S., Henderson, M., Barnard, M. and Hart, G. (2001) 'Violence by clients towards female prostitutes in different work settings: questionnaire survey', *British Medical Journal*, 322: 524–5.

Coy, M. (2006) 'This morning I'm a researcher, this afternoon I'm an outreach worker: ethical dilemmas in practitioner research', *International Journal of Social Research Methodology: Theory and Practice*, 9 (5): 419–32.

Coy, M. (2008) 'The consumer, the consumed and the commodity: women and sex buyers talk about objectification in prostitution', in V. Munro and M. Della Giusta (eds), *Demanding Sex: Critical Reflections on the Regulation of Prostitution*. Aldershot: Ashgate, pp. 181–98.

Coy, M. (2009) 'This body which is not mine: the notion of the habit body, prostitution and dis(embodiment)', *Feminist Theory*, 10 (1): 61–75.

Davis, K. (1997) 'Embodying theory: beyond modernist and postmodernist readings of the body', in K. Davis (ed.), *Embodied Practices: Feminist Perspectives on the Body*. London: Sage, pp. 1–26.

Department of Health (2000) *Safeguarding Children Involved in Prostitution: Supplementary Guidance to Safeguarding Children*. London: HMSO.

Doucet, A. and Mauthner, N. (1998) *Voice, Reflexivity and Relationships in Qualitative Data Analysis*. Background paper for workshop on 'Voice in Qualitative Data Analysis'. Available online at: http://www.coe.uga/edu/quig/proceedings/Quig98_proceedings/doucet_mauthner.html (accessed 6 August 2007).

Edwards, S. S. M. (1993) 'Selling the body, keeping the soul: sexuality, power, theories and realities of prostitution', in S. Scott and D. Morgan (eds), *Body Matters: Essays on the Sociology of the Body*. London: Falmer Press, pp. 89–104.

Epele, M. (2001) 'Excess, scarcity and desire among drug-using sex workers', *Body and Society*, 7: 161–79.

Farley, M. (2004) 'Bad for the body, bad for the heart: prostitution harms women even if legalised or decriminalised', *Violence Against Women*, 10 (10): 1087–125.

Farley, M. (2005) 'Prostitution harms women even if indoors: reply to Weitzer', *Violence Against Women*, 11: 950–64.

Farley, M., Cotton, A., Lynne, J., Zumbeck, S., Spiwak, F., Reyes, M. E., Alvarez, D. and Sezgin, U. (2003) 'Prostitution and trafficking in nine countries: an update on violence and post-traumatic stress disorder', *Journal of Trauma Practice*, 2: 33–74.

Gavey, N. (2005) *Just Sex? The Cultural Scaffolding of Rape*. London: Routledge.

Gilfus, M. E. (1999) 'The price of the ticket: a survivor-centred appraisal of trauma theory', *Violence Against Women*, 5 (11): 1238–57.

Giobbe, E. (1991) 'Prostitution: buying the right to rape', in A. Wolbert Burgess (ed.), *Rape and Sexual Assault III: A Research Handbook*. New York: Garland, pp. 143–60.

Häkkinen, A. (1999) 'Clients of prostitutes – an historical perspective on Finland', in L. Keeler and M. Jyrkinen (eds), *Who's Buying? The Clients of Prostituion*. Helsinki: Council for Equality, Ministry of Social Affairs and Health, pp. 13–24.

Hatty, S. E. (1992) 'The desired object: prostitution in Canada, United States and Australia', in S. Gerull and B. Halstead (eds), *Sex Industry and Public Policy*. Proceedings of a Conference held 6–8 May 1991. Canberra: Australian Institute of Criminology. Available online at: http://www.aic. gov.au/publications/proceedings/14/hatty.pdf (accessed 6 August 2007).

Herman, J. (1997) *Trauma and Recovery: The Aftermath of Violence from Domestic Abuse to Political Terror*. New York: Basic Books.

Hoigard, C. and Finstad, L. (1992) *Backstreets: Prostitution, Money and Love*. Cambridge: Polity Press.

Jeffreys, S. (1997) *The Idea of Prostitution*. Melbourne: Spinifex Press.

Jordan, J. (2008) *Serial Survivors: Women's Narratives of Surviving Rape*. Sydney: Federation Press.

Kelly, L. (1987) 'The continuum of sexual violence', in J. Hanmer and M. Maynard (eds), *Women, Violence and Social Control*. Basingstoke: Macmillan, pp. 46–60.

Kelly, L. (1988) *Surviving Sexual Violence*. Cambridge: Polity Press.

Lee, M. and O'Brien, R. (1995) *The Game Is Up: Redefining Child Prostitution*. London: Children's Society.

Lees, S. (1993) *Sugar and Spice: Sexuality and Adolescent Girls*. London: Penguin.

Lees, S. (2002) *Carnal Knowledge: Rape on Trial*. London: Women's Press.

McKeganey, N. and Barnard, M. (1996) *Sex Work on the Streets*. Buckingham: Open University Press.

Merleau-Ponty, M. (1962) *Phenomenology of Perception*. London: Routledge.

Monto, M. and Hotaling, N. (2001) 'Predictors of rape myth acceptance among male clients of female street prostitutes', *Violence Against Women*, 7 (3): 275–93.

Nixon, K., Tutty, L., Downe, P., Gorkoff, K. and Ursel, J. (2002) 'The everyday occurrence: violence in the lives of girls exploited through prostitution', *Violence Against Women*, 8 (9): 1016–43.

Nussbaum, M. (1995) 'Objectification', *Philosophy and Public Affairs*, 24 (4): 249–91.

O'Connell Davidson, J. (1996) 'Prostitution and the contours of control', in J. Holland and J. Weeks (eds), *Sexual Cultures*. London: Macmillan, pp. 180–98.

O'Connell Davidson, J. (1998) *Prostitution, Power and Freedom*. Cambridge: Polity Press.

O'Connell Davidson, J. (2002) 'The rights and wrongs of prostitution', *Hypatia*, 17 (2): 84–98.

O'Connell Davidson, J. (2005) *Children in the Global Sex Trade*. Cambridge: Polity Press.

O'Neill, M. (2001) *Prostitution and Feminism*. Cambridge: Polity Press.

O'Neill, M. and Campbell, R. (2001) *Working Together to Create Change: Community Consultation Research on Prostitution*. Available online at: http://www.safetysoapbox.com.

O'Neill, M., Goode, N. and Hopkins, K. (1995) 'Juvenile prostitution: the experience of young women in residential care', *Childright*, 113: 14–17.

O'Neill, M. with Giddens, S., Breatnach, P., Bagley, C., Bourne, D. and Judge, T. (2002) 'Renewed methodologies for social research: ethno-mimesis as performative praxis', *Sociological Review*, 50: 69–88.

Pateman, C. (1988) *The Sexual Contract*. Cambridge: Polity Press.

Pheterson, G. (1993) 'The whore stigma: female dishonour and male unworthiness', *Social Text*, 37: 39–64.

Phoenix, J. (1999) *Making Sense of Prostitution*. Cambridge: Polity Press.

Pink, S. (2001) *Doing Visual Ethnography*. London: Sage.

Radin, M. (1996) *Contested Commodities: The Trouble with Trade in Sex, Children, Body Parts and Other Things*. Cambridge, MA: Harvard University Press.

Raphael, J. and Shapiro, D. L. (2004) 'Violence in indoor and outdoor prostitution venues', *Violence Against Women*, 10 (2): 126–39.

Ribeiro, M. and Sacramento, O. (2005) 'Violence against prostitutes: findings of research in the Spanish-Portuguese frontier region', *European Journal of Women's Studies*, 12: 61–81.

Richardson, D. and May, H. (2001) 'Deserving victims? Sexual status and the social construction of violence', *Sociological Review*, 47 (2): 308–31.

Sanders, T. (2005) *Sex Work: A Risky Business*. Cullompton: Willan.

Scott, S. (2001) *The Politics and Experience of Ritual Abuse: Beyond Disbelief*. Buckingham: Open University Press.

Scutt, J. (1994) 'Judicial vision: rape, prostitution and the "chaste woman"', *Women's Studies International Forum*, 17 (4): 345–56.

Shaw, S. (2002) 'Shifting conversations on girls' and women's self-injury: an analysis of the clinical literature in historical context', *Feminism and Psychology*, 5 (12): 191–219.

Silbert, M. H. and Pines, A. M. (1981) 'Sexual abuse as an antecedent to prostitution', *Child Abuse and Neglect*, 5: 1–5.

Valentine, G. (1989) 'The geography of women's fear', *Area*, 21: 385–90.

Wasco, S. M. (2003) 'Conceptualising the harm done by rape: applications of trauma theory to experiences of sexual assault', *Trauma, Violence and Abuse*, 4 (4): 309–22.

Wesely, J. (2002) 'Growing up sexualised: issues of power and violence in the lives of exotic dancers', *Violence Against Women*, 8 (10): 1182–207.

Williamson, C. and Folaron, G. (2001) 'Violence, risk, and survival strategies of street prostitution', *Western Journal of Nursing Research*, 23 (5): 463–75.

Chapter 9

Reviewing rape and rape allegations in London: what are the vulnerabilities of the victims who report to the police?

Betsy Stanko and Emma Williams[1]

Introduction

This chapter takes a close look at allegations of rape reported to the police in London. The aim is to explore in detail the contexts of rape for those victims who come to the attention of the police and to examine any subsequent implications these contexts have on the outcome of a criminal allegation of rape. Changes in policy and law continue to be based on the majority of 'unreported rape' victims. However, we suggest that information that the police *do* hold about rape victims could ground change in observable, verifiable information about the outcome of justice. We further suggest that this detailed information challenges the current legal debate about what underlies 'the problem of conviction' for rape. Better understanding the information held by the police and examining what it tells us about the vulnerability of the victims of rape (who are already in contact with the police) could support policy and legal changes that place victim care at the heart of the dilemma about how we currently administer justice.

Internationally, both the law and its institutions have been criticised for assessing the credibility and truthfulness of victims of rape and sexual violence using stereotypical assumptions about gender-appropriate behaviour and moral conduct (Adler 1987; Estrich 1987; Jordan 2004; Kelly 2002; Lees 1997, 2002; Stanko 1982). The debate over the past thirty years centred on defining the acceptable boundaries of harmed female[2] and male sexuality. It was predominantly the feminist work of the 1980s that stretched these boundaries by revealing both a more realistic picture of male violence against women and the infrequency of the fit of the 'perfect victim' with the way rape occurs. By the early 1990s, a large-scale survey conducted by the US National Victim Centre and Crime Victims Research and Treatment Centre (1992) revealed 84 per cent of assaults were committed by a known assailant (Greenfield 1997). With the development of more sensitive victimisation methodologies to capture data on sexual assault, the more researchers and policymakers understood that the problem of coercive sexual encounters is not dominated by the 'stranger' lurking in a dark alley. Rather, a better understanding of sexual assault emphasised the familiarity and familial in an assailant's access to and power over the victim (Gavey 1999; Kelly 1988; London Rape Crisis Centre 1984; Russell 1982; Stanko 1990).

In essence, research findings shattered the stranger danger mythologies and highlighted instead that women are far more likely to experience assault from partners, husbands and those whom they know (Stanko 1984). This research challenged the common presumption that rape could not occur between two parties who might have been intimates at any one time. As Gavey (1999) has suggested most unwanted sexual experiences were considered as 'just sex'. The historic legal boundary of what constituted sexual violation was drawn from men's ownership of wives and daughters (Brownmiller 1975). Simply stated legally, a husband could not rape his wife. If unmarried, only chaste women might be believed when alleging rape. Not only was the law criticised, but the criminal justice system, the key institution associated with public safety, was also accused by feminists of failing to recognise certain woman (for example sex workers and women raped by partners or husbands) as victims. But law and policy changed, recognising rape in marriage in England and Wales in 1991 and setting out police and action plans with the intention of 'putting the victim' at the heart of the criminal justice system.

Despite concerted policy effort to remove legal barriers to reporting and improving the treatment of victims of sexual offences and rape, still only a minority of incidents are reported to the authorities. Painter's (1991: cited in Kelly *et al.* 2005: 14) study in the UK solely aimed at examining unreported rape found that one in four women had experienced rape or attempted rape during their lifetime. Similar to the US research, the most common perpetrators were ex and current partners and 91 per cent of the victims told no one at the time. An analysis of British Crime Survey data (Myhill and Allen 2002; Walby and Allen 2004) indicates an increase in rape victims' willingness to tell someone about the incident. But women are still more likely to tell a friend or family member than the police or any other official. Even for those raped less than five years ago (supposedly more likely to benefit from the transformed way the criminal justice system treats rape complainants), less than half of these victims told anyone at all (see Kelly *et al.* 2005: 14–15 for further discussion).

The reasons for women not reporting today are as complex as they were before any legal changes. Rape myths stretch far beyond the confines of the criminal justice system. They are still very much a part of the fabric of everyday life, affecting how rape victims, assailants and the public view the crime of rape. Recent research on mock jurors in rape trials involving intoxicants, for example (Finch and Munro 2006), exposes the deeply seated perceptions about gender and appropriate sexual behaviour. These mock jurists were willing to 'forgive' men's sexual behaviour and acquit the assailant of rape in most situations. Criminologists have suggested that the media too play a critical role in reinforcing dominant rape myths and existing social relations, particularly in relation to false rape complaints (Soothill and Walby 1991). Depictions of rape in the media continue to undermine what researchers have documented about women's experience of sexual violence. When it comes to rape and sexual assault, there remains a presumption that women lie or are somehow mistaken in naming what they experienced as sex as 'illegal' sex. Indeed more recent media portrayals have suggested the emergence of a new type of victim – that of the innocent man – created as a result of women's malice and revenge (see Jordan 2004 for further discussion and Jenny Kitzinger's chapter this volume).

The present chapter sets out to address systematically the rape contexts reported to the police as allegations. The first hurdle once an allegation is made to the police is the recording of the rape allegation as a crime by the police. Home Office guidelines advise that the police accept a report of a complainant of rape unless the complainant 'retracts completely and admits to fabrication' – known as a no crime[3] (Home Office Circular, 69/86). A plethora of research (Gregory and Lees 1999; Harris and Grace 1999; Kelly *et al.* 2005) continues to find high rates of no criming – a major contribution to the attrition of rape allegations. Research also documents an overestimation of the scale of false allegations by both police officers and prosecutors and suggests that this overestimation creeps into judgments about the legal classification and decisions to prosecute rape allegations. Even the most recent research documents the fact that the highest proportion of cases is lost at the earliest stages, predominantly during the police investigation. The most significant contributors to this early loss of cases are due to complainants withdrawing their allegations and police classifying reports as false allegations (Kelly *et al.* 2005).

This chapter explores the above contributions to the attrition of rape allegations. It also adds a new dimension. We suggest that the vulnerability of the victims who do report rape to the police contributes significantly to the outcome of the allegation in the criminal justice process. By vulnerability, we mean that the context of the rape occurs in situations where the victim is disadvantaged – in terms of social believability – as a witness. Legal credibility is enhanced by social 'believability' (Stanko 1982). Victims who must 'convince' a jury should be articulate, unafraid in a court room, not intimidated by a revenging assailant or his friends/family, mature and psychologically stable and have clear recall of the event. Vulnerability affects how victims are exposed to rape, how victims feel exposed once raped and how these two forms of 'exposure' might influence decisions, investigations and jury deliberations. By tracking the outcome of allegations to the police, this chapter demonstrates that 'vulnerability' does have an influence on the outcome of justice in rape allegations.

Methodology

The data presented here were collected for an internal review about the handling of rape within the Metropolitan Police Service (MPS). It was commissioned to provide better understanding of the kinds of allegations being reported to the MPS – and the situations facing victims reporting them – which in turn would lead to the improvement of the services offered to victims of rape and enhance the standard of the investigation delivered.[4] By knowing the concerns of the users of the police service, the MPS can better tailor improvements in its treatment of complainants and enhance its investigative efforts.

This analysis of 697 allegations of rape recorded by the Metropolitan Police Service Crime Report Information System (CRIS) during April and May 2005 tracked the outcome of these allegations through the criminal justice system. Of the original 697 cases identified, ten were rapes that occurred outside of the MPS area and were subsequently referred to other national forces. The research team found an additional ten CRIS records to be duplicate entries. These 20 allegations were eliminated from the analysis, making the sample of allegations explored 677. A team of analysts read each of the CRIS records and coded these onto a common database.[5] Analysis focused on key emerging themes such as time taken to report the offence, location of the offence, age of the victim, attendance at a London sexual assault referral centre, the presence of alcohol, mental health issues and victim–assailant relationship. Key to the analysis was clustering the contexts of the allegations into four main categories of 'vulnerability': victims under 18 years old, victims who were drinking or misusing drugs, victims with mental health issues (such as learning difficulties) and victims who were or had been an intimate partner of their assailant. Eighty-seven per cent of the allegations fell into at least one of the above four categories.

The data about the rape incidents were obviously limited to the information contained and recorded in the crime reports, which primarily record lines of inquiry and the progress of the police investigation. These records are subject to disclosure in any court proceedings and it is probable that investigating officers limit what is recorded as a consequence. We recognise that the reports provide only a 'snapshot' of the investigation. We did not speak with investigating officers about any omissions. The CPS case tracking system was used to document the final outcome of each case. There was of course missing information in many of the reports. Despite these limitations, information about the vulnerability of the victims using the above categories was often readily available.

Findings: rape allegations reported to the MPS in April and May 2005

In setting out the dilemma for the management of 'rape' in England and Wales as a problem of justice, scholars are making transparent the complexities of decision-making by police officers, by third party supporters and by the victims themselves – all of whom are making decisions within criminal procedures and traditions in Anglo-Saxon legal advocacy that highlight the 'illegality of forced sex'. There is a common acceptance of the fact that few rape allegations come to the attention of the police. There is also an acceptance that police officers do not and cannot control the kinds of rape incidents reported to them. Any incident brought to the attention of the police provides a glimpse at the kinds of situations victims and their third-party supporters 'name' as rape. These are the 'sexual events' that – at least according to the complainants – are in the spotlight for legal condemnation. In this chapter, these reported examples are a thematic guide to understanding where vulnerability meets the intersection of law, sexuality and criminal harm when rape is alleged.[6] Broadly, the MPS rape review provides a unique glimpse of rape allegations immediately following their initial recording. These reports pose a picture of rape that in our opinion must serve to challenge the public debate and open the discussion about 'the crisis' of rape attrition in the UK.

A descriptive look at the sample of allegations

Who reports
In just over one quarter of the allegations, a third party reported the offence. That means that someone else – a parent, friend or other third party (occasionally the sexual assault referral centre (SARC)[7]) – feels that the behaviour of the assailant deserves scrutiny from the police. The MPS rape review showed that third party reports are more likely to result in a withdrawal of the complaint by the victim. Also these reports are less likely to be investigated because victims specifically request anonymity in their attendance at the London SARCs. We conclude that third-party reporting is a routine contribution to the attrition of rape allegations in London. While other third parties feel that police intervention is important, the victims themselves may feel less able to face scrutiny – from police, from friends and family, from their assailant, from themselves.

Age of victim
Nearly one quarter (23 per cent) of the victims were aged 15 or younger. Just over a third (35 per cent) were aged between 16 and 25 years of age. (When looking at the issue of younger victims, one in three victims is under 18 years old.) Just under another third (30 per cent) were aged 26–40 years. Only one in eight (12 per cent) were 41 and over. Youth, as a special form of vulnerability, will be tested against the other three categories of vulnerability to see whether age influences the outcome of a rape allegation.

Ethnicity
The broad ethnic categories of those reporting rape in London do not match the London population estimates. Black complainants (including Afro-Caribbean, African and other) are nearly a quarter (23 per cent) of the victims, while making up approximately 12 per cent of the population.[8] Asian complainants make up only 7 per cent of the victims, in contrast to 13 per cent of the London population. White complainants represent 59 per cent of the victims, in contrast

to making up 71 per cent of the population in London. The remaining 8 per cent of the complainants are from other black and minority ethnic groups, a higher percentage than their make up in London's population (4 per cent). If we are to assume that the unreported, hidden incidents of rape are evenly distributed in the population, then this suggests that different groups of women turn to the police for assistance. For the purposes of this chapter, we explore composite vulnerabilities as the critical intersectionality of race, gender and the composite of factors (including the influences of individual decision-makers).

Gender
Women/girls make up 92 per cent of those who alleged rape in April/May 2005 in London; men/boys comprise 8 per cent of the victims.[9]

Where the rape allegedly occurred
Approximately two-thirds of the rapes occurred in either the victim's or the suspect's residence. Of these, the victim's residence is more likely to be the venue for the offence.[10] Where victims alleged the rape occurred in an 'open space' or street (20 per cent of the reported rape allegations) it was observed that there is a slightly higher chance of the allegation being classified as a no/not crime. This is influenced by the small number of recorded 'false' allegations[11] where the rape took place in some vaguely identified outside 'space'.

Relationship between victim and assailant
In nearly two out of three reported incidents, the victim knew the attacker. One quarter (24 per cent) of the victims reporting rape was in or was formerly in an intimate relationship. Another 39 per cent of the offenders were recorded as 'acquaintances' of the victim. Assailants were listed as 'strangers' to the victims in just over a quarter (26 per cent) of the offences.

The outcome of allegations of rape in London (April–May 2005)
Attrition is defined as the reduction in the number of allegations through to each stage of the criminal justice system. The key points of attrition are: allegation to crime; crime to arrest; arrest to charge; charge to conviction. Of the 677 rape allegations, the conviction outcome was as follows:

- of all rape allegations: 5.3 per cent resulted in a conviction;
- of all crimed allegations: 7.9 per cent resulted in a conviction;

- of all arrested suspects: 13.7 per cent were convicted;
- of all charged suspects: 31.3 per cent were convicted.

Vulnerabilities and rape

Vulnerability means being exposed to attack or harm, physically or emotionally. Catharine MacKinnon once mused: 'to be rapable, a position which is social, not biological, defined what a woman is' (1983: 651). We define vulnerability as a form of 'exposure to rape', and as quite discrete for the purposes of our discussion here. The review of rape allegations in London found that the majority of complainants had vulnerabilities (and were thus more exposed to exploitation of rape) because they were:

- either under 18 years old at the time of the attack;
- had a noted mental health issue (in the police record);
- was currently or previously intimate with the offender; or
- had consumed alcohol or drugs just prior to the attack.

In only 13 per cent of the rape allegations did victims *not* have one of the above vulnerabilities which exposed them to the rape.

As Tables 9.1 and 9.2 below show, these vulnerabilities contribute significantly to the outcome of a rape allegation in the criminal justice system. This desk-based research is not able to offer an exact formula for 'fixing' the problem of vulnerability, nor does this chapter intend to do so. Its aim is to demonstrate that at the very least allegations of rape are reported by victims who are – from the start of the process – largely disadvantaged by the circumstances of the rape event itself. This means that legal decision-making and outcome is dominated by a shadow of doubt cast by the vulnerabilities of the victims who report rape to police. As we have argued earlier in this chapter, there is an abundance of doubt about whether complaints of rape are 'real' or not. Public debate is steeped in doubt, and can be seen in the accounts of rape reported in the media and shown on television. More contradictory, media accounts of civil conflict across the world thrive on reporting the common plight of locally raped women. But the victims who report rape in the UK are overwhelmingly exposed to an offence which is rarely considered a matter for legal condemnation in civil society (Stanko 1985).

Vulnerability also applies to how the victims themselves feel about being exposed to and by a criminal justice system. There were a number of occasions when a police report would suggest that the

Table 9.1 Predicted probability of attrition depending on the number of vulnerabilities (taken from Stanko 2007)

	Number of vulnerabilities			
	None	1	2	3 or more
Possibility of attrition classified as no crime	23.8%	29.8%	36.7%	44.1%
Attrition at crimed-to-charge stage	74.2%	74.5%	74.9%	75.3%
Attrition at post-charge stage	31.6%	40.3%	49.7%	59.0%

victim did not wish to continue with the legal process. There were other police reports that stated that the victim avoided any further contact with investigators (such as not returning phone calls, refusing to answer doors) and the investigation was closed. Table 9.1 shows the criminal justice outcome in the MPS review of rape allegations. Attrition is the greatest between the points of classification of the report as rape by the police and the charge of a suspect by the CPS with a crime: *75 per cent of all allegations of rape are eliminated at this stage.* Post CPS charge, an additional 42 per cent of rape allegations drop out at this stage or end in acquittal at trial. Vulnerability, we argue, affects the likelihood of attrition. Victims with multiple vulnerabilities are the most disadvantaged and are less likely to see their allegations result in a conviction for rape.

There are variations between the criminal justice outcome and different vulnerabilities. The overall percentage of all allegations that result in conviction remains below 6 per cent. Once an allegation is classified as a crime, the likelihood of conviction of the offender is just under 8 per cent. Table 9.2 demonstrates the odds of drop-out at different attrition points of the criminal justice system. What this shows is that victims under 18 and those whose offenders are intimates/ former intimates are more likely to have their allegations classified as a crime of rape by the police. Victims who have consumed alcohol, while less likely to have their allegations recorded as a crime, are more likely to have any resulting case result in a conviction once it reaches the prosecution stage. Table 9.2 also shows that victims with mental health issues are most disadvantaged in the process: they are three times less likely to have their allegations classified as a crime of rape and have reduced odds of reaching a conviction at the subsequent two stages of the criminal justice decision-making process.

Table 9.2 Vulnerability and the odds of attrition (taken from Stanko 2007)

Type of vulnerability	Classification stage	Crimed-to-charge-stage	Post-charge stage
Under 18	0.73	0.81	1.36
Alcohol consumption	1.41*	0.68	0.79
Mental health issue	3.18**	1.42	1.45
Intimate relationship	0.72	1.22	3.04**

*Statistically significant p < 0.05.
**Statistically significant p < 0.001.

Discussion

Throughout the MPS rape review, the research team came across many examples of 'good' victim care by the police. One young woman, raped by a man who offered her a ride home when she missed her bus, had been drinking. The investigating officer found CCTV evidence to back up her version of events and located the rapist's van. The CPS charged the man and the courts convicted him despite his allegations that the woman was a prostitute. Investigations of the incidents reported to the police are clearly guided by its legal setting – a hearing in a court of law – within which the legal determination of rape is ultimately determined. Problems in 'proving' rape – often raised by police and prosecutors as the justification for decisions to recommend that the allegation not be heard in a court – are similar to the kinds of doubts of victims themselves (see examples in the appendix to this chapter). The MPS review found numerous examples in the crime reports that victims did not want to go to court. Research suggests that simulated juries make judgments that bear an uncanny resonance with victims' own doubts about whether the jury would believe them. Finch and Munro's (2006) extensive series of mock jury deliberations on alcohol and drug-related rape show that it took quite dramatic wrongdoing on the part of the defendant to divert the focus of jurors away from the complainant's behaviour and onto what the defendant did. Perhaps abusive men know that taking sexual advantage of drunken women or vulnerable women will not be criminally sanctioned (Godenzi 1994). Other men have relied in the past on the hope of courtship and marriage to 'forgive' abuse and hurt (Ferraro 2006).

As noted earlier, 87 per cent of the victims who reported rape to the Metropolitan Police had one of the four vulnerabilities: they were under 18 at the time of the rape, were under the influence of alcohol or drugs at the time of the rape, had mental health issues or were former partners of their assailants. We suggest that many of the victims withdraw their cooperation from the legal system because they cannot face such invasive scrutiny that has become the 'folklore' of the aftermath of rape. Perhaps in the name of sensitivity to victims, criminal justice decision-makers – police in particular – may feel sympathy for a victim who is reluctant to face a rough adversarial justice system. Perhaps decisions made not to prosecute an arrested and charged suspect 'in the public interest' may be justified by a prosecutor who is concerned that the victim is too fragile or vulnerable to take the witness stand. But how often this happens, and how much it actually influences decisions, are speculation on our part and should be the subject of further research. Ultimately this is an empirical question.

While debate about 'the rape attrition crisis' rages, women and men are reporting rape to the police. The MPS review found that one in three of the 677 allegations of rape in April and May 2005 was recorded as 'no crime'. Of those 'no crimed', 30 per cent (or 72 allegations) were classified as 'false allegations'. This means that the other 70 per cent of the allegations no crimed were judged to be reports of some kind of distressing incident, distressing enough to warrant an approach by the victim to the police for help with something that was alleged to be 'rape'. The overwhelming problem in determining the distinction between legal and illegal sex therefore is not the truthfulness of the victim. After all, victims are reporting distressing incidents; the police are recording and classifying that incident, initially as rape. It is this initial classification that enables the MPS to track the outcome for this review. The rape victim – as many commentators have argued over the past 20 years – remains the 'legal subject' on whose body and through whose body is drawn the conditions of establishing a criminal case (Stanko 1982, 1985). Brownmiller's (1975) groundbreaking work led to heated debate and clearly helped facilitate change for the better for the treatment of some rape victims. Her observations deserve revisiting. Brownmiller states in her book *Against our Will*: 'A female definition of rape can be contained in a single sentence. If a woman chooses not to have intercourse with a specific man and the man chooses to proceed against her will, that is a criminal act of rape. Through no fault of woman, this is not and never has been the legal definition' (Brownmiller 1976, Bantam edition 1976: 8)

Scholars have discussed the power of the concept of 'real rape' (Estrich 1987; Kelly *et al.* 2005). Other researchers have over the years established how few victims report their attacks to the police (see, for example Walby and Allen 2004). That power of the concept 'real rape' (Estrich 1987), we suggest, has not diminished in law, regardless of whatever legal changes have taken place in statute and in policy. That power locates legal decision-making on evaluating what the victim did, what she/he might have done and how she/he might have consented to rather than resisted the assailant's entitlement to sex. The power further rests in spotlighting how the victim might come across in a court of law giving evidence. Even when the police believe a crime was committed (and in two-thirds of the rape allegations the allegation is classified as a crime worthy of investigation), few incidents reach a court of law. Even fewer result in a conviction of the assailants.

Conclusion

The MPS rape reviews (Stanko 2005, 2007) found four critical issues clustering in the rape allegations reported to the MPS and these all have adverse impact on the outcome: domestic violence, young adults' accounts of peer sexual assault, mental health and alcohol-related sexual contact.[12] Most acts of rape reported to police as a consequence fail to be judged as illegal. The police are faced with the complexities of managing rape allegations that are steeped in these different kinds of vulnerability. While there may be other witnesses on some occasions, most reports of rape are experienced as a 'private' encounter, in situations that are not too dissimilar to consensual sex, with other social and psychological disadvantages. The impact of these vulnerabilities can be seen in the fact that many victims walk away from their initial allegation and sometimes withdraw their allegations – we suggest – because they may find that it is difficult for them to articulate 'non consent' in a way that can be understood within the contemporary perceptions where men are given the benefit of the doubt. Some of the women are actively encouraged by police to withdraw because the police are trying to protect the victim from the brutality of the advocacy system of justice (Williams 2004). Some of the investigations are hampered by the vulnerabilities. Some of the investigations are poor as a consequence. 'Ladettes', sexual freedom, mutually satisfying heterosexuality – times have changed since feminists argued for sexual liberation in the 1960s and 1970s. What has not changed since these times is the logic of the entitlement of men to sex and this definition of sexuality is sustained in the public domain by many members of the public.[13]

While debate about the 'crisis of attrition' has placed criminal justice actors in the dock (and rightly), there is a reluctance to speak about the toll participating in the legal process has on victims. Such a toll, documented a quarter of a century ago by Chambers and Millar (1983), remains as evidenced in the MPS rape review which found that many victims – once they had reported to the police – wanted out. In one in four of the allegations someone other than the victim reported the offence to the police. Colleagues, friends and family encourage a victim to report to the police after hearing what happened or seeing the injuries (see case examples in the appendix to this chapter). These third parties felt that 'something' was not right about the way the man treated the woman. The rape review also found a number of incidents of rape allegations where the victim reported 'something' to the police as a rape but could not remember the details because alcohol clouded her recall of the event (85 of the allegations reviewed). Just over one in three of all the allegations (235) involved victims where the investigation recorded the victim had been drinking prior to the alleged rape (see Lovett and Horvath in this edition). We feel that the failure to gain convictions for rape may suggest that the situation for victims, usually women – made vulnerable by youth intimidation, drink, mental illness or domestic violence in particular – remains especially difficult because rapists may very well be targeting that vulnerability in their conscious actions. Indeed the range of 'vulnerabilities' identified in this chapter leaves the victims vulnerable to both the assault itself and subsequently to attrition as a result of the challenges to their credibility as witnesses placed on them by the original circumstance of the case.

The police – the recorders of the allegations scrutinised for this chapter – manage the consequences of the above. Police investigations of rape need to document the evidence and this fact-finding process navigates through the difficulties vulnerabilities bring to the majority of allegations brought to the attention of the MPS. What this review shows is that in the face of such vulnerability, victim care must underpin the approach to the gathering of evidence. This continues to be a challenge.

Returning to our original questions raised at the beginning of the chapter, how are we to understand the declining conviction rate for rape in England and Wales? Is the decline of convictions due to the fact that more victims trust the police and report personal hurt and harm? Can law manage the messiness of everyday sexual behaviour if sexual harm can only be understood when consent is not a possible defence (the classic stranger lurking in an alley)? The authors of this chapter urge that a systematic and transparent system of tracking decision-making in rape allegations can offer a way of documenting the outcome of rape allegations, and possibly challenge the dominant debate about rape as it is waged in the public domain. Women and men *are* reporting rape every day in the UK. This MPS review highlights the acute vulnerability of the victims who report rape. There has been a number of rape 'Action Plans' adopted by the government in the past number of years. Research on domestic violence complaints shows that advocates facilitate better outcomes for victims (Hester and Westmarland 2006). Perhaps lessons learnt from this research should be applied to victims of sexual violence. However open the government may be to demanding change, our review shows that any progress is painfully slow. Few victims of rape find redress through the criminal justice process.

Appendix

The following are composite examples of allegations reported to the MPS. The inclusion of these examples highlight some of the complexities involved in the indicative examples of vulnerability reported to the police in London.

Example 1: domestic violence-related rape allegation

Eva[14] arrived at work with bruises on her neck. A colleague, who Eva had been confiding in, knew that Eva's boyfriend had been abusing her. She encouraged Eva to call the police. Eva told the police that she ended her relationship with her partner two weeks ago but was still living with him in the flat. She speaks limited English and needed to find a new place to live. She is currently employed as a cleaner, and had limited funds and contacts from which to find alternative accommodation. The night before she was in bed, and her ex-boyfriend, also from her country of origin and who had been drinking, demanded sex. He started to strangle her. She nearly lost consciousness and couldn't breathe. She tried to call the police using her mobile phone, which he took from her. He grabbed her hair, pushed her on to the bed and raped her. He continued throughout the night having sex with her, eventually he fell asleep early in the morning. She had to work the next day, rose early and left for work at 5:30 a.m. Her colleague, concerned enough from her bruises and marks on her neck, encouraged her to call the police. There is medical evidence of marks to her neck.

Two weeks later the victim requests that the charges be dropped, as she says she still loves the suspect and doesn't want him to go to prison. She has moved out of the flat, but is still in contact with the suspect via text messages.

Example 2: alcohol-related rape allegation

Rosa had been clubbing with her cousin Britt in one of London's outer boroughs known as a lively spot for young people. She was spotted by one of the bouncers very upset. She was quite drunk. She said that she was dancing with this guy and agreed to leave the bar with him. He was joined by one of his friends and they headed to his car. She agreed to have sex with Mark in the back of the car but asked that his friend go away. Mark wanted her to have sex with his friend Thomas too. She said no. Thomas then got on top of Rosa and had sex with her as well. He said 'you know you want it', then called her a tease. Then Mark took another turn having sex. Thomas tried again but she managed to get out of the car. Mark asked Rosa why she was crying as he walked her back to the club.

Example 3: familiarity/peer intimidation-related rape allegation

Police were called to a GP surgery when a young woman attended the clinic for the morning after pill. Gladys was distressed and informed the doctor that she had been raped. She said that two people visited her house yesterday to watch TV. Her grandmother was asleep upstairs, and her two brothers were also in the loft. Gladys was left alone with the friend's friend, and he starting kissing her. She said that she shouted 'get off' but he put his hand over her mouth. He then pulled up her skirt and forced his penis into her vagina. The suspect just got up and left, walking out of the flat. Gladys' friend returned soon after, but Gladys did not tell her what had happened. Gladys did tell a teacher who made the appointment at the surgery. The teacher also called the grandmother, who was with her at the time of reporting to the police. Her parents were then called and spoke to the police. The parents were concerned as Gladys was in the midst of taking her GCSE exams and had another exam the next day. As a result, there was a decision not to attend the SARC immediately. As the investigation proceeded,

Gladys admitted that she used to go out with Derek, but that she had never slept with him. She was until this incident a virgin. Gladys felt forced to have sex. Gladys' parents were supportive and wanted Gladys to carry on with the criminal investigation. Gladys, however, felt that the stress of a court case would be very detrimental to her. She is a bright student and wishes to get on with her life. Derek's story was that Gladys had agreed to have sex and the investigation was unlikely to discover which party was telling the truth.

Example 4: mental health-related rape allegation

Emma said that she visited Mike's house to give him back the £5 he lent her. She knows Mike, as they all live in the same block of flats and have been friends for years. She says that when she went to the address the suspect locked the front door behind her. She was pushed onto the bed and was raped. Emma returned home, saw her parents and took the dog for a walk. While she was walking the dog she called the police on her mobile phone. Emma was taken to hospital, examined by a doctor and given painkillers. Emma has serious learning difficulties and is under the care and support of a local social services team. She was living on her own but returned to her family home after complaining of a rape by a builder near her last flat. Her social work team are very concerned that her actions may put her in vulnerable situations with men. However, the social work team feel that she has the capacity to decide whether or not she wants to have sex. The victim reported the situation to police herself. Following CPS advice, there is a decision that it is not in the public interest to proceed with the case.

Notes

1 The views expressed in this chapter are solely those of the authors. They do not represent those of the Metropolitan Police Service.
2 Rape of men became defined as rape in 1991. For the purposes of this article, we are focusing primarily on the 92 per cent of allegations of rape reported by females.
3 'No crime' is where a notifiable offence has been classified on the CRIS (crime report information system) and a decision is subsequently made that it should not have been recorded as a crime.
4 Stanko *et al.* (2005).

5 Thanks to Jennifer O'Connor, Ubaid Rehman, Daniela Wunsch and Marie Doran from the Strategic Research Unit MPS.

6 Moreover, rape must establish 'illegal' sex within a context where 'legal' sex has a wide range of practices, some of which may be considered as 'abusive', 'forceful' or involve sexual practices that few in the population willingly indulge. Nonetheless, the jury is required to sort out the 'illegal' from the 'legal' sexual contact, and a great deal of the 'sorting' revolves around the notion – and 'proof' – of consent.

7 A SARC is located in a hospital, and is where a victim of sexual assault can be forensically examined and offered counselling and other types of assistance. London has three SARCs.

8 2001 Census figures, Office for National Statistics, London.

9 We focus this paper on the female complainants. All of the male complainants were attacked by men.

10 Of the 450 rape allegations taking place in either the victim's or the suspect's residence, the victim's residence is listed as the venue in 273 of these incidents, i.e. 60 per cent of the incidents where victim/offender residence is listed as the place where the alleged crime took place.

11 In 72 of 677 (11 per cent) allegations, the police noted that the complainant admitted or the evidence suggested that the allegation was 'fabricated'.

12 This does not mean that there are not a number of other issues, such as childhood sexual abuse and 'stranger rape', among others. It does mean that these issues clearly overshadow many of these in the day-to-day work of rape investigators in London.

13 In the UK a number of television 'reality' shows chose 'rape' as the issue around which mock trials facilitated the public debate about rape. The authors do not feel that this debate was enlightened by these shows.

14 All the names are randomly assigned.

References

Adler, Z. (1987) *Rape on Trial*. London: Routledge & Kegan Paul.

Adler, Z. (1991) 'Picking up the pieces: a survey of victims of rape', *Police Review*, 31: 1114–15.

Brownmiller, S. (1976) *Against Our Will: Men, Women and Rape*. New York: Bantam Books.

Chambers, G. and Miller, A. (1983) *Investigating Sexual Assault*. London: HMSO.

Estrich, S. (1987) *Real Rape: How the Legal System Victimises Women Who Say No*. Boston: Harvard University Press.

Ferraro, K. (2006) *Neither Angels Nor Demons: Women, Crime and Victimisation*. Boston: Northeastern University Press.

Finch, E. and Munro, V. (2006) 'Juror stereotypes and blame attribution in rape cases involving intoxicants', *British Journal of Criminology*, 45: 25–38.

Gavey, N. (1999) '"I wasn't raped, but ...": revisiting definitional problems in sexual victimisation', in S. Lamb (ed.), *New Versions of Victims: Feminists Struggles with the Concept*. New York: New York University Press, pp. 57–81.

Godenzi, A. (1994) 'What's the big deal? We are men and they are women', in T. Newburn and E. Stanko (eds), *Just Boys Doing Business?* London: Routledge, pp. 135–52.

Greenfield, L. (1997) *Sex Offences and Offenders: An Analysis of Date Rape and Sexual Assault*, US Department of Justice Bureau of Justice Statistics, NCJ-163392.

Gregory J. and Lees, S. (1999). *Policing Sexual Assault*. London: Routledge.

Harris, J. and Grace, S. (1999) *A Question of Evidence? Investigating and Prosecuting Rape in the 1990s*, Research Study No. 196. London: Home Office.

Hester, M. and Westmarland, N. (2006) *Tackling Domestic Violence: Effective Interventions and Approaches*, Home Office Research Study No. 290. London: Home Office.

Jordan, J. (2004) *The Word of a Woman? Police, Rape and Belief*. New Zealand: Palgrave Macmillan.

Kelly, L. (1988) *Surviving Sexual Violence*. Cambridge: Polity Press.

Kelly, L. (2002) *A Research Review on Reporting, Investigation and Prosecution of Rape Cases*. London: HMCPSI.

Kelly, L., Lovett, J. and Reagan, L. (2005) *A Gap or a Chasm: Attrition in Reported Rape Cases*, Home Office Research Study No. 293. London: Home Office.

Lees, S. (1997) *Ruling Passions*. Buckingham: Open University Press.

Lees, S. (2002) *Carnal Knowledge: Rape on Trial*, 2nd edn. London: Women's Press.

London Rape Crisis Centre (1984) *Sexual Violence: The Reality for Women*. London: Women's Press.

MacKinnon, C. (1983) 'Feminism, Marxism, method and the state: an agenda for theory', *Signs: Journal of Women in Culture and Society*, 8: 635–58.

Myhill, A. and Allen, J. (2002) *Rape and Sexual Assault of Women: The Extent and Nature of the Problem – Findings from the British Crime Survey*. London: Home Office Research Study.

Russell, D. (1982) *Rape in Marriage*. New York: Macmillan.

Soothill, K. and Walby, S. (1991) *Sex Crime in the News*. London: Routledge.

Stanko, E. (1982) 'Would you believe this woman?', in N. Rafter and E. Stanko (eds), *Judge, Lawyer, Victim, Thief: Women, Gender Roles and Criminal Justice*. Boston: Northeastern University Press, pp. 63–82.

Stanko, E. (1984) 'Fear of crime and the myth of the safe home', in K. Yllo and M. Bograd (eds), *Feminist Perspectives on Wife Abuse*. Newbury Park, CA: Sage, pp. 75–88.

Stanko, E. (1985) *Intimate Intrusions*. London: Routledge.

Stanko, E. (1990) *Everyday Violence*. London: Pandora.

Stanko, E. (2007) *MPS Rape Review: The Attrition of Rape in London*. London: Strategic Research and Analysis Unit, Metropolitan Police.

Stanko, E., Paddick, B. and Osborn, D. (2005) *A Review of Rape Investigations in the Metropolitan Police Service*. December.

Walby, S. and Allen, J. (2004) *Domestic Violence, Sexual Assault and Stalking: Findings from the British Crime Survey*. London: Home Office Research Study.

Williams, E. (2004) *Project Sapphire Report – Victim Withdrawal*. London: Metropolitan Police Strategic Research Unit.

Part 3

The Criminal Justice System

Part 3

The Criminal Justice System

Chapter 10

Seeking proof or truth: naturalistic decision-making by police officers when considering rape allegations

Stephanie O'Keeffe, Jennifer M. Brown and Evanthia Lyons

Introduction

There has been considerable criticism of the way police officers go about investigating rape allegations (Jordan 2004; Temkin 1997). These include the charge that police approach such allegations within a 'culture of scepticism' (Kelly *et al.* 2005) in which the veracity of the allegations are doubted unless they conform to the stereotype of a 'real' rape, defined by Estrich (1987) as that being committed by a stranger, outside and with a weapon. In the United Kingdom, it is thought this contributes to the 'no criming' of cases, whereby police officers believe there is insufficient evidence to proceed or the complainant admits to fabrication such that they decline to pass the case papers onto the prosecuting authorities. This contributes to the attrition rate when cases fail to reach court. Brown *et al.* (2007) challenge the notion that such decision-making is borne of unthinking scepticism but rather the police engage in a process of considering legal standards required to prove the case or express concerns about the truth of an allegation.

Research examining police attributions of guilt tend to use survey or quasi-experimental designs. While this research does provide consistent information accounting for the kinds of characteristics that result in negative credibility judgments it does not provide a good representation of how police investigate reports of rape and how they make decisions, for example what decisions are of real importance in rape investigations and how judgments of truth are related to the investigative process and investigative behaviour in particular. This chapter explores in more detail the decision-making processes that the police employ when investigating a complaint of rape. This is undertaken with the theoretical formulation of naturalistic decision-making (NDM). The chapter presents an exposition of this approach and describes the results of an empirical investigation conducted within this framework.

Naturalistic decision-making

NDM grew out of an increasing dissatisfaction with the limitations of classical models of decision-making (Klein *et al.* 1993). In summary, this critique argues that decisions are not simply some optimising from a fixed set of alternatives undertaken in a vacuum but occur within a social context with varying degrees of social influence and complexity and with impactful consequences for the decision-maker (Broadstock and Michie 2000; Crego and Alison 2004). These authors suggest that traditional decision-making approaches fail to take into account ethical and cultural values or the views of influential others that are important to the decision-maker. Police investigative decision-making clearly not only operates within a set of legal procedures and codes of practice but is also subject to a set of expectations and beliefs about rape and is of great consequence to the complainant. Thus we conceptualise investigative decision-making as a high-stakes, dynamic, interpretative, social process occurring within an interactional context. The decision-makers have agency and do not simply operate prescriptively in terms of conforming to the principles of mathematical logic, as conceptualised in more classical decision-making models.

The naturalistic paradigm was found to fit these important assumptions. However, as Norros and Klemola (1999) point out, NDM research has yet to offer a coherent method to get at the complex details of decisions made in real-life settings. These researchers used video recordings and expert commentaries of actions during the clinical administration of anaesthesia to elucidate decision-making but this relies on inferences about the decision-makers. Other approaches simulate decision situations. For example, Dunn *et al.* (2002) employed concurrent 'think aloud' commentaries by emergency personnel which overcomes the inference problem but allows after-the-fact rationalisations which may not be consistent with real-time decision making. Crego and Alison (2004) facilitated anonymous group discussions among police officers, where officers recorded information on a laptop and their anonymised comments were shared by the whole group. This neutralises the high-stakes element out of real-world decision-making. These different approaches vary in their attempts to capture the richness of data, generalising findings and obtaining in-situ live commentaries. But all acknowledge the difficulties in doing so. Thus this chapter develops a method of retrospective commentary about real cases and by using concepts from grounded theory, explained later, we construct a composite of the decision-making processes. The focus of our research then is a better understanding of how police officers make decisions in rape investigations. In this we hope to retain the consequential aspects of decision-making, rely on the decision-makers' own commentary, avoid some of the pitfall of post hoc rationalisation by asking for accounts in a non-judgmental way and discuss real rather than simulated events. We are interested in examining how police decision-makers actually function, not how they ought to function, and to see the effects of police socialisation in action through the manner of their storytelling.

NDM suggests that more automatic processes may precede the more analytic processes used to diagnose and evaluate a decision. For example, cognitive and emotional aspects of a decision such as experience and knowledge have a fundamental and automatic impact on information processing. The interest lies in how people make decisions in the context of their work. NDM recognises that the decision process tends to be messy. Most decision-makers have difficulty comprehending the range of elements contributing to the decision and tend to simplify in order to deal with them. The decision-maker may not do the best job possible, but rather does a good enough job to keep sufficient information about the event in focus rather than an optimal strategy of maximising the information in all permutations of a possible relationship.

NDM recognises that decision-making is essentially social and that decisions have to take others into account. Both training and socialisation affect the way a person interprets a given situation (Trice and Beyer 1993). The police have an especially strong socialisation process that influences their working culture, which inculcates informal norms, values and attitudes (Fielding 1988; Fielding and Fielding 1992). Beliefs about deception as integral to police rape investigations appear consistent in the research literature in whatever jurisdiction is studied, e.g. Krahé (1991) and Greuel (1992) in Germany, Winkel and Koppelaar (1992) in Holland, Temkin (1997) in England and Jordan (2004) in New Zealand. Le Doux and Hazlewood (1995) found that while officers (from the USA) were not insensitive to the plight of rape victims, they were suspicious of those having had previous and willing sex with the assailant.

Such research consistently reports that situational factors (e.g. characteristics of the victim, suspect and incident circumstances), as well as application of the 'received wisdom' of rape myths, affect attributions of blame (see Chapter 2 by Bohner *et al.* this volume). The limitations with this corpus of research is that it does not explain the ways in which beliefs and attributions are directly related to decision goals, information processing, investigative behaviour or decision outcome, or how police occupational context and societal norms affect attitudes, attributions, motivations or decisions. We attempt to do this by a thorough examination of police decision-making. We argue this is critical to understanding how cases are presented to the prosecuting authority and in court and how this may influence the high attrition rate for this offence.

There are several NDM working concepts that need to be explained. Key among these are

- experience and social knowledge;
- the decision frame;
- heuristics and information processing;
- story building.

Experience and social knowledge

To make sense of events a decision-maker must mentally put them in the proper context and give them meaning, which is done by drawing on past experience. This knowledge supplies the context, the ongoing story that gives coherence to experiences, without which everything would appear unrelated (Beach 1997). However, such knowledge comprises individual and cultural interpretations of past events rather than just a catalogue of objective truths. Individuals have a rich store of such social knowledge about people, events and objects, all of which informs judgmental procedures. Knowledge can be general and represent general theories or attitudes, e.g. women who work in prostitution are unreliable and dangerous. Knowledge can also be more schematic or structural, e.g. a person's understanding of how they do a job, what has to be done first, second and so on. Different constructs (e.g. attitude, stereotype, schema, script) are used by different researchers to describe different kinds of knowledge and beliefs and these in turn inform judgment and decision-making.

The decision frame

A decision frame is used in the literature to describe how people structure a decision. Embedding observed events in a context to give them meaning is called framing. A frame is a mental construct consisting of salient current events and associated past events, experiences and beliefs (Minsky 1968). A more informal definition would be that frames are the decision-maker's interpretations of what is happening in a given situation. A frame tells the decision-maker what to expect. The frame may be in error but until feedback or some other information makes the error evident, the frame is the foundation for understanding the situation and for deciding what the outcome will be. People frame situations differently and different decision frames put the focus on different types of information (Wagenaar and Keren 1986).

Heuristics and information processing

Laboratory research examining how people violate logical and statistical principals of probability assessments found that people used several rules of thumb or heuristics to avoid information overload (Tversky and Kahneman 1973, 1981, 1982). Heuristics act as mental short cuts and are generally employed without reflection or consideration of their usefulness. The most common judgmental short cuts used by decision-makers include the availability and representativeness heuristics. The representative heuristic is employed when assessing the probability of an event on the basis of how closely it resembles some other event or set of events. The importance of recognition underlies the application of heuristics. Klein *et al.* (1993) have done extensive research on recognition-based decision-making. They outline the importance of strategies such as pattern or feature matching and mental simulation, whereby the decision-maker projects a course of action or retrospectively makes sense of events. Klein *et al.* found that the more experience the decision-maker has in the area in which decisions arise, the greater the role of recognition. The availability heuristic is when people predict the frequency of an event or the proportion within a population who might be affected based on how easily an example can be brought to mind. Simply stated, where there is a widely held belief such as 'women lie about consensual sex' and it is used either to 'prove' the general proposition that rape can only occur under certain stereotypical circumstances or supports a bias that 'good' women cannot be raped then the availability heuristic is in play. Under these circumstances the ease of imagining an example or the vividness and emotional impact of that example becomes more credible than actual statistical probability. Because an example is easily brought to mind or mentally 'available', the specific instance is considered as representative of the whole rather than as just a single example in a range of cases.

Story building

Story building has also been described as central to decision-making in real-life scenarios. This is where a decision-maker attempts to synthesise the features of a situation into a causal explanation that can be subsequently evaluated. Pennington and Hastie (1986) developed a model of decision-making that explained how jurors impose narrative story on trial information and evidence in which causal intentional relations between events are central. Story models or scenario models have a clear relevance to police investigative decision-making where the decision-maker has to reconstruct and make sense of past events.

The research we are reporting in this chapter employs these NDM tools to understand more clearly how and what beliefs help inform a police officer's decision frame when investigating rape. We examine if and how heuristics work in practice thereby providing a better understanding of investigative decision-making in rape situations. We describe a decision frame that accounts for the resources and processes of the police decision-maker. We also discuss the findings in terms of the theoretical and methodological implications and their applied value from a police operational perspective.

Due to restrictions on the length of this chapter it will not be possible to detail results relating to the more social aspects of this process and the impact of occupational and societal cultural norms. Findings dealing with delegation of duties, team and group behaviour, organisational constraints and societal constraints will not be covered. Nor are we able within the space of this chapter to detail differences in approach by men and women police officers.

Our analytic strategy also draws on 'grounded theory' principles (Glaser and Strauss 1967; Strauss and Corbin 1990). Grounded theory provides a form of deconstructive analysis. The procedure provides a strategy to tap a decision-making process which is 'multilayered' and allows for conflicting interpretation and meanings to be drawn out. Grounded theory's data-handling strategies enable the researcher to move from initially unstructured material to a collection of structured theoretical observations. The advantage of employing grounded theory is that it provides a highly systematic, innovative and powerful method for handling and analysing qualitative interview data. The method initially consists of coding or labelling incidents within the data. A central aspect of the analysis is to compare each incident with all other instances both within and between categories (constant comparison). Writing memos is also a central aspect of grounded theory development. Content analysis (Krippendorf 1990) was also used to examine differences in frequencies of categories across officers. Interview transcripts were read a number of times to identify key terms in the text. Data were broken down into discrete parts, closely examined and compared. As many categories of analysis as possible were made. As text was methodically and iteratively coded it enabled the formulation of conceptual categories and properties underlying the developing theoretical model to emerge. The management of coding was achieved initially by using both traditional index cards and employing NUD*IST VIVO (a computer-aided qualitative data analysis tool) as the number of categories being generated became very large, over 400.

Comparisons and links were made between individual categories of data and also between and within datasets. Rather than merge similar groups of categories and lose subtle differences between them, categories were organised into higher-level sets as follows:

- deployment;
- idiosyncratic differences;
- experience;
- crime seriousness;
- investigative aims;
- false report beliefs and disposition;
- impression formation and motivational aims;
- statement taking;
- occupational culture;
- practical process;
- recommendation/eventual decision;
- training.

Individual case profiles for each participant were also developed. This technique provided a useful checking mechanism and allowed comparisons to be made both across and also within transcripts. Finally when the model was developed it was cross-checked with each scenario of rape described by officers to ensure the goodness of fit to the entire range of scenarios described by officers.

Study details

All officers (N = 33) were drawn from Ireland's National Police Service, An Garda Síochána. All were of constable rank. In order to examine potential effects of occupational socialisation, officers with three different lengths of service in the police force were targeted. Both men (N = 15) and women (N = 18) officers were recruited who

- were in the last year of their police training and had not yet graduated from Garda college (probationer Gardaí[1] (group 1, N = 13);
- had five years' service (group 2, N = 11); and
- were officers with 15 years' service (group 3, N = 9).

The longer-serving officers were selected from a list of all Gardaí who had graduated from the Garda College 5 and 15 years previously. All of the female Gardaí in the older groups had direct experience of rape investigation – half of the females in the youngest group had experience of taking rape statements. None of the probationer male Gardaí had experience of taking rape statements and half of the older groups had experience of being involved in rape investigations.

We sought information about:

- age, education, and other background information;
- role definition;
- levels of occupational identification;
- information processing;
- decision-making and belief structures when investigating reports of rape;
- schema-based social attributions;
- Garda policy and legal framework.

Interviews were conducted in an office of the Garda Station where the participant worked, were audiotaped and lasted between 55 and 90 minutes. Interviews with probationer Gardaí were conducted in the College. All interviews began by asking officers to describe the last report of adult female rape they dealt with or heard of and to take the interviewer through the decision-making process.

Generating the decision making model

Numerous findings relating to officers' knowledge, attitudes and beliefs about their job emerged from the analysis. The term evaluative knowledge structure (EKS) was used to encompass these findings. As illustrated in Figure 10.1 the EKS for these police officers is divided into social knowledge, victim-centred attitudes and the primary decision goal.

Social knowledge, beliefs, attitudes and decision goals are not mutually exclusive but do exist as separate entities. The decision-making frame is made up of numerous interrelated belief structures (e.g. attitude toward *x*, knowledge of *y*, schema of *z*), within which a specific report of rape is embedded. Knowledge elements of the frame exist independently of a particular case but merge and feed directly into the way in which a specific complaint is evaluated. This extensive knowledge base provides the raw material and evaluative filter through which a complaint is received and the decision frame defined. The knowledge structure affects the salience, availability and prioritisation of information, while the relative weight ascribed to automatic social judgments of truth, moderates the way in which the case is dealt with and prescribes the conclusions that can be made. The following quote provides an example of how beliefs concerning how a rape victim should present when making a complaint feed into the officer's assessment of the case:

> She was very strong ... I was like 'dodgy, dodgy', but just a very strong girl, so she wasn't the type of person I was expecting you know the weeping girl in the corner and then you know something happened in her childhood and it will all come out ... I remember saying to the sergeant I don't know is she telling the truth because she was so strong. I thought she was almost too exact and the story contrived. (Group 1, #12)

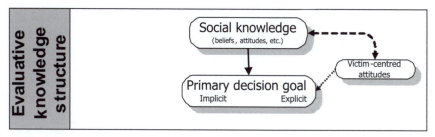

Figure 10.1   Evaluative knowledge structure

One of the major moderators is the 'primary decision goal'. This has two aspects: a veracity goal which seeks either to 'prove' the complaint or to elicit the 'truth' about the complaint. Key features defining the primary decision goal are beliefs in a high level of false reports of rape, a suspicious disposition toward reports of rape, beliefs in motivations of deceit, and prior experience or acquired knowledge about withdrawal and false rape allegations. This part of the model is illustrated in Figure 10.2.

Beliefs about the problem and prevalence of false rape allegations emerged early in the analysis, and interestingly were made in the recognition that there is an uncomfortable inevitability about officers' probability estimations of falsehood. Participants in group 1 and group 2 were divided between those that believed there to be 'a lot' of false rape reporting (n = 8) and those that believed the level of false reports was 'not that much' (n = 7). There were also members of both of these groups that believed the level to be about half or less than half. Participants in group 3 with 15 years operational experience generally thought the level of false rape reporting was either 'half and half' or 'not that much'.

I suppose you decide yourself whether the allegation is true or not, you know a lot of times as well you can get complaints where nothing happened at all … in my experience almost half [allegations are false]. (Group 1, #4)

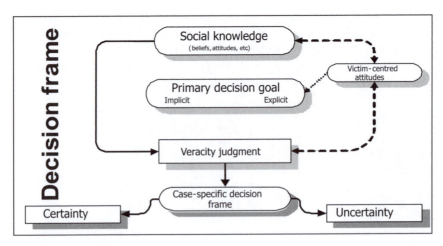

Figure 10.2 Decision frame

From my own experience I would say 70:30. 70 as in it's made up or its panic or whatever. Personally I would always be very cagey without showing it. (Group 2, #9)

And it is terrible to be so negative, but I come across it [false accusations] fairly regularly… I think I've had more bogus than genuine which is terrible. I'd say nearly six out of every ten are not, are very dubious … (Group 3, #8)

Use of the term 'terrible' in this context implied that the rate of false allegations was both unfortunate but was also an indictment of the accuser. Responses from most officers indicated wariness and suspicion toward reporters of rape. It would appear that instead of accepting complaints as genuine (as dictated by the force's procedure) officers instead receive complaints with the probability of a false report firmly in mind. One participant in the longer-serving group described this skepticism in terms of a 'credibility gap' that the victim has to bridge. The police officer's logic here appears to be that it is the complainant's responsibility to prove, persuade or convince the investigator that she is telling the truth.

Detection of deception and veracity-seeking intentions appear to be conceptualised by most officers as their primary investigative decision goal. Veracity decisions were expressed with varying degrees of explicitness, from the participant who stated that the investigative goal for rape cases is always to decide if 'she is telling the truth' to the participant who says detection of deception is not the main requirement in a rape investigation although credibility always has to be assessed. The main requirement for this participant is establishing the corroborative proofs for the case.

The second most frequently mentioned investigative goal was to establish the corroborative proofs of the case. The following extracts illustrate veracity-seeking primary investigative decision goals in answer to the question: 'What is the first decision you have to make about the case?'

Well you need to get at the genuineness of it and see how credible the witness is. (Group 2, #10)

You have a victim in here and first of all she has to get over the credibility gap, be believed by the police and then she has to sit in front of 12 people and be believed by them. (Group 3, # 2)

239

The first decision is if it is true or is it false. (Group 3, #4)

There was a strong consensus among officers of the motives, circumstances and behaviour of a woman who makes a false report of rape. Officers had a number of shared, learned scripts that define both the individual who makes a false rape allegation (stereotypes) and specific characteristics of the false allegation (event schemata). A content analysis revealed the extent to which officers mentioned certain beliefs they perceived to be motivating factors that give rise to false rape allegations. These are presented in Table 10.1 below. The numbers represent the number of officers who mentioned each category (not the frequency of how often participants mentioned each category).

It is important to note that most officers mention more than one possible reason why they think women are motivated to make false complaints of rape. These stereotypes play a critical role in the social judgment phase as they provide an interpretative basis for information processing and orient decision-makers' attention as well as permitting assessment of similarity between beliefs and the situation. For example:

If she says they were doing a steady line [in a relationship] or whatever, consent is dodgy then in your own mind it may be dubious or whatever like but maybe she's just getting back at him, sleeping around or. (Group 1, #11)

A lot of these women from my impression go off-side [are unfaithful]. They have boyfriends and girlfriends and they go

Table 10.1 Motivations attributed to complainants by officers

Motivational factors	Group 1 (0 yrs) n = 13	Group 2 (5 yrs) n = 11	Group 3 (15 yrs) n = 9	Total n = 33
Revenge	10	3	6	19
Fear of pregnancy	3	5	3	11
Attention seeking	3	5	3	11
Emotional Problems	3	4	2	9
Guilt due to infidelity	2	3	3	8
Psychiatric issues	0	6	2	8
Evil personality	2	1	0	3

off-side with some fella and the next thing 'oh-oh, I was out all night, I'm going to have serious problems here', feeling guilty you know? (Group 3, #6)

Officers having at least five years' service tended to put more emphasis on dispositional factors such as problems specific to the woman, psychiatric difficulties and the need for attention whereas the more inexperienced group focused more on situational factors associated with elements of the event and story. All groups were inclined to mention the possibility of pregnancy and guilt regarding an extra-relational affair.

Underlying these descriptions is the tacit understanding that false allegations are made against persons known to the complainant.[2] Officers believed and expected that many false rape allegations would subsequently be withdrawn by the complainant. Concomitantly, there was an expectation that false reporting has a short duration and this expectation forms an identifiable component of shared schemata of false rape allegations, giving rise to an *expectation-confirmation bias*. This occurs if the complainant does withdraw her report, such that the investigator then confirms his/her earlier suspicions. The experience is then interpreted and categorised by the investigator as a false report and will be employed in future conversations and investigations of rape. It is likely that this expectation-confirmation bias accounts, in part, for the inflated perceptions of high levels of false rape reports. This interpretation is further reinforced by stories of false rape accounts told by colleagues where the ground truth[3] is unknown, yet the officer confidently describes and categorises the report as having been definitely false. Officers, for example, described scenarios where clearly some incident had happened, or the victim was under age, yet the report was still categorised by the participant as wholly false.

In saying that too you'd find the people that would actually come in to cry rape or whatever and then withdraw their complaints, its kind of withdrawn in a moment of impulse and they haven't thought their story through. (Group 1, #13)

The second part of the model concerns the kinds of processing that occur once a complaint of rape is received by a Garda. This is the social judgment phase and marks the beginning of the 'investigative stages' shown in Figure 10.3.

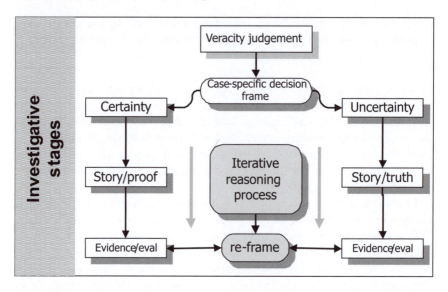

Figure 10.3   Investigative stages

When a report of rape is made, depending on the constellation of beliefs held by the Garda and the relative weight ascribed to veracity judgments as dictated by the primary decision goal, an initial veracity judgment is made. What results is the definition of the case-specific decision frame – either the officer believes the woman to be telling the truth or is uncertain as to whether the woman is telling the truth. Whether the officer initially judges the woman to be telling the truth or not (veracity judgment) depends on the type of beliefs held by the decision-maker *and* importantly the extent to which the officer perceives their role (primary decision goal) as establishing if the allegation is true or not. Veracity judgments, described by participants as 'instinctual' or based on 'gut feeling', are made by Gardaí using a number of heuristics, namely the availability and recognition heuristics. These heuristics are tied to elements of the EKS (attitudes, schema, etc.), whereby a series of veracity triggers or cues lead to a condition of certainty or uncertainty in the investigator. The case-specific investigative decision frame is characterised by certainty when the Gardaí believes the complaint to be genuine, or with uncertainty when the Garda is unsure.

> It depends on the person, as I say some people you know for a fact they are genuine and other people are iffy [dubious] …

it's just instinct I suppose, you just kinda say 'hmmmm, I don't know. (Group 1, #7)

Actual descriptions of rape cases that participants had experience of also conformed to this analysis:

I remember when I initially walked into the hospital my first impression of her was 'hmmm, don't know if I like the look of her', just police instinct you do, don't know now, and I'm talking to her and still wasn't convinced. (Group 1, #12)

Officers described a number of veracity cues that they employed in order to make intuitive credibility judgments (see Table 10.2).

These were categorised as *non-verbal, story-based cues* and *intelligence-based cues* (information derived from third-party sources). Non-verbal cues that lead to veracity judgments include how the person looks and behaves visually (age, injury, professional status, social class, dishevelled) and how they behave and react to the situation (body language, agitation, distress, nervousness, calm).

It goes back to body language, but people never cease to amaze me, you know we had another girl here who joked and took

Table 10.2 Number of participants in each group mentioning cues to deception

Cues to deception	Group 1 (0 yrs) n = 13	Group 2 (5 yrs) n = 11	Group 3 (15 yrs) n = 9	Total n = 33
Emotional affect	11	7	7	25
Story consistency	7	9	6	22
Acquaintance	10	4	4	18
Drugs/drink	5	6	3	14
Body language	6	2	5	13
Working class	6	4	2	12
Injury	3	2	5	10
Previous allegations	4	1	3	8
Sexual contact	5	3	0	8
Way they talk	4	2	1	7
Promiscuity	4	0	2	6
Timing of report	1	3	1	5
Age	3	0	0	3

it very casual, you know what's the story here? This girl had been raped and buggered you know? And you say to yourself, 'I don't think I'd [be like that]'. (Group 3, #2)

Very few genuine that come in here, mostly due to alcohol. (Group 2, # 4)

Am, dress ... I mean it's a factor that comes into it [deciding if the allegation is true/not], the runners, hood, earrings, jewellery, simple little things like that we'd know, you'd associate with am, I don't even want to say poorer areas because socio-economic, nothing like that, but just you'd associate those crimes with ... (Group 1, #2)

Story-based cues to deception include characteristics of the report made, i.e. details of the story and events surrounding the rape, the way in which the injured party tells the story and the way she speaks, but, most importantly, what she says and against whom the complaint is made. Verbal cues generally manifest themselves as elements of the told story that the investigators categorise as indicative of truthfulness or not. Other veracity cues include information supplied by third parties, e.g. about the injured party's family or about herself (that she had made a report before). These again manifest themselves as elements of the story that the investigator considers being indicative of truth or lies. These tend to occur earlier on in the investigative process.

If somebody comes in we haven't seen before and reports a rape and we have to discover if it's true or not, we begin to elicit quite a bit of information from her and the only way you can trip her up, or not to trip her up but to confirm her story is to go back and see if it matches what you have written down on your notes and it's just a matter of am, to confirm your story all the time. (Group 2, #1)

I was of the opinion that she was claiming that the man had performed oral sex on her against her will and it was my belief that if this was the case, she could have got away or injured him in some way. (Group 2, #8)

The third section of the model concerns the procedural features of the investigation, i.e. a formal interview and statement. This is illustrated in Figure 10.1 in two parts that run parallel, as each describes the investigative process but are located within different case-specific decision frames. On the one hand, automatic veracity judgments can result in the investigator feeling confident that a crime has occurred (or willing to accept a complaint as true). This leads to a 'condition of certainty' regarding the veracity of a complaint and the officer is then motivated to seek and delineate corroborative proofs of the complaint. On the other hand, case-specific veracity judgments can result in the investigator feeling uncertain with respect to the truth of an allegation and the investigative aim becomes one of reducing uncertainty and detecting deception. Findings strongly suggest that investigative conditions of uncertainty are common with rape allegations and are broadly defined in terms of varying levels of doubt. Feelings of uncertainty were categorised at differing levels of strength, from officers who said they had a 'gut feeling' that something was wrong to those that remarked 'she was definitely lying' to a participant that said 'that something was amiss'.

This part of the model describes the information processing strategies that occur during investigative procedures. One of the main strategies, employed by all officers, was the generation of story structures and causal models, particularly when taking the victim's statement of complaint. Statement taking is a conduit, not only for making decisions (e.g. to arrest an alleged offender if reasonable grounds exist) but also for testing the validity of previous judgments directly related to the decision frame of the investigation. For example, factors such as the appearance of the complainant, whether injury is apparent, what type of area she comes from, the type of rape she is reporting, whether she has reported before and whether she is drunk or has taken drugs create a veracity impression and the statement is subsequently employed to test and verify veracity hypotheses. Noticeably, it is mainly the younger probationer officers who mention this function. For example, if the complainant is able to give a lot of detail, the officer taking the statement will interpret this as an indication that she could not have made up such a story.

A further issue is that of consent. This was verbalised by officers saying that they have to find out how the complainant expressed her lack of consent (i.e. did she resist, scream, shout), consent being one of the points that has to be legally covered for the investigation file and for court. There was widespread acknowledgment among the more experienced officers, that a 'good' statement is one where the issue of 'consent' is described and outlined clearly and in full. This category is related to the need to establish if a crime has really occurred but it is also related to the demands and constraints of the law.

Officers used a number of methods while taking the statement to reach veracity decisions. The behaviour of the complainant is observed throughout the interview and behaviour is evaluated according to the case-specific decision frame of the investigator. Testing methods vary from sending in different interviewers and comparing notes to confronting the complainant with the investigators' doubts and observing her reaction. Officers also described trying to confirm whether the story elicited at different times and with different people is consistent, they may attempt to 'trip her up', employ repeat questions (question asked twice at different times), and use directive questions such as 'how did you know it was that time?' The following are a number of extracts that illustrate the above points.

> I think it would be easier to spot a liar than someone a person who is telling the truth. You could trip, you have to test them with questioning. I know it's not a nice thing to do, but you have to test their story like, so when you're writing notes and whatever it's very hard to tell a lie, a long lie because you know you won't have that good a memory, you'll be writing a statement that is six or seven pages long and they're telling lies, you can pick up lies ... (Group 1, #1)

The two groups of more experienced officers have a more sophisticated understanding and detailed knowledge of the ways in which information is best elicited from complainants and gave more examples of methods to elicit further detailed responses in an interview setting. This is consistent with the findings of decision-making research demonstrating that expert decision-makers with more experience have a greater repertoire of information and can recall more complex sets of manoeuvres from which to choose (Dunn et al. 2002).

Story construction is followed by iterative sequences of evidence interpretation and evaluation. One of the main investigative tasks is to try to find information that will corroborate the allegation made by the complainant. Finding corroborative evidence that supports the veracity of a story means that the decision-maker will believe and feel more certain that the story is true. The strongest type of evidence is that which can be presented in a court of law as proof for some element of the case, e.g. forensic evidence or evidence from eyewitnesses. Officers perceive this kind of evidence as a powerful indication (often incontestable) of truth. Where this evidence is absent, doubt continues to be cast over the allegation and this has consequences for the final deliberative stage of the investigation. Officers further sought quasi-legal evidence in an attempt to accurately construct and corroborate the story. This type of information (that does not concern a point of law) is thought to provide indirect evidence and support for the validity of a story.

At any point during the investigation it is possible for the investigator to re-frame his or her decision. Officers described numerous examples of rape cases they had dealt with where their initial case-specific decision frame was later reversed as new information was evaluated, new evidence found or the victim managed to persuade the investigators that her story was true. An important finding was that social knowledge, in the form of the evaluative knowledge structure, permeates through the entire investigative process and affects primary decision goals, the case-specific decision frame, the statement process, information processing and the final deliberative stage.

The final section of the model addresses the later deliberative stages of the investigative process, where all investigative information has been amassed, subjected to varying cognitive decision strategies and prosecution recommendations are made and is shown in Figure 10.4. In Ireland the investigating Garda makes a prosecution recommendation on the investigation file. Unlike the system in the UK, the Gardaí Síochána have to forward every rape file (where they believe there to be a case), to the Director of Public Prosecutions (DPP) who formally decides the nature of the charge and whether the state will prosecute the alleged offender (HQ Circulars 60/80, 54/85, 149/85 and Code 46.51). The main investigating officer, however, makes a recommendation in the first instance to the state solicitor's office, and then to the prosecuting authorities. The recommendation covers the direction of the charge and their reasons for the same. Investigation files are sent to the District Officer before being referred to the DPP. The Superintendent is required to oversee that the file is in proper order and check that they concur with the investigating officer's recommendation. A reasoned analysis of the merits of the case should be outlined – either by the investigating member or the Superintendent.

The final deliberative stage is an extension of the investigative stage but, irrespective of the investigative decision frame, corroboration is the most preferred method employed by officers in arriving at a recommendation decision. Investigative aims motivate the decision-maker to elaborate corroborative proofs of the case.

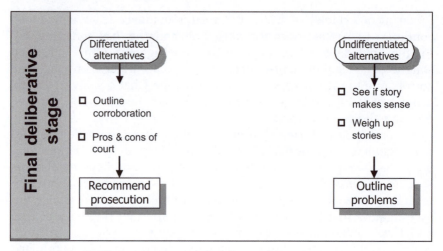

Figure 10.4 Deliberative stage of decision making

Conclusion and implications

This chapter provides an account of police decision-making using an NDM framework. Four decision-making stages were identified and the totality of the model is presented in Figure 10.5. The final element in the model is a feedback loop which arises from the decisions made, and the experience adds to the store of social knowledge, either confirming or disconfirming beliefs about rape and the women who report allegations. This is particularly important in terms of the confirmation bias around the notion of false allegations. If the officer believes that a majority of women fabricate allegations of rape and the investigation results in no further action or withdrawal of the allegation then this strengthens the officer's presumption that women lie about rape. If they believe the allegation and it is closer to the stereotype of 'real' rape then this too becomes another instance that confirms the general principle of what a rape looks like.

In this decision frame, recommendation decisions are generally made on cases where there are differentiated alternative stories due to a belief (and/or proof) that the allegation is true (or possibly entirely false). Conversely, in a decision frame of uncertainty, the decision-maker is often left with undifferentiated alternative stories to consider because 'hard' corroborative evidence is unavailable/could not be found. Many rape cases fall into this category but depending on the investigative decision frame, 'soft' evidence (both quasi-legal and extra-legal)[4] can play a more important role in these cases. In

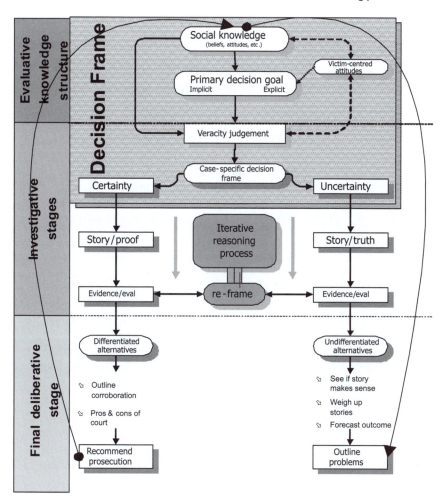

Figure 10.5 Investigative decision-making in cases

conditions of certainty, however, officers described stories that were differentiated for one or all of three reasons:

- the decision-maker has evidence to legally provide the proofs of the case;
- the decision-maker knows the complainant (and hence believes her);
- the decision-maker believes one person's story to be more truthful than the other (generally for personal reasons).

A more involved and complex set of heuristics and cognitive reasoning strategies is employed to reach a recommendation decision in this decision frame. Officers describe how they use their own implicit theories of human behaviour to make sense and evaluate the stories constructed. In this way they see if the story told 'fits in' with their own presumptions, theories and hypotheses. These assumptions drive the interpretation of information and the conclusions reached. In addition, officers describe how they 'weigh up' stories, again on the basis of what seems likely according to the decision-maker. Another important strategy is to predict the likely outcome of the case, in terms of what the prosecuting authorities are likely to think and how the case would 'go down' in court (in terms of how the witness would withstand the trial and how a jury would view the case).

> You need something else, something independent to make somebody make up their mind, you know? Evidence from somebody else or a piece of forensic evidence. If you didn't have something good to go on the DPP won't run with it. (Group 3, #6)

> It's something you discuss with other people [colleagues] and you weigh up the evidence and you make your decision on that then. (Group 3, #7)

> Her friend had come in at the same time and they all verified her story and it was all there. Her story was true, it's just that she showed no emotion [complainant not believed at first]. (Group 2, #7)

Most Gardaí said they were primarily assessing the level of corroborative evidence to see if it justified a prosecution. It is interesting to note that deciding if an allegation is true or not is often an integral part of deciding if a prosecution will be recommended or not.

This study found decision frames of uncertainty led to recommendations of uncertainty.

> I would write the whole recommendation from every bit of evidence that I had, from the way the people were with me and the whole thing … It's up to the judge and jury after I have my job done. (Group 1, #5)

This model elaborates and explains how attitudes, beliefs, stereotypes and general social knowledge are drawn on when formulating the officer's investigative goals, which in turn are related to veracity judgments. These processes operate within a complex working environment and map the antecedents of judgments of blame. By using a grounded theory adjunct to NDM, we have outlined a mechanism for *how* social knowledge is related to veracity judgments (and the construction of the case-specific decision frame) via role and goal definition in the investigation of rape. This mechanism strongly suggested that knowledge structures are not merely cognitive devices but also play an important motivational role, which together not only provide a basis for what the police attend to, but also for anticipating the future and specifying and directing their role in it.

Police officers provided a tightly constructed rationale for why they believed women make so many false rape reports and why it was their role to decide if the allegation is genuine. The most significant 'attitude-behaviour' link, in terms of its substantive impact, was between social knowledge, story construction and final prosecution decisions. Stories were the key structural features of the final recommendation stage and were evaluated using a number of often complementary decision-making strategies. For example, officers 'matched' the story narrated by the complainant with perceived 'likely' stories, given the information at hand. This involved the decision-maker assessing if the story constructed matched, represented or was similar to what the decision-maker expected in the situation. The decision-maker relied on the content of their schematic representations of rape scenarios in addition to other information employed when evaluating the story (e.g. corroborative evidence,[5] implicit theories, and information from other sources or stereotypes).

We found that the decision-maker determines the course of the interview with a complainant, what questions should be asked, how they should be phrased and with what tone of voice. They choose whether 'to get a bit tough' or to be gentle, to empathise or to confront the complainant. All of these actions have a considerable effect on the investigative process and the story constructed. The model further explains how and why certain kinds of information are sought and how information is evaluated in the way it is.

We have not sought in this chapter to constitute what makes a good decision (thought to be a desirable requirement of NDM by Broadstock and Michie 2000); rather we hope by understanding the decision process to identify vulnerable sites where potential 'errors' in decision-making may occur.

We recommend that officers be trained as evidence-gatherers rather than truth-seekers. It is important to counter the stereotype of 'real' rape elucidated by Estrich (1987) and encourage officers to be more open-minded about the many and varied circumstances under which a woman can be raped. As well as including in the training syllabuses psychological aspects of memory (what facilitates or inhibits remembering) and the psychological trauma associated with rape that may affect a complainant's demeanor, it is important to emphasise that women are often raped by men they can identify and with whom they may have been in a prior relationship. As consent is often a contested issue, there is a need to obtain as much corroborative forensic evidence as possible. This means encouraging women to come forward quickly in order to identify and preserve as many crime scenes as are implicated in the allegation.

Policies are clearly designed to encourage belief in the complaint unless the officer has strong contra-indications, but it still seems to be the case that disbelief is the default position. Encouraging officers to systematically collect the evidence and leave veracity judgments to the courts may also be instrumental in tackling the attrition rates of rape cases. Significant changes in practice can only come about through changes in organisational priorities, e.g. by examining deployment policies (who takes the initial statement and in what location), the legislative principles governing rape trials (there is a feedback loop to investigation through the view that rape complainants need to hold up to cross examination in court), and societal attitudes towards consent especially when dating and drinking mores are concerned.

Notes

1 All of these officers had nine months' operational experience as part of their training.
2 There was one exception: Group 2, #8 suggested that false allegations are made against someone unknown to the person. All other officers described scenarios where both parties were known to one another.
3 Ground truth is a term used to describe the objective reality of the event.
4 Extra-legal criteria refer to factors that are separate from the incident and relate to the lifestyle, background and 'reputation' of the complainant.
5 This refers to legal, quasi-legal and extra-legal evidence – as perceived and evaluated by the investigator.

References

Beach, L. R. (1997) *The Psychology of Decision Making: People in Organisations.* Thousand Oaks, CA: Sage.

Broadstock, M. and Michie, S. (2000) 'Processes of patient decision making: theoretical and methodological issues', *Psychology and Health*, 15: 191–204.

Brown, J., Hamilton, C. and O'Neill, D. (2007) 'Characteristics associated with rape attrition and the role played by scepticism or legal rationality by investigators and prosecutors', *Psychology, Crime and Law*, 13 (4): 355–70.

Crego, J. and Alison, L. (2004) 'Control and legacy as functions of perceived criticality in major incidents', *Journal of Investigative Psychology and Offender Profiling*, 1: 207–25.

Dunn, J., Lewandowsky, S. and Kirsner, K. (2002) 'Dynamics of communication in emergency management', *Applied Cognitive Psychology*, 16: 719–37.

Estrich, S. (1987) *Real Rape: How the Legal System Victimises Women Who Say No.* Boston: Harvard University Press.

Fielding, N. G. (1988) *Joining Forces: Police Training, Socialisations and Occupational Competence.* London: Routledge.

Fielding, N. G. and Fielding, J. (1992) 'A comparative minority: female recruits to a British constabulary force', *Policing and Society*, 2: 205–18.

Glaser, B. G. and Strauss, A. L. (1967) *The Discovery of Grounded Theory.* Chicago: Aldine.

Greuel, L. (1992) 'Police officers' beliefs about cues associated with deception in rape cases', in F. Lösel, D. Bender and T. Bliesener (eds), *Psychology and Law: International Perspectives.* Berlin: Walter de Gruyter, pp. 234–9.

Jordan, J. (2004) *The Word of a Woman? Police, Rape and Belief.* London: Palgrave.

Kelly, L., Lovett, J. and Regan, L. (2005) *A Gap or a Chasm? Attrition in Reported Rape Cases*, Home Office Research Study No. 293. London: HMSO.

Klein, G. A., Orasanu, J., Calderwood, R. and Zsambok, C. E. (eds) (1993) *Decision Making in Action: Models and Methods.* Norwood, NJ: Ablex.

Krahé, B. (1991) 'Police officers' definitions of rape: a prototype study', *Journal of Community and Applied Social Psychology*, 1: 245–54.

Krippendorf, K. (1980) *Content Analysis.* Newbury Park, CA: Sage.

Le Doux, J. C. and Hazelwood, R. R. (1995) 'Police attitudes and beliefs concerning rape', in A. W. Burgess and R. R. Hazelwood (eds), *Practical Aspects of Rape Investigation: A Multi-disciplinary Approach.* New York: CRC Press, pp. 37–45.

Minsky, M. (1968) *Semantic Information Processing.* Cambridge, MA: MIT Press.

Norros, L. and Klemola, U.-M. (1999) 'Methodological considerations in analysing anaesthetists' habits of action in clinical situations', *Ergonomics*, 42: 1521–31.

Pennington, N. and Hastie, R. (1986) 'Evidence evaluation in complex decision making', *Journal of Personality and Social Psychology*, 51: 242–58.

Strauss, A. and Corbin, J. (1990) *Basics of Qualitative Research: Grounded Theory Procedures and Techniques.* Newbury Park, CA: Sage.

Temkin, J. (1997) 'Plus ça change: reporting rape in the 1990s', *British Journal of Criminology*, 4: 507–28.

Trice, H. M. and Beyer, J. M. (1993) *The Cultures of Work Organizations.* Englewood Cliffs, NJ: Prentice Hall.

Tversky, A. and Kahneman, D. (1973) 'On the psychology of prediction', *Psychological Review*, 80 (4): 237–51.

Tversky, E. and Kahneman, D. (1981) 'The framing of decisions and the psychology of choice', *Science*, 11: 453–8.

Tversky, E. and Kahneman, D. (1982) 'Evidential impact of base rates', in E. Tversky, P. Slovic and D. Kahneman (eds), *Judgements Under Uncertainty: Heuristics and Biases.* New York: Cambridge University Press.

Wagenaar, W. A. and Keren, G. B. (1986) 'The seat beat paradox: effects of adopted roles on information seeking', *Organisational Behaviour and Human Decision Processes*, 38: 1–6.

Winkel, F. W. and Koppelaar, L. (1992) 'Perceived credibility of the communicator: studies of perceptual bias in police officers conducting rape interviews', in F. Lösel, D. Bender and T. Bliesener (eds), *Psychology and Law: International Perspectives.* Berlin: Walter de Gruyter, pp. 234–9.

Chapter 11

Police interviews of rape victims: tensions and contradictions

Lesley McMillan and Michelle Thomas

Introduction

It is widely recognised that the evidence provided by victims[1] in rape cases is critical, not least because, aside from the defendant, there are rarely any other witnesses to the assault (Kebbell *et al.* 2007). Research attention has often been given to complainants providing their evidence in court (Kebbell *et al.* 2007; Konradi 1996). However, the process of giving evidence begins almost immediately upon reporting to the police, when complainants give an initial account of what has happened, and later on a more detailed account when they are interviewed by a police officer to provide a witness statement. It is this statement that helps shape the police investigation and is a key source of evidence that is referred to by both the prosecution and defence when complainants give their evidence in court.

Despite its significance throughout the criminal justice process, the complainant interview is very rarely focused on the literature on rape and sexual assault. In this chapter we would like to make a contribution to addressing this omission by examining the role and function of the police interview from the perspective of the different parties involved in the judicial process: police officers, judges and rape complainants themselves.

It has been argued that the information obtained from interviews with victims and witnesses of crime often forms the cornerstone of an investigation both in terms of finding out what has occurred and who perpetrated the crime (Milne and Bull 2006). However, the very process of collecting this information has been described as an 'obstacle course' that has to manage problems with the witness's memories, as well as the difficulties associated with taking and recording statements (Milne and Bull 2006: 9). There is some evidence to suggest that interviews with victims and witnesses have not always been accorded the same priority in terms of resources and training as those with suspects and offenders. Despite the centrality of this interview to the success of the investigation (Fisher *et al.* 1987; McLean 1995; Milne and Bull 2006), officers do not always feel adequately trained (Dando *et al.* 2008) and questioning styles used by the police are sometimes not effective in eliciting full and detailed accounts (Clarke and Milne 2001; McLean 1995; Milne and Bull 2006).

The means by which an interview is documented has also been found to influence the amount and type of information recorded. Video-recorded interviews can be advantageous as they can be less time-consuming than written statements, allowing the interviewer to concentrate on the information collection process as opposed to both asking and recording questions, and also provides a record of the specific questions that were asked as well as the witness's responses (Milne and Bull 2006). Furthermore, a statement recorded in this manner more accurately reflects the words and responses of the witness or victim, in contrast to written statements which may be recorded according to the interviewing officer's perceptions of what is relevant, confirmatory, appropriate language and so on (Milne and Bull 2006; Rock 2001). The more accurate the statement, the more effective the investigation and prosecution is likely to be (Milne and Bull 2006). From the perspective of the complainant a video interview can be additionally advantageous as it avoids the need for them to repeatedly give their account (Home Office 2000).

Recent legislation and guidelines in England support the use of video interviews in serious sexual offences. The Youth Justice and Criminal Evidence Act 1999 identified adult victims of sexual assault as potentially vulnerable or intimidated witnesses and stipulated that interviews with this group should be video-recorded (with the option of using this video interview as their evidence-in-chief in criminal trials). The Home Office 'Achieving Best Evidence' (ABE) guidelines (2000) also recommend the use of video-recorded evidence as evidence-in-chief for complainants in rape and sexual assault cases. The experience of providing evidence in a witness/ victim statement is of course a central part of the complainant's experience with the police. Several studies have highlighted the significance of sensitive and sympathetic handling of cases by the police with regard to women's experience of reporting rape and that this is likely to influence whether or not they chose to withdraw from the legal process (Jordan 2001; Kelly *et al.* 2005; Temkin 1997, 1999). The increase in numbers of reported rapes suggests increased confidence in the way police might handle a complaint (Regan and Kelly 2003). However, little research has been undertaken since the changes to police procedures for dealing with rape in the 1980s. There is some evidence that police handling of rape and sexual assault complainants has improved with many women generally satisfied with their experience with the police (Adler 1991; Lees and Gregory 1993; Temkin 1997). Examining the reporting process in some detail, Temkin interviewed 23 women who had reported rape to the Sussex police during the years 1991–3. Temkin found that the process of statement taking was a key factor in women's experience of reporting, with importance attached to having a female officer, for consideration to be given to the timing of statement taking in relation to the assault, for them to be given opportunities to rest and recuperate as and when necessary and to be given the opportunity to give their statement without interruption from investigating officers. The experience of being treated with disbelief was found to be particularly distressing. Home Office research found that feeling able to give their evidence accurately was the most important predictor of satisfaction for vulnerable and intimidated witnesses (including rape victims) (Hamlyn, Phelps and Sattar 2004).

In this chapter, drawing on data from two different studies, we will examine the police interview in rape and sexual assault investigations from the perspectives of the different parties involved in the criminal justice process. We will begin by considering the interview from the perspective of serving police officers, including their views of the role and function of the interview, and the advantages and disadvantages of video-recorded interviews, before moving on to look at the functions of the police interview in the courtroom context. We will then look at data collected from women who have reported being raped or sexually assaulted to the police in order to consider their experiences and expectations regarding the police interview. Before doing this we will briefly outline the methods used to collect the data we refer to in this paper.

Study details

Data that informs this chapter come from two ESRC-funded studies. The first study involves three sources of data (interviews with police officers, data from a review of police rape files and field notes) and the second study uses one source of data (interviews with women who reported rape to the police). Police interview data was collected as part of a larger ESRC-funded (Res-061-23-0138) study involving both authors, which aimed to explore factors influencing attrition in rape cases. The original research took a case study approach and, as such, all data for the study were collected in the English county of Sussex. Sussex police fully supported the study and for the purposes of the research generated a list of all police officers in the force who had dealt with at least one rape in the last 12 months, either as an 'Officer in the Case' (OIC) investigating officer, or as a Sexual Offence Liaison Officer (SOLO). We drew a purposive sample from this list to cover geographical policing divisions in the force area and gender. A total of 35 SOLO officers and 11 investigating officers were contacted of whom 11 SOLOs and 9 investigators agreed to take part in a semi-structured interview.[2] A further 13 officers e-mailed and volunteered to be interviewed after receiving the e-mail from the Superintendent. A further seven senior officers[3] (Detective Chief Inspectors and above) were also interviewed. This resulted in a total of 40 interviews, consisting of 7 female and 6 male SOLO officers, and 7 female and 20 male detectives.[4] Officers ranged in age from 22 to 52 years, and had between 2 and 28 years of service in the police. All interviews were tape-recorded and transcribed verbatim. The authors individually read and reread the transcripts and then separately developed analytic categories based on the data and the existing literature. These categories were then compared and discussed and categories subsequently refined, revised and developed as appropriate. Transcripts were coded using the qualitative data analysis package NVivo, and were analysed systematically using analytic induction (Frankland and Bloor 1999).

As part of this study of rape attrition courtroom observations were undertaken by the authors at four rape trials in Sussex courts. Detailed field notes were taken throughout the trials and after 'conversations in the field' with various parties in the judicial process (such as OICs, judges, barristers and ushers). These field notes were systematically analysed.

The research also involves a review of all reported rapes to Sussex police within a specific 12-month period. These case files include complainant statements and transcripts of complainant interviews (where tape- or video-recorded) and these also informed the discussion on the experience from the police and complainant perspectives. At the time of writing 182 cases reported had been reviewed, approximately half of those reported in this period.

Interview data from women who have reported sexual violence to the police are taken from another ESRC-funded study conducted by McMillan that examined feminist organisations providing welfare support for women who have experienced sexual and domestic violence (e.g. Rape Crisis) and was a comparative study of Sweden and the UK. The study involved mixed methods and included 25 interviews with women working or volunteering in these services. Of these 16 had personal experience of violence, eight of whom had reported rape or sexual assault to a UK police force. The data informing the complainant aspect of this chapter is taken from these eight interviews. During the interviews women described the process of reporting to the police and their experience of it, as well as the experiences of other women they have supported as a result of their role in support organisations such as Rape Crisis.

Findings: police perspective

Although rape investigations follow national guidelines, strategies and policies may vary across different forces. At the time of data collection the Sussex Police Force Strategy dictated that upon the report of a rape or serious sexual offence, a specially trained Sexual Offence Liaison Officer (SOLO) would be deployed and this officer would be responsible for taking a first account, accompanying the complainant to a 'victim suite' and assisting in the forensic medical examination and liaising with the detective in charge of the case (OIC) (Sussex Police Rape and Sexual Violence Strategy 2007). In keeping with Home Office guidelines, in Sussex interviews with rape complainants are typically taken under Achieving Best Evidence (ABE)[5] format. Reflecting the significance of the interview and the seriousness of the offence, the Sussex Police rape protocol requires that an interview with a rape complainant is undertaken by a 'Tier 3' interviewer, or a Tier 2 interviewer where a Tier 3[6] interviewer is unavailable and expediency is critical (Sussex Police Rape and Sexual Violence Strategy 2007).

Functions of the interview

All police officers saw the complainant interview as crucial in the gathering of evidence in order to progress the investigation.

Information provided by the complainant in the interview informed the police strategies in a variety of ways, from forensic decisions regarding the submission of samples for analysis, search strategies at the crime scene, identification and location of witnesses to the event or circumstances before or after the event, and indeed identification and arrest of the suspect. These strategies could initially be informed by the brief question and answer (QandA) account taken by the SOLO officer, which is an initial description of the main aspects of the assault solicited from the victim as soon as possible after report, and can inform the investigation particularly in relation to forensic strategies and then honed and focused during the detailed interview.

Timing of the interview

In order to facilitate the most effective investigation, it is perhaps unsurprising that officers typically preferred that the interview be conducted as soon as possible after the incident has been reported. However, in reality the timing of the interview depends on a number of factors such as whether the complainant was under the influence of drugs or alcohol at the time of reporting, the availability of a suitably trained officer to conduct the interview and the availability of an appropriate location for the interview. In particular, the timing of the interview was often decided by the needs and preferences of the complainant themselves, as these officers noted:

[The interview] tends not to [be done immediately] because once you've done the medical and you've done all that side of things often the victim is not really sort of up to being interviewed. (Senior detective, male)

Depending on how the victim feels, you either will shut the suite down and leave it there, or if they're up for it, [...], sometimes I will start doing the beginnings of an interview in detail, but it's dictated by them. (Senior detective, female)

[... W]e wouldn't be doing the ABE interview that closely after the medical, there might be a number of reasons why, they might be drunk, they might be just too traumatised, but we want to do it fairly soon [...] (Senior detective, male)

Importance of detail

The level of detail required by the police was a very common theme in our police data, as these officers explained:

> You look for everything, even if it's not relevant at the time, there might be some nugget in there that leads you down that different path that gets you more evidence. (Detective, male)

> [...] I'm trained to go into extreme detail with regards what happens, what position, where were your hands, what did you feel, smell, touch, that sort of thing. (Detective, male)

The process of establishing what was often described as 'fine-grained detail' was illustrated by one officer as follows:

> Some rape allegations you'll say 'ok, so you've got to this room, you're wearing jeans and you're wearing a top and you're wearing a cardigan, and so you tell me what happened then?' and they say 'well I just got naked and we were on the sofa and sex happened', 'ok what we need to do is go back and revisit that point', and the detail just isn't there, and when you want to sort of probe, 'ok you say your knickers come off, how did they come off? Did you take them off or were they taken off? How were they taken off?, if they were taken off', things like [....] (SOLO, female)

The importance of collecting such a detailed account was reflected in both the time it could take to conduct the interview and also the selection of appropriately trained officers. As one officer told us:

> I'll interview – you can be with somebody for half a day, take the account, [...] it's not just any old plod who goes out, and we'll do our damnedest to find the evidence if it's there [...] (Detective, male)

Officers saw this process of collecting a very detailed account as essential to the investigation, and crucial to establishing investigative strategies and putting together a robust case. In order to produce as strong a case as possible it was seen as vital that they address and probe any inconsistencies or gaps in the complainant's account. Some officers recognised that the production of a clear, consistent and detailed account could be problematic for someone who had recently been sexually assaulted. As one officer told us:

> It's the middle of the night, they had been drinking alcohol and it was a traumatic experience, so it's not uncommon to have those little gaps. (Detective, male)

And indeed it was acknowledged that 'it is alien to most people to use the amount of detail required in a police interview' (OIC, Michelle Thomas (MT) field notes). However, if the gaps were too frequent or the inconsistencies too great, then this could lead officers to question, not only the potential strength of the case they could build up, but also the veracity of the complaint itself.

Veracity

The notion of establishing 'truth' and 'veracity' is a common theme in the context of police interviews with suspects. There is literature which suggests that suspect interviews are not always a neutral process where information is gathered in order to establish the 'truth' but rather are a complex interaction between the parties (Quinn and Jackson 2007) and where assumptions of 'guilt' can shape interviewing style and lead to an 'accusatorial style of interviewing' (Mortimer and Shepherd 1999). The concept of 'guilt' may not be considered relevant in an interview with a victim of sexual assault; however, the establishment of truth remained pertinent. Indeed our data suggested that officers viewed the interview as a means of not simply 'establishing the facts' but also assessing the veracity of the complainant's allegation. In particular, the ability to provide detail was noted by many officers as an important means of assessing whether an assault had occurred or whether the complainant was making a false allegation. As two officers reflected:

> I'm not a lie detector, I don't know whether people are telling the truth or not, but what I do, and how we interview is we get down to what we call 'fine-grained detail', that's what Advanced Interviews do, they want to know the nuts and bolts of exactly what happened. Now the more detail you try and get from someone, the more easy it is to prove whether they are lying or not. (Senior detective, male)

It's that fine-grained detail I think. It's when you ask someone what happens and … lots of people can tell you something but then to expand on that with fine-grained detail and to be able to sort of flesh it out … because it's that fine-grained detail that makes it believable […] (Detective, male)

The consistency of the account both internally within the interview itself and between the first account 'QandA' and the interview was also seen as a means of establishing whether the report was genuine.

Interviewer: What sort of things make you believe somebody or not believe them?
Respondent: Inconsistencies in their story. So you will ask them something and they will give an answer and then you will rephrase it a bit differently and ask them the same question again and you'll get a different answer. And sort of timing of things will be inconsistent. (SOLO, female)

Describing a recent case that had been charged and was awaiting trial, one officer explained why he considered this to be a 'good case':

So she gave this initial account to the neighbour and then obviously the police arrive and they ask her some questions, she gives another account, slightly fuller account, which mirrors exactly her initial account. Then later on she was interviewed again on tape, videotape, and gives another really really detailed account, really good account of what had happened, again, mirroring exactly the first two accounts. (Detective, male)

Credibility

Since the advent of Shadow Charging[7] the Crown Prosecution Service (CPS) has taken over the responsibility for deciding whether or not a defendant should be charged. This means that officers have to produce a case that will satisfy the CPS criterion for charging. The complainant interview forms a critical part of the case that is put forward to the CPS and could inform decisions on a range of levels.

When liaising with the CPS regarding charging decisions the perceived 'credibility' of the complainant was a critical factor. Many police officers saw that CPS perceptions of complainant credibility were shaped by the production of a consistent, detailed account.

Challenging those inconsistencies with the complainant was seen as a means of presenting them as a more credible witness and thus also presenting a stronger case to the CPS, as one officer recalled:

> Because, when you're dealing with so many you just know, you know the ones that are really strong, this was like a 'proper rape' you know, a good case of rape, there were some inconsistencies in her account, and they [the CPS] wanted to drop it based on some inconsistencies, but together, this is about us working in partnership, we work through those inconsistencies and I said 'well we'll re-interview her about those'. (Senior detective, female)

A small number of officers also mentioned how they felt that the video interview 'performance' could influence CPS opinions of whether a complainant would make a 'good witness' and that this could be problematic. As one officer told us:

> I think that's something that the CPS don't understand, they might see a video that lasts an hour and a half, an hour, [...] and on that person that they've only met through that machine, through that videotape, they will make their judgment of what that person's like [...] (Senior detective, male)

Interview as a performance for court

Indeed, the data suggested that interviewing officers were conscious of the video interview as a tool, not simply for the police to collect information to further their investigation, but also as a piece of evidence that may impact on both the CPS and influence the jury. Reflecting on and assessing recent interviews they had conducted, two officers spontaneously considered the potential of the interview as video evidence should a case come to trial. They told us:

> Yeah it [the interview] was very good and as far as playing the interview to a jury I think it came across really well. (Detective, male)

> I was the interviewer and she came across as, 'when it suited her she turned the tears on', it would have been a classic case of her evidence in chief would have done her no good whatsoever. (Senior detective, male)

Indeed it seemed the use of the video interview as evidence-in-chief could render the complainant vulnerable to 'rape myths' concerning the 'appropriate' range and level of emotions that should be experienced and displayed by someone reporting a rape, and could lead to the video interview becoming a form of performance or even an 'audition' for the CPS, and later, if the CPS decide to charge, for the judge and jury in court. As one officer told us:

> As I say they [the CPS] had an issue with reliability [...] how she came across. I've now had the opportunity to review the second ABE video interview of the victim, she represents as more composed and clear in her recall, though still suffering some emotional distress when she actually recounts the sexual intercourse occurring. (Detective, male)

And another told us:

> She reported it and we did the video interview here, and when I did the interview with her I kept saying to her 'so how did that make you feel?', and she kept saying 'like I wanted to stab him, so angry I just wanted to kill him, if you give me a knife now I'm going to stab him', and that's all she said, and I thought 'this is not, it's not looking good, because you play back to a court she's just going to look like an angry, frustrated ..., rather than a vulnerable victim, she's going to look quite angry and frustrated', [...] (SOLO/detective, female)

A small number mentioned their beliefs in the loss of impact a video interview had on the jury as opposed to a complainant giving live evidence. As one officer reflected:

> I never think it's as good, not as effective, juries don't seem to be as receptive to watching a video as someone live, you don't get the emotions. (OIC, MT field notes)

Interview impact on the complainant

Many officers were not indifferent to the demands placed on rape complainants of undergoing an interview, particularly as the interview requires significant detail. As one officer told us:

> I mean my opening words to whoever I interview for a rape is saying 'afterwards both of us, we're going to be absolutely shattered and you need time out after this because I'm going to have to do a lot of concentration, a lot of recall, and all the work is down to you and you alone because you've just got to give me absolutely everything that I want […]. (SOLO/detective, female)

However, a number of officers made reference to their belief that not only did the video interview significantly improve the experience of taking the statement from the perspective of the interviewing officer, but also from the perspective of the complainant. As this officer commented:

> Taking a long statement from somebody it can take days, you're sort of there saying 'hang on I'm writing something out', so I think there's an improvement. (Senior detective, male)

> Well, the video interviews are good I would say, on the whole, because it's recorded, it's more natural and fluid than writing, because obviously someone would tell you something you write it down and there are big gaps which sort of interrupts the flow of it. (Detective, male)

One officer even felt that the process and experience of providing a statement to the police could have potentially therapeutic qualities:

> I feel like it is just like I am selling them some sort of line but it's almost … when you get them to speak to you, I always try and explain to them 'look you telling me pushes the burden of what's happened from you onto me', do you know what I mean? It's the old 'get it off your chest routine', but in a more scientific way, and I have had numerous victims that say 'yeah, I feel better now for telling you because now the burden, the onus is on you to deal with it, not me'. (Senior detective, male)

Several recognised the potential for the video to be used as evidence-in-chief as a means for reducing the stress associated with a court appearance for a complainant. As one commented:

> I think the evidence in chief by video is far more a refreshing way of doing it and a more accurate way of doing it, and after

that they can be cross examined on what they have to say. And like anything, the defence have their turn and then the prosecution will re-examine them again if there are any issues. So I think that will make it better for victims [...]. (Senior detective, male)

The interview in court

Our interviews with police officers showed that there was an awareness of how a complainant might be perceived in a court based on their 'performance' in their video interview. This view was reflected in comments and during our courtroom observations. However, these data also highlighted potential incompatibilities between the collection of detailed evidence to further police investigations and an interview which makes effective and compelling evidence in the courtroom context. This was seen as particularly the case where video-recorded interviews were used as evidence-in-chief in court and related to the duration of the interview and the careful, and sometimes repetitive, collection of minute detail surrounding the assault. In a conversation during the observation of a rape trial one judge spoke to us directly about this conflict:

The judge talked about inadequate police interviews when recordings of interviews are shown to the jury. He said that the impact is lost when questioning is ineffective and the interview/ video runs on for 2 hours plus and that there was often much repetition – that events are summarised and then gone over in detail and then gone over again and so heard three times and the jury is effectively 'lost'. (MT, field notes)

He also commented on the quality and effectiveness of the actual 'filming' of the interview and how this was an area he felt could be improved:

The judge talked at length about issues relating to video links (there was some uncertainty about whether this would be used in the current trial). He said that when watching video interviews the jury forget that 'they are not at home watching with their takeaway'. He went on to talk about the problems of poor visual and sound quality of recordings and described the jury as 'just watching a stick insect' (referring to the distance the complainant is filmed from). He said that something is lost via video link – heads appear tiny, you lose eye contact and lose impact. He reflected that he wondered whether the police were actually informing complainants about 'special measures' and the possible impact they might have on a jury. He said he felt that with video link juries were more likely to acquit and that this could be explained to the complainant. (MT, field notes)

However, we also saw that 'live' evidence could also lose its impact because of the needs of the criminal justice process.

[The complainant] is giving a very personal and emotional account in quite fine detail and this is punctuated by the Crown Barrister repeatedly saying 'right pause there' [to give people time to record what she was saying] – I just think this must be very difficult for a complainant to 'tell their story' – and indeed for the jury to 'hear' it. The account goes on and there is lots of pausing for people to make notes. All the 'pause there' are awful – even if they are deemed necessary. (MT, field notes)

The Crown Barrister goes on to ask more very detailed questions and the complainant breaks down. There is quite a contrast between the cool, factual approach of the Crown Barrister and the emotion of the complainant. The Crown Barrister interjects with an abrupt 'Keep your voice up!' There is so much detail, for example about the layout of the downstairs of the house, I can see this is necessary but this sort of detailed factual information is in strange contrast to the very emotional descriptions. The judge occasionally interjects to clarify detail and he is also making a lot of notes. (MT, field notes)

Complainant's perspective

Importance of free narrative

While police interviews have a function in the investigative process and courtroom process, they also form a central part of the experience of reporting a traumatic life event to the police from the perspective of the complainant. Data from our interviews with women who reported their sexual assault to the police highlighted their desire to be able to give a free narrative account of their assault during the interview process. Women who were able to do this reported a more positive experience with the policing process than those who felt their story was interrupted or questioned too specifically during it. For example, one woman reported:

> I needed to tell MY story MY way, but I wasn't allowed to do that. I would be, um, telling it but then interrupted to clarify something or go back to a different point ... it distracted me, and confused my own memory of it. It made me angry that he wouldn't just listen.

In contrast, women who felt they were given the space to give a free narrative reported a more positive experience, for example:

> She just said 'tell me what happened, from start to finish, in your words and I'll listen', and I did ... I felt such relief afterwards, that she'd heard me. We went back over, well ... most of it, all of it, but I told it first my way.

Expectation and 'burden' of detail

As we have seen evidenced in the interviews conducted with police officers, there is concentration on specific details within the account of the complainant, and these are given high importance by the police. Data from transcripts of complainant interviews conducted by Sussex Police, and from our interviews with women who had reported to a number of forces throughout the UK, suggested that the necessity of detail was experienced as a burden by complainants and the questioning directed at retrieval of detail could be distressing for some. The following verbatim interaction taken from an interview with a rape complainant in Sussex shows clearly the importance placed on detail within an account, and the expectation or pressure likely to be placed on the complainant for explicit detail in the account, which may or may not be readily available to the victim.

> DS (*Detective Sergeant*): I want to, to go into lots of detail. Now, the sort of detail I'm gonna ask you to do is, um, if you imagine that glass there [indicates glass on the table]. Most people, if you were describing that to somebody in a conversation you'd just say 'there was a glass on the table and it had water in it'.
> C (*Complainant*): Mmm hmm.

DS: But actually, what I need you to do is to picture the glass and say it's actually probably about eight inches tall. It's round, completely round. It's got little squares on it that are, like, er, white, etched into the glass. There are lines that come off at ninety degrees off of these squares. Er, and the diameters are probably about three inches across. And the water in the glass is probably about two inches down from the top. That's the sort of detail I'm gonna need you to try and concentrate on in a minute when I hand over to you.

C: But I don't know if I remember everything like that, that detail ... but what if I can't, don't have it in my mind ... what if I let you down?

(Case file)

Our own interview data with women who had experienced the rape reporting process highlighted this concentration on detail and the difficulties it presented. Two women commented:

He kept asking where his hands were when he grabbed me and I didn't know, I just know he grabbed me ... all I remember is the fear, the panic ... not where his hands were, but he kept saying 'where were his hands?', 'you must know where his hands were' 'n I thought 'I've got no idea'. He kept asking me to tell him.

They wanted so much information from me and I never had it. I had to describe the car – the car he was in when he collected me but all I could say was it was blue, I mean, like I cared what colour the dashboard was! I mean they asked that ... and I felt stupid that I didn't know and they kept pushing over and over. Why were they asking me about the dashboard? What's that got to do with it?

Inability to remember or articulate

It is acknowledged in literature on trauma that '... sometimes confusion about facts, complicity, and peril are part of trauma's emotional aftershocks' (Coffey 1998: 44), and as such trauma recall on the part of the complainant may not include all the details. It is clear from our data taken from transcripts of complainant interviews conducted by Sussex police that specific details are not always available to the complainant at the time of interview. For example:

I'm sure both of them were involved but I can't exactly remember how they got me to the floor, um …. [pause]. I can't remember whether they told me 'sit down' or … [pause] I really don't know. (Case file)

I don't remember what colour his eyes were … dark, I think … but, I don't really know. (Case file)

Our interview data with women who had reported sexual violence to the police in the UK showed that women were often unable to tell the story of their assault with the kind of linearity one might expect in a conventional story. Their recall of events often jumped from place to place in the story, and women themselves were concerned that it did not result in a 'good' story from the point of view of the police.

I couldn't remember everything – my mind would jump about …. you see I could remember the end, and the beginning, but the middle part … I had, you know, gaps, and then I would remember something from the start that I thought would be important, something he said, so jump back there. It couldn't have been easy to follow …. still now, no, it's not a normal memory, not like how you'd remember going to the shops.

All I had was a collection of visions, or images really, it wasn't an event. I was trying to describe them and I could tell they were thinking 'she's going to be no use', or that they probably didn't believe me. I just had no sense of time.

Given that '… silence is the typical response of those who are sexually assaulted' (Stanko 1997: 76), it is not surprising that women who do report to the police often find it difficult to articulate their experience of sexual violence during interview. Many comments made by complainants in their police statements reflected this difficulty:

I can't get it out of my mouth if you know what I mean. It's too embarrassing. (Case file)

I don't know how to put it. I want to say it, but I don't know how.

Do you know what I mean? (Case file)

I don't know how to get it out. (Case file)

These comments were peppered throughout many complainant statements and clearly exemplify that disclosure of sexual violence, and in particular details of the intimate violations that are at the heart of sexual violence, can be very difficult for complainants. Interviews with women who had reported to the police provided further evidence of the difficulty in articulating what Gilmore calls 'complex stories of injury' (2001), as these women said:

> I had to sit with someone who was half my age, describe how his penis entered my vagina in minute detail, how it felt, where it hurt ... I just felt so humiliated, and the detail ... did I see his penis? What did it look like? Was it erect? I understand why he asked, but I felt so embarrassed and ashamed. I couldn't answer some questions ... pretended I didn't remember.

> I think it would always be hard, impossible maybe. These are things we don't talk about, language you don't use, certainly not with a stranger – talking about my vagina, my body – I could barely find words for what they wanted, needed, me to tell them about.

Anxieties surrounding perceived veracity

The expectation of detail in accounts and complainants' inability to either remember specific details or to articulate the experience during interview caused concern for women that they were subsequently disbelieved and that they had failed to tell a 'good' and believable story. All eight women who discussed their experience of reporting sexual violence to the police stated they found the questioning of specific detail to be intrusive and felt their stories were being questioned rather than simply clarified, as these quotes illustrate:

> I didn't feel believed at all [...] to be honest, it felt like an interrogation.

> It left me feeling I hadn't convinced them about what happened that day ... I wasn't sure they were on my side, 'cause, you know, someone on your side would believe what you were saying, not question everything you said. I got tied in knots, couldn't remember it clearly anymore, 'n I started to wonder if I'd remembered it wrong because they asked so many times. I just thought they're not going to help me ... they didn't believe me.

He said I had to convince him it had happened how I was saying it did 'n basically that he had to be sure before he went anywhere with it. It was, it was my responsibility to prove it; I felt crushed.

Summary and implications

Sussex police rape strategy states that: 'The objective of the investigative plan is to bring the offender to justice and to mitigate the trauma of the experience by providing the appropriate support to the victim thereby ensuring the victim is in the strongest position to give the best evidence in court' (2007: 7). This statement indicates a police commitment not only to a robust investigative process but also to victim care. Evidence that police do have concerns about victim care is reflected in the sensitivity of the timing of the interview and the training afforded to victim interviewers. Home Office guidelines also reflect this duality of concerns, providing guidelines for *achieving best evidence* while recognising that some witnesses may be particularly vulnerable (Home Office 2000).

Paradoxically it can be this dedication to promoting a complainant's case that can render the experience negative for the complainant as efforts to build a robust account can lead to complainants feeling interrogated and disbelieved by the officers interviewing them. That said, in common with other studies (Temkin 1997), we found evidence that there still existed a widespread belief among officers that a significant proportion of rape complaints were false allegations and that the inability to produce a consistent and detailed account could sometimes lead officers (internally if not explicitly) to question the veracity of the complaint.

Throughout the extracts from interviews with police officers evaluative judgments about victim interviews are evident, with officers often referring to 'good' interviews or 'good' cases. The perception of an interview as 'good' appeared to reflect the aims of the police to undertake a thorough investigation and produce a case that would be charged by the CPS and lead to a subsequent conviction in court. Thus a 'good' interview was one where the complainant could provide a detailed and consistent account, ideally with points that could be corroborated by other evidence (for example, whereabouts at certain times corroborated by CCTV footage). To be considered a 'good interview' this account should ideally be consistent, not only internally within the police interview, but also in the telling and retelling to other audiences, such as the SOLO officer when taking the account, and any other individuals the victim may have told about the assault. The notion of a good interview, therefore, was not necessarily tied up in an assessment of the veracity of the complaint, but rather the likelihood of the case resulting in a charge or, to use a police term, whether or not the case would be 'a runner'. Our data suggested that this assessment was based on the officer's assessment of their ability to build up a strong case, with evidence to support the complainant's account. Thus a complaint could be considered to be genuine and yet not be a 'good case' or a 'good interview', but the production of a 'good account' could influence and shape perceptions of truth and veracity in relation to the complaint.

It is widely acknowledged that disclosure of trauma and the subsequent telling of trauma stories is not easy, and this is certainly the case in relation to sexual violence (Coffey 1998; Lewis Herman 1992; Stanko 1997). When reporting sexual violence to the police, complainants are required to detail their experience in a way that tells the story of what actually happened, what can be called 'historical truth', and for that story to also have some aspects of 'verifiable truth', details that can be checked and rechecked, for it to be considered a 'good' or 'useful' story for the criminal justice process (McMillan 2007). The nature of gendered and sexual violence means there are rarely any witnesses and it is, in part, the police's attempt to establish a historical and verifiable truth that leads to the concentration and importance placed on detail. In our adversarial legal system, in the few cases that come to court, these are the very aspects that will be open to scrutiny. Our data suggests, however, that it may not always be possible for complainants to provide the required level of detail in a way that satisfies criminal justice personnel, and what complainants feel they need from the interview and statement process is not always met. Our data also suggests that a positive experience with reporting rape was shaped by the need to 'tell their story', in an uninterrupted and free-flowing manner. This need could be in conflict with the structured, rigorous and detailed approach adopted by officers in their efforts to deliver an effective investigation. Women could feel that there was a disproportionate focus on peripheral and in their view unnecessary detail, very much at odds with the emotional and personal nature of the account. Indeed, a consistent response from the women who discussed their experience of reporting to the police was that concentration on specific details was distressing for them, as they often did not know, or could not recall, the information being requested.

Of course some of the detail requested by the police is undoubtedly vital in order to identify or eliminate suspects and build up a robust case. However, our research findings suggest that the need for such details is not always adequately explained. We know from our own data as well as existing literature that feeling believed is of considerable significance to rape complainants and can have a tremendous impact on their experience of the criminal justice process (Jordan 2001). Left unexplained the thorough and probing nature of the questioning and the challenging of any inconsistencies could be experienced as an indicator that the interviewing officer did not believe their account or indeed their allegation. For some women the 'telling of the story' also serves a therapeutic purpose; however, this can be undermined by the thorough questioning and probing viewed as vital by the police to the quality of the interview. There is of course a tension here given that the primary role of the police interview is to elicit a detailed enough account of the assault in order to support a prosecution and there is no explicit aim of catharsis for the victim. This adds weight to the use of Sexual Assault Referral Centres where the victim can have opportunities to 'tell their story' to the police for the purpose of the criminal justice process, but also to an appropriately trained counsellor who can provide the therapeutic element.

The introduction of video interviewing in England and Wales has come about through a commitment to providing justice to victims and a desire to enable them to give 'best evidence'. We do not have data at this point to explore this video interview from the perspective of the complainant; however, recent research suggests that many victims and witnesses would welcome such special measures as the use of a video interview as evidence-in-chief (Burton et al. 2006; Hamlyn et al. 2004). Moreover, several officers in our study reported a belief that the opportunity to be interviewed without the constant delays and interruptions necessitated by written statement taking improved the experience for both themselves and the victim.

The use of the video interview as evidence-in-chief was generally seen by police officers as a positive thing, sparing the complainant from having to go through the process of giving their evidence twice. However, this stance was challenged by our data from the courtroom, where concern was expressed that the video had a lesser impact on the jury. This, in part, was seen as due to inadequate stylistic/technical abilities on the part on the police, with complainants filmed at a long distance making it impossible to see facial expressions and responses along with poor sound quality on the recording. Furthermore, the attention to detail and the rigorous and at times repetitive questioning required by the police to further their investigation was seen as detrimental to both keeping the attention of the jury and to presenting the complainant's case in an effective way. This view was supported by our courtroom observations of trials. It has been argued that interviews recorded in very close temporal proximity to an assault can provide more compelling evidence (Office for Criminal Justice Reform 2006). However, our data suggested that often victims of sexual assault continue to be judged according to prevalent 'rape myths' regarding expected and 'appropriate' emotional responses to the assault and that complainants who did not show these accepted and anticipated emotions could potentially be regarded as less credible witnesses or even suspected of making false allegations. Thus while the opportunity to use the video interview as evidence-in-chief may improve the process of the criminal justice system for the complainant, it could potentially have a negative impact on the outcome of the case in terms of conviction of the defendant. Such concerns have been reported in other studies (Office for Criminal Justice Reform 2006); however, there is no evidence to date that the medium in which evidence is presented affects the likelihood of a 'guilty' verdict (Davies 1999) but more research is needed in this area. The contrasting views of police officers, who believe detailed and rigorous accounts from the victim are very important, and those of judges, who believe such interviews are often too lengthy and too detailed and as such put jurors off, suggests a lack of dialogue between agencies in the criminal justice system. It also suggests that using the full video interview in court may not be the most appropriate approach, and where possible and levels of vulnerability do not preclude it, victims could be supported to give evidence in person, which would avoid jurors seeing the lengthy video interview in full.

Conclusion

It appears from our data that the police interview is laden with expectations and functions that are not always compatible: it must accurately elicit and record very detailed information, provide an arena for a complainant to 'tell their story' in a manner that does not add to the trauma of the assault and the process of reporting, present the complainant as a 'good' and 'credible' witness to the CPS and later the jury and also provide effective, emotive and 'dramatically pleasing' evidence in court. Jordan (2001) notes that there has always been a tension for the police in terms of finding a balance between meeting victims' needs and the requirements of the investigative process. Writing about her research on rape reporting in New Zealand, Jordan argues that to some extent police and complainants are operating in 'different worlds' – the police being concerned with outcome and complainants focused on process. It seems that such a tension also exists in the case of the police interview, where it has to serve a number of functions that are at the very least incompatible if not in direct conflict.

There are, however, a number of practical steps that can be taken in order to alleviate some of the tensions between the different expectations and needs of the police interview. Our data suggests further training for police officers conducting complainant interviews may be needed. This should include training on the nature of traumatic memory and the difficulty complainants might have in remembering specific detail or telling a linear and 'good' story of the event. Training should also address the perceived link between detail and truthfulness, and to challenge this assumption.

When conducting interviews with victims of sexual assault officers should explain the need for detailed questioning and reassure complainants that this style of questioning and the need for detailed clarification does not reflect disbelief or suspicion but rather reflects their desire to work with the complainant to conduct as thorough an investigation and build as robust a case as possible in the hope of bringing the perpetrator to justice.

Resources should also be directed towards providing police equipment and training for video interviewing in order to produce the most effective recording of the complainant's interview. Previous research has found that the use of large-screen plasma televisions to present testimonies have a stronger impact on the jury and reduce the likelihood of acquittal compared to evidence displayed on smaller screens (Taylor and Joudo 2005). As such resources should be also extended to the courtroom so that appropriate and optimum equipment is available in all cases. Attrition rates in rape and sexual assault cases continue to be unacceptably high and the significance of the police interview in addressing this should not be overlooked.

Acknowledgments

Grateful thanks to Sussex police for their support for the research, and to the women who have experienced sexual violence and shared their stories during interview.

Notes

1 We recognise that the term 'victim' is value laden and not always accepted by those who have experienced sexual assault. However, we use this term in this paper as an acknowledgment of the seriousness of the assault. We also use the term 'complainant' and will use these terms interchangeably where appropriate in order to avoid repetitious use of language.
2 More SOLO officers were contacted than investigating officers due to the lower response rate from this group.
3 For the purposes of protecting officer anonymity, for quotations from interviews we have defined 'senior officers' as holding the rank of Detective Sergeant and above.
4 Where detectives had previously been SOLOs they were interviewed primarily about their current role.
5 Achieving Best Evidence guidelines are issued by the Crown Prosecution Service and describe good practice for interviewing witnesses and victims in order to enable them to give the best possible evidence in criminal proceedings. It provides guidance on preparation and planning, about how interviews should be recorded (by video or a written statement) and guidance on preparation for court (Home Office 2000).
6 There are five tiers of police interviewers, of which 'Tier 1' is the most basic and the level to which all officers are trained. 'Tier 5' is the most advanced.
7 Introduced initially in 2003 and nationwide across England and Wales by April 2006.

References

Adler, Z. (1991) 'Picking up the pieces: a survey of victims of rape', *Police Review*, 31 May, pp. 1114–15.
Burton, M., Evans, R. and Saunders, A. (2006) *An Evaluation of the Use of Special Measures for Vulnerable and Intimidated Witnesses*, Home Office Findings No. 270. London: Home Office.
Clarke, C. and Milne, R. (2001) *National Evaluation of the PEACE Investigative Interviewing Course*, Police Research Award Scheme, Report No. PRAS/149. London: Home Office.
Coffey, R. (1998) *Unspeakable Truths and Happy Endings: Human Cruelty and the New Trauma Therapy*. Baltimore, MD: Sidran Press.

Dando, C., Wilcock, R. and Milne, R. (2008) 'The cognitive interview: inexperienced police officers' perceptions of their witness/victim interviewing practices', *Legal and Criminological Psychology*, 13: 59–70.

Davies, G. (1999) 'The impact of television on the presentation and reception of children's testimony', *International Journal of Law and Psychiatry*, 22: 241–56.

Fisher, R., Geiselman, R. and Raymond, D. (1987) 'Critical analysis of police interviewing techniques', *Journal of Police Science and Administration*, 15: 177–85.

Frankland, J. and Bloor, M. (1999) 'Some issues arising in the systematic analysis of focus group interviews', in R. Barbour and J. Kitzinger (eds), *Developing Focus Group Research: Politics, Theory and Practice*. London: Sage.

Gilmore, L. (2001) *The Limits of Autobiography: Trauma and Testimony*. Ithaca, NY: Cornell University Press.

Hamlyn, B., Phelps, A. and Sattar, S. (2004) *Key Findings from the Surveys of Vulnerable and Intimidated Witnesses 2000/01 and 2003*, Home Office Findings No. 240. London: Home Office.

Hamlyn, B., Phelps, A., Turtle, J. and Sattar, S. (2004) *Are Special Measures Working? Evidence from Surveys of Vulnerable and Intimidated Witnesses*, Home Office Research Study No. 283. London: Home Office.

Home Office (2000) *Achieving Best Evidence in Criminal Proceedings: Guidance for Vulnerable or Intimidated Witnesses Including Children*. London: Home Office.

Jordan, J. (2001) 'Worlds apart? Women, rape and the reporting process', *British Journal of Criminology*, 41: 679–706.

Kebbell, M. R., O'Kelly, C. M. E. and Gilchrist, E. L. (2007) 'Rape victims' experience of giving evidence in English courts: a survey', *Psychiatry, Psychology and Law*, 14 (1): 111–19.

Kelly, L., Lovett, J. and Regan, L. (2005) *A Gap or Chasm? Attrition in Reported Rape Cases*, Home Office Research Study No. 293. London: Home Office.

Konradi, A. (1996) 'Preparing to testify: rape survivors negotiating the criminal justice process', *Gender and Society*, 10 (4): 404–32.

Lees, S. and Gregory, J. (1993) *Rape and Sexual Assault: A Study of Attrition: Multi-agency Investigation into the Problem of Rape and Sexual Assault in the London Borough of Islington*. London: Islington Council.

Lewis Herman, J. (1992) *Trauma and Recovery: From Domestic Abuse to Political Terror*. London: Pandora.

McLean, M. (1995) 'Quality investigation? Police interviewing of witnesses', *Medicine, Science and the Law*, 35: 116–22.

McMillan, L. (2007) *Feminists Organising Against Gendered Violence*. London: Palgrave.

Milne, B. and Bull, R. (2006) 'Interviewing victims of crime, including children and people with intellectual disabilities', in M. R. Kebbell and G. M. Davies (eds), *Practical Psychology for Forensic Investigations and Prosecutions*. Chichester: Wiley, pp. 7–24.

Mortimer, A. and Shepherd, E. (1999) 'Frames of mind: schemata guiding cognition and conduct in the interviewing of suspected offenders', in A. Memon and R. Bull (eds), *Handbook of the Psychology of Interviewing*. Chichester: Wiley, pp. 293–315.

Office for Criminal Justice Reform (2006) *Convicting Rapists and Protecting Victims – Justice for Victims of Rape: A Consultation Paper*. Available online at: http://www.homeoffice.gov.uk.

Quinn, K. and Jackson, J. (2007) 'Of rights and roles: police interviews with young suspects in Northern Ireland', *British Journal of Criminology*, 47: 234–55.

Regan, L. and Kelly, L. (2003) *Rape: Still a Forgotten Issue*. London: CWASU, London Metropolitan University.

Rock, F. (2001) 'The genesis of a witness statement', *Forensic Linguistics*, 8: 44–72.

Stanko, E. (1997) '"I second that emotion": reflections on feminism, emotionality, and research on sexual violence', in D. Schwartz. (ed.), *Researching Sexual Violence Against Women: Methodological and Personal Perspectives*. London: Sage, pp. 74–85.

Sussex Police (2007) *Sussex Police Rape and Violence Strategy*. Brighton: Sussex Police.

Taylor, A. and Joudo, D. (2005) *The Impact of Pre-recorded Video and Closed Circuit Television Testimony by Adult Sexual Assault Complainants on Jury Decision Making: An Experimental Study*. Canberra: Australian Institute of Criminology.

Temkin, J. (1997) 'Plus ça change: reporting rape in the 1990s', *British Journal of Criminology*, 37 (4): 507–20.

Temkin, J. (1999) 'Reporting rape in London: a qualitative study', *Howard Journal of Criminal Justice*, 38 (1): 17–41.

Chapter 12

A vicious cycle? Attrition and conviction patterns in contemporary rape cases in England and Wales

Vanessa E. Munro and Liz Kelly

Rape has been defined as a unique crime, presenting a distinct set of challenges to both criminal justice and wider social policy (Kelly *et al*. 2005). When a claim of rape is accredited, it is often acknowledged to be a serious violation – not only a physical assault but also an intrusion upon intimate boundaries and personal autonomy. At the same time, however, identifying an incident of sexual intercourse as non-consensual and, in turn, labelling the behaviour of its perpetrator as criminal, have frequently given rise to difficulty, particularly in cases in which – as is typical – the assailant and victim are known to each other. A victim's disclosure of rape may be prohibited by internal feelings of shock, humiliation and/or self-blame, as well as by concerns about how the people closest to her, and her social community more broadly, are likely to respond (Jordan 2004; Kelly 2002). Arguably, in no other crime is the character and credibility of the complainant subject to such intrusive scrutiny, as conventions regarding the intended, and inferred, meaning of her dress/behaviour, for example, are routinely invoked. The gender dynamics involved in rape – both that, in England and Wales, it requires a male perpetrator and that there is an overwhelming preponderance of female victimisation – also merit special attention in order to situate the offence and institutional/popular responses to it in the context of modern socio-(hetero)sexual norms.

Despite considerable efforts in recent decades to improve the response to rape across both police forces and Crown Prosecution Service (CPS) regions in England and Wales (HMCPSI and HMIC 2007; HM Government 2007), the provision of support services and investigative expertise varies widely (Coy *et al.* 2007). Though a victim's evaluation of the prospects of being believed and treated with respect by criminal justice officials will be an influencing factor in determining the likelihood of reporting (Jordan 2004; Kelly 2002), evidence has been uncovered of institutional sexism and individual subscription to gender stereotypes that coalesce in support of the preservation of a 'culture of scepticism' (Kelly *et al.* 2005; Yancey Martin 2005). Indeed, in 2008, John Yates – an Assistant Commissioner in the Metropolitan Police and the Association of Chief Police Officers' (ACPO) spokesman on rape – invoked this exact phrase in explaining the poor performance of police and the mediocrity of many investigations (Dyer 2008), a point that is all the more significant in light of revelations of inadequate police investigation in the recent cases of two serial rapists, John Worboys and Kirk Reid (Hughes 2009; Laville 2009). Moreover, research conducted by Liz Kelly and her colleagues has revealed that while the recent ambition to increase reporting has gradually been realised, this has been accompanied by a fall in the proportion of rape cases that are being prosecuted and result in a conviction (Kelly *et al.* 2005). From a position in the late 1970s when one in three reported rapes resulted in a conviction, by the mid-1990s, this figure had dropped to fewer than one in ten. And although the most recent data (2006) reveals a reduction in reporting, alongside a small reversal in the plummeting conviction rate, it should be recalled that this sits in comparison to a record low conviction rate of 5.3 per cent (1 in 19 reported cases) in the previous year (see Figure 12.1).[1]

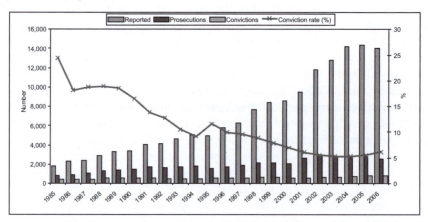

Figure 12.1 Attrition in reported rape cases in England and Wales 1985–2006

Attrition research, which explores the conviction rate in relation to reported rapes by tracking the progress (or, more accurately, the lack of progress) of complaints within the criminal justice process, highlights a worrying tendency for rape cases to 'fall out' of the system, particularly in the early stages. A number of explanations might be offered to account for this, including the withdrawal of victim cooperation, the decision by police to 'no crime' a complaint, or the decision by police and/or prosecutors that an investigation should be discontinued on evidential grounds. Previous research illustrates that 70–80 per cent of a large sample of rape complaints made to English police since 2000 have fallen out of the system at the investigation stage (Feist *et al.* 2007; Kelly *et al.* 2005). Similar processes have also been documented across all the adversarial systems in Europe and the Nordic countries (Kelly and Regan 2001; Regan and Kelly 2003), as well as in the US (Spohn and Horney 1996), New Zealand (Jordan 2004) and, most recently, South Africa (Vetten *et al.* 2008).

Alongside this focus on early-stage attrition (including police and prosecutorial decision-making), the rape trial itself has also been the subject of scrutiny in England and Wales (Adler 1987; Lees 2002; Temkin 2007). Critical attention has been directed, for example, at exposing sexist and/or 'victim-blaming' attitudes among the judiciary (Temkin and Krahé 2008), and challenges have been made to defence strategies that seek to discredit the complainant by introducing irrelevant detail in regard to her sexual and medical history (Burman *et al.* 2007; Kelly *et al.* 2006; Parraig and Renner 1998). The substantive criminal law – and, in particular, the retention of an offence definition that requires proof of the complainant's non-consent – has been challenged for continuing to invite a focus upon the victim's behaviour: both for what it was intended by her to communicate, as well as for what the defendant might have reasonably taken it to mean (Tadros 2006; Temkin and Ashworth 2004). In addition, the adversarial environment of the criminal courtroom and the lack of independent representation afforded to the complainant have been criticised for facilitating her 'secondary victimisation' (Bacik *et al.* 1998; Regan and Kelly 2003).

Reforms under the Sexual Offences Act 2003 notwithstanding, it remains largely a matter for the jury to apply their combined good sense, experience and knowledge of human nature and modern behaviour in rape trials in order to determine the key components of criminal liability. Despite this, prohibitions under the Contempt of Court Act 1981 have prevented research with 'real' juries in England

and Wales, and have left commentators to bridge the gap between judicial direction and verdict outcome with conjecture. Extrapolating from, among other things, social attitude surveys (for example, Amnesty International 2005), researchers have hypothesised on the factors that may influence jury deliberation in rape cases, but this has left unaddressed central questions relating to jurors' understanding and application of the relevant legal tests in concrete cases (Finch and Munro 2008). The lack of transparency, and accountability, thus associated with the jury is potentially problematic, particularly given its centrality to the administration of criminal justice. What is more, in a context in which police and prosecutors – mindful of the imperative not to proceed to trial in cases that do not offer a reasonable prospect of conviction – deploy predictions of juror response in order to justify not taking rape complaints forward (Brown *et al.* 2007), this lack of certainty regarding the factors that influence, if not determine, jury deliberation clearly takes on a peculiar significance.

In contrast to much of the previous literature on rape prosecution, which – though extremely valuable – has tended to focus *either* on early-stage decision-making *or* on courtroom practice, this chapter develops a more holistic analysis of contemporary patterns of attrition and conviction in England and Wales. In a context in which the realities of rape are often far removed from – and significantly more complex than – the stereotypical frame against which complaints are measured (by the criminal justice system, the media and society at large), what we call 'non-conforming' cases (i.e. those falling outwith the stereotype) are regularly abandoned at an early stage of investigation, often on the basis that jurors at any subsequent trial are believed to be unwilling to convict. Bringing together findings from previous, independently conducted research, this chapter explores the extent to which this claim is relied upon in police and prosecutor decision-making and evaluates its legitimacy by reflecting upon the substantive content of (mock) jury deliberations.

The next two sections trace the ways in which certain markers of non-conformance – including the consumption of intoxicants by the complainant and the existence of a previous relationship with the defendant – appear to influence police, prosecutor and (mock) juror assessments of credibility and consent. The methods and modes of analysis employed in the empirical projects relied upon in this chapter – though appropriate for their own purposes – are clearly quite different. In the first section, the focus is on statistical trends across a large case-tracking database. Meanwhile, the second section qualitatively explores the content of (mock) jury deliberations across two rape trial simulations. Despite this, triangulation of the studies' respective findings, together with pre-existing literature on rape reporting, investigation, prosecution and conviction in England and Wales, generates some valuable insights into the circularity of criminal justice decision-making in this area.

Rape attrition: complainant, police and prosecutor decision-making

The primary source of data for this section is a case-tracking database compiled during a project for the Home Office Crime Reduction Programme (CRP).[2] This whole sample comprised 3,527 cases reported between late 2000 and the end of 2002 to three Sexual Assault Referral Centres (SARCs) and three police comparison sites (with no SARC) in England. All cases were tracked prospectively: data was collected on the assault, the victim, the perpetrator(s), the forensic examination, as well as the services accessed, the legal process and its resultant outcome. The results reported on here come from a follow-up study, funded by the Economic and Social Research Council (ESRC). This comprised three elements: retrieving some missing case outcome data, creating new analytic variables and undertaking new analyses. The new fields of analysis were:

- presence of alcohol and level of intoxication;
- the initial approach/contact between victim and perpetrator;[3]
- whether the assault took place within six routine spheres of daily life (personal, social, public space, residential, work/school and contacts with authority).

Multivariate analysis was used to explore the influence of these various factors upon the patterns of attrition across the processes of reporting, investigation and prosecution of cases. In addition, apparent connections between these case/complainant characteristics and targeting for sexual assault were examined. The detailed statistical analyses can be found in the final report to the ESRC (Lovett *et al.* 2007). Here, general findings are presented to illuminate the attrition process.

The central question posed in the study was the extent to which the stereotypical construct of rape – as a crime committed by strangers, in the public sphere and, in at least some versions (Estrich 1987), including the use of a weapon and the infliction of resultant injuries

– predicted case outcomes. To operationalise this, assaults captured in the sample were coded across three 'types':

- 'stereotypical rape' defined as rapes/attempted rapes committed by anyone known for less than 24 hours (14.5 per cent, n = 513);
- 'non-stereotypical rape' defined as rapes/attempted rapes committed by known men (61.7 per cent, n = 2177); and
- 'other assaults' which included cases missing the assault type and non-penetrative sexual assaults (23.7 per cent, n = 837).

Initial analysis revealed that almost a quarter of the 'stereotypical rapes' took place in the victim's home rather than a public place (22.4 per cent, n = 115), and this led to the creation of a further variable: 'stereotypical rape 2'.

Victim profile, reporting and conviction

Given the well documented under-reporting of sexual crime (Kelly 2002; Walby and Allen 2004), the decision to report to the police was analysed as the first attrition point[4] and a comparison was made with cases in which the victim attended a SARC but made no formal criminal justice complaint. Among the key findings here was that the ethnic origin, marital status and employment status of the complainant correlated with case outcomes. Black victims were most likely not to report to the police (37 per cent), while Asian victims were most likely to do so (only 14.3 per cent did not report). Despite this high reporting rate, however, 80.2 per cent of cases involving Asian victims suffered attrition. Furthermore, cases involving black victims were the least likely to result in conviction – 2.4 per cent compared to a conviction rate of 7.6 per cent in regard to white complainants. Even though these differences are not vast, there is sufficient evidence here to suggest that the relationship between experiencing and/or reporting rape, criminal justice attrition and the complainant's racial/ethnic origin may require further investigation, and that more may need to be done in order to redress the apparent danger that black and minority ethnic (BME) victims may have less access to justice. Other findings at this first stage of analysis included that cases involving married victims were the least likely to suffer attrition. In addition, cases involving student victims were most likely to end in conviction, while those involving unemployed victims were least likely to do so.

The relationship between the victim and the perpetrator also affected the case outcome. Cases where the perpetrator was a family member, current partner, friend or in a professional relationship with the victim were less likely to be reported to police. However, when such cases were reported, all – apart from those involving current partners – were more likely to result in convictions. Allegations where the perpetrator was a recent acquaintance or a stranger were most likely to 'drop out' of the system during the investigation, in large part due to the police's failure to identify the assailant.

Exploring the stages and processes of attrition

Only rape allegations that were reported to the police and for which a case outcome was retrieved are discussed in this section (n = 1,925). Table 12.1 shows the proportion of cases lost at each of five designated attrition points. In line with other studies (Feist *et al.* 2007), this reveals that victim withdrawal is the single largest category, closely followed by an assessment (often taken by police in dialogue with the Crown Prosecution Service) that there was insufficient evidence to proceed.

Further analysis indicates that complainants are most likely to withdraw their allegation when the offence occurs in situations of familiarity (defined as relationships and contexts which are part of the victim's everyday life). Factors that increased the victims' vulnerability – for example, substance misuse or ongoing abuse – were also associated with complainant withdrawal. Ethnicity also played a role, with black and other ethnic minority victims being somewhat more likely to withdraw their allegations than white victims. While these correlations were all statistically significant (Lovett *et al.* 2007), they do not illuminate the processes through which such decisions were made. Data from a sub-sample of the complainants shows that their decision-making was influenced by the responses of those around

Table 12.1 Attrition in sample of reported rape cases

Attrition point	%	n
Victim withdrawal	36.3	699
Insufficient evidence	35.2	678
No evidence of assault/false allegation	15.6	301
Acquittal at trial	6.7	129
CPS discontinuance	6.1	118
Total	100	1,925

them, especially the 'messages' they believed were communicated by the criminal justice personnel with whom they had contact.[5] Feeling disbelieved and/or disrespected alongside losing faith in the ability of the criminal justice system to effectively investigate and/or to protect their privacy were all likely to prompt withdrawal (Kelly *et al.* 2005).

While rape stereotypes did influence attrition, they did so in complex, multi-layered and even paradoxical ways. In the early investigation, while 'stereotypical rapes' were undoubtedly considered more 'believable' by police officers (Kelly *et al.* 2005), they were less likely to be detected (due to failure to identify the perpetrator), and thus featured strongly in the insufficient evidence category. Also strongly represented at this stage were police designations of the victim's account as inconsistent. This is likely to reflect a more subtle feature of the 'stereotypical rape' construct – not controlled for in our analysis – since, despite evidence that trauma can generate memory lapses, distortions in the appreciation of time sequences and disassociation which would make recall difficult (Taylor 2004), many police officers still appear to assess 'genuine victims' as those who are able to provide a coherent and consistent narrative account (Kelly *et al.* 2005).

Findings in this study in regard to trial conviction or acquittal rates should be viewed with caution due to the small number of cases involved at this final stage of the prosecution process. Of the 2,138 cases reported to the police, tracking yielded trial outcomes for 285, of which a minority (n = 140; 49.1 per cent) resulted in a conviction, and the rate was even lower for rape charges (44 per cent). Conviction was most likely in cases involving family members, a friend/relative/partner or known other, or a person in a position of authority and/or where the victim was a minor.[6] Conviction was least likely in cases where first contact took place in clubs and where victims were followed/jumped/accosted, and where the victim had consumed drugs or lived in a vulnerable housing type. If alcohol had been consumed by both victim and perpetrator, or the police characterised the victim as having abused substances or having mental health issues, the chances of conviction were substantially lowered (see also Stanko 2007). Perpetrators who had been previously convicted or accused of sexual assaults were more likely to be found guilty. This is a common finding in criminal justice outcome studies across a range of offences and is accounted for by the increased likelihood that the police investigate vigorously once prior history is known.

Reflections on 'stereotypical' rape and attrition

This prospective case-tracking study reveals that stereotypical constructions of rape, rape victims and rapists continue to inform institutional responses, albeit in more complex formulations than previously recognised. The stereotypical construct of rape, as operationalised in this study, was not entirely predictive of outcomes, especially when cases reached trial. It is now possible to obtain convictions that were previously impossible – either because of changes in the law (criminalisation of marital and male rape) or changes in how some categories of complainants are viewed (for example, women in prostitution). At the same time, however, the findings of this study do indicate that the legacies of the stereotype continue to inform the early stages of attrition, where it affects victims' willingness to report and/or stay in the criminal justice process, as well as police and prosecutorial decision-making. Victim vulnerabilities play a crucial role in framing attrition (Stanko 2007; for further discussion, see Stanko and Williams in this volume), appearing to make some victims less credible to criminal justice professionals and even acting as cues to 'drop' cases. While there is, thus, some small room for optimism in the fact that – if they make it through the eye of the needle – stereotypes of rape are not always predictive of trial outcomes, this study indicates that, in practice, few such cases of non-stereotypical rape ever find their way into the courtroom.

Rape conviction: (mock) juror deliberation

In this section, the findings of two rape trial simulation studies (funded by the ESRC) will be drawn upon. Scripted trial scenarios, lasting approximately 75 minutes, were re-enacted by actors and barristers in front of an audience of 24–26 jury-service eligible volunteers from the community. After having received judicial instructions, participants were streamed into three different jury rooms and their deliberations (which lasted up to 90 minutes) were recorded and analysed. In the first study, seven trial scenarios were scripted in which the issue of sexual consent was complicated by the complainant's intoxication. Variables were introduced depending upon the means by which she became intoxicated or the nature of the intoxicating substance (Finch and Munro 2006, 2007). In the second study, nine scenarios were used and variables depended upon the complainant's level of physical resistance, the delay between the incident and the police report, and the apparent demeanour of the complainant in the courtroom, as well as the extent to which participants had been provided with educational guidance (Ellison and Munro 2009a, 2009b, 2009c).

Bringing together the findings from these studies generates a sizeable dataset involving nearly 400 mock jurors deliberating across 48 different juries. At the same time, it is important to bear in mind some inevitable limitations of this experimental method – in particular, the mock trial was streamlined in its duration and content, restrictions were imposed on both deliberation time and jury size, and participants knew that, ultimately, nobody's fate was held in the balance (Finch and Munro 2008). It should also be noted that the background facts underpinning the trials differed across the two studies, as did the actors and barristers playing the key roles. While caution should thus be exercised in extrapolating these findings to the 'real' jury room, they support the suggestion that – in line with the assertions above regarding police and prosecutors – there are certain markers of non-conformance with the stereotypical rape construct that lay assessors may find problematic.

Lack of evidence of physical injury

Both mock jury studies confirm previous research which suggests that – despite the fact that many victims of sexual assault offer no physical resistance and suffer no serious physical injury (Du Mont and White 2007) – claims of non-consensual intercourse which are not accompanied by this evidence are less likely to be accredited as rape (Krulewitz and Nash 1979; Ong and Ward 1999; Taylor and Joudo 2005). In scenarios in which the complainant displayed no physical injury, jurors routinely emphasised the significance of this in reaching their not guilty verdicts. Their commitment to the belief that a 'normal' response to sexual attack is to struggle physically often persisted, even in cases in which the complainant was heavily intoxicated or had 'frozen' in fear during the attack. Jurors often exhibited unrealistic expectations regarding a woman's physical capacity to inflict defensive injury – as one juror put it, for example, 'the smallest and quietest of people, when you're in a situation you don't want to be in, you find something within you to give him a damn good kicking.' And even in those situations in which jurors were willing to accept that a complainant who was so intoxicated as to be 'slipping in and out of consciousness' might be unable to offer physical resistance, they nonetheless expected her to display clear verbal resistance in order to communicate non-consent. As one put it, 'even though her whole body was slumped, she was still slurring. She could still speak. Even if she was slumped, she could still have said no.' It was clear, moreover, that in expressing their expectation of physical injury, jurors often had a particular type or level of injury in mind. Indeed, in trial scenarios in the second study, in which there was some evidence of bruising and scratching upon the complainant, many jurors remained unconvinced, if not of the complainant's lack of consent then at least of the lack of a reasonable belief in consent on the part of the defendant. Jurors went to considerable lengths to provide alternative explanations for such injuries and emphasised that if the complainant had not consented to sex, she would have resisted more forcefully and received and/or inflicted more injuries as a result.

Complainant's consumption of intoxicants

While in the first study, complainant intoxication was the central focus, in the second study, the significance of the fact that the parties were *not* drunk – and the difference which this might have made to jurors' evaluations – was raised in all the deliberations. In line with previous research which suggests that when a man and a woman drink together, this serves as a cue which may be (mis)perceived as a sign of sexual intent (Abbey and Harnish 1995; George *et al.* 1988; Wall and Schuller 2000), jurors in both studies routinely emphasised the social significance of shared alcohol consumption. Jurors insisted that offering a male companion wine, rather than coffee or tea, 'sort of says something'. In addition, they supported the position that women who have consumed alcohol will be more sexually disinhibited and more likely to enjoy being seduced than a non-drinking counterpart. As one juror put it, 'if she [the complainant] was drunk, she was more than likely flirting a lot.' The tone of deliberations was marked by the suggestion that women who are intoxicated are more likely to consent to sex, which they may subsequently regret when sober (grounding a false rape allegation). In addition, the notion that drunken women should take responsibility for the 'mixed signals' that their behaviour might unintentionally emit was also often deployed alongside a seemingly contradictory claim that men who are intoxicated should be seen as less responsible for their actions, since their drunkenness may have impeded their ability to heed the woman's reluctance or to curb their 'natural' sexual urges (see, for example, Finch and Munro 2007; Norris and Cubbins 1992; Richardson and Hammock 1991; Schuller and Stewart 2000;). Thus, as one juror in the first study argued – albeit in disregard of fundamental principles of criminal liability – 'he (the defendant) was in a fairly sober state of mind, so you know, he should have been able to judge: if he'd been fairly drunk as well, then I don't think it would be a question of rape.'

The existence of a previous relationship

In both studies, the complainant and defendant were loosely acquainted with one another but they were not – and had never been – in a sexual relationship. While some jurors contrasted this type of acquaintance rape with an assault by a stranger, and implied that the latter was more serious and/or traumatic, there was also an explicit recognition by many that, in reality, rape is most likely to be perpetrated by someone known to the victim. This suggests a potentially wider notion of 'what rape looks like' among jurors than is assumed by those police and prosecutors who, in anticipation of a slim chance of conviction, decline to take forward allegations involving acquaintances/partners. At the same time, though, it is important to note that this did not necessarily work in the complainant's favour in the concrete context of the deliberations. Indeed, many of the jurors continued to focus on her behaviour towards the defendant in the run up to the incident, especially her spending time alone with him, accepting his compliments/drinks, and – in the second study – consenting to his request for a goodnight kiss. Such behaviour, which was seen to reflect a level of previous consensual intimacy, was often relied upon to indicate the presence of/reasonable belief in consent, despite the assertions of many participants that 'consent to a kiss is not consent to sex'. Allied to this, jurors routinely emphasised that they wanted to know more about the previous relationship between the parties – and specifically about the extent to which it had been flirtatious – which again suggests that, while the fact of a previous acquaintance *per se* may not be problematic, much of its irrelevance will hang on its being an exclusively distant and platonic one.

The fact of a previous allegation

Research has revealed that a woman who has previously experienced rape is likely to be perceived more negatively and be attributed higher levels of blame than a victim who has not (McCaul *et al.* 1990; Schultz and Schneider 1991; Tyson 2003). While there was no suggestion in either of the studies that a previous rape allegation had been made, jurors were certainly anxious to know more about the complainant's general (and sexual) character. In particular – and of potential relevance here – participants wanted to be able to establish if she was 'the sort of woman' who was prone to sexual promiscuity, liable to revoke a drunken consent retrospectively when sober, or sufficiently vengeful to fabricate a rape allegation out of anger. It is reasonable to hypothesise, then, that the fact of a previous but unproven rape allegation – which may have been interpreted as a false claim, despite some jurors' explicit awareness of the difficulties of securing a conviction – would be unlikely to work well for the complainant, fuelling the jurors' impulse to 'fill in' evidential gaps in relation to the present case with conjecture regarding her overall character and credibility.

Narrative inconsistency in the complainant's account

Experiences of trauma can distort reports of time sequences and generate memory blocks that may be either temporary or permanent (Granhag and Stromwall 1999; Welch and Mason 2007). In addition, the shame or embarrassment that rape can elicit – as well as the concern that conduct prior to the attack may be viewed negatively – all contribute to making it difficult to give a full and candid initial disclosure. Despite this, there is evidence which suggests that any subsequent additions to, or inconsistencies in, the complainant's narrative of what occurred risk jeopardising her credibility (Taylor 2004). While this was not a specific focus of attention in either of the present studies, the consistency, confidence and accuracy of the complainant's testimony was regularly commented upon by the jurors in the second study. While this often worked to the advantage of the complainant, there were some jurors who suggested that she was in danger of being 'too precise' and who questioned the feasibility of such detailed recall, particularly in a context in which she testified to having 'disassociated' from the event. In regard to the intoxicated complainant in the first study, while the reasons behind her incomplete recall were often accepted by jurors, the upshot of this was that it often placed her in a double-bind: either she was so drunk that she could not remember what had occurred and so could not be certain that she had not consented *or* she was able to recall what had occurred, in which case she was not so heavily intoxicated as to have been unable to communicate her lack of consent at the time (through verbal/physical resistance).

Judging the jury

In England and Wales, the Sexual Offences Act 2003 calls upon the jury to consider whether the complainant 'agreed by choice' in circumstances in which she had the freedom and capacity to make a choice, as well as to determine whether the defendant either knew she was not consenting or relied on a mistaken belief in her consent which was unreasonable in the circumstances. Lack of physical injury ought not to be a barrier to non-consent, just as the presence of complainant intoxication should not imply sexual interest. Likewise, in a context in which the majority of rapes are perpetrated by assailants known to the victim and in which experiencing trauma can generate confusion and lapses in the recollection of events, the relevance of a previous relationship or narrative inconsistency is contestable. Despite this, these studies of (mock) juror deliberations reveal that such considerations may – as police and prosecutors have predicted – play a role in framing assessments of both credibility and consent, which in turn will determine verdict outcome.

Breaking the cycle: future law and social reform

Discussion over the previous two sections has suggested some interesting correlations between patterns of attrition and the content of (mock) jury deliberations. In both contexts, it seems that aspects of the stereotypical construct of rape continue to inform decision-making. While there are some patterns or individual cases that appear to successfully challenge traditional assumptions, it is also clear that there are certain categories of victim, and certain forms of rape scenario, that are disadvantaged from the outset in current criminal justice responses. Triggers relating – among other things – to the vulnerability of the complainant (including her consumption of intoxicants), the existence of a previous relationship with the perpetrator, the narrative consistency and novelty of her account, as well as the presence of physical injury will continue, in complex and interconnected ways, to influence the prognosis for case progression, prosecution and conviction in rape cases.

At one level, the conclusion that predictions made by police and prosecutors in regard to jury deliberation are often well-founded justifies the patterns of attrition outlined above – at least to the (questionable) extent that it can be seen to be better for rape complainants who have no realistic prospect of seeing their attacker punished to avoid the stress associated with criminal prosecution. At the same time, however, this fails to critically reflect upon the broader consequences of these self-perpetuating and self-justifying patterns of criminal justice decision-making. By restricting the opportunity for non-conformist scenarios to proceed to court in the first place, this selective prosecutorial approach removes from the public gaze the majority of rape complaints which fail to fit the stereotype. In so doing, it reinforces a public (and thus a potential juror's) conception of rape that too often retains its narrow contours. When this is then applied in any specific case, it lends an air of self-fulfilling prophecy to previous predictions by *generating* this reluctance to convict in non-conforming cases. By relying on an institutional culture of scepticism and a conservative method of precedent-driven second guessing, this cyclical process of prediction and attrition thus effectively reproduces the systematic impunity of certain categories of sexual offender and/ or offending.

Initiatives aimed at encouraging official reporting of rape, together with those seeking to improve the treatment received by complainants throughout the investigation and trial process, have certainly had some positive impact. The increasing use of gender-matched and specialist investigators, the introduction of special measures to protect vulnerable witnesses from intrusive questioning in the courtroom and the formal acknowledgment by the government of the victim's legitimate interest in the progress of her case – though far from offering a panacea – are all to be welcomed, and have clearly yielded benefits for some individual rape complainants. At the same time, however, there is little doubt that more must be done in order to redress the 'justice gap' in rape cases. Recent proposals by the government to introduce guidance designed to disavow jurors of misconceptions in regard to rape, rapists and rape victims continue to be debated, but would surely represent an important step forward in ensuring less prejudiced evaluations of credibility and consent (Office for Criminal Justice Reform 2007; see also Ellison and Munro 2009c). Likewise, the repeated commitment by the current Solicitor General, Vera Baird QC, that mechanisms must be developed and implemented to ensure better case building in rape cases – by both the police and the CPS – are also to be welcomed. The fact that such reforms emerge in a context in which the past decade has seen considerable legislative and procedural innovation in regard to sexual offences in England and Wales, as well as heightened media attention on this issue, suggest that the question of justice for rape victims remains – quite rightly – a policy priority.

More must yet be done, however, in order to expose and interrupt the (vicious) circularity that lies at the heart of much of the current criminal justice response to rape in England and Wales. While the progressive intentions of recent law reform initiatives are to be welcomed, there has too often been a tendency to prioritise 'quick-fix' solutions over more socially situated engagement. Though clearly a demanding task, it is only by acknowledging the complexity of the cyclical dynamic between stereotypical rape and reality that we can begin to deconstruct at social, institutional and legal levels the means by which it is affirmed, perpetuated and too often rendered unremarkable. Among other things, this requires that criminal justice agencies, and those working with victims of sexual violence, develop frameworks for support, investigation and prosecution that are responsive to the lived experience of rape rather than its stereotypical construct. It requires that instances of sexual offending, in all their multiplicity, are engaged with, and that the depressing reality of the mundane nature of sexual violence is acknowledged by the criminal justice system, the courts, the media and society at large. In addition, the fact that most rapists are ordinary men must be more candidly confronted, and we must reflect on the social responsibility that we share for our failure to challenge problematic perceptions both of male sexual entitlement and of female sexual passivity.

Notes

1 Data are not compiled for the UK, since Scotland has a separate and subtly different legal system, and to a lesser extent so does Northern Ireland. The Scottish data mirrors that for England and Wales, and indeed has a lower conviction rate in 2007, but data from Northern Ireland has not been accessed.

2 Consisting of evaluation of four funded service innovations, evaluation of Sexual Assault Referral Centres and detailed examination of the attrition process.

3 The variables here included whether there was any prior contact, i.e. was it a stereotypical 'blitz' rape with no social contact at all between victim and perpetrator before the attack. Where this was not the case, the location and type of contact/approach were coded. Examples include: homes – of victim, perpetrator, friend, someone else; educational institution; workplace; social event; public place.

4 The concept of 'attrition points' was developed in the Home Office study in which the initial data collection took place (Kelly *et al.* 2005) and refers to the key points in the chronology of cases at which a significant number of cases are lost.

5 Two hundred and twenty-nine agreed to take part in the study, completing questionnaires and/or participating in in-depth interviews.

6 This was in part due to increased guilty pleas in cases involving minors.

References

Abbey, A. and Harnish, R. (1995) 'Perceptions of sexual intent: the role of gender, alcohol consumption and rape supportive attitudes', *Sex Roles*, 32: 297–313.

Adler, Z. (1987) *Rape on Trial*. London: Routledge & Kegan Paul.

Amnesty International (2005) *Sexual Assault Research: Summary Report*. Available online at: http://www.amnesty.org.uk.

Bacik, I., Maunsell, C. and Gogan, S. (1998) *The Legal Process and Victims of Rape*. Dublin: Dublin Rape Crisis Centre.

Brown, J., Hamilton, C. and O'Neill, D. (2007) 'Characteristics associated with rape attrition and the role played by scepticism or legal rationality by investigators and prosecutors', *Psychology, Crime and Law*, 13 (4): 355–70.

Burman, M., Jamieson, L., Nicholson, J. and Brooks, O. (2007) *Impact of Aspects of Evidence in Sexual Offences Trials: An Evaluation Study*, Research Findings. Edinburgh: Scottish Government.

Coy, M., Kelly, L. and Foord, J. (2007) *Map of Gaps: The Postcode Lottery of Violence against Women Support Services*. London: End Violence against Women Coalition.

Du Mont, J. and White, D. (2007) *The Uses and Impacts of Medico-Legal Evidence in Sexual Assault Cases: A Global Review*. Geneva: World Health Organisation.

Dyer, C. (2008) 'Rape cases: police admit failing victims: Senior Met officer blames scepticism and inertia for low conviction rate', *The Guardian*, 4 March.

Ellison, L. and Munro, V. (2009a) 'Reacting to rape: exploring mock jurors' assessments of complainant credibility', *British Journal of Criminology*, 49 (2): 202–19.

Ellison, L. and Munro, V. (2009b) 'Of normal sex and real rape: exploring the use of socio-sexual scripts in (mock) jury deliberation', *Social and Legal Studies*, forthcoming.

Ellison, L. and Munro, V. (2009c) 'Turning mirrors into windows? Assessing the impact of (mock) juror education in rape trials', *British Journal of Criminology*, 49(3): 363–83.

Estrich, S. (1987) *Real Rape: How the Legal System Victimizes Women Who Say No*. Boston: Harvard University Press.

Feist, A., Ashe, J., Lawrence, J., McPhee, D. and Wilson, R. (2007) *Investigating and Detecting Recorded Offences of Rape*, Home Office Online Report 18/07. Available online at: http://www.homeoffice.gov.uk/rds/pdfs07/rdsolr1807.pdf.

Finch, E. and Munro, V. (2006) 'Breaking boundaries? Sexual consent in the jury room', *Legal Studies*, 26 (3): 303–20.

Finch, E. and Munro, V. (2007) 'The demon drink and the demonised woman: socio-sexual stereotypes and responsibility attribution in rape trials involving intoxicants', *Social and Legal Studies*, 16 (4): 591–614.

Finch, E. and Munro, V. (2008) 'Lifting the veil: the use of focus groups and trial simulations in legal research', *Journal of Law and Society*, 35: 30–51.

George, W., Gournic, S. and McAfee, M. (1988) 'Perceptions of postdrinking female sexuality: effects of gender, beverage choice and drink payment', *Journal of Applied Social Psychology*, 18: 1295–317.

Granhag, P. and Stromwall, L. (1999) 'Repeated interrogations – stretching the deception detection paradigm', *Expert Evidence*, 7: 163–74.

HM Government (2007) *Cross Government Action Plan on Sexual Violence and Abuse*. London: HMSO.

HMCPSI and HMIC (2007) *Without Consent: A Report on the Joint Review of the Investigation and Prosecution of Rape Offences*. London: Central Office of Information.

Hughes, M. (2009) 'Black cab rapist struck again and again after police mistakes', *The Independent*, 14 March.

Jordan, J. (2004) *The Word of a Woman: Police, Rape and Belief*. London: Palgrave.

Kelly, L. (2002) *A Research Review on the Reporting, Investigation and Prosecution of Rape Cases*. London: HMCPSI.

Kelly, L. and Regan, L. (2001) *Rape: The Forgotten Issue? A European Attrition and Networking Study*. London: Child and Woman Abuse Studies Unit.

Kelly, L., Lovett, J. and Regan, L. (2005) *A Gap or a Chasm? Attrition in Reported Rape Cases*, Home Office Research Study No. 293. London: HMSO

Kelly, L., Temkin, J. and Griffiths, S. (2006) *Section 41: An Evaluation of New Legislation Limiting Sexual History Evidence in Rape Trials*, Home Office Online Report 20/06. London: Home Office.

Krulewitz, J. and Nash, J. (1979) 'Effects of rape victim resistance, assault outcome, and sex of observer on attributions about rape', *Journal of Personality*, 47: 558–74.

Laville, S. (2009) 'Metropolitan Police facing crisis after failures in Kirk Reid rape inquiry', *The Guardian*, 27 March.

Lees, S. (2002) *Carnal Knowledge: Rape on Trial*, 2nd edn. London: Women's Press.

Lovett, J., Uzelac, G., Horvath, M. and Kelly, L. (2007) *Rape in the 21st Century: Old Behaviours, New Contexts and Emerging Patterns*, Final Report to the Economic and Social Research Council.

McCaul, K., Veltum, L., Boyechko, V. and Crawford, J. (1990) 'Understanding attributions of victim blame for rape: sex, violence and foreseeability', *Journal of Applied Social Psychology*, 20: 1–26.

Norris, J. and Cubbins, L. (1992) 'Dating, drinking and rape: effects of victims' and assailants' alcohol consumption on judgments of their behaviour and traits', *Psychology of Women Quarterly*, 16: 179–91.

Office for Criminal Justice Reform (2007) *Convicting Rapists and Protecting Victims: Response to Consultation*. London: Office for Criminal Justice Reform.

Ong, A. and Ward, C. (1999) 'The effects of sex and power schemas, attitudes towards women, and victim resistance on rape attributions', *Journal of Applied Social Psychology*, 29: 362–76

Parraig, A. and Renner, K. (1998) *Do Current Criminal Justice Practices Lead to Unjust Outcomes for Adult Victims of Sexual Assault?* Available online at: http://www.careleton.ca/~erenner/nsap.html.

Regan, L. and Kelly, L. (2003) *Rape: Still a Forgotten Issue*. London: CWASU/ RCNE. Available online at: http://www.rcne.org.

Richardson, D. and Hammock, G. (1991) 'Alcohol and acquaintance rape', in A. Parrot and L. Bechhofer (eds), *Acquaintance Rape: The Hidden Crime*. New York: Wiley & Sons, pp. 83–95.

Schuller, R. and Stewart, A. (2000) 'Police responses to sexual assault complaints: the role of perpetrator/complainant intoxication', *Law and Human Behaviour*, 24: 535–51.

Schultz, D. and Schneider, L. (1991) 'The role of sexual provocativeness, rape history and observer gender in perceptions of blame in sexual assaults', *Journal of Interpersonal Violence*, 6: 94–101.

Spohn, C. and Horney, J. (1996) 'The impact of rape law reform on the processing of simple and aggravated rape cases', *Journal of Criminal Law and Criminology*, 86 (3): 861–84.

Stanko, E. (2007) *The Attrition of Rape Allegations in London: A Review*. London: Metropolitan Police Service.

Tadros, V. (2006) 'Rape without consent', *Oxford Journal of Legal Studies*, 26 (3): 515–43.

Taylor, C. (2004) *Court Licensed Abuse, Patriarchal Love and the Legal Response to Intrafamilial Sexual Abuse of Children*. New York: Peter Lang.

Taylor, N. and Joudo, J. (2005) *The Impact of Pre-Recorded Video and Closed Circuit Television Testimony by Adult Sexual Assault Complainants on Jury Decision-Making: An Experimental Study*, Australian Institute of Criminology Research & Public Policy Series No. 68. Canberra: AIC.

Temkin, J. (2007) *Rape and the Legal Process*, 2nd edn. Oxford: Oxford University Press.

Temkin, J. and Ashworth, A. (2004) 'The Sexual Offences Act 2003: rape, sexual assaults and the problems of consent', *Criminal Law Review*, pp. 328–46.

Temkin, J. and Krahé, B. (2008) *Sexual Assault and the Justice Gap: A Question of Attitude*. Oxford: Hart.

Tyson, G. (2003) 'Adolescent attributions of responsibility and blame for date rape', *Australian Journal of Psychology*, 55: 218–37.

Vetten, L., Jewkes, R., Sigsworth, R., Christofides, N., Loots, L. and Dunseith, O. (2008) *Tracking Justice: The Attrition of Rape Cases Through the Criminal Justice System in Gauteng*. Johannesburg: Tshwaranang Legal Advocacy Centre, South African Medical Research Council and Centre for the Study of Violence and Reconciliation.

Walby, S. and Allen, J. (2004) *Domestic Violence, Sexual Assault and Stalking: Findings from the British Crime Survey*, Home Office Research Study No. 276. London: Home Office Research, Development and Statistics Directorate.

Wall, A. and Schuller, R. (2000) 'Sexual assault and defendant/victim intoxication: jurors' perceptions of guilt', *Journal of Applied Social Psychology*, 30 (2): 253–74.

Welch, J. and Mason, F. (2007) 'Rape and sexual assault', *British Medical Journal*, 334: 1154–8.

Yancey Martin, P. (2005) *Rape Work: Victims, Gender and Emotions in Organization and Community Context*. New York: Routledge.

Chapter 13

Addressing the attitude problem in rape trials: some proposals and methodological considerations

Barbara Krahé and Jennifer Temkin

Introduction

In England and Wales, Parliament has actively sought in the last thirty years to address the many defects in the way that the criminal justice system responds to rape and has been assisted in doing so by the police and the Crown Prosecution Service as well as other agencies. Other countries have similarly introduced measures to improve the way rape victims are treated by the criminal justice system. Nevertheless, the 'justice gap' whereby only a small proportion of rape cases is reported to the police, only a small fraction of those reported is sent for trial and even fewer cases result in conviction has remained a serious problem across many western countries (Regan and Kelly 2003). This leads inevitably to the question of what more can be done. Empirical research has investigated some of the problems which bedevil this area, but there clearly remains a knowledge deficit when it comes to strategies for improvement. There is plenty of evidence to suggest that stereotypes and myths about rape affect decision-making about sexual assault, undermining the position of the complainant and playing an important part in the attrition process (Temkin and Krahé 2008). Therefore research programmes are needed that explore effective means of preventing such stereotypic beliefs from feeding into decision-making about rape cases to ensure that they are considered on the basis of the facts and the evidence. It is not the purpose of this chapter to set out an exhaustive research agenda, merely to highlight several issues in connection with the trial itself which would benefit from further scrutiny.

We begin by illustrating the problem of attrition in rape cases by considering its occurrence at the trial stage in England and Wales. We then go on to discuss three possible strategies for ameliorating this problem and the appropriate methodologies for testing their validity. First, given that trial by jury is firmly embedded in the handling of rape cases in the common-law world, we look at some ways of tackling the impact of rape myths on *jury decision-making*, namely by screening jurors, introducing expert evidence and making juries account for their decisions. Secondly, we consider the possibility of replacing juries with *trial by judge* alone and finally, we discuss the appointment of more *female judges*. Rather than providing conclusive answers, the purpose of this chapter is to suggest a path towards evidence-based policy decisions.

Attrition at the trial stage

It is widely acknowledged that attrition is at its greatest at the reporting stage with most women declining to do so. Thereafter, it is at the police stage that most cases fall out of the system, with no-criming and victim withdrawal being some reasons for this (Feist *et al.* 2007). However, attrition at the trial stage is also a problem, not merely for the number of cases that end in acquittal in comparison with other violent and sexual offences, but for the effect this has on decision-making down the line where cases may be discarded by police and prosecutors because it is anticipated that they will fail to persuade a jury (Brown *et al.* 2007).

In the latest criminal statistics of defendants tried and sentenced at Crown Court in 2007 for all offences of violence against the person and sexual offences, convictions exceed acquittals in every offence category, mostly by a considerable margin (Ministry of Justice 2007: Table S2.1(A)). The one exception is rape of a female where acquittals exceed convictions (Ministry of Justice 2007: Table S2.1(A)). Table 13.1 presents the proportion of convictions and acquittals in a sample of offences.

As Table 13.1 shows, rape of a female stands out as the only category of sexual offence where acquittals notably exceed convictions. Furthermore, the statistical category of rape of a female, introduced as a result of the Sexual Offences Act 2003,[1] includes rape of females above 16, under 16 and under 13. Unpublished data provided by the Office for Criminal Justice Reform at the authors' request reveals

Table 13.1 Conviction and acquittal rates for different violent and sexual offences

	Convictions	Acquittals	% convicted
Violence against the person: total	14,806	5,910	71
Murder	369	99	79
Manslaughter	226	47	83
Sexual offences: total	3,412	2,409	59
Rape of a female	783	912	46
Rape of a male	77	41	65
Sexual assault of a female	1,156	933	55
Buggery	43	16	73

that 93 convictions involved children under 13. In these cases, the prosecution does not have to prove the absence of consent and has only to prove that sexual intercourse took place, which makes successful prosecution far easier than in other rape cases. Thus, by including figures for rape of a child under 13 within the category of rape of a female, the overall figure for convictions tends to disguise the true conviction rate for females above that age. It also serves to inflate the figures. Previously, some of this conduct was separately designated as sexual intercourse with a child under 13. Similarly, the new 2003 definition of rape includes some sexual assaults previously designated as indecent assaults which will also serve to inflate the conviction figures for female rape.

Tackling the impact of rape myths on jury decision-making

It is recognised in legal circles that the jury can be a problem in rape cases. In a recent study of judges licensed to conduct fraud trials, one remarked: 'I have agreed with juries in all of my serious fraud trials. I am far more likely to agree with juries in complex fraud cases than I am in sex cases' (Julian 2007: 754). Of the judges and barristers interviewed by Temkin for the Home Office sexual history study (Kelly *et al.* 2006), 10 out of 24 regarded juries as a barrier to convictions in rape cases (Temkin and Krahé 2008: 132). These recent examples echo those quoted by Kalven and Zeisel (1966),[2] suggesting that little has changed over the past decades.

It is widely acknowledged that juries are susceptible to 'extra-evidentiary influences', of which the adherence to stereotypical beliefs or 'myths' about rape is particularly problematic (see Chapter 2 of this volume). Such beliefs undermine the credibility of the complainant and are widely endorsed in the general population from which jurors are drawn (see Temkin and Krahé 2008: ch. 2, for an overview). Research has demonstrated that individuals who score high on rape myth acceptance (RMA) tend to carry their prejudices with them when asked to evaluate rape situations and are disinclined to judge these situations on the basis of the facts alone. Such persons, if appointed to juries in sufficient numbers, are a serious impediment to obtaining convictions. A large body of evidence has shown that decisions about the guilt of an alleged offender are affected by jurors' pre-existing attitudes (see Lecci and Myers 2008, for a summary). These attitudes may influence the way in which jurors attend to and interpret the information presented to them in the course of the trial. For example, a mock-jury study by Krahé (1988) found that individuals with high RMA scores did not differ from those with low scores when asked to consider the likelihood of defendant guilt in a case where the victim behaved in accordance with female gender role prescriptions prior to the attack but were more likely to blame the victim and less inclined to blame the perpetrator if the victim had engaged in behaviour at odds with the female role. Furthermore, a series of studies by Temkin and Krahé (2008; Krahé et al. 2007: Study 2) showed that identical case information was evaluated differently depending on individuals' endorsement of rape myths, with those highly accepting of rape myths blaming the complainant more and being less certain about the guilt of the defendant. As noted by Devine et al. (2009), extra-evidentiary factors are more influential the less clearly the available evidence points at a particular verdict. It seems that when the evidence is ambiguous, jurors are 'liberated' from the constraints imposed by the trial information and refer to more general beliefs, assumptions and sentiments. This situation is true for many rape trials that typically centre on the question of consent and where there is a dearth of surrounding evidence. Moreover, some research using trial simulations has shown that mock jurors have a tendency to consider a broad spectrum of improbable scenarios that shift the blame from the perpetrator to the victim (Finch and Munro 2005).

Screening jurors

One potential strategy for keeping prejudicial attitudes about rape out of rape trials would be to screen out potential jurors who show a high acceptance of rape myths. Screening for attitudes, such as misconceptions about rape, which may result in bias against one party or another is permitted in some states of America as part of the *voir dire* procedure and can lead to the disqualification of individual jurors.[3] Screening can take place either in the form of direct face-to-face questioning or in the form of written responses to questionnaires (see Lieberman and Sales 2007, for a comprehensive discussion of jury selection). The National Center on Domestic and Sexual Violence has issued 'Voir dire and prosecution tips for sexual assault cases' that explain to prosecutors what to look out for as indications of bias in jurors (National Center on Domestic and Sexual Violence 2007). Similar question lists have been prepared by the National District Attorneys' Association (2007). Their purpose is to identify prospective jurors who might be biased in their approach to the case, either in favour of the complainant (e.g. because of their own previous rape experiences) or in favour of the defendant (e.g. because of adherence to rape stereotypes or myths).

However, there is a shortage of empirical research exploring the effectiveness of different screening procedures (Diamond and Rose 2005). On the basis of their review of the evidence, Hans and Jehle (2003) concluded that traditional *voir dire* procedures involving a limited set of questions posed to prospective jurors in a group setting are often ineffective because jurors may be reluctant to disclose personal information or attitudes they think are generally regarded as socially undesirable. The authors favour an expansive *voir dire* in which a broader range of questions is used than at present and prospective jurors are questioned individually and in confidence.

To support such proposals for change, research is required comparing juror questioning in different settings and formats (face-to-face versus confidential questionnaires, individual versus group settings, close-ended versus open-ended questions) to compare their efficacy in detecting juror bias. For example, in order to argue in favour of confidential juror surveys as opposed to questioning jurors about their rape-related attitudes in front of others, evidence would be needed that potential jurors responding in private to a written questionnaire display higher levels of RMA than jurors asked to respond publicly to the same set of items. In a study examining different question formats for detecting racial bias in potential jurors, Schuller *et al.* (in press) found that the way the question was asked made a difference. A standard closed-format question ('Would your ability to judge the evidence in this case be affected by the fact that the person charged is Black?') did not do the job as well as a more reflexive, open-ended question ('How might your ability to judge the evidence in the case be affected by the fact that the defendant is Black?'). These findings indicate that the way in which screening is done crucially determines its effectiveness.

A critical prerequisite for juror screening is the availability of suitable screening tools. These tools not only have to cover the different facets of attitudes undermining an impartial assessment of case information, they also need to provide critical thresholds or cut-off points for deciding whether a potential juror should be admitted or rejected. Rape myth acceptance scales used for research purposes do not meet these requirements. They enable researchers to categorise participants into high versus low RMA groups based on the mean RMA score of the total sample. This makes an individual's classification as high on RMA dependent on the distribution of the RMA scores in the particular sample, and samples are usually too small and not randomly selected to be considered representative of the population as a whole. More rigorous principles of psychometric testing need to be observed in order to develop and validate a screening instrument suitable for individual selection or deselection of potential jurors. This includes the establishment of a normative distribution of RMA scores on the basis of a large sample that yields standardised scores or percentiles against which an individual's score can be interpreted, similar to the distribution of scores on a standard intelligence test against which to compare an individual's IQ score. While the development of a screening tool for RMA could follow the practice established in other areas of psychological testing, a more difficult and contentious issue would be to define the threshold of unacceptably high levels of RMA. Should a juror be disqualified from serving on a rape trial if his or her acceptance of rape myths was above the 50th percentile, indicating that he or she is more accepting of rape myths than half of the norm population given the same measure, or should the threshold be defined differently (lower or higher)?

Further research would be required to decide whether screening out individuals with extreme attitudes toward rape would be sufficiently effective in suppressing the impact of rape myths. Evidence is needed that juries consisting of members screened for low acceptance of rape myths are less influenced by the real rape stereotype or by extraneous information about the parties than a comparison group of unscreened jurors. Experimental methods that facilitate a comparison of these critical differences while holding the case-related information constant are best suited to this task. A tried and tested method is the use of scenarios or 'vignettes' that contain information about a rape case (Bieneck 2009). Typically, the scenario method involves relatively short scenarios. There is no question of this method duplicating a trial and no opportunity for participants to assess the witnesses, draw inferences or evaluate the evidence after they have heard the witnesses. On the other hand, the scenario method has the advantage of enabling researchers to build critical variables into the rape scenarios that they expect to influence participants' judgments, such as information about any previous relationship between victim and assailant, while holding the remaining aspects of the case constant. This gives researchers a high degree of control over the stimulus material and enables them to identify the interactive effects of juror attitudes and features of the case. For example, if it was shown that information about a previous sexual relationship between the defendant and the complainant reduced perceptions of defendant liability compared to a stranger rape in the unscreened group but not in the screened group, this could be seen as evidence that the impact of rape stereotypes can be reduced through the screening procedure.

It may be concluded that developing and implementing screening procedures would be a complex process the effectiveness of which is difficult to predict from the outset. At present, jury selection to screen out people with extreme attitudes towards rape would run counter to current practice in England and Wales where jury screening is strictly limited (Lloyd-Bostock and Thomas 2000).

Introducing expert evidence

A second strategy for improving jury decision-making in rape cases that may be easier to evaluate is the introduction of expert evidence as a means of dispelling rape myths as they come into play in a rape trial. Calling upon experts in rape cases has a tradition in the American legal system (Lonsway 2005) and is currently contemplated as one method of educating juries (see, for example, Office for Criminal Justice Reform 2006). Experts could be brought in on behalf of the prosecution to give general evidence, for example about common reactions of victims of rape, including the frequency of late reporting[4] and unemotional responses (Office for Criminal Justice Reform 2006). The argument in favour of expert testimony is based on two assumptions. One is that certain information about the complainant's behaviour during and after the alleged assault undermines complainant credibility in the eyes of jurors. The other is that expert testimony can be used to improve jurors' understanding, leading to less biased perceptions of complainant credibility (Ellison and Munro 2008). There is indeed ample evidence from studies using the scenario technique that a complainant's behaviour during and after an assault does affect perceptions of her credibility. For example, information that the complainant was intoxicated at the time of the assault, that she did not physically resist or that she delayed reporting has been shown to increase mock jurors' perceptions of complainant blame and to decrease their perception of victim credibility (see Temkin and Krahé 2008: ch. 2). A different methodology was adopted by Ellison and Munro (2008) who scripted a series of nine mini-trials that were enacted in front of three different juries per case with the key roles played by actors and barristers. The cases were varied so as to provide different information which potentially undermined perceptions of complainant credibility. The authors found that absence of victim injury, delayed reporting and calm complainant demeanour at the trial raised suspicions about the credibility of her complaint (see Chapter 12 of this volume).

There is less evidence regarding the second underlying assumption, namely that expert evidence is a successful tool for dispelling juror misconceptions about rape. Studying expert evidence in the context of a simulated rape trial, Marable (1999) showed that expert testimony addressing rape myths was more effective than testimony focusing on the rape trauma syndrome in increasing mock jurors' confidence that the defendant was guilty. Schnopp-Wyatt (2000) showed that expert evidence that offered an opinion as to whether or not the complainant had been raped[5] was more influential on mock jury verdicts than expert testimony that presented research findings or discussed hypothetical examples. These studies show that the effectiveness of expert evidence depends very much on its specific content, e.g. whether it focuses on syndrome evidence or on rape myths, and the form in which it is presented. But there is no guarantee that expert witnesses will clarify matters for the jury. Indeed, it is possible that they would introduce further complexity and uncertainty into an already ambiguous situation. This is true, in particular, for adversarial justice systems where the prosecution and defence introduce expert witnesses who deliver contradictory messages (Brekke *et al.* 1991). Indeed, research demonstrates that whatever the impact of the evidence of a prosecution expert, this is swiftly diluted if the defence uses its own expert (Spanos *et al.* 1991–2; for further discussion see Temkin and Krahé 2008: 62–3, 165–7). Furthermore, the type of general expert evidence contemplated by the Office for Criminal Justice Reform which was confined to the common reactions of victims of rape would not sufficiently tackle victim-blaming attitudes which are the heart of the matter. Thus, while there is much to be said in favour of the admission of expert evidence as a means of bringing to public attention some of the myths of rape, it must be conceded that there is no solid evidence yet that it would have a substantial impact on conviction rates. Studies are required that systematically vary the form and content of expert testimony to establish when it is able to counteract stereotype-based information processing. Studies involving simulated rape trials are the method of choice here because they enable researchers to use identical case material so that differences in verdict can be attributed conclusively to differences in the way expert testimony was presented. The study by Ellison and Munro (2008) illustrates that it is possible to achieve a good degree of realism within the constraints of the simulation method by creating videotapes of trial enactments involving professional lawyers and requiring mock jurors to engage in group deliberation before returning their verdict.

An alternative method of seeking to educate the jury away from certain rape myths is currently being explored by a working group set up by the Solicitor General for England and Wales (Baird 2008). The group is looking at the possibility of drafting a special judicial instruction concerning the psychological reactions of rape victims, or alternatively providing an information leaflet or DVD for jurors. The advantage of conveying information through such methods is that juries would not have to contend with conflicting accounts from prosecution and defence experts. On the other hand, the information conveyed would presumably have to be fairly basic and anodyne in order to be fair to both sides. A judicial instruction would be incontestable by the parties at trial although it could affect the way the defence conducts the case.

The effectiveness of a judicial instruction, information leaflet or DVD in reducing the influence of jurors' RMA on their assessment of victim credibility and perpetrator liability could be examined through the simulation method. Three groups could each be given one of them and then compared with a control group which received no such assistance. Participants' RMA would need to be measured. If decisions were found to be less dependent on participants' RMA in any of the three groups rather than the control group, this would provide at least tentative evidence for the effectiveness of this approach. This would warrant further exploration in more realistic contexts, for example using shadow juries that are exposed to the same information in the courtroom as the real jury assigned to the case.

Juror accountability

Stereotypes and misconceptions about rape can impinge on verdicts because jurors lack the ability or the motivation to engage in a careful, data-driven examination of the facts and the evidence as presented in the course of a trial. Expert evidence may be regarded as a strategy for improving jurors' *ability* to make sense of the evidence and arrive at data-based decisions. Different strategies are needed to boost jurors' *motivation* to engage in a cognitively demanding scrutiny of the available information rather than falling back on well-rehearsed, less demanding stereotype-based judgments. Psychological research on social information processing has shown that one way of motivating individuals to engage in thorough, data-based information processing is to make them account for their decisions (Tetlock 1992). As shown in a study by Tetlock and Kim (1987), where individuals are told beforehand that they will be asked to justify the judgments they have been instructed to make, this acts to suppress schematic information processing. Applied to the issue of promoting data-driven processing of rape complaints, this line of research suggests that jurors should be less likely to rely on their rape-related attitudes and less influenced by extra-evidentiary cues related to rape stereotypes if told beforehand that they would have to justify their decisions.

Preliminary support for this assumption comes from a study by Krahé *et al.* (2007). In this study, participants were asked to make judgments about a set of case scenarios involving sexual assault. Before being given these scenarios, one group was told that they might have to justify their judgments afterwards, whereas a control group was not given this instruction. It was found that where the instruction was given, this reduced the impact of rape myth acceptance in situations most at odds with the real rape stereotype, namely those involving rape by an ex-partner. This research suggests that there might be some mileage in informing the jury at the outset of the trial that it will be asked to give reasons for its decision as a method of ensuring that the evidence in the case is carefully processed. However, making juries account for their decisions is contrary to the common-law tradition. Research is needed to see if the use of an accountability instruction to induce a more careful, data-driven appraisal of the evidence can be replicated in other studies to substantiate the benefits of making such a change.

Abolishing the jury in rape cases in favour of judge-only trials

A possible solution to the jury problem which scarcely dare speak its name is abolition of the jury in rape cases. There are arguments in favour of doing so. The jury system in its present form in England and Wales and elsewhere is becoming increasingly hard to justify. It is hard to control jury access to the Internet whatever warnings judges may give, so that jurors may find out more about the case and the players in it than it is fair for them to know. Juries are not required to give reasons for their decisions and cannot be educated in the way that it is possible to educate judges. Quite apart from the negative attitudes to rape victims held by some members of the public which are likely to result in wrongful acquittals, jurors may in some cases be swayed by their emotions which can give rise to wrongful convictions (see generally Doran and Jackson 1997; Jackson and Doran 1995). A further advantage of non-jury trials would be the improvement of their tone and conduct. Defence counsel would have far less incentive to use their well-worn strategies for undermining the complainant if there was no jury as an audience. Hence the experience of victims would be immeasurably improved.

Despite what would appear to be the many advantages of trial without a jury such a solution was, with two exceptions, not favoured by the judges and barristers interviewed in the sexual history study (Temkin and Krahé 2008: 179). The judges interviewed were, for the most part, wholeheartedly committed to the system of trial by jury for reasons of principle but also because they preferred to leave the task of fact-finding to juries and were reluctant to shoulder the blame for unpopular decisions. Even in fraud trials, notorious for their length, complexity and expense, trial by judge alone has been robustly opposed (see Julian 2008) and the Fraud (Trials Without a Jury) Bill introduced in 2006 has not been enacted. Yet there may be more reasons for abolishing the jury in sex than in fraud trials. One of the most important issues in fraud trials is whether juries can *understand* the evidence. Juries can be helped to do so by tailoring the issues through efficient case management and by careful presentation of the evidence. Fraud trials differ from sex trials in not carrying with them the same degree of baggage in terms of prejudice, myths and stereotypes. Prejudice is far harder to deal with than lack of understanding and is not susceptible to the same remedies.

However, the real research question for present purposes is whether trial without a jury in its present form would actually affect conviction rates. The general expectation is that trial by judge alone or by a panel of judges would certainly have that effect simply because experienced judges would be better able to draw appropriate inferences and less likely to be led astray by defence counsel. But the proposition has yet to be subjected to much in the way of empirical scrutiny. Judges, it might be thought, could be just as prejudiced in their own way as juries. Indeed, in a speech to mark International Women's Day in 2003, Vera Baird, the Solicitor General and chair of the Fawcett Society's Commission on Women and the Criminal Justice System, commented adversely on the clause in the Criminal Justice Bill which was then going through Parliament which would have allowed defendants to opt for trial by judge alone. In her view this would be to give them an extra right and, given that 95 per cent of trial judges were male, the judge would be 'chosen from a body of men who are not known for high levels of gender awareness ... So male defendants will pick their tribunal – one may think against the interests of women complainants.' In support of her argument she asserted that 'Judges in recent years – not old fuddy-duddy judges, but relatively young and highly intelligent ones – have none the less been guilty of making immensely sexist remarks in rape trials' (Baird 2003).[6]

The question of whether judge-only trials would be successful in reducing the impact of rape stereotypes on the decision-making process can only be decided on the basis of empirical evidence.[7] Such evidence is as yet limited, not least because of the difficulties in implementing valid and reliable research designs. In Canada, where defendants can opt for judge-alone trials, Read et al. (2006), using archival analysis, compared judge-only conviction rates with jury conviction rates in historic child abuse cases. They found a considerably higher conviction rate in trials by jury. The fatal flaw with this methodology is that jurors and judges were not assessing the same cases. Because choice of trial was not randomly determined but chosen by the defendants themselves, it cannot be ruled out that the difference between juries and judges was due to differences in the nature of the cases which affected defendants' choices. As Kalven and Zeisel noted, 'it is of small interest to learn how judge and jury decide *different* cases; the question is how judge and jury would decide the *same* case' (Kalven and Zeisel 1966: 46).

The classic study by Kalven and Zeisel (1966) avoided this problem by collecting judge and jury verdicts for the same cases and thus allowed for a direct comparison between judge and jury decisions.[8] Their findings revealed that conviction rates in a range of 42 crime categories were higher when verdicts were made by the judge rather than the jury. Overall, judges and juries agreed in 75.4 per cent of cases, but when they disagreed, cases where the judges would have convicted and the jury acquitted were much more frequent (16.9 per cent) than those where the judge would have acquitted and the jury convicted (2.2 per cent; in the remaining 5.5 per cent of cases the juries were hung; Kalven and Zeisel 1966: 56). This pattern translates into a 'net leniency bias' of juries relative to judges of 14.7 per cent.[9] Looking specifically at sexual assault cases, the juror leniency bias for forcible rape was 18 per cent, and for statutory rape 32 per cent (Kalven and Zeisel 1966: 70). Thus the Kalven and Zeisel data support the position that juries are more reluctant to convict than judges, not just across a range of offences but specifically in sexual assault cases. The study demonstrates that differences in judge and jury acquittal rates are most likely to occur in cases of 'simple rape' between non-strangers which do not involve extrinsic violence or several assailants. For the 42 simple rape cases in their sample, the net leniency bias was found to be 60 per cent, way above the 18 per cent found in their total sample of forcible rape cases (Kalven and Zeisel 1966: 253). The authors found that judges cited jury perceptions of the 'contributory fault of the victim' as one of the reasons for jury leniency, particularly in rape cases (Kalven and Zeisel 1966: 249–54) where juries were effectively importing notions of contributory negligence from tort law.[10]

Apart from the fact that the Kalven and Zeisel study was conducted in the 1950s and therefore does not reflect changes in legislation implemented since then,[11] it has a number of methodological deficiencies, such as a non-random selection of cases, the absence of a mechanism for checking whether judges had, as instructed, recorded their verdicts before the jury returned theirs,[12] and a reliance on judges' perceptions of the reasons for their disagreements with juries. Nonetheless, the study provides a blueprint for a research strategy capable of yielding evidence-based conclusions about judge-only trials.

A systematic analysis of jury and non-jury trials in rape cases would entail comparing the results of judge-only trials with trials by jury in a range of different cases. It would also ideally contrive to make these comparisons with other forms of trial such as trial by judge with a small lay panel as is the system in Germany (Bliesener 2006). But as Kalven and Zeisel have pointed out, in carrying out research of this kind the methodological options are strictly limited. Ultimately, however, to provide sure answers to the empirical questions discussed above, it is essential to ask judges in a sufficient number of actual trials for the verdicts they themselves would have given *before* the jury returns its verdict. There is no legal reason why research of this kind could not, with permission of the judicial authorities,[13] be carried out in England and Wales provided the anonymity of the judges was secured and provided the finer details of the cases were not revealed in such a way that the case could be identified. However, empirical research designed to test jury as against judge decision-making clearly has its practical difficulties and would require a considerable degree of judicial cooperation. It would, moreover, be necessary to have a spread of cases so that comparisons could be drawn between different types, for example child and adult, acquaintances and strangers, those involving alcohol or historic abuse and those where the defendant has previous convictions for sexual offences.

Studying judge–jury agreement in actual cases could be complemented by the more cost-effective method of using trial simulations. Videotapes of staged trials could be shown to judges and laypersons eligible for jury service so that both would assess the same evidence. The drawback would be that both jurors and judges would be aware that their decisions would not have consequences for the parties involved. On the plus side, however, it would be possible systematically to vary key aspects of the cases to examine, for example, whether jury leniency is particularly pronounced when the case deviates from the stereotype of the real rape.

If there was conclusive evidence that juries were more lenient than judges in rape trials, explaining this difference would not be straightforward. Juries lack legal training and experience. Any disagreement between judges and juries could be attributed to this factor. However, the explanation could be quite different. Juries arrive at their verdict through a process of group deliberation. By contrast, the judge, in a judge-only trial, would be asked to deliver his or her own individual verdict. It is well established in social psychological research on 'group polarisation' that group decisions tend to be more extreme than decisions made by individuals and that the direction of the shift is determined by the position initially favoured by the majority of the individuals involved (Brown 2000). This suggests that if the majority of jurors in a given case are at least mildly accepting of rape myths, such beliefs are more likely to be perceived as socially acceptable and arguments consistent with rape myths more likely to be exchanged in the course of the jury's deliberations. This increases the chances of an acquittal relative to the odds that any single juror would have acquitted the defendant. The same process could be assumed to operate if judges were asked to deliberate as a group before reaching a verdict. Thus, to identify the underlying reasons for jury leniency, a proper analysis of judge–jury disagreement needs to include a comparison of juries with judges who also deliberate as a group. Depending on the outcome of such research, different implications for managing rape trials would result. If juror leniency could be attributed to the effects of group decision-making, then asking for individual decisions might be an option. If, however, the juror leniency bias remained even in comparison with group decisions made by judges, differences in professional training and experience would be the more plausible explanation and this would lend support to calls for judge-only trials.

Female judges

While in England and Wales judges do not decide guilt or innocence in rape trials, they do make crucial decisions on the admissibility of evidence and the conduct of the trial. Their non-verbal cues may also have an impact on juries. Unlike their American counterparts, they provide a detailed summing-up to the jury at the end of the trial in which they go through all the evidence, explain the law and point out the salient issues. Judges therefore perform a vital role in jury trials. In countries with an inquisitorial justice system, the role of the judge in determining the verdict is even more prominent. In England and Wales it still remains the case that the overwhelming majority of trial judges are male. Thirteen per cent of circuit judges are female, 87 out of a total of 653.[14] Research with samples from the general population or with university students suggests that men are more likely than women to subscribe to myths about rape and to victim-blaming attitudes (Anderson *et al.* 1997; Temkin and Krahé 2008: ch. 2). On the basis of this evidence, the question arises whether similar gender differences can be found among judges and whether an increase in the number of female judges would enhance rape conviction rates. The socialisation process which women go through as barristers and then as judges could well have the effect of reducing the gender difference in rape myth acceptance (see Temkin and Krahé 2008: 197). Empirical evidence on gender differences in RMA among lawyers is scarce. In a study with graduate law students in Germany, men were more accepting than women of rape myths (Krahé *et al.* 2008: Study 2). In turn, higher acceptance of rape myths was linked to a stronger tendency to blame the complainant across a range of rape scenarios, reflecting an indirect role of gender via differences in RMA. In contrast, no gender differences in rape myth acceptance were found in a sample of graduate law students in England studied by Temkin and Krahé (2008: Study 2), clearly indicating the need for further research.

In order to test whether the strategy of appointing more female judges to try rape cases would have any impact on the attrition problem, research could be conducted with a sample of male and female barristers who have reached the point in their careers at which they might be considered for appointment to the circuit bench. Again, only experimental research that presented identical case information to each group could provide conclusive evidence. Realistic trial simulations could be created for this purpose. If there was a consistent gender difference, with men being less inclined than women to find a defendant guilty, this would create an evidence base from which policy decisions could be derived. However, using gender as a 'marker' for prejudicial attitudes is a crude measure because there is a wide range of views within each gender group and some men are less accepting of rape myths than some women. Therefore, in addition to comparing the male and female barristers' guilty verdicts, measures of RMA should be included in the research design to clarify the extent to which differences between men and women can be attributed to underlying differences in the acceptance of rape myths.

In order to ensure that those with rape-supportive attitudes, whether male or female, do not try rape cases, the obvious step forward would be to institute a screening process. However, even assuming this were considered to be an appropriate course of action, screening, as discussed above in relation to juries, is problematic. If this is not an option, the alternative is to appoint more female judges provided it can be shown that female judges are less likely on the whole than their male counterparts to have stereotypical views about rape.

Conclusion

If, as is generally accepted, there is a justice gap in rape cases, and if this is a situation which requires improvement, then proposals for doing so need to be evidence-based. This chapter has discussed some research designs for testing a variety of possible options and has pointed out some of the pitfalls.

In terms of methodology, experimental research designs provide the best approach for identifying causal relationships between the introduction of certain measures, such as juror screening or expert testimony, and changes in decision-making about rape cases. Field experiments using real cases are not an option in this area because of legal restrictions but also because cases differ from each other in a wide range of aspects to which any observed differences in verdicts could potentially be attributed. Studies comparing jury and judge responses in real trials are important for gauging juror bias, but they present problems in terms of obtaining random or representative case samples and need to be complemented by methods offering more rigorous control. Therefore the methodological options discussed in this chapter rely heavily on hypothetical material in the form of case vignettes and trial simulations. Once a particular measure has been found effective under these controlled yet artificial conditions, the next step is to examine the feasibility of implementing them as part of the law in action and carefully to monitor the consequences of their introduction. This monitoring process also needs to include unwanted side effects, for example the opportunity to evade jury service which jury screening could present.

Of the many problems underlying the justice gap, the chapter has highlighted stereotypical attitudes about rape as a major obstacle to unbiased and fair decisions about rape cases. To counteract the influence of rape myths on decisions made by juries, screening out individuals with a strong belief in rape myths, introducing expert evidence to educate juries about rape and dispel misconceptions about victim behaviour, as well as asking juries to account for their decisions have been discussed as potential improvements. A more radical suggestion, namely replacing trial by jury with judge-only trials, has also been considered. Finally, on the basis of evidence that men are more likely than women to accept rape myths, appointing more female judges has also been examined. Some of these options would no doubt today be considered beyond the pale. Only research will tell whether they are not merely politically unacceptable but of no particular value in seeking a measure of improvement to rape trials. On the other hand, empirical research of the sort outlined in this chapter may reveal the efficacy of taking certain steps. It will then be for policymakers to make informed choices.

Notes

1 See: http://www.opsi.gov.uk/acts/acts2003/ukpga_20030042_en_1.
2 'There are cases in which the situation is clearly aggravated by extrinsic violence, but the jury is still lenient to the defendant. In one such case, the judge tells us: "This was a savage case of rape. Jaw of complainant fractured in two places." Nevertheless the jury acquits when it learns that there may have been intercourse with the complainant on prior occasions' (Kalven and Zeisel 1966: 251).
3 *Voir dire* is the process by which the suitability of prospective jurors may be challenged.
4 It has now been established that the judge may explain to the jury that delay in reporting may be a response to rape: see *R v. Doody* [2008] EWCA Crim 2394.
5 Current proposals do not envisage the admission of such evidence in courts in England and Wales.
6 The clause in the Bill was eventually dropped in favour of a more limited version which does not apply to rape trials (Criminal Justice Act 2003, Part 7; see: http://www.opsi.gov.uk/acts/acts2003/ukpga_20030044_en_1).
7 For the suggestion that inquisitorial systems have higher conviction rates, see Regan and Kelly (2003: 13).
8 They looked at 3,576 actual trials which took place in 1954–5 and 1958 of which 106 were rape trials. A large sample of judges received a questionnaire by mail and 555 agreed to participate. They were asked to report, for cases tried before them, how the jury decided the case and how they would have decided it had it been tried without a jury. The judges were instructed to record their verdict before the jury returned theirs. They were also asked to give some descriptive and evaluative material about the case, counsel and the parties and to comment on the reasons for disagreements between judge and jury. Reports were received from every US state except Rhode Island.
9 Kalven and Zeisel calculated the net leniency bias of juries as the difference between the more lenient judgments by juries (judge convicts, jury acquits) and the more lenient judgments by judges (judge acquits, jury convicts) which was $16.9\% - 2.2\% = 14.7\%$.
10 In the civil law of tort, the defendant's liability for damages may be reduced if the victim has been negligent but contributory negligence of the victim is not a concept which applies in criminal law.
11 However, a later study by Heuer and Penrod (1994) produced highly similar results.
12 See note 8.
13 Contrast Kalven and Zeisel who simply approached judges individually, – see note 8.
14 See: http://www.judiciary.gov.uk/keyfacts/statistics/women.htm. Specially licensed circuit judges are mainly responsible for trying rape cases.

References

Anderson, K. B., Cooper, H. and Okamura, L. (1997) 'Individual differences and attitudes toward rape: a meta-analytic review', *Personality and Social Psychology Bulletin*, 23 (3): 295–315.

Baird, V. (2003) *International Womens Day, 6 May 2003*. Available online at: http://www.labouronline.org/wibs/166155/cf7789c4-63a7-3a34-bd2b14 f06d23e35e?PageId=a02c2de8-713e-c1e4-ed72-66bd5fecee96 (accessed 2 December 2008).

Baird, V. (2008) Letter, *Counsel Magazine*, April, p. 5.

Bieneck, S. (2009) 'How adequate is the vignette technique as a research tool in psycho-legal research?', in M. E. Oswald, S. Bieneck and J. Hupfeld-Heinemann (eds), *The Social Psychology of Punishment of Crime*. Chichester: Wiley, pp. 255–71.

Bliesener, T. (2006) 'Lay judges in the German criminal court: social psychological aspects in the German criminal justice system', in M. F. Kaplan and A. M. Martin (eds). *Understanding World Jury Systems through Social Psychological Research*. Hove: Psychology Press, pp. 179–97.

Brekke, N. J., Enko, P. J., Clavet, G. and Seelau, E. (1991) 'Of juries and court-appointed experts: the impact of nonadversarial versus adversarial expert testimony', *Law and Human Behavior*, 15 (5): 451–75.

Brown, J. M., Hamilton, C. and O'Neill, D. (2007) 'Characteristics associated with rape attrition and the role played by scepticism or legal rationality by investigators and prosecutors', *Psychology, Crime and Law*, 13 (4): 355–70.

Brown, R. (2000) *Group Processes*, 2nd edn. Oxford: Blackwell.

Diamond, S. S. and Rose, M. R. (2005) 'Real juries', *Annual Review of Law and Social Science*, 1: 255–84.

Devine, D. J., Buddenbaum, J., Houp, S., Studebaker, N. and Stolle, D. P. (2009) 'Strength of the evidence, extraevidentiary influence, and the liberation hypothesis: data from the field', *Law and Human Behavior*, 33 (2): 136–48.

Doran, S. and Jackson, J. (1997) 'The case for jury waiver', *Criminal Law Review*, 44 (3): 155–72.

Ellison, L. and Munro, V. (2008) 'Reacting to Rape: Exploring Mock Jurors' Assessment of Complainant Credibility'. Unpublished manuscript.

Feist, A., Ashe, J., Lawrence, J., McPhee, D. and Wilson, R. (2007) *Investigating and Detecting Recorded Offences of Rape*, Home Office Online Report 18/07. Available online at: http://www.homeoffice.gov.uk/rds/pdfs07/rdsolr1807. pdf (accessed 2 December 2008).

Finch, E. and Munro, V. E. (2005) 'Juror stereotypes and blame attribution in rape cases involving intoxicants', *British Journal of Criminology*, 45 (1): 25–38.

Hans, V. P. and Jehle, A. (2003) 'Avoid bald men and people with green socks? Other ways to improve the voir dire process in jury selection', *Chicago-Kent Law Review*, 78: 1178–201.

Heuer, L. and Penrod, S. (1994) 'Trial complexity: a field investigation of its meaning and its effects', *Law and Human Behavior*, 18 (1): 29–51.

Jackson, J. and Doran, S. (1995) *Judge Without Jury: Diplock Trials in the Adversary System*. Oxford: Oxford University Press.

Julian, R. F. (2007) 'Judicial perspectives on the conduct of serious fraud trials', *Criminal Law Review*, 54: 751–68

Julian, R. F. (2008) 'Judicial perspectives in serious fraud cases – the present status of and problems posed by case management practices, jury selection rules, juror expertise, plea bargaining and choice of mode of trial', *Criminal Law Review*, 55: 764–83.

Kalven, H. and Zeisel, H. (1966) *The American Jury*. Boston: Little, Brown.

Kelly, L., Temkin, J. and Griffiths, S. (2006) *Section 41: An Evaluation of New Legislation Limiting Sexual History Evidence in Rape Trials*, Home Office Online Report 20/06. Available online at: http://www.homeoffice.gov.uk/rds/pdfs06/rdsolr2006.pdf (accessed 2 December 2008).

Krahé, B. (1988) 'Victim and observer characteristics as determinants of responsibility attributions to victims of rape', *Journal of Applied Social Psychology*, 18 (1): 50–8.

Krahé, B., Temkin, J. and Bieneck, S. (2007) 'Schema-driven information processing in judgements about rape', *Applied Cognitive Psychology*, 21 (5): 601–19.

Krahé, B., Temkin, J., Bieneck, S. and Berger, A. (2008) 'Prospective lawyers' rape stereotypes and schematic decision-making about rape cases', *Psychology, Crime and Law*, 14 (5): 461–79.

Lecci, L. and Myers, B. (2008) 'Individual differences in attitudes relevant to juror decision making: development and validation of the Pretrial Juror Attitude Questionnaire (PJAQ)', *Journal of Applied Social Psychology*, 38 (8): 2010–38.

Lieberman, J. D. and Sales, B. D. (eds) (2007) *Scientific Jury Selection*. Washington, DC: American Psychological Association.

Lloyd-Bostock, S. and Thomas, C. (2000) 'Juries and reform in England and Wales', in N. Vidmar (ed.), *World Jury Systems*. Oxford: Oxford University Press, pp. 53–91.

Lonsway, K. A. (2005) *The Use of Expert Witnesses in Cases Involving Sexual Assault. Violence against Women Online Resources*. Available online at: http://www.mincava.umn.edu/documents/commissioned/svandexpertwitnesses/svandexpertwitnesses.pdf (accessed 7 December 2008).

Marable, B. E. (1999) 'Influence of expert testimony and victim resistance on mock jurors' decisions and judgments concerning acquaintance rape', *Dissertation Abstracts International: Section B: The Sciences and Engineering*, 59 (9B), p. 5096.

Ministry of Justice (2007) *Criminal Statistics Annual Report 2007*, Volume 2, Part 1, Table S2.1(A). Available online at: http://www.justice.gov.uk/publications/criminalannual.htm (accessed 11 December 2008).

National Center on Domestic and Sexual Violence (2007) *Voir Dire and Prosecution Tips for Sexual Assault Cases*. Available online at: http://www. ncdsv.org/images/SexualAssault-VOIRDIREANDPROSECUTIONTIPS. pdf (accessed 7 December 2008).

National District Attorneys Association (2007) *Voir Dire Questions*. Available online at: http://www.ndaa.org/apri/programs/vawa/voir_ dire_questions.html#samplequestion (accessed 3 December 2008).

Office for Criminal Justice Reform (2006) *Convicting Rapists and Protecting Victims. Justice for Victims of Rape. A Consultation Paper*. Available online at: http://www.homeoffice.gov.uk/documents/cons-290306-justice-rape-victims?view=Binary (accessed 3 December 2008).

Read, J. D., Connolly, D. A. and Welsh, A. (2006) 'An archival analysis of actual cases of historic child sexual abuse: a comparison of jury and bench trials', *Law and Human Behavior*, 30 (3): 259–85.

Regan, L. and Kelly, L. (2003) *Rape: Still a Forgotten Issue*. London: Child and Women Abuse Studies Unit. Available online at: http://www.rcne.com/ downloads/RepsPubs/Attritn.pdf (accessed 3 February 2009).

Schnopp-Wyatt, E. N. (2000) 'Expert testimony in rape trials: prejudicial or probative?', *Dissertation Abstracts International: Section B: The Sciences and Engineering*, 60, p. 6425.

Schuller, R., Kazoleas, V. and Kawakami, K. (in press) 'The impact of prejudice screening procedures on racial bias in the courtroom', *Law and Human Behavior*.

Spanos, N. P., Dubreuil, S. C. and Gwynn, M. I. (1991–2) 'The effects of expert testimony concerning rape on the verdicts and beliefs of mock jurors', *Imagination, Cognition and Personality*, 11 (1): 37–51.

Temkin, J. and Krahé, B. (2008) *Sexual Assault and the Justice Gap: A Question of Attitude*. Oxford: Hart.

Tetlock, P. E. (1992) 'The impact of accountability on judgment and choice: toward a social contingency model', *Advances of Experimental Social Psychology*, 22 (3): 31–7.

Tetlock, P. E. and Kim, J. I. (1987) 'Accountability and judgment process in a personality prediction task', *Journal of Personality and Social Psychology*, 52 (4): 700–9.

Part 4

Concluding Remarks

Chapter 14

Do you believe her and is it a real rape?

Jennifer M. Brown and Miranda A.H. Horvath

Introduction

Rape is a unique crime insofar as there is both a psychological and physical violation of its victims, independent corroboration may not be available and the conviction rate is appallingly low. Rape is also a paradoxical crime. Allegations of rape are often contested. As Stanko and Williams point out in their chapter, the distinction between criminal and legal sex is cloudy and the difference sufficient to warrant the deprivation of liberty is judged through scrutiny of the consent of the victim rather than the behaviour of the man. To be labelled either a rapist or a liar is highly stigmatising yet there is a public perception that the greater harm may be done to a man wrongly called a rapist than to a woman wrongly called a liar. The data revealed by Stanko and Williams (and by Maddy Coy) show that the more vulnerable victims, who might reasonably expect the protection of the law, actually fare worst and are least likely to have their cases presented in court. A further aspect to consider is the criminal status of rape. While the cultural coding of behaviour as criminal may be relative, the ambivalence about rape together with its other distinctive features makes this a particularly problematic crime.

When we initiated our SORI seminar series we looked at theories, methods, substantive findings and practical applications in relation to rape. The chapters in this edited collection reflect and supplement the discussions from our SORI meetings. The authors of the present volume have brought together a number of conceptualisations and formulations when thinking about and explaining sexual assault and rape. This final chapter will offer some reflections on these ideas and approaches and suggest an agenda for action derived from the work presented in the book's contributions.

A key conceptualisation that pervaded our discussions and is evident throughout the book's chapters is the notion of the 'justice gap' for women suffering a sexual assault. Temkin and Krahé (2008) describe this as the dramatic gap between the number of offences recorded by police officers and the securing of convictions in court. This is also referred to as the attrition problem. Attrition is the identification of instances within the sequencing of reporting, recording, prosecuting and trying of rape where cases are dropped. Temkin and Krahé (2008) identify stereotypic beliefs and attitudes as key to understanding the problem of attrition. This has also been one of the threads running through all the chapters in the present collection.

Attitudes have been conceptualised as comprising three elements: affect, cognitions and behaviour. The way a person feels and thinks is said to influence behaviour, although sometimes people may think or act differently from the way they feel. Theorists suggest that there is an evaluative dimension by which people evince negative or positive feelings towards some person or issue. Stahlberg and Frey (1996) note that the term beliefs is reserved for opinions held about some attitude object while behavioural intention describes some predisposition to engage in attitude-relevant behaviour. These attitudes and beliefs are critical factors in the decision-making processes made by women when choosing to report the offence in the first place, by police and prosecutors in exercising their professional judgments in investigating and evidence testing of cases and jurors when deliberating over the guilt or innocence of a defendant. We argue that these beliefs are a product of rape myths about what constitutes a criminal case of rape and are pervasive within society and influence all the actors, i.e. the victim, the offender/defendant, police investigator, prosecutor and members of the jury. Thus a victim who believes that the type of women who are raped are different to her, i.e. her attitudes towards rape victims are negative, may thus form the behavioural intention not to report her assault. A police officer investigating rape may form the belief that many women fabricate their allegations and form the behavioural intention not to proceed with the investigation. This can be encapsulated in the observations of a woman detective constable who commented that the two questions she is asked by her (male) senior officer investigating a case of rape are: Do you believe her? Is it real rape? Jurors may believe that drinking alcohol or flirting may have shifted the weight of responsibility for sex to the victim rather than her assailant and they then form the behavioural intention to exonerate the man from the charge of rape.

We have found Estrich's (1987) articulation of 'real rape' helpful in focusing on reasons and explanations for the huge disparities between the numbers of women estimated to have suffered a sexual assault and those willing to report, the dropping out of cases by police and prosecutors and the apparent reluctance of juries to convict.

Estrich describes the 'jump from the bushes' stereotype in which an unsuspecting woman is forced to have sex without her consent by a man she does not know and who has a weapon with which he threatens or uses to overcome her resistance. Estrich also observes that a 'real rape' victim reports her attack directly to the police without washing away any of the forensic traces of her attacker. Estrich points out, as do other scholars (e.g. Temkin and Krahé 2008), that the presence of all these elements in rape is relatively rare. The research evidence highlights that women are far more likely to be assaulted by people they know under circumstances that may involve socialising and possibly drinking, as demonstrated in Jo Lovett and Miranda Horvath's chapter. Yet women themselves, police investigators, prosecutors and juries appear to use the 'real' rape scenario as some notional standard such that deviations seriously undermine a judgment that what occurred was a rape. The chapters in this collection attempt to find explanations and mechanisms for the operation of these decision-making processes.

Mapping the justice gap

Hamilton (2004) maps the attrition process and identifies key stages where cases drop out of or never get into the criminal justice system (see Figure 14.1 below). In order to convey to the reader the extent of the justice gap we draw on Coleman et al. (2008) who estimate that about 100,000 women are raped every year in England and Wales. Figures available from the British Crime Survey report that about 12,000 cases are annually reported to the police which corresponds to Myhill and Allen's (2002) suggested figure that as many as 90 per cent of rapes go unreported.

Once a rape has been reported between half and two-thirds of cases are dropped by the police and are either no crimed or no further action is taken (Kelly et al. 2005). Of the remaining cases that are

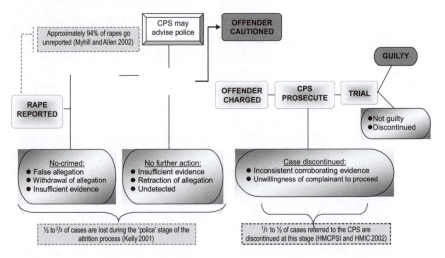

Figure 14.1 Places within the criminal justice system where rape cases are dropped (taken from Hamilton 2004)

considered by the Crown Prosecution Service a further third to a half of cases are dropped (HMCPSI and HMIC 2002). Once in court about half the cases result in a guilty verdict although this only represents about 6 per cent of the original number of cases coming to police attention.

The vicious cycle

Called the cycle of blame by Sinclair and Bourne (1988), Vanessa Munro and Liz Kelly in their chapter refer to a 'vicious cycle' in which stereotypic thinking about rape (influenced by acceptance of rape myths) continues to inform decision-making throughout the criminal justice process. Rape myths may inhibit women from reporting rape, police officers confirm their beliefs in high rates of false reporting when there is an insufficiency of evidence or women withdraw their allegations, prosecutors anticipate jurors' responses to cases in which the evidence deviates from the 'real' rape scenario and juries continue to acquit which reinforces rape myths and discourages women from reporting. We suggest that this vicious cycle creates a self-perpetuating feedback loop in which the prejudicial disbelief of women's experience is confirmed by the attrition process within the criminal justice system. It is women who are considered deviant if the rape is not of the 'real rape' type. The representation of rape is in part drawn from media depictions and the content of sexual scripts which feed into a set of myths about rape. Acceptance of these myths is associated with lessening belief that a sexual encounter is criminal the further removed it is from the stereotype. The vicious cycle of rape myth perpetration is supported by a further mechanism, just world beliefs. Bohner and colleagues discuss this in their chapter. A belief in a just world assumes that adverse outcomes are not visited upon people with good intent. When applied to rape this gives rise to a syllogistic fallacy. Bad things do not happen to good people; a bad thing (rape) happens to a person, therefore the person must be bad (i.e. colluded in her own victimisation). This leads to notions of the deserving and undeserving victim. We can illustrate this vicious cycle as shown in Figure 14.2.

Just world and rape myth beliefs operate at societal, organisational as well as individual levels. Societally, there is a rape-supporting culture by virtue of sets of beliefs, developed through socialisation and promoted through the media, that contribute towards the construction of rape myths and scripts which lay out expectations about the roles for men and women in sexual encounters which make saying no difficult for women. Structurally within police organisations and prosecution agencies, there is an agenda about

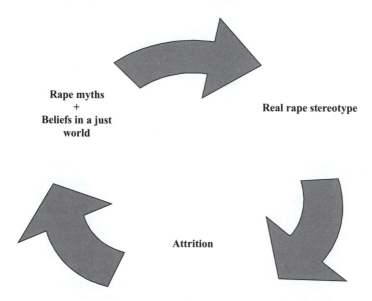

Figure 14.2 Vicious cycle of rape myth perpetuation

cost to the public purse which influences the criteria for decision-making to proceed with a prosecution. Individuals, in their various roles within the criminal justice system are susceptible to rape myths which the chapters in the present book demonstrate influence their formulation of what constitutes rape. This suggests some radical rethinking if interventions are to be designed to break the cycle and the need to take into account these psychological, structural and cultural influences.

Emotive connotations associated with rape

Giner-Sorolla and Russell offer an elegant and persuasive analysis that the emotions of disgust and anger are aroused by rape. They argue rape presents threats to the integrity of a person (autonomy), to community cohesion and to cultural or theological values in the form of purity or chastity violations. Threats to autonomy invite anger and a wish to punish or rebuke the offender. Threats to sexual norms in the form of violation evince disgust and evoke aversion or avoidance. Threats to the community (or organisations) provoke contempt or a combination of anger and disgust. Their formulation proposes that individuals engage in an evaluative process to judge whether behaviour is acceptable or not. It would appear from the work of O'Keeffe and colleagues people utilise short cuts to their evaluations, i.e. heuristics, which bias their judgments of acceptability. If there is a cultural stereotype of 'real rape' which has certain critical features such as the presence of coercive force, an act committed by a stranger and resistance by the victim, then this constitutes a relatively high threshold to trigger an emotional reaction whereby there is anger directed at the perpetrator and sympathy expressed for the victim. The operation of culturally embedded myths about rape seem to act to attenuate the harm experienced by the woman, thus minimising the autonomy threat, and to maximise the blame attributed to the victim, thus creating a reversal whereby the man becomes the victim of an unstable, vindictive or sick woman. Thus it is his sexual entitlement, whose origins may be found in property rights over women, which has been threatened. Consequently the anger and wish to humiliate and punish is directed at the woman. Preservation of a man's autonomy and defining sexual norms in his terms limit threats to community cohesion. The responsibility for regulating sex and so minimising the threats lies with women, at its most extreme in the concept of honour. This is explained by Aisha

Gill in her chapter as being achieved through 'the conduct, actions and social performance of women'. 'Misbehaviour' by women, i.e. the exercise of their sexual autonomy, is defiling and 'brings shame and dishonour to the male members of the entire community'. Rape in Urdu is referred to as *meri izzat looti gayi/meri izzat lut gayi* which literally translated means 'I could not prevent them from stealing my honour'. This justifies retributive honour-based violence thereby restoring community cohesion.

Rape myths

In their chapter, Bohner *et al.* delineate the notion of rape myth acceptance (RMA) as one mechanism contributing towards the preservation of the culturally embedded real rape stereotype and the reluctance to accept different versions of women's assault experiences as legitimate.

They define rape myths as beliefs about rape that serve to deny, downplay or justify sexual violence that men commit against women. Typically rape myths blame the victim for their rape (women have an unconscious desire to be raped or provoke rape through their appearance), express disbelief in claims of rape (exaggerate assault behaviour), exonerate perpetrators (what does a woman expect if she is wearing skimpy clothes) and imply only certain types of women get raped (those who drink, hang out in bars). Myths operate as devices to simplify a complex world. They help people to explain and understand confusing and contested events, to maintain cognitive consistency, to fend off threats to self-esteem and to rationalise problematic behaviours. Endorsement of rape myths predicts greater perceived responsibility towards victims and exoneration of perpetrators. The trauma experienced by victims is perceived as less severe. An outcome of subscribing to rape myths is to lower the likelihood of reporting a rape to the police.

Acceptance of rape myths also predicts that a particular piece of information is used prejudicially against the victim such as her drinking or being drunk. Rape myth acceptance (RMA) also enables people to infer from absent information, i.e. if a woman knows the defendant, then high RMA is associated with the belief that she consented to the sex rather than it being coerced. Bohner and colleagues find that where there is clear evidence of rape, such as with 'the jump from the bushes' type, RMA is not influential but it is when the evidence is ambiguous, as often is the case, or where there is a good deal of irrelevant information. As Susan Estrich notes, rape is uniquely a crime where corroboration in the form of independent witnesses or supportive forensics is often not available.

Rape myths become part of a self-supporting system whereby the absence of convictions supports the belief that women falsify claims or men's behaviour does not justify the charge. The fear then by women that they will not be believed is confirmed, thus is likely to contribute to their reluctance to report. As Stanko and Williams and Munro and Kelly point out, not only do victims anticipate juries' responses to accounts of rape but simulated jury studies show that victims are pretty accurate in their attributions that jurors are sceptical about the criminal aspects of the sex that had been described in court.

Victims also know that police and prosecutors give weight to the context and circumstances of rape which influence the decision to proceed with a prosecution. The accounts of police decision-making by O'Keeffe *et al.* provide evidence that professionals within the criminal justice system have access to the real rape stereotype embedded in social knowledge and that they engage heuristics in their information processing. O'Keeffe and colleagues show how police investigators use the availability or representativeness heuristics to assess the probability of a complaint being a case of criminal activity based on how closely it resembles their model of 'real' rape. As a consequence their investigative strategies seek to test the truthfulness of the woman's account or they attempt to generate proof that it happened as she said. McMillan and Thomas provide some examples from their police officer research participants of this proof-seeking or truth-seeking dichotomy: 'I'm not a lie detector but what I do ... is to get the fine-grained detail. Now the more detail you get the more easy it is to prove whether they are lying or not' contrasts with 'We do our damnedest to find the evidence if it's there.' O'Keeffe *et al.* found that the social knowledge absorbed by the officers influenced their degree of empathy towards the complainant which was also illustrated in the McMillan and Thomas data. One officer spoke of her desire to support the victim: 'When you get them to speak to you, I always try and explain look you telling me pushes the burden of what happened from you onto me', whereas another explained: 'Because you are dealing with so many you just know the ones that are really strong ... A proper rape ... you know a good case of rape.'

The vicious cycle is strengthened by the restricted number of cases that prosecutors forward to court and by the not guilty verdicts which confirm jurors' scepticism. So victims are in a double bind.

On the one hand, they may be inhibited from reporting a rape if they think that they are not the type of women who might be expected to be raped. On the other hand, if the woman has been drinking or was raped by someone she knew, this deviates from the 'real' rape stereotype and is likely to be viewed with disbelief. This situation is further compounded by the confirmation bias that women must be lying because there are so few convictions. The paucity of guilty verdicts also allows men to rationalise their own aggressive sexual behaviour or justify the pressures put on women to have sex they do not want and, as such, men then normalise such sexual encounters and do not interpret these as rape.

Sexual scripts

Hannah Frith in her chapter draws attention to another over-simplification: namely that signalling sexual consent or non-consent is a straightforward saying yes or no. Frith, like Estrich, argues that a key feature of a 'real' rape is the importance to the perceiver as to whether a rape has occurred is the idea that the woman must have resisted. This notion of resistance is at the heart of discussion about consent, which in rape cases is often contested. Estrich suggests that it is unreasonable to expect a woman to resist if she is terrified and copes by complying with the unwanted sex.

How women should behave rather than how they do behave is embedded in templates or scripts which are the social rules implied in negotiations of sexual encounters. The scripts generate the kinds of activities and sequencing that typify sexual encounters and attribute different roles to men and women. Men are the sexual pursuers and initiators of sex and women are the gatekeepers granting permission. Such scripts are held to be supportive of rape because the scripts can give permission for men to pursue their sexual objectives aggressively (and without responsibility). Stanko and Williams in their chapter suggest that actually men's normal sexual behaviour and coercive sex differ relatively little thus it is the woman who has to make the allegation that what happened was not normal sex. Such scripts do not easily allow women to change their minds or renegotiate their consent because this disrupts the expected sequencing of behaviour. Reliance on the script may result in confusion because women fail to say no clearly or men fail to act on or understand their refusal and the resultant sex is the result of misreading signals. Adherence to the script makes sexual refusals difficult. Thus if young people learn a script, from resources available through the media, socialisation, peers, this then guides their early sexual encounters which is then confirmed by those encounters.

Frith found that young women had ideas about the stages and sequencing of sex, that this is commonly available knowledge which is consensually agreed and that they draw on general instances about the kinds of things men do or say to confirm the nature of sexual encounters. This is a case of art (in the form of expectations confirmed through these devices) becoming real life. This leads to the idea that it becomes difficult for women to say no and shifts blame onto women who do not then know how or when to say no clearly. Men are 'let off' since they claim to be confused by this apparent ambivalence of women to say no clearly and because refusal deviates from the script. There are cultural rules that attribute undesirable qualities to women if they attempt to renegotiate sex and say no once they indicate their consent to having sex by being cast as a tease, flirt or tart. In negotiating no it seems young women offered justifications for their inability rather than unwillingness to say no. In other words they seek excuses or justifications rather than being able to be clear that they do not want sex with this man on this occasion. Thus the miscommunication notion within this formulation is another rape myth.

Aisha Gill also tries to find an explanation as to why Asian women do not report rape because they do not believe the behaviour they experienced constitutes rape. She looks at cultural scripts in which 'honour' accentuates ideas of dictating ways that men and women behave and violence remains unreported because it is the norm. To provide an account of oppressive behaviour presents a woman with a characterisation of having to deviate from the accepted norm whereby husbands have a right to do their will and women misattribute the violence they suffer. The story of Min the girl abused in the Temple tells us how pervasive this is and that women collude to live by male concepts of honour. The social norms here are also rape-supporting in that they inhibit women speaking out and to do so causes fractures and disruptions in the social fabric. Often women are economically dependent and power differentials between men and women limit the latter's options.

Maddy Coy's chapter discusses another extreme version of vulnerability through women's accounts of prostitution and various forms of sexual violence. Selling sex does not mean that aspects of the encounter are beyond what was negotiated and are not what the woman consented to, or that having had numerous sexual encounters, women cannot recognise abusive sex outside those encounters which are commercially transacted.

Vulnerabilities

Stanko and Williams discuss the idea of multiple vulnerabilities experienced by women such as mental health issues and the effects of alcohol. They point out that women are supposed to protect themselves from dangerous exposure yet while it is the offender who makes the choice to cross a boundary between consensual and consenting sex there is still a condemnation of the victim.

In Maddy Coy's chapter vulnerability is identified in the sexual violence experienced by women who are often classed as 'undeserving' victims by their involvement in prostitution. As she says 'women who sell sex are ... regarded as legitimate targets of sexual violence because of who they are and what they do.' This too can create a social norm of acceptable sexual violence. Interestingly, Coy points out that research finds some men who pay for sex have a higher endorsement of rape myths.

Media

Jenny Kitzinger describes resources that feed, fuel and shape rape-supporting attitudes. She argues that the media present a highly partial view and promote myths and stereotypes. The print media has a long history of salacious reporting of sexual crime. Media exposure is an important source that provides public awareness and can and does blame victims and excuse men. The Women's Liberation Movement and programmes such as Roger Graef's fly-on-the-wall documentary about Thames Valley Polices' oppressive interviewing of a rape victim have influenced the media agenda in that most journalists now recognise sexual violence as a critical social issue. Nevertheless, Kitzinger contends there is a new criticism emerging of media coverage. This includes court-based discussions which perpetuate victim blaming and perpetrator exoneration, which stereotype and simplify the complexities of rape and which position both victim and offender as other.

Disputed and contested cases fit into the media agenda of exciting and dramatic stories and there is an increasing coverage of stories about false allegations. The emphasis is on the stranger, serial or

335

multiple perpetrator rape which serves to engage and amplify the stereotype. The woman is portrayed as contributing to her own victimisation by drinking or socialising with her alleged attacker. Thus rape is portrayed as exceptional, unusual and not normalised or routine. There is an imbalance in the reporting with women's behaviour subjected to detailed scrutiny while the sexual details extracted from or attributed to men are minimal. There is an emphasis on and a responsibility attributed to women not to dress immodestly or to drink too heavily. Stories of fabricated allegation cast men as the victims.

Myth busting

The chapter by Betsy Stanko and Emma Williams presents convincing evidence that directly counters many existing myths. For example, two-thirds of the rapes in their sample took place in the victim's or suspect's home, not in a dark alley; 40 per cent of the victims said an acquaintance raped them and 24 per cent indicated that the perpetrator was a former intimate partner not a stranger. Perhaps more worryingly, a third of victims were under 15 years of age and victims with a greater number of vulnerabilities (of which being under 16 years old is one) were twice as likely to have the charge no crimed or dropped at the post-charge stage of the investigation compared to women with no vulnerabilities. Finally, approximately 10 per cent of allegations were classified as false so the problem is not the truthfulness of the victim, rather the difficulty in determining whether the sex that took place was criminal or not. But cases hinge on the woman's testimony rather than the man's to figure out truthfulness.

Jo Lovett and Miranda Horvath set out to challenge myths in relation to rapes where alcohol and/or drugs are involved. Their data shows quite clearly that while it is still widely believed that drugs such as Rohypnol are being used by men to incapacitate women and then sexually assault them, the research evidence is compelling that this is relatively rare and that the intoxicant properties of alcohol is a far more likely substance to be implicated in rape. Much is also still made of date rape yet their analysis of the contexts and arenas in which sexual assaults occur shows that relatively few cases involved people who were on a date and that rape occurs in a much wider variety of contexts. In fact rapes are more likely to occur where alcohol is consumed in social and public arenas with minimal prior contact between the victim and perpetrator, hence alcohol is acting as a facilitator of interaction between them.

These two chapters, along with others in the book, highlight the strength of evidence now available to researchers and practitioners which can be used to bust myths which inhibit progress in reducing the justice gap for victims of rape.

Practice implications

We suggest that critical to the argument presented above is the notion of attitudes. For there to be real progress in closing the justice gap, attitudes need to be tackled at the societal level from where jurors are drawn as well as criminal justice professionals.

Gerd Bohner and his colleagues show clearly how pervasive rape myths are but perhaps more importantly find that rape myth acceptance plays distinct functions for men and women. For women levels of rape myth acceptance determine whether they include or exclude themselves from the threat of rape. Women rejecting rape myths accept any woman can be raped whereas women who accept rape myths believe that only certain types of women (i.e. not them) are raped. Believing in rape myths for these women allows them to reduce their anxieties about the threat of rape thereby protecting their self-esteem. Endorsement of rape myths by men serves to rationalise aggressive sex and justifies corresponding behaviours. Further, rape myth acceptance by men also serves to neutralise the adverse impacts and permits a trivialisation of rape. Moreover, believing that others have high rape myth acceptances increases rape proclivity thus promoting a social norm for aggressive sexual behaviour.

Stroebe and Jonas (1996) propose that the most influential determinant in sustaining an attitude position is perceived personal relevance. It follows then that any interventions designed to lower rape myth acceptance need to address the functions this serves for both men and women. Women who already have low rape myth acceptance are prone to negative affective reactions, so interventions designed to challenge rape myths will need to address women's fears of rape and find other mechanisms to limit their worry about this crime and their assessments of the likelihood of becoming a victim. Women who manage their fear of being raped do so by rejecting the likelihood that they will become victims. As has been demonstrated there is a greater range of scenarios than these women may care to admit that might result in rape.

The work by Gill and by Frith shows there is a strong possibility that coercive sex may be recast as unwanted sex and not construed as rape. It will be a challenging task to design messages in such a way that allows a realistic understanding of the many and varied circumstances in which rape may occur but without increasing women's fear or increasing their likelihood estimates of being a victim. Campus-based education programmes aimed at reducing sexual violence seem to have had some success in changing cognitions but the reported effects appear relatively short-lived. Bohner and his colleagues suggest designing interventions that tackle the idea that aggressive sex is normative. Frith's research may also link in here by proposing a shift in the stigmatising as tease or tart women who change their minds or are trying to signal no to sex that they do not want. Finding high-status male role models to promulgate messages about non-aggressive normative sex may be a place to start.

Undoubtedly the media have a role to play in societal education. As Frith in her chapter points out, the media were crucial in shifting attitudes and were influential in the UK in stimulating work by the Women's National Commission and the new Home Office guidance on police handling of rape in the 1980s. She states 'media coverage made a crucial contribution to a spiral of recognition helping to fundamentally transform private and public thinking and discussion. It ... helped sexual violence, including rape by one's own father or step father, to enter public discourse.' However, as Kitzinger highlights, the media also have a tendency to limit or reduce discussion on the widespread nature of sexual violence and cast attackers as monsters, animals or beasts. Frith's proffered solutions are to shift the news agenda from events-based to issues-based allowing for more thoughtful features about rape. The addition of a sexual violence specialist in newsrooms who is experienced in the complexities of sexual violence would be one way to advance this change of emphasis in news coverage.

The chapters by Vanessa Munro and Liz Kelly and by Jennifer Temkin and Barbara Krahé suggest both social and law reform. The former are encouraged by initiatives to limit the second guessing by prosecutors and shifting the conservative decision-making by increasing the range of rapes that are presented in court. Using gender-matched specialist investigators and introducing protection for especially vulnerable witness are developments to be welcomed. This is a start in reducing the self-fulfilling prophetic nature of restricting prosecuted cases to those that conform to the real rape stereotype because jurors are believed to be unwilling to convict cases that deviate from this. Using campaigns to persuade behavioural change has limited success (as witnessed by Temkin and Krahé's evaluation of the Home Office anti-rape posters). Dramatic changes of behaviour have resulted from legal sanctions such as the seat belt laws or legally enforced prohibitions such as smoking in pubs or using a mobile phone when driving. There are problems with legal sanctions, not least the need to monitor adherence and the impact on the desired behaviour were the sanction to be lifted. If persuasion rather than coercion is used then Stroebe and Jonas (1996) argue that the behaviour remains under intrinsic control and does not need monitoring.

Jennifer Temkin and Barbara Krahé suggest that offering expert testimony about the nature of rape and its impact on victims to jurors might be introduced as a means of dispelling rape myths. This may help to explain why a woman did not resist or why she failed to report the rape immediately. However, they remain uncertain as to how effective this would be and pose the possibility that such evidence may cloud an already complex situation and lead to greater confusion. They are also not sanguine about the possibility of eliminating jurors who show high rape myth acceptance. This is because there is relatively little convincing evidence about the efficacy of screening procedures. Eliminating juries altogether in favour of judge-only trials rather assumes judges themselves are free from rape myth acceptance.

Betsy Stanko and Emma Williams indicate four specific issues that limit the likelihood of cases proceeding to prosecution: domestic violence, peer intimidation, mental health and alcohol-related sexual contact. They advocate greater levels of support to encourage women in these situations to bring their allegations to the police and greater efforts by the police to secure appropriate evidence.

An agenda for action

There is a great deal of intellectual theorising and empirical research invested within the chapters of this book. We believe this not only presents challenges to both the research community and criminal justice practitioners, but to society in general from whom all the relevant actors reflected in the contributions are drawn. The cross-disciplinary collaboration represented by the contributing authors has permitted the development of new insights and has the potential to offer more. Our final reflections consider next steps. We therefore present some thoughts about future research and seek also to inform practice.

The research efforts into rape will be greatly facilitated by theory development. The prospect offered by some synthesis between theories of emotion and the role played by rape myth acceptance and just world beliefs would present a fuller understanding of values within society that are at best ambivalent about rape and at worst rape-supporting. This would allow a more detailed conceptualising of the vicious cycle and, once verified by research, would allow more evidence-based interventions to be made at strategic points in the criminal justice process. Use of theoretical frameworks such as naturalistic decision-making, grounded theory and other qualitative frameworks provide more systematic formulations within which to develop explanatory conceptualisations.

In this book we have, deliberately, focused our attention on adult women as victims and men as perpetrators. There are of course other rape victims such as children and men themselves. The rape of the elderly, gerontophilia, might also be the subject of further study. A research programme examining these in detail to establish similarities and differences in experiences to those of adult women would enhance our knowledge base. Offenders represent another critical group to study. As Stanko and Williams point out, the difference between normative and criminal sex from the offender's point of view is slim. Fuller understanding of normative sex and the points at which it deviates into a criminal act would be instructive. As one woman police detective pointed out, the woman is subjected to detailed scrutiny of the intimate details of the sex that allegedly took place, whereas police interviews with suspects treat this rather perfunctorily. Focusing on men's discourses about sex more generally and those of offenders in particular would enhance the body of accumulating knowledge about sexual politics.

From a practice perspective, there clearly needs to be a better interface between academics and criminal justice professionals. The academic community needs to understand the practical problems facing practitioners and the difficulties of operationalising empirical findings into policy. There is also a requirement to disseminate findings in accessible language that supports evidence-based practice. A programme of practitioner/academic engagement to develop practical solutions to challenging stereotypes and combat rape myth acceptance could lead to the development of training materials. Innovations such as expert evidence could be made available to courts to inform barristers, judges and jurors about the psychological impacts of rape.

Clearly there is more work to be done in developing the law. In England and Wales there have been attempts to clarify consent which invoke notions of capability, freedom and the genuineness of that consent. Yet there is still an ambiguity about the role of alcohol in terms of capability. There is ambiguity too in the notions of reasonableness when it comes to consent. There is a difference between the black-and-white requirements of the law and the shades of grey involved in psychological meanings attached to behavioural intentions and actions. The innovations reviewed in the chapter by Temkin and Krahé as adjuncts to the legal process have yet to realise their potential to inform decision-making in trials and further development is needed.

At a broader societal level, theoretically informed education campaigns about the realities of sexual violence and the variations in circumstances that constitute rape could be designed and evaluated. These would have to be relevant to the target audience and inform people so as to break the vicious cycle of self-conforming biases. Designing awareness-raising and risk-avoidance communications will require creativity and imagination. Linking in with the psychological risk perception literature may well be a useful starting place to garner ideas about how this might be done.

Finally, there are structural organisational issues that are said to create the 'cult of scepticism' when police review allegations of rape. Part of this may be attributable to factors that inform decision-making criteria such as the demands for a reasonable prospect of achieving a guilty verdict or no criming policies that need to be challenged. As Betsy Stanko and Emma Williams point out, there is research to be done in looking at investigators' judgments about the fragility of the complainant and her ability to make a credible witness in court.

If the justice gap is to be narrowed and women are encouraged to come forward in greater numbers then there will be a capacity problem. Resources to support rape victims and investigate and prosecute crime are already stretched and demands on the criminal justice sector in general mean there is little slack. If efforts to combat stereotyping and improve best evidence collection thus far are anything to go by then we might expect present resources to be inadequate to meet a rising demand. We may well have to create more radical solutions to overcome attrition problems and manage the changing expectations that will allow women to get justice at last.

341

References

Coleman, K., Kaiza, P., Hoare, J. and Jansson, K. (2008) *Homicide, Firearm Offences and Intimate Violence 2006/7*, 3rd edn. London: Home Office Research and Development Statistics Directorate, Information and Publications Group.

Estrich, S. (1987) *Real Rape: How the Legal System Victimizes Women Who Say No*. Boston: Harvard University Press.

Hamilton, C. (2004) 'A Research Investigation into Attrition in Rape Investigations'. Unpublished MSc dissertation, Guildford: University of Surrey.

HMCPSI and HMIC (2002) *A Report on the Joint Inspection into the Investigation and Prosecution of Cases Involving Allegations of Rape*. London: HMCPSI.

Kelly, L. (2001) Routes to (In)justice: A Research Review on the Reporting, Investigation and Prosecution of Rape Cases'. Unpublished manuscript.

Kelly, L., Lovett, J. and Regan, L. (2005) *A Gap or a Chasm? Attrition in Reported Rape Cases*, Home Office Research Study No. 293. London: HMSO.

Myhill, A. and Allen, J. (2002) *Rape and Sexual Assault of Women: The Extent and Nature of the Problem – Findings from the British Crime Survey*. London: Home Office Research Study.

Sinclair, C. H. and Bourne, L. E. (1998) 'Cycle of blame or just world: effects of legal verdicts on gender patterns in rape-myth acceptance and victim empathy', *Psychology of Women Quarterly*, 22: 575–88.

Stahlberg, D. and Frey, D. (1996) 'Attitudes: structure, measurement and functions', in M. Hewstone, W. Stroebe and G. Stephenson (eds), *Introduction to Social Psychology: A European Perspective*, 2nd edn. Oxford: Blackwell, pp. 205–39.

Stroebe, W. and Jonas, K. (1996) 'Principles of attitude formation and strategies of change', in M. Hewstone, W. Stroebe and G. M. Stephenson (eds), *Introduction to Social Psychology: A European Perspective*, 2nd edn. Oxford: Blackwell, pp. 240–75.

Temkin, J. and Krahé, B. (2008) *Sexual Assault and the Justice Gap: A Question of Attitude*. Oxford: Hart.

Index